THREAT PERCEPTION IN A GLOBALIZING WORLD

THREAT PERCEPTION IN A GLOBALIZING WORLD

With Special Reference to India

Editor

Prof. Mohd. Moazzam Ali Muztarib

GYAN

Threat Perception in a Globalizing World : With Special Reference to India

ISBN: 978-81-212-1185-7

Rs. 950

Published in 2013 in India by
Gyan Publishing House
23, Main Ansari Road, Daryaganj,
New Delhi-110002
Phone : 23282060, 23261060
Fax : (011) 23285914
E-mail : books@gyanbooks.com
Website : gyanbooks.com

Leser type Setting : Lucky Graphic, Delhi
Printed at : G. Print Process, Delhi

Dedicated to the fond memory of

Abbajan (Mr. Mohd. Mohiuddin Ali)

and

Ammi (Mrs. Moti Begum)

Also by the same author:

The Collapse of Soviet Union: Nationality Causes (2004)

Contents

Preface

The topic of the international seminar : Changing Threat Perception in a Globalising World With Special Reference to India, on which the book is based, was the result of wide consultations. Special mention has to be made of the doyen of Defense Studies in India, Prof. A. Narsimha Rao. As the Coordinator of SAP (Special Assistance Programme of the UGC) for a year, I faced massive resistance to the idea of an international seminar on the subject of International Relations/Defense Studies. Very serious compromises had to be made in matters of funding. A very small amount from the SAP funds was finally made available.

A seminar should not be just an exercise in speech making, verbal duels and bonhomie of which no record was kept. I was therefore keen not just to invite important academics (Indian and foreign), journalists, foreign secretaries, Army-Navy-Air-force personnel, but I strongly requested all of them to put on paper their valuable thoughts which many of them did and thereby helped shape this book.

Prof. Shashikant Jha, Dr. Abid Hussain, Dr. M.N. Rajesh and Dr. Peter Smerkel could not submit finished papers.

I was keen that colleagues and research scholars also participated in sufficient numbers. Some colleagues and research scholars presented papers which are included in this volume.

A book-length treatment on the subject of threat perception is uncommon. What adds to the value of the book is the inclusion of articles written by important defense personnel, some of whom held very high positions. The foreign scholars have pursued novel paths. The galaxy of Indian professors who have contributed articles are, in fact, the leading writers in their respective fields. Their views are of abiding interest to academics and non-academics alike. It is hoped that the book will receive an appropriate response it deserves.

Hyderabad, July 5, 2012 **Mohd. Moazzam Ali Muztarib**

Acknowledgements

The number of people who made it possible to hold this seminar successfully is indeed very large. I fear that I may miss out some. I would begin by thanking the UGC for the grant of the SAP programme to the Department of Political Science, University of Hyderabad. The idea of the seminar was contingent upon the grant of SAP. Although a very small amount was utilized from the SAP for the seminar, the group of teachers associated with international relations could not have thought of organising the seminar if SAP was not there.

The then Vice-Chancellor of the University of Hyderabad, Dr. Seyed Hasnain, besides encouraging me, also agreed to support the effort with a small financial grant.

The Ministry of External Affairs was generous with a grant without which it was impossible to hold the seminar. The organisers of the seminar owe a great debt of gratitude to the Ministry. Mr. Topno was very positive and encouraging. The theme of the seminar generated a lot of interest in the Ministry's bureaucratic circles. I am told by those in the know of things that the higher ups in the bureaucracy were very appreciative of the theme and the participants.

The ICSSR, Delhi, deserves thanks for a small but extremely useful grant for the seminar. The staff in the ICSSR, Delhi, was very encouraging and cooperative barring an exception which I would rather ignore.

The first person to thank is Prof. A. Narsimha Rao, my teacher and former professor of Political Science, Osmania University. I hereby record my deepest sense of appreciation for him. All the top people from the defense services and a former Foreign Secretary, Mr. H.E. Ambassador Venkateswaran, participated in the seminar thanks to the tireless efforts of Prof. Narsimha Rao.

Professor Chintamani Mahapatra, my friend, former classmate and a colleague in the IDSA and presently a professor in JNU, was of great help. My access to a galaxy of foreign secretaries was greatly facilitated by him. He even personally met some of them to ensure their participation. He himself participated and presented a paper in the seminar which is duly included in this book. I record my sincere thanks to him.

Mr. Anil Mishra, my former classmate in JNU and presently teaching in Delhi University, worked hard to fix up an appointment with the Vice-President of India, hon'able Hamed Ansari, whom I met briefly to invite him to inaugurate the seminar. The Vice-President, however, could not make it to the seminar but was kind enough to send a telegram extending his best wishes for the seminar.

Dr. M.N Rajesh, my young friend and colleague in the University of Hyderabad, helped in arranging all the articles, formating them and making soft copies of some of them etc. I am hereby acknowledging his help. Two of my P'h.D. students extended very valuable support. They are : Dr. Niranjan Mohapatra (presently teaching in the Assam University, Diphu Campus) and Dr. Anshuman Behera (presently associated with the IDSA, New Delhi). At that time they were research scholars in the Department, doing their Ph.D under my supervision. My student, Mr. Mathew Simon, helped me a lot in seminar work. Dr. Kanneganti Ramesh Babu (formerly my student, then SAP research assistant and presently associated with the Indian Institute of International Studies, (formerly the ASRC), Osmania University, Hyderabad, was very helpful in varieties of ways. He looked after all the guests and participants who had come from all parts of the country and abroad. In fact, Niranjan, Anshuman, Mathew, Ramesh and SAP research assistant, Mr. Murthy, met me regularly for months in connection with the preparations for the seminar. Every detail was worked out with meticulous care. I own all of them a great debt of gratitude.

My teacher, Professor Madhusudhan Reddy, was always generous with his advice. He attended all the sessions of the seminar and chaired an important session. He deserves generous thanks.

All those who Chaired various sessions of the seminar like Prof. Narsimha Rao, Ambassador Chinmaya Gharekhan, Prof. Madhusudhan Reddy, Prof. Prakash Sarangi, Prof. P. Eashvariah, and the foreign participants, Prof. Peter Emberly, Dr. Katrin Uba, Dr. Peter Smerkel and the participants from outside of Hyderabad (please see the list of contributors) – all deserve a grateful acknowledgment and warm thanks for their efforts. The list of the contributors is included in the book.

All the defense personnel who participated in the seminar deserve special mention and appreciation.

I record with a deep sense of sadness the demise of my dear friend of long standing, Prof. Shashikant Jha. He encouraged me always and was kind enough to attend the seminar and make a presentation.

I record with great sense of grief the passing away of Dr. Abid Hussain in a London hotel on June 21st, 2012. A great administrator and diplomat, Dr. Abid Hussain, a universally acclaimed orator, had graced the Seminar by delivering a scintillating Inaugural Address. His Hyderabadi manners and cordiality, impeccable conduct and sense of humour will always be remembered.

In the end, I would record my deeply felt appreciation of the constant, invaluable help, support and encouragement, provided by my wife, Mrs. Salma Moazzam. Her unfailing cooperation and patience made all the difference to me. My daughters, Areeba Ahsanat Moazzam, Zeba Tamkanat Moazzam and my son, Mohd. Fareesuddin Ali Moazzam helped me in myriad ways difficult to detail here.

Prof. Mohd. Moazzam Ali Muztarib

and warm thanks for their efforts. The list of the contributors is included in the book.

All the defence personnel who participated in the seminar deserve special mention and appreciation.

I record with a deep sense of sadness the demise of my dear friend of long standing, Prof. [illegible]. He encouraged me always and was kind enough to attend the seminar and made a great [illegible].

I record with great sense of grief the passing away of Dr. Abid Hussain in a London hotel on June [illegible], 2012. A great administrator and diplomat, Dr. Abid Hussain, a universally acclaimed orator, had graced the occasion by delivering a scintillating Inaugural Address. His Hyderabadi manners and cordiality, impeccable conduct and sense of humour will always be remembered.

In the end, I would record my deeply felt appreciation of the constant, invaluable help, support and encouragement, provided by my wife, Mrs. Salma Moazzam. Her unfailing cooperation and patience made all the difference to me. My daughters Areeba Ahsanal Moazzam, Saba Tabassum Moazzam and my son Mohd. Fareequddin Ali Moazzam helped me in [illegible] ways difficult to detail here.

Prof. Mohd. Moazzam Ali Moazzam

List of Contributors

1. **H.E. Ambassador A.P. Venkateshwaran**, Former Foreign Secretary, Government of India.
2. **H.E. Ambassador Chinmaya Garekhan,** India's Former Permanent Representative to the UN and an Advisor to the Prime Minister on West Asia.
3. **Prof. Mohd. Moazzam Ali Muztarib,** Dept. of Political Science, University of Hyderabad.
4. **Brigadier V.P. Munjal,** Dean, FIET, MCEME.
5. **Commander Vivek Dahiya.**
6. **Mr. Nitin Gokhale,** Senior Editor, Defense and Strategic Affairs, NDTV.
7. **Maj. General (Rtd.) R.K. Bagga**, AVSM, Advisor IIIT, Hyderabad.
8. **Prof. Peter Emberley,** Carleton Univesity, Canada.
9. **Dr. Katrin Uba,** Uppsala University, Sweden.
10. **Dr. Peter Smerkel,** Uppsala University, Sweden.
11. **Prof. Chintamani Mohapatra,** Former Chairman, Centre for American and Canadian Studies, JNU.
12. **Prof. P.L. Dash,** Former Head, Centre for Central Eurasian Studies, Mumbai University, Calina, and presently India Chair, Tashkent University, Uzbekistan.
13. **Professor R.S. Yadav,** Dept. of Political Science, Kurukshetra University.

14. **Prof. Kondapally Srikant,** Centre for Chinese Studies, JNU, New Delhi.
15. **Prof. A.K. Pasha,** Chairman, Centre for West Asian Studies, JNU, New Delhi.
16. **Prof. M.J. Vinod,** Bangalore University, Bangalore.
17. **Prof. P.V. Rao,** Former Director, Centre for Indian Ocean Studies, Osmania University.
18. **Dr. Sujit Lahiri,** Associate Professor, Punjab University.
19. **Dr. Anshuman Behera,** Researcher , IDSA, New Delhi.
20. **Dr. Niranjan Mohapatra,** Assistant Professor, Assam University, Diphu Campus.

1

General Introduction

Mohd. Moazzam Ali Muztazib

The panel of speakers at the seminar was distinguished and large and hence parallel sessions were held. Dr. Abid Hussain, Air Marshal V.R. Iyer, AVSM, A.O.P., IAF, Prof. Shashi Kant Jha addressed the sessions but could not send finished papers. Ambassador A.P. Venkateswaran, Ambassador C.R. Gharekhan (also included in the Book) and Ambassador Dr. Abid Hussain were most impressive and illuminating in their addresses in the inaugural session. Their valuable insights made for a great, memorable start. Dr. Abid Hussain's wit and anecdotes would always be remembered. The areas covered by the participants were both important and varied. The Participants from the defense background had obviously some constraints but in spite of that they presented very informative papers and answered all the prickly and searching questions addressed to them during the seminar sessions with intelligence and patience. A good example is the paper presented by Brig. V.P. Munjal who was precise on issues of concern to India without showing personal preferences. Maj. Gen. (Rtd.) R.K. Bagga, AVSM, advisor to IIIT, Hyderabad, is very concise in his article. He gives tables to elaborate his points. Commander Vivek Dahiya, a very vivacious and witty participant, has used some catchy phrases like the 'Death of Distance' (the title of the book by Frances Cairncross, 2001) or 'electronic pearl harbour' etc. He extends very many advises. He has portrayed many scenarios which are interesting. Prof. Peter Emberly's comprehensive, philosophical narrative of threats and their perception with reference to the West and to the modern times is very scholarly. Dr. Katrin Uba has gone in for a novel approach by focusing on the privatization – related threat perception of the Indian labour movement and other stake holders of the Indian economy. She highlights the economic aspects and relates them to threat perception. This informative article not only carries the conclusion concisely and clearly written but also suggests the ways to carry out further research in the area. Dr. Peter Smerkel could not send his finished paper but his views are well recorded in his synopsis. Prof. R.S.Yadav has gathered a lot of useful information. Security is looked at from a broader perspective. Prof. Vinod Joseph's article on trafficking in persons and its impact on the security of South Asian states is well thought out and covers a new ground. He has avoided providing many footnotes but the references are found right in the main text of the article. Prof. P.L. Dash is a seasoned writer. He has written on neighbourhood concerns that globalization has brought into sharp focus. As usual his grasp of the subject is perfect. Prof. P.V. Rao, has concentrated on the Indian navy, its perceptions and policies which are well documented. He elaborates on maritime doctrines adopted by India. He seems satisfied with what India is doing. Prof. Chintamani Mohapatra begins very provocatively by asking fundamental question like what is a threat? Does it cease after it materialize ? He goes on to elaborate his theme as a seasoned specialist. Prof. A.K. Pasha, is an acknowledged expert on West Asia and his knowledge of the region is widely appreciated. India's threat perception with regard to the Middle East is elaborated, giving many important details. Prof. Kondapally Srikant is among the few excellent China hands we have in India. His knowledge of the Chinese language makes his writings very authentic. His aptitude to go into details is a notable feature. The threat perception involving China is elaborately dealt with by him. Dr. Niranjan Mohapatra has dwelt on the Indo-Russian threat perceptions and joint responses made by the two countries. Dr. Sujit Lahiri has written on terrorism and Islamic fundamentalism. He gives important details and makes many suggestions which are of interest. Dr. Anshuman Behera specializes on Nepal. The threat perception involving Nepal is dealt with by him with the knowledge of an expert that he is.

Since most of the contributors are senior and seasoned writers, I have chosen not to prune their presentations much. However, I wish to state that the responsibility for the facts stated/used, the errors, if any, and the information provided in the footnotes is entirely the responsibility of the writers concerned.

2

Threat Perception in a Globalizing World with Special Reference to India

Prof. Mohd. Moazzam Ali Muztarib

For the defense/security related think tanks the world over, the question of threat perception is the staple diet.[1] They keep churning out threat scenarios/ projections frequently enough to, inter alia, plead for more expenditure on defense.[2] Strategic Studies, the sub-field of the discipline of International Relations, survives largely on its projections on threats and enemies whom, as Carl Schmidt maintained, we fight all our lives. But in this article, it is not the enemy/enemies within but without that are focused upon. During the Cold War, full length books were also written on the subject by both the Americans and the Soviets.[3] But the role of intellectuals is suspect in foreign policy making, according to some scholars,[4] notwithstanding the names of Kissinger, Kennan, Galbraith and many others.

Threat Perception as a concept, although, ubiquitously noted in International Relations studies, has not received adequate academic attention it deserved, as a perusal of encyclopedias and classical collection of articles shows.[5] In contrast, the concepts of security and security perception are better explored as the "degree of protection against danger, damage, loss and crime."[6] Threat Perceptions are varied and may pertain to a whole country or a policy. Threat Perception is hard to define although attempts have been made.[7] The Realists and Social Psychologists carved out different routes to understanding threat perception.[8] Threat Perception as a concept and as an exercise has significant uses. It keeps a country agile, alert and alive to putative dangers from within and without. It can help avoid wars. If one's threat perception is transmitted across to the enemy, it may possibly result in a negotiating process or the activation of conflict managements/control mechanisms, bilaterally, regionally and globally. Threat Perception may not always be in an offensive frame. It can be defensive as well. A free and frank dialogue can always help remove misunderstandings, clarify matters and clear the air and ultimately obviate war and promote peace- the central concern of the discipline of

International Relations Studies. A sensible foreign policy can save huge expenditure and resources and this can be partly achieved through a sensible threat perception mechanism. Disarmament for Development thesis can then be operationalized. Threat Perception can promote alertness all around, which is salubrious to all. It helps to envision and address all possible eventualities leading to a better preparedness. Territorial, economic-trade, socio-cultural, environmental, cyber and other dimensions of threats and their perception are all explored in this article within the broad canvass of international relations. Threat Perception can serve to sensitize a state to its deep vulnerabilities.

Small, weak and failing states feel perennially threatened. For the Realists, desire for power, itch to dominate, proclivity to imperialism/hegemony are the basic sources of threats. Various constructs of threat perception, to be credible, have to obviate a coward's obsessive fears and a paranoid megalomaniac's hallucinations and ideologue's/intellectual's phantoms. Unless there exists sufficient factual basis, perspicacity and urgency about a clear and present danger/dangers backed by profundity of analysis about threat perception, adequate preventive steps in time cannot be taken and hence crisis may overwhelm. False alarms can only precipitate matters, serve to ignite hasty, wrong responses, pushing states into unwanted crises, even wars. While states cannot ignore threat perceptions or make light of them, precautions against the drawbacks, touched upon above, are a must. However, it is quite apt and appropriate to argue that a lack of seriousness about threat perception can heighten vulnerability of a state to crippling proportions.

When threats are examined, do we take a threat posed to country as a whole or a policy/posture or both? Both the possibilities exist and since the whole exercise of threat perception is largely perceptual, many lacunae exist in working out a blueprint of/preventive measures of threat perception. Threats can be spurious, ideological and can even be invented to dupe the domestic constituency into going to war. Media hype (a la Chomsky's *Manufacturing of Consent*) has the power to transform what is false into something credible and real. Goebbels is not after all totally irrelevant: a thousand time repetition of untruth can make it appear like the truth. WMD-Al Qaida link logic and subsequent media hype in the case of Iraq is a good recent example. A kind of threat perception can be inculcated into the minds of large or even a whole population as was the case with the former Soviet Union: capitalism in its imperialist incarnation headed by the US posed a perennial threat to the very existence of the Soviet Union. Conflict with capitalism can be postponed but not avoided. The Cold War will culminate in an unavoidable confrontation with Capitalism. The Fascist and Nazis had their own aggressive, race based versions inculcated in to the minds of a whole society. In the case of the US, Muslims are an implacable, permanent enemy and the 'war on terror' is inexorable and endless. There can be threats from non-state actors/sources like terrorist outfits, drug and other trafficking agencies, organized crime, piracy etc.

Threat Perception in an international ambiance involving a mix of democratic and non-democratic states and non-state actors/sources, has to be differently viewed given an opinion by Natan Scharansky, President George W. Bush and others that democracies do not go to war and, by inference, are not obsessed with threat perceptions. If only the Middle East were to be re-made (President Bush Jr.'s agenda) into states with democratic regimes, war from the Middle East can be eliminated and Israel and Arabs could live in peace.[9]

On my visit to Vienna (Sept., 2006), my friend, Irwin Numayer, exuded happiness that the Europeans have not fought a war amongst themselves for over four decades (wars inflicted by the Europeans on the non-European soil are case apart) thanks to democratization of the Eastern Europe and the integration of Eastern and Western Europe in to the European Union.

Henry Kissinger highlights some other aspects based on the nature of changing global environment which is characterized by, (1) democratization of politics, (2) globalization of economies, (3) confusion over what is 'foreign', (4) instantaneousness of communication, (5) crisis of sovereignty-sensitive Westphalia system and the transformation of the nation-state concept.[10] On the other hand, the principle of intervention devised by the US has gained legitimacy. The unipolar world and American exceptionalism stand to threaten non-Western states. (The case of Iran is a recent grave excess. Iran has no nuclear weapons making programme as Iraq before had no WMD programme and yet Blair and Campbell allegedly manipulated the secret services, falsified their report to exaggerate the threat of WMDs[11]), But harsher sanctions are imposed on it in May, 2012.[12] Territory has lost much of its significance leading Frances Cairncross to declare *The Death of Distance in 2001.* Some writers speak of post-national, post-territorial state and *mobile sovereignty*.[13] Tiny Singapore and Israel have performed exceptionally well. Under the Third Wave of democratization[14] lasting up to the late 1990's, 120 countries (60 per cent) have preferred electoral democracy.[15] Since much of the Muslim world still remains outside the pale of electoral democracy, it is the special target of the US-Israel combine.[16] The concept of Threat Perception has to be looked at afresh by taking cognizance all of these developments.

The expression, 'Threat Perception', on the face of it, appears simple enough and not in need of an elaborate definitional exercise. Threats to national-cultural-civilizational identities representing un-compromizable core values, territory, population, vital interests - economic, political and socio-cultural -

are often perceived and preparations are made to meet the threats. Threat Perception involves a deep negative sense of vulnerability which may result in loss, huge or significant, and which may start a drift towards war. While wars in the nuclear age have become futile, yet conventional wars are still fought and the security question remains important, perhaps much more so than the food and employment security, for most states.[17] The stimuli and responses to threat in individuals and states have similarities as they share a good deal of common ground. In many ways, states are individuals writ large. When an individual feels threatened, he takes recourse to defensive (or offensive) measures so as to fend off the threat. But a threat may be magnified many fold by premonitions and fears. Russell maintains that, "fear makes man unwise in the three great departments of human conduct: his dealings with nature, his dealings with other men, and his dealings with himself."[18] In the 12th century, there existed no conception of sovereignty in Europe.[19] And the Post Westphalia Treaty (1648) states, with all the appurtenances of sovereignty, felt threatened causing endless wars. The world we live in comprises unequal states- big and small, powerful and weak. Martin Wight classified them into dominant powers, great powers, world powers, minor powers, sea powers etc. To which we may add the category of super powers of the Cold War era having global reach to defend their interests. These powers bequeathed multipolar and unipolar configurations of forces at global level, creating different structures of international relations. Martin Wight provides details about them.[20] Threats emanate from bilateral, regional and global levels. Threats from global sources have assumed serious proportions in recent times. The US has embarked on an interventionist course at the cost of ignoring the UN.[21]

Recognition by other states is a pre-requisite for the existence and acceptance of a state. Since most states are state-nations, national and state boundaries do not coincide leading to endless uneasiness, tensions and problems, even splits, affected by fissiparous tendencies. Kosovo is not recognized by Russia and Kashmir is treated as a disputed territory by Britain and the US. For long, apartheid afflicted South Africa, on the one hand, and Israel, on the other, were not recognized by a host of countries. It took the US long to recognize Russia (from 1917 to 1933) and China (from 1949 to 1979). If Palestinian leadership declared independence (120 countries recognize Palestine which made an unsuccessful bid for UN membership in September, 2011), Europe and the US are sure to deny recognition to such a state.[22] The US has used veto in the Security Council 42 times to save Israel.[23] A state without recognition feels isolated and threatened. Sovereign and separate identity of a state, like that of individual in Hobbesian scheme of things, is perennially under attack or fear of attack. Threat perception here is endemic to the existence of a state. The war of all against all, a sense of anarchy, is an underlying reality, more so in a unipolar world passing through the times of 'globalization' with economic factors ruling the roost. Threats at bilateral, multilateral, regional and global levels have to be necessarily taken into account. Pakistan was recently threatened with sanctions by the US if Pakistan did not opt out of the gas pipeline involving Iran. It was asked to opt for TAPI pipeline which skirted Iran or face sanctions.[24] Even the strongest state has its own premonitions of threats and vulnerabilities. The US is the most security conscious state in the world. One or a combination of states can pose a threat. In the age of ICBMs, MIRVs, and the projections of space based weapons, on the one hand, and MNCs and other non-state actors like the NGOs, INGOs, WTO etc. and host of supranational organizations like the UN, Commonwealth organization, CIS, EU, NATO etc. and multi-national trade arrangements like the ASEAN, NAFTA etc. and many other multilateral arrangements like the Shanghai Cooperation Organization, BRICS, the Axis ideas like Russia-India-China axis, Japan-India – US axis, Japan-India-Australia-US axis etc., on the other, have rendered state boundaries, in many ways anything but relevant. The formulation of borderless, globalized world are bandied about. Kenichi Ohmae finds the nation-states in paralysis and giving way to what he calls 'region-states' for the good of the people.[25] Cyber criminals, hackers and the MNC's pose serious threats.[26] The downsizing of sovereignty-sensitivities has become rife. Horseman and Marshall conclude: today, 'Sovereignty is fractured and nation-state diminished.'[27] Few states can afford to pursue independent foreign policies in a unipolar world. But threats galore and perceptions about them endemic.

How to problematize the concept of perception ? In terms of pinning it down or exposing its inadequacies, complexities or its dimensions which are too varied to be reconciled ? What kind of problematique the concept 'perception' is ensconced in? The term 'perception' is so complex, has so many dimensions – philosophical, psychological and empirical - and misperceptions have played such a havoc in international relations that a detailed treatment of it becomes necessary and the same is attempted below.

Adler observes that , "The majority of mankind is probably visual minded." But, "Perception" warns Adler, "is never to be compared with a photographic image because something of the peculiar and individual quality of the person who perceives is inextricably bound up with it. One does not perceive everything that one sees. No two human beings react in quite the same way to the identical picture....These perceptions need not be strictly identical with actuality.....individuality and uniqueness of a human being consists in what he perceives and how he perceives. Perception is more than a simple physical phenomenon; it is a psychic function from which we may draw the most far going conclusions concerning the inner life."[28] While Zezek's critique of Foucauldian formulation of discourse analysis in contradistinction to the Marxian ideology paradigm remains moot,[29] the dimensions of the term perception forces us to take recourse to discourse parameters. The discursive treatment of the concept of perception alone is rewarding since there are no definitive conclusions to be arrived at. Awareness about Dualism adds new complications where there could be minds without brains and brains without minds. If the two met, which Descartes thought they do, "it involves a handshake across a metaphysical divide."[30] Is perception a reliable tool ? What is perception anyway? How do we perceive? David Hume divides all perception into *impressions and ideas* and the impressions can be original and secondary. He distinguishes the impressions into impressions of sensations and reflection. "Perceptions arise in the soul, from the constitution of the body from the animal spirits or from the application of objects to the external organs." Perceptions arise without any antecedent in the soul.[31] Perceptions therefore can be part of a psychic process. If the perception is to be sense-based (which is what is the position taken by the Empiricists[32] and from Locke to Russell in England)[33] , we have to be sensitive to the fact that our senses are far from reliable. Hobbes had warned long ago : "deception of senses" leads to appearances or "apparitions" and the great deception of senses has to be "sense corrected."[34] If Tony Blair is to be believed, 'politics was a mix of intellect and instinct'[35] neither of which is amenable to scientific treatment. H.G. Wells had long lamented the general low level of intelligence and great reliance being put on leaders whereas "grown men do not need leaders."[36] But the real life is more complex. The appearance of sky and earth meeting at a distant point for sure or spherical shape of planets are optical illusions. In the age of quantum physics and mechanics (based on the measurement of the position and velocity of subatomic particles)[37], 10-dimensional universe, string and super string theories culminating in the theory of chaos, matter is found to be of less substance and hence demoted and replaced with concepts, organization, complexity and information. In the age of information, matter and materialism are declared dead.[38] This is what the so called New Physics is all about. Russell was said to be very appreciative of the wonders of Quantum Mechanics.[39] Matter is unimportant, things happen randomly, nothing is predictable and enduring. Heisenberg's uncertainty principle reigned supreme. For all the apprehensions of Einstein, God was indeed playing the dice. Fuzzy logic had taken over. All kinds of permutations, combinations, mutations through natural, random selection made physics a dicey subject. Quarks changed their position on seeing them and if velocity is measured, the distance between the components of atoms and their position is lost. We can't seem to know enough. We don't know for sure whether things will change after the scientists at CERN, who are set to announce the discovery of the so-called God-Particle (Higgs Boson) in mid-July, 2012, a long awaited discovery.[40] In the meantime, Quirkology may gain in popularity where theory of relativity is explained this way: Einstein once said, 'Sit with a beautiful woman for an hour and it seems like a minute, sit on a hot stove for a minute and it seems like an hour – that's relativity'[41]. "one doesn't have to be a prophet to predict consequences....Reason will be replaced by Revelation.....Knowledge will degenerate into a riot of subjective visions"[42] 'Naïve Realism' (the common sense picture of the physical world, as Ayer puts it, p. 83) under the influence of which we tend to believe what we see or perceive, is falsified by physics. Russell proclaimed that grass is green, stone is hard, snow is cold are all wrong statements under the '*causal theory of perception*'.[43] The common sense view of the world and that of physicist's view of the world appear to be in clash because ....not only that what we see/perceive may just be an appearance, the place (the problem of space) where we place the object of observance also seems to be wrong: "This is not to say that things are always where they seem to be."[44] Mind-body controversy has assumed new dimensions and the problem of consciousness and its role in perception building compounds complications.[45] The Idealists (they regard whatever that exists, "must be in some sense mental"[46]) like Hegel would accord precedence to Idea and mind, the Realists and Marxists would proclaim that mind makes sense only in a body alive, mind without body does not make sense.[47] The question of perception involves mind and consciousness. Why/how mind perceives remains obscure. Wilson records that up to 1970, most scientists thought that the concept of mind be better left to philosophers.[48] Everything that we know and can know about existence is located in the brain and brain, in the words of Wilson, "is a machine assembled not to understand itself but to survive."[49] But if you ask what is mind? The scientists dance around the question as very little is known as yet. No powerful, enduring theory of mind exists, making mind a mystery. However, Wilson ventures to write, "mind is stream of conscious and sub-conscious experience. It is at root the coded representation of sensory impressions and the memory and imagination of sensory impressions. The information composing is most likely sorted and retrieved by vector coding, which denotes direction and magnitude.....Consciousness consists of the parallel processing of vast numbers of such coding networks."[50] This is hardly the most clarifying definition for the social scientists. Similarly, defining emotion, impulse, stimulus, is equally hard, although attempts are made in that direction.[51] The cognitive process is too complex to be left to a few definitions. Consciousness remains as elusive as ever when it comes to defining it in universally acceptable terms. "Consciousness is the virtual world composed by the scenarios....the mind is a self-organizing republic of scenarios that individually germinate, grow, evolve, disappear and occasionally linger to spawn additional thoughts and physical activity."[52] Perception and consciousness are hands in glove. But "consciousness has temporal and spatial limits in the universe." Moreover, consciousness is tied to bodies. "To be conscious is essentially to have sensations of 'what is happening to me': in other words, of what is happening at the boundary between me and not-me."[53]

Like ideology, perception can be a false consciousness, (even a dream)[54] but a definitive debate on the term and a conclusive understanding of it remains out of the realm of possibility making discourse analysis attractive proposition to pursue. Hence, what has been undertaken is a discourse on perception. The term perception presents problems, as has been shown above, most of which are insurmountable. If someone's perception is presented with a dash of rhetoric, the combination can be deadly. Rhetoricians are masterful craftsmen of persuasion and the changers of perceptions. They can sow the seeds of suspicion, dislike, discord and hatred through their suave tongues.[55] The scientists are no better and theoretical physics deceives and deceives dangerously according to Arthur Koestler. Examples abound specially in the domain of politics.[56] From one point of view, everything is a matter of perception. Roger Penrose in his *Emperor's New Mind* wonders at one place: "How can one be wrong about what one actually perceives? Surely, one's actual perceptions are just the things of which one is directly aware, by definition; so one cannot be 'wrong' about it." But his certainty gives way to doubts subsequently. [57] Intelligence and consciousness are mutually inclusive, (p.526) with consciousness having some active effect (p. 528). Some writers call consciousness a raw sensation.[58] Consciousness is so important that Penrose thinks, "a universe governed by laws that do not allow consciousness is no universe at all." (p. 580). Humphrey quotes Roger Penrose to the effect: "it is the ability to divine or intuit truth from falsity in appropriate circumstances-to form inspired judgments – that is the hallmark of consciousness."[59] Inspiration (occasional flashes of new insights), 'odd feeling of elation' (p. 544) that can come from the unconscious (which is a function of consciousness?) and reported by many great minds (p. 541)[60]. Paul Dirac says that his *keen sense of beauty* is that which enabled him to divine his equation for the electron. 'Ability to divine things,' 'importance of aesthetic qualities' or 'aesthetic convictions' (p. 545) is all. Then there exists the *unconscious*. The role of the *unconscious* leads Penrose to observe that, 'I must concur with the view that unconscious processes are important.' (p. 546). He also believes that the *unconscious* does not throw ideas at random but 'there is impressive selection process' whereby only those ideas that have a 'chance' alone surface. (p. 546). Many unusual ideas come up but cannot stand the scrutiny of 'critical judgment of wakeful consciousness.' (p. 546). Mozart, writes Penrose, wondered how such ideas come in a flash and become part of creative work but said, "Whence and how do they come? I do not know and I have nothing to do with it." (p. 546). The globality of inspirational thought is noteworthy (p. 447). Schopenhauer believed that, "thoughts die the moment they are embodied by words" (but verbalization, Penrose argues, is necessary for thought, p. 548). Vision, sensation and consciousness reinforce each other and it is the consciousness that breeds and sustains perception. "Sensation is indeed in a different category to perception", argues Humphrey. It is not intuitively obvious that, "visual sensations and visual perceptions are different categories of experiences."[61] But both affect perception but may not be in equal measure. "The chief function of vision is perception."[62] Francis Bacon's Theory of Idols involved identification of defects of reflections that pass through an uneven mirror which our mind is. We are prone to get distorted images i.e. the idols, which cause distorted images, we can avoid this by training our minds.[63] If one probes deep into the question of perception, one runs into the psychological, philosophical and epistemological terrain as well. Merleau Ponty, in his much acclaimed work on perception, attacks the sense-datum theory, maintaining that the notion of 'pure sensation' corresponds to nothing in our experience. Distinguishing between layers of impressions within experiences is not justified. "The mistake made by empiricists is to introduce sense-data as objects, whereas it is a 'pre-objective realm that we have to explore in ourselves if we wish to understand sense experience."[64] Ponty goes on: "All knowledge takes its place within the horizons opened up by perception..."[65] He maintains that, "the traditional analysis missed the phenomenon of perception."[66] Ponty is upset that empiricists deduce datum from what happens to be furnished by the sense organs and in this way, 'perception is built upon with states of consciousness as a house is built with bricks, and a mental chemistry is invoked which fuses these materials into a compact whole."[67] Morleau-Ponty insists that thought does not exist independent of words and therefore it is hard to see how a phenomenon can have meaning without being conceptualized.[68] Another difficulty is that, 'there is, in the mass of sensations and memories, nobody who sees'.[69] Morleau-Ponty's arguments led him ultimately to, what Ayer calls, "thickset of idealism" which allows him to argue in favour of things existing outside one's own experience.[70] Neither sense-datum nor idealism satisfactorily solve the problems of perception. Paul Schilder warns us that, "the concept of perception needs scrutiny."[71] When we speak of perception, we generally think of sense perception by which we mean sensation which is an abstraction. Kafka, according to him, rightly criticized this way of looking at things and Schilder argues that, "there is no constant correspondence between simple objects of the outside world, stimuli and simplest experience."[72] It is therefore, "incorrect to say that perceptions are built of sensations......sensations are by no means the natural units of psychic life, particularly not in the sense that psychic life is built of such simple sensations. There is a widespread opinion, more or less tacitly held, that only sensations are realities and that they become perception by being displaced into the outside world through projection."[73] But in an empirical, sense-based knowledge representing sense perception/impression, we work with (in Anglo-Saxon empirical tradition) and any other route to knowledge (like the Continental Idealism, pursuit of origins and essences of things, Kantian philosophy, involving critique of pure, practical reason, Phenomenology, [74] , the German penchant for 'Will' etc., resorting to intuition, wisdom of sages, scriptures, divine knowledge through the institution of prophet-hood etc.), being branded as metaphysical and unscientific, it is hard to accommodate many psychological and philosophical dimensions involved. Knowledge based on brute facts (whose validity cannot be questioned) derived from sense data and not being 'judgmental' is something that is valued in the English speaking world.[75] This they do notwithstanding the fact that our senses are deficient and unreliable. The idea is to avoid subjective intuition and rival interpretation preferred by the traditional and logical empiricists.[76] Scientists like Einstein embrace Russell's arguments.[77] For Russell, perception is naturally something mental. But what we perceive and what we experience are different things. Seeing the sun and sun itself are two different things. "The astronomer's sun is inferred, it is not hot or bright, and it existed eight minutes before what is called seeing it. I see the sun and it makes me blink, what I see is not 93,000,000 miles and eight minutes away, but is causally (and therefore spacio-temporally) intermediate between the light waves striking the eye and the consequent blinking." "Naïve realism" needs to be avoided. Similarly, "If my seeing of the sun is identical with the sun I see, then the sun that I see is not the astronomer's sun. For exactly the same reason, the tables and chairs I see, if they are identical with my seeing of them, are not located where physics says they are, but where my seeing is. You may say that my seeing, being mental, is not in space; if you do, I will not argue the point. But I shall none the less insist that there is one, region of space-time with which my seeing is always causally bound up, and that is my brain at the time of seeing. And exactly the same is true of all objects of sense-perception."[78] "The dualistic view of perception, as a relation of a subject to an object, is one which, following the leadership of William James, empiricists have now for the most part abandoned. The distinction between "seeing the sun as a mental event, and the immediate object of my seeing, is now generally rejected as invalid and in this view I concur." The problem of perception remains tricky and far from simple. Schilder states that, "....the world of experience is discontinuous. I have shown elsewhere that we can hardly make the world as a whole the object of our actions."[79] Further, "fundamentally, perception, images, and thoughts always have a subjective and an objective aspect. What we call sensation is the subjective aspect of perception. For the objective side of images and thoughts we have no term."[80] When an object is removed from sight, writes Hobbes, "we still retain an image of the thing seen." Latins call this *imagination* and the Greeks *fancy* but it signifies appearance (which can be deceptive, perceived variedly). "Imagination, therefore is nothing but decaying sense." Old and past sense turns into memory and imagination and memory merge and become one. "Much memory, or memory of many things, is called experience."[81] These observations have relevance for perception which can be based on obsolete data, old appearances (Hitler underestimating US power not expecting it to intervene in the war), besides prejudices, ideological and other.

No perception is free from imagination and Hobbes calls imagination, "nothing but decaying thought." If perception is an imperfect, even unacceptable concept, the same is widely used. If one seeks to differentiate between perception arising out of/based on sense-based hard scientific data or perception soiled with unscientific elements like gut feelings, hunches, premonitions, fears (real or imaginary), reflections and speculations, historical sense (a Pole will be bullish/ stubborn or a Caucasian vengeful and unforgiving etc.), one is apt to realize that no perception can be cent per cent scientifically based. The 'unscientific' elements do creep in. Only wisdom (an unscientific entity) can at times help. But the world is governed with so little wisdom. What is called "naïve realism" (the doctrine that things are what they seem) is also false.[82] Einstein points out that, "man has intense desire for assured knowledge. That is why Hume's clear message seemed crushing: the sensory raw material , the only source of our knowledge…."[83] But Einstein is sensitive to Hume's dilemma: "whatever in knowledge is of empirical origin is never certain." To make matters worse, we tend to mix concepts and propositions with factual data.[84] Hume's fear of metaphysics which may lead to what Christopher Evans called *cults of Unreason (1974),*[85] does not go well with Einstein.[86] Problems are bound to be there. Perception often gets fused with imagination. Imagined friends and enemies may not turn out to be the real friends and enemies. For Einstein, "imagination is more important than knowledge."[87] Jules Verne never left the quiet of his house but his imagination produced works like *A Journey to the Center of the Earth (1864)* and his other famous works. Those who scoffed at it had this to hear from him, "Whatever one man is capable of conceiving, other men will be able to achieve."[88] This is true in the case of science fiction as well. We know that Arthur C. Clark's imaginative science-fiction led to satellite building. Some of the leading ideas and theories like Black Holes, Big Bang theory, Quantum Physics, String theory etc. originated in coffee house debates and discussions where free play was given to imagination. "That phrase 'no meaning' introduces the latest phase of thinking in physics which is called the queen of sciences by Paul Davies and which has led the way for all other sciences.[89] Some critics call it 'ironic science', speculation as much as experimentation, where there is no real evidence for the (often) outlandish ideas being put forward."[90] Much of theoretical Physics take recourse to imagination. New Physics "finds closer accord with mysticism than materialism."[91] Fritjof Capra wrote *Tao of Physics to* fuse Eastern mysticism and the modern Physics.[92] Paul Dirac finds accommodation of beauty in calculations as progress and Bohm declared: "Physics is a form of insight and as such it's a form of art."[93] "Mathematics is the poetry of logic" intoned Paul Davies.[94] Kant relates imagination ("indispensable to function") to soul without which no cognition (and hence understanding) is possible.[95] When Hitler's advisors reeled out facts to show that the combined might of Britain and France was so much more than Germany's, Hitler excoriated : our job is not be slaves to facts but to rise above them; that is how great/superhuman deeds are accomplished. His perception had the day and Vienna was subdued. It is hard to maintain that unscientific perceptions are totally devoid of any value. Then where do we go from here? The continental philosophy went to the other extreme by inquiring into the origins and essences of things. Phenomenology, the offshoot of which is Existentialism, became dominant philosophy of the European continent, devised the Doctrine of Intentionality. Husserl's teacher, Franz Brentano, expostulated that, "what is distinctive of mental phenomena is their being directed towards an object which might or might not objectively exist." Brentano divided mental phenomena into three fundamental classes: representations, judgments and affective attitudes of acceptance or rejection.[96] Brentano's '**psychognosy**' inspired Husserl to publish philosophy of arithmetic which became an object of criticism by Frege. Husserl accepted criticism of Frege (in his book *Logical Investigations*, 1900) and combined analysis of knowledge, intentionality and meaning rejecting any subordination of mathematics to psychology.[97] Husserl gave priority to philosophy of psychology by delineating acts of consciousness and their objects, "to which he gave priority over all other forms of enquiry coining the term Phenomenology where, "the investigation of phenomena was treated as a conceptual rather than empirical proceeding." Phenomenology consisted in the 'intuition of essences' similar to Moore's analysis of concepts pointing increasingly towards idealism.[98] Here, Descartes' *Cogito Ergo Sum* made it subjective idealism, although different from solipsism (self existence is the only certainty).[99] From the foregoing account, the following points may be deduced.

Problems of Perception in the Real World

Perception is not a photographic image of the object perceived. Human mind is an uneven mirror as Fracas Bacon argued. Its reflections are defective, full of what Bacon called 'idols'. Cleansing them of these idols alone can ensure appropriate, accurate images. Training of minds is therefore required.

Perception is individual and differs from person to person. There is a unique quality to perception: why an individual perceives and how he perceives remain distinct to the individual concerned.

Perception can represent prejudices. Balraj Madhok and Lal Krishn Advani, being refugees, will show deep negative prejudices against Pakistan. A Marxist-Leninist will either underplay or downrightly reject any perception of threat from China at all. The Chinese official position is the version he would accept. For him, 1962 war with China will remain *India's China War*. An

Indian hard core nationalist will see threats all around, from Pakistan, China and all the small neighbours, suspicious of India and the internal threats from the Christians and Muslims etc. Sri Lanka, Bhutan, Nepal and Bangladesh will be prone to pro-Chinese proclivities and play India against China or at least play China/Pakistan card. The think tanks in India would see only threats since their shops cannot run without perceived enemies. They will magnify threats and recommend huge spending on defense so that India can meet any threat and any eventuality. India's defense budget of 1,93,407 crore rupees (1.9% of the GDP) is high enough.[100] India now (in 2010) is world's top arms buyer, buying arms worth $5.8 billion.[101] The Indian army chief's recent statements about 14 crore bribe being offered to him,[102] the substandard weapons the defense personnel are equipped with, thanks to corrupt and scandalous deals[103] and India not being combat ready, will be lapped up. Many of them will make calculations about limited nuclear war. Various schemes of deterrence would be suggested involving huge expenditure. A country like Israel can never perceive Arab neighbours in a friendly light. The Arab countries represent a perennial threat. Here, perennial war remains the only perception as Israel sees it.

Perceptions can be misperceptions which can stoke the fire of tensions, war of nerves culminating eventually in war in many instances. Napoleon III-Bismarck provocation over Venetia and Luxemburg[104] or Hitler's proclivity to underestimate the power of the US and the possible US intervention in war.[105] Both Napoleon and Hitler perceived war on two fronts feasible and Russia was the victim. Misperceptions and apprehensions of all the major powers on the eve of WW I is also an instance. Vietnam was to be a cake walk and within a couple of weeks it was all to be over after American victory if Halberstorm's book *The Best and the Brightest* is to be believed. Afghanistan was no different and America remained bogged down in both the wars for more than a decade. Down to our time, misperception about the Soviet power during the Cold War (the Soviet economy, at its height, was no more than 18 per cent of the American economy) and the resultant grand Strategies, military doctrines, grandiose deterrence schemes, war games and the development of concepts like 'second strike' and 'massive retaliation' and 'limited nuclear wars' etc. provided another instance. Behind the Cuban missile crisis were mutual misperceptions and apprehensions.[106] In the case of Iraq, the non-existent Weapons of Mass Destruction (WMD) (admitted now by Tony Blair: ("We thought that there was active WMD programme and there wasn't't")[107] entered the threat perception which Bush pushed and Blair found credible. In their autobiographies, Bush shows no compunction, while Blair exhibits qualms of conscience.[108] But millions were killed in Iraq and Afghanistan. About Iran today, the same misperceptions continue which may lead to war. Even after Bin Laden's killing, the Americans are trying hard not to leave Afghanistan after 2014. Their threat misperceptions are responsible for it. The current misperceptions about Islam/ Muslims has begat Islamophobia for the US and the Western Europe prompting the likes of Andrei Brewick to kill scores of innocent Norwegians. These misperceptions may lead to many more catastrophes which will feed up on each other. It is the new Don Quixote fighting the windmill of Islam.

Certain perceptions are artificially created, cultivated and sold through controlled media. The hyping of the so-called terrorism and unending 'war on terror' to achieve the preconceived goals of pre-emptive strikes and regime change suffuses with such elements.[109] America needed an enemy after the Cold War to justify its massive expenditure on arms and intelligence gathering and an artificial and wrong enemy was invented and sponsored i.e. the Muslims. The US believes : 'We are an empire now. And when we act, we create our own reality.'[110] Most Muslim countries cannot even produce an equivalent of Kalashnikov. The war on terror is taking its own toll on the West: general brutalization, curtailment of democracy, human rights, tighter government control.[111]

The hiatus between perception and actuality, between perception and reality remains huge, sometimes insurmountable. Zulfekar Ali Bhutto's perceptions that Pakistani people would prefer to eat grass than not have nuclear bomb. The perception of parity here is coupled with the perception of threat from a nuclear India. The reality is, both the countries with all their nuclear weapons, have never been able to live up to the image of nuclear powers and remain under the effective domination of the US.

Perception besides being a physical phenomenon, is also a psychic phenomenon. Psychology of an individual/leader plays a great role. Hitler thought that Czechoslovakia appeared like dagger in the belly of Germany on the map and hence needed to be weeded out.[112] Hitler's obsession with racism and Aryan supremacy completely blinded him and determined his perception. These ideas, interestingly, were formed when he was just 21 and he admitted that he had not changed his ideas at all since then. Besides, the psychology of fear serves to distort one's perception. One may begin to see non-existent phantoms and react in a paranoid way. Tsar Ivan the Terrible killed his own son. He used to have a list of people who were around him to be killed just like the White House today. The lists of people to be killed on Afghan-Pakistan border through Drone aircrafts are supplied by the White House.[113] Under democracy, the opponents were supposed to be treated decently and not killed. This principle is abandoned by the US today. The world is witness to many a leader without mental balance, even insane ones. Nero's famed tears and playing of an musical instrument on the burning of Rome are well known. Stalin suffered from these symptoms as clinical assessment of him showed in *An Anatomy of Human Destructiveness* by Eric Fromm. He was always full of suspicion, never trusted anyone. He posed as an ally before Churchill and Roosevelt but behind the back his mind was always working on establishing Russian dominance over the West. World War II was a war for world's markets. There was nothing to choose between Germany and Allies as both will not hesitate a moment to finish off Russia if they could. Hence, when WW II will sufficiently bleed both the configurations, Russia will intervene and subjugate the West for the socialist cause. Ceausescu of Romania was another example and so was Mao as latest writings on Mao show him to be.[114]

Perceptions and impressions get mixed up. The reliability of impressions is very uncertain. Impulses, emotions, sentiments and the defects of cognitive processes also serves to distort perception. For Nehru, 1962 came as a shock. He never believe nor ever expected the Chinese aggression. He was shattered. Panchsheel and 'Hindi Chini Bhai Bhai' (Indians and Chinese are brothers) slogans lost their sheen. Chamberlain's appeasement strategy misfired and the perception that Hitler could be appeased into accepting the status quo and avoid going to war proved a chimera.

Perceptions can be handiwork of intuition, hunches, premonitions etc. Wisdom, vision, divining, elating inspirations, surmises and guesses, gut feelings, images and thoughts all go into perceptions, even empirical analyses and evaluations. Superstitions can creep in too. Nancy had rendered Reagan quite superstitious. For him, Russian was an evil empire and socialism was an evil, satanic creed. He had an instinctive dislike for everything Soviet. He even played the hoax of Star War weapons, a new generation of space based expensive weapons. Gorbachev was spooked according to some. For all the claims that empiricists in the Anglo-Saxon world make for empiricism and brute facts, empiricism and data based on empiricist methods is far from reliable. Hume-Kant approaches dwelt on this problem as we have shown. Our senses are far from perfect tools to rely on. Naïve realism cannot work either. Morleau-Ponty and others that we have cited above provide enough material in this regard. It is not for nothing that Heisenberg's uncertainty principle has shown the great staying power. Hence, the perceptions based on the sense-data have to be taken with a pinch of salt.

Perception based on technologies are not problem free either. Blunders committed in Iraq, Afghanistan in the name of carpet bombing, drone aircrafts killing scores of innocent people, even children, have made nonsense of the claims of precision. For all its technological sophistication, the US got bogged down in Vietnam, Iraq and Afghanistan. Too many innocent lives were lost. What kind of assessments the US defense establishments make with all the most sophisticated technologies at their command? How many times the US was forced to extend apologies for its misperceptions and misconduct. Many of the 169 to 625 Guantanamo Bay tortured prisoners, half of them found innocent, have smeared the American record as the protector of human rights worldwide as former President Carter rightly points out.[115] Under democratic philosophy the opponents are to be treated fairly and decently. American anti-terrorist laws are making nonsense of these ideas, making the US the most unpopular country in the world.[116]

Perception may mistake appearance for reality. The appearance of the Trojan horse and the reality of soldiers hiding inside the horse are two different things. Appearance of calm on the peaks hid the reality of Pakistan soldiers occupying 48 peaks before the Kargil war. Musharraf gives a different version.[117] Kargil did not take place in isolation. It was tit for tat for him. Siachen was no man's land which India grabbed.[118] The appearance of calm on the borders hid the reality today of Chinese soldiers violating the border and making deep incursions into the Indian territory. This was graphically shown on an Indian TV channel CNN-IBN.

Perception could contain ideological elements and become a false consciousness. Lenin characterized the First world War as a war among the imperialists to gain control of markets and the workers had nothing to do with such a war. The workers should stay away from the war efforts of the bourgeoisie in the European countries. But workers everywhere enlisted and fought for their countries. The slogan that the workers have no country also proved wrong. Lenin, until his death, believed that the revolution in the West was just round the corner and it will come to the aid of the fledgling Soviet regime. Trotsky shared such a belief. Ideologies are like lenses, the wearing of which colour your seeing, imagination, perception and thought. The perception of friends and enemies gets coloured too. Lenin thought that the Polish workers will be sympathetic to the Soviet workers but Polish workers ferociously fought the Soviet army comprising workers. The idea that workers have no country was ideological and not real. After the bitter experiences during the Civil War in 1918 during which period 14 bourgeois armies marched into the RSFSR, Lenin worked out a two camp theory-the capitalist camp and the socialist camp. The capitalist camp had worked out a 'capitalist encirclement' of the young Soviet socialist regime. It was made part of the 1924 constitution. The Soviet state had to break out of this encirclement. The analysis was heavily ideological as was shown by the fact that one of my teachers working on the material released in his times in London, found a margin entry in Churchill's hand enquiring : 'who is Lenin ?'

Perception can be artificially created. Populist hype and media management can make them appear real. The hatred of Saddam Hussain and Gaddafi, the bogey of weapons of mass destruction, Saddam-Al Qaida linkage, Osama hiding in Afghanistan mountains, 9/11 being Al Qaida work and Osama was directly responsible for it, may be counted among so many misperceptions created and hyped through managed media described as *Manufacturing Consent by* Noam Chomsky.

There can be perception based on intentionality. Knowledge, meaning and intentionality may give a different twist to the making of perception. For Hitler and Mussolini, war was a purgative. Wars beget superhuman actions. Peace was like a disease. All great races either expand or perish. The oceans will stink if there were no storms. Aryans were the chosen race. Lebensraum was a natural corollary. For Mussolini, Rome lived. If Rome could provide civilisational lead in ancient times, it could provide it yet again. Nationalism and racism were a heady brew, a deadly combination. The aggressive foreign policies Rome and Berlin pursued represented intentionality. Knowledge and meaning were loaded into it all. Things were pre-ordained for the Fascists and the Nazis which were to be accomplished through intentionality. Theirs was a destiny-based perception. History was on their side. They represented the wave of the future.

If perceptions are to be credible, all these pitfalls have to be kept in mind. One slips into the realm of art. Here, experience, intelligent guesses, wisdom, intuition (although all of them unscientific) play a crucial role. For all of its faults, perception cannot be abandoned. No country can do without a framework of threat perception.

The linkages between 'threat perception', 'national security' and 'foreign policy studies' are intimate, real and strong. Threat perception could be imaginary or real. Threat perception, to be objective, credible, and closer to reality, has to transcend a coward's nightmare and a jingoist's hallucination as pointed out before. Such Psychology begat beliefs like this: Without the conquest of Russia, the mastery over Europe will not be complete. Napoleon's attack on Russia in the early 19th century and Hitler's unprovoked attack on an ally like Russia in 1941 may be cited as examples. To the examples given about Hitler and Mussolini, another one may be added. Brezhnev desired to surround the USSR with satellite states to secure the USSR and the Brezhnev Doctrine of limited sovereignty could be harnessed to serve that purpose partly if not fully. Such ideas were false. A sufficient realistic basis and a sufficient factual basis lends credibility to a threat perception configuration/ model.

Threat perception encompasses both 'internal' and 'external' dimensions. In this paper, however, we have concentrated on the external dimension. Threats may be perceived on matters bilateral, multilateral, regional as well as global. Iran is threatened primarily by the US-Israel combine both of which are not territorially contiguous. So is the case of North Korea. They both are termed as 'rogue states'. 'Failed states' is another category that can invite foreign intervention of some kind or the other. The new tools like sanctions, UN vote, gun boat diplomacy, establishment of no flying zones, affecting regime change through sabotage or 'rent a crowd tactic' are all threats which cannot be ignored. Iran's threat perceptions are external and the new tools mentioned above being closely watched. It was argued by some that the desire for nuclear weapons by Iran and South Korea was directly linked to and whetted by the fear of the US attack and the need to thwart/face it. Threat perception can engender abnormal, sometimes queer responses like the case of North Korea. The World Order (representing Uni-polar, Multi-polar, or pole-free anarchical configuration of forces at the global level at a given point of time) colors the threat perceptions. Hostile alliances like the NATO for Iran or other multilateral/ global arrangements like the auspices of the UN can exacerbate threats or its perceptions. The regional environment also plays a role in generating threat perception of a kind. More concrete is the threat perception rooted in bilateral matters/environment. Over and above these considerations, economic threats have come to occupy a central stage in the times of 'globalization'. Jeans, Jazz, Coca Cola, Burgers, KFC, other items of junk food and artificial needs and consumerism can cause cultural threats. There are scholars who have devoted themselves to pursue cultural international relations of whom Huntington was a prime example. Threats and their perception can therefore be varied, assuming political, military, economic, socio-cultural and cyber dimensions. To some, America represented an evil society, an evil culture, the influence of which had to be countered in all spheres. America is out to change the world in its own image and safeguard it by assuming the role of a global cop. On the other hand, Huntington thought the world has come to accept/emulate the model of politics and economics America represented. In fact, America is aped all over the world. It is only in cultural matters that the greatest resistance has come, from the Muslim world in particular, and hence that world has to be made to fall in line. Gone are the days when the West contemplated cooperating with the Muslim world in the face of the Soviet invasion of Afghanistan in 1979.[119] Culture matters and cultural fault lines would become the battle lines of future. The threat comes from the Western/American socio-politico-cultural values/ norms not accepted by the an array of countries.

Threat and its perception remains rife in foreign policy making. The foreign policies pursued by the states around the world remain threat/threat perception driven. Threat perceptions and foreign policies stand mutually reinforcing. The security concerns/issues, the concepts of friends and enemies, allies and opponents are all interconnected and all of them find their echo in threat perceptions debates. The existence and persistence of threats and their perception is a recurring phenomena in international relations studies. A sub-discipline like the Strategic Studies is suffused with the ideas of threat perceptions and ways and means to ward off threats. The concepts of security and threat perception are closely related. In strategic studies, security is a core concept.[120] This is more so when we have an anarchical situation on hand. Kenneth Waltz thinks that, "in anarchy, security is the highest end."[121] The fact that the concept of security defies definition and one has to wade through a variety of ambiguities, many writers have given up on the concept of security.

Buzan chooses to call security a contested concept.[122] If we speak of national security, the nation to be taken as inclusive of all its people? The contradictions involve defense and security issues, between individual and national security and between national security and international security. Do we need to take a holistic view or national or individualistic views? Security has to be ensured through force/power or through peaceful means ? At a given point of time, what is to be secured, which level of security to be sought? These are tricky questions to tackle.[123] Arnold Wolfers, Hedley Bull, Bernard Brodie, Frank Trager, Frank Simonie have all found it difficult to apply the concept of security.[124] In a changing global environment, (say globalization or unipolar world configurations) what approach to be taken ? Sometimes it has led some writers like Arnold Wolfers to declare that, it "may not have any precise meaning at all."[125] In other words it does not mean anything at all. However, absence of precise definition need not serve as a handicap and Buzan suggests that we can look at the question through 'the perceptual lens of security' like we look at security through power and peace lenses. Just like the concept of Balance of Power emerges by looking at international relations through Power lenses.[126]

Threats and their perception stems both from within and without. To detract the attention from domestic problems, the states/individual politicians may extrapolate threat as coming not from within but from without like Clinton ordering bombarding of Iraq to detract attention from Lewinsky affair. The states may weave/cite phantoms like Communism or 'war on terror' etc. into threat perception. Such threat perceptions are spurious but may lead to distorting/damaging situations/imbroglios. For some states, threats come from outside through external interventions/invasions (Iraq, Afghanistan etc.) or what has come to be known as 'rent a crowd' tactics as in the case of some former Soviet republics Ukraine, Kirghizstan, Georgia etc. (and in the case of former East European states like the 'Velvet' revolution in Czechoslovakia) undergoing the so-called color revolutions like the Orange revolution.

Can a threat be precisely defined and measured ? Not really. Hence threats remain ipso facto perceptual. Since we are concerned with not domestic but external threats, we can ask: when can a country feel secure? When its hegemony is uncontested at regional/international levels? Pax Britannic or Pax Americana, unipolar world where one super power calls the shots, dictates terms to the entire international/regional or individual country as epitomized in Medeline Albright's words, "nothing goes without us." But even then 9/11 happened. Or alternatively, one surrounds oneself with yes regimes in the neighborhood and beyond as was sought to be done by Brezhnev partly through Brezhnev Doctrine? Either arrangement is not full proof. Reagan's Star War weapons proved to be a hoax but even if such a system of space based weapons can be devised, the same can be dented as was evident from the plan Putin handed over to NATO chief not long ago. Can threats be of the order to necessitate a system of deterrence involving 'second strike', 'massive retaliation' through Armageddon leading to total annihilation?

A world free from threats, security concerns, wars and violence is enticing to imagine through a collective security system or other means. Konrad Lorenz believes that what can win the day is the diffusion of right values.[127] Threats can be minimized and money saved by pursuing a sensible, flexible, intelligent, and accommodative foreign policy. It often does not happen. Ban Ki-Moon skirts Iran, ills of the unipolar world, US 'exceptionalism' and interventions and other political issues and speaks of sustainable development- the goal declared at Rio summit 20 years ago and the second one that followed in June, 2012, for the 7 billion people of the world.[128] The scientists involved in making the atomic bomb thought that if the atom bomb idea worked, it will lead to "no more wars' and 'a world without war' as Oppenheimer puts it.[129] If only security could be ensured for all through some agreeable Collective Security arrangements; conflict resolution devices; universally accepted International Law and viable international organization/organizations, the world could be rid of the scourge of war itself leave alone threat perceptions. But the world we live in, where the national and state boundaries do not coincide and where Westphalia sovereignty related sensibilities reigns supreme, it sounds something of a pipe dream. World Watch Institute Report[130], Club of Rome Project[131], Feminist movements, peace research and disarmament studies[132] have not made the requisite dent on the thinking of states and politicians.

Security and threat perception can be both imaginary and real. Configuration of power/forces at international/global levels, regional and bilateral levels at a given point of time provide ammunition to the debates on threat perception and security issues serve as a decisive determinant of foreign policy. Threats from contiguous neighbors no longer serves as the staple of threat perception imagery. Iran and South Korea are not contiguous to the US nor were Iraq and Afghanistan. Iran and Israel are not contiguous either. Iran and South Korea's nuclear ambitions are traceable, inter alia, to the threats perceptions from the US. The nuclear weapons, so it was imagined/thought, could help ward off or at least serve as a restraint and a bargaining chip vis a vis the US. Why do the states continue to feel threatened? To answer this question, the historical and psychological roots have to be traced. Here, fear is the key. It is sometimes argued that state is individual writ large. If Hobbes' mother gave birth to twins, himself and fear[133] and if one declares the distrust of society by locking one's door[134] and timorous Hobbes relocating himself to France in the wake of civil war conditions prevailing in England in 1640 (the Glorious Revolution of 1866 was in the making), Hobbes basic reason for the flight was fear or the perception of it, for his royalist views. Chester C. Maxey writes that Hobbes was being timorous and his fears were somewhat misplaced. He was relatively unknown and nobody would have threatened his life.[135] So is the case with many states which suffer from threat perceptions, both real and imaginary, and act in a paranoid way precipitating conflict. Threat perception, like security concerns, involve primarily threat to territory and population. The loss of these two entities results in the loss of cultural identity, which includes the loss of ideological, religious identities. Distinct language, traditions, ways of life, customs can not only be lost but get subordinated to the conquerors' culture and language. Fear of the loss of cultural identity and the fear of subjugation to the conqueror's ways is an all pervading fear. Destruction, loss of life presents another fear. The great sensitivity stems from these factors. The weak states live in constant fear. Threats and their perception are varied and differ from state to state and hence a universally applicable model or mapping of it pertaining to threat perception is hard to work out. Circumstances at bilateral, regional and international levels differ too. What Buzan thinks i.e. "unique structure of the circumstances of the state concerned"[136], informs threat perception. The understanding of threat is based on multifarious perceptions of threat. There can be threats other than political. A set of economic threats in the forms of tariffs, embargoes, blockades, dumping, sanctions etc. can play havoc during both war and peace times. The economic instruments of foreign policy have acquired new teeth in the times of globalization we are living in. The threat of cultural invasion remains real. Jeans, Jazz, Coca Cola, Burgers and junk food, Hollywood movies and American lingo poses a great threat to native traditions, language and culture. Those doing cultural international relations like Huntington lend support to the idea of what they understand as modernity, progressive changes to be accepted and integrated by the non-Western societies. What is good for American should be good for the world and the world has accordingly to be changed into American image. This is taken as cultural onslaught to be resisted by many around the world. It is therefore evident that threats and their perception involves political, economic, socio-cultural domains. Threats to a way of life based on a religion, ideology or tradition are intrinsic to threat perception. Stronger states may have lesser quantum of threat perception compared to the weak states. Weak states also suffer from dependency syndrome. Buzan is right in maintaining that, "the distinction between weak and strong states is vital to any analysis of national security."[137] Today, very few states can afford to stand independent and sovereign in the classical sense. LPG, neo-conservative ideas have a sway and structural reforms, economic and trade regimes are taking their toll. Pursuit of independent foreign policy has become the privilege of a few strong states, even they are prevailed upon by the US most of the time. States are divided, sub-divided at the whim of the powerful. Sudan, East Timor or three partitions of Poland in the past may be adduced as examples. Any defiance is punished through sanctions, worst still through intervention or downright invasion and occupation. Threat perception has come to acquire totally new dimensions. Sovereignty of most of the states stands threatened. Multinational corporations have made nonsense of sovereignty. Naomi Klein's *No Logo* captures most of these,[138] often disturbing, developments. The economic restructuring dispensation is all-pervasive aiming to create a borderless world. Under these circumstances threats and their perception have to be looked at very differently. The internal security dimension has come to acquire greater significance. Buzan is partly right in maintaining that, "Unless the internal dimension is relatively stable as a prior condition, the image of the state as a referent object for security fades into a meaningless blur."[139] Fear psychosis is all pervading in a unipolar dispensation. States live in fear. The Big Brother is watching and watching perennially with the most sophisticated weapons of mass destruction and technologies under its command.

New Dimensions of Threat Perceptions in a Globalizing World

Threat perception involves a sense of deep vulnerability which may cause harm, damage, war, or loss of identity.[140] Under a globalizing world, the nature of threats and their perceptions have undergone radical changes.

- Up to now, threats were thought of in politico-military, geo-political terms. Armed conflicts between sovereign states for territorial gains or establishment of domination, twisting the arms of the states to do the bidding of the dominant state. The threats were politico-military and the dominant instruments were armament and war. Religions. Ideologies, vital territorial, economic and other interests, pursuit of power and enhancement of powers were dominant other means to achieve political objectives through instruments other than war. But the world is getting transformed into a borderless and interdependent world.

Robert McNamar, while recommending the arms build up for the US in the years of Cold War, suggested an alternative humanist understanding of security. He warned that, 'peace has nothing whatsoever to do with military hardware.' And that helping the developing countries, working for effective partnership and take steps to reduce the risk of war are necessary too.[141] However, the weak states always forged alliances with the strong/major powers to meet the threats. The world was configured in terms of friends and enemies.

Conquest, Imperialism (British style), hegemonic suzerainty (of the ancient Chinese empire involving no physical occupation but just tribute paying), the British imperialism followed by the American one were the dominant modes of domination over others. Gramsci's idea of hegemony, popularized by Robert Cox, is sometimes used to play down the role of violence in this subsequent mode of domination. This hegemony/domination has continued and taken different forms.

- Under globalizing dispensation, some new developments have emerged which are not exactly politico-military in nature. Right during the First World War, the interdependence of European states due to economic reasons and international division of labour resulting in interdependence of a high level, was felt. This is magnified in recent years many fold. Thomas L. Friedman, in famous book *The World Is Flat- The Globalized World in the Twenty-First Century* (2006) adduces 10 reasons why the world has gone flat and why conflict/ war can be too costly. Interdependence/integration, connectivities and global supply chains have rendered conflict/war an insane proposition. He outlines what he calls *The Dell Theory of Conflict Prevention, Golden Arch Theory of Conflict Prevention* that serves as antidotes to conflicts. Two countries having Dell, MacDonald and other MNCs would not think in terms of conflict.

Economic interdependence (of course, with no equal playing field) is actively forged with the neo-conservative LPG dispensation. The MNC's rule the economic domain both nationally and globally. FDI is seeking to dominate the global market. The idea of a borderless world with free and open access to markets of all the countries is being projected as the dominant idea of the day beamed from the First World to the Third worlds. The sway of economic factors is unmistakable. Threats are perceived differently under this dispensation. Economic threats have come to dominate the minds of the strategists. Market strategies are more important than the military strategies. ASEAN, NAFTA, SAFTA, Groups-8, Group-20, BRICS, Shanghai Cooperation Council, Strategic Partnerships, Axis arrangements – add new dimensions to threats and their perceptions. War has become very costly and often does not achieve the purpose for which it was fought. Wars acquire a logic of their own. Economic instruments of foreign policy like economic regulations, trade manipulations, creating economic satellites, economic spheres of influence, establishment of dependencies etc. are increasingly resorted to. A system of economic rewards and punishments is sought to be imposed. The techniques used in this regard include : manipulations of tariffs, quotas, economic boycott, embargoes, loans, credits with strings attached and currency manipulations, blacklisting, preemptive buying etc.[142] The trade with Cuba is still blockaded by the US. The US imposed crippling sanctions against Iraq causing the death of tens of thousands of people, particularly causing child malnutrition leading to the death of millions of children. Israel imposed embargoes and blockade on Gaza people is still causing untold hardships, even deaths to the people there. The Gaza sanctions still continue. Currently Iran is facing crippling sanctions imposed by the US and backed by the Europeans. These days sanctions, economic regimes, structural adjustments, economic reforms, economic aid to extract political objectives, lure of the FDI etc are frequently used by the sole super power and economically developed countries. Many other economic techniques are listed by John Perkins that include dispatching economic hit-men around the world.[143]

Another development is what may be described as the emergence of borderless world.[144] The Internet, information revolution, ICBM's, MIRVs, Nuclear protective shields etc make nonsense of borders in many ways. In a world without borders, the concepts of security, threats and their perceptions all stand changed.

Perhaps the most important development is the transformation of the concept of 'friends and enemies' which informs much of the foreign policy making, constituting the core and kernel of foreign policies. For Carl Schmidt, we spend all our lives fighting enemies. For long, specially after the Cold War, Islam and Muslims are sought to be projected as the principal enemies of the West. The Muslim world is still very backward and does not count for much in economic terms. Oil money has not fostered indigenous economic development. The resources they have are already largely controlled. But the rest of the world, is no longer perceived as divided into friends and enemies. For all their apprehensions, the US and China get along and dare not declare themselves as enemies. Huge US stakes of the US MNC's and Chinese holdings of over a trillion dollar American bonds ensures that. The Rubicon is not crossed. The tiffs here and there over Taiwan, Middle East (China and Russia voted against the US resolution on Syria), stealing of US weapon's secrets chafe but disruptive chasm never caused. Russia for all its apprehensions and protests over NATO's expansion eastward, war in Georgia, not allowing Ukraine and Georgia to become NATO members, US-EU moves in Central Asia, sponsoring of colour revolutions by the US in the 'near abroad', nuclear shield based on Eastern Europe, squabbles over Middle East etc. still appears accommodative. Putin may not attend the recent G-8 meeting in 2012 (duly retaliated by Obama) but keen to do business with the US and welcome American FDI. Post Bush 're-set' in Russo-American relations was harped upon when Putin and Obama met in Rio on the sidelines of Sustainable Development meet in June, 2012. Russian inferiority complex vis a vis the West is of such an order that at the whiff of a suggestion of accommodation being made, Russia will jump to the Western side. Putin would love to be seen shaking hands with the US President. Both Russia and China are keen to do business with the US. India and China similarly wish to be seen as friends rather than enemies. Even Pakistan and India have become accommodative and friendly thanks to American pressure and domination. If any of the countries cited above is asked who are their friends and enemies, they are sure to turn evasive. The economic considerations remain dominant and if a perceived enemy is eliminated, the loss in economic terms will be damaging. You may attempt to outsmart/ pressurize but not eliminate a country which is a perceived enemy. Europe learned the hard way that a great power like Germany should not have been totally undermined, humiliated and eliminated. France, urging all the other European powers to do so after the world wars was found to be wrong. Germany's spectacular resurgence and aggressiveness had a crippling effect on Europe. Moreover, there is a remarkable tendency under which former friends have turned adversaries and former adversaries have become friends. Who could have imagined a few years ago that Russia, China and the US would become accommodative, at times, even friends. Yeltsin and Deng may be taken as examples. The Europeans chose to forget their past enmities and forged a European Union and the traditional enemies, particularly over Alsace-Lorraine, Germany and France, became arch friends in the EU ? We are living in a different time. The elite countries are no longer divided and fighting but united against the rest, chiefly the non-Western world. Dependencies and satellite states have remained. (Globalization is a one way street sans equal playing field beamed from the First World to the rest of the world which has to open their markets, carry out economic reforms, make structural adjustments, welcome FDI – all to facilitate the smooth flow goods and services from the first world to reach the rest of the world). In the post-Opium Wars of 1842 and 1856, the principal demand mad was: open China for trade. This demand is today extended to the rest of the world. Gun boat diplomacy is back, assuming new and sophisticated forms. The global cop this time is far more powerful than the British (who ruled the waves right up to the 20th century) ever were. All resource rich countries are under threat. Great attention paid to Central Asia, West Asia and Afghanistan (recently found to be resource-rich) is explained by the fact the resources of the world are sought to be controlled and centralized and monopolized by the developed world. 'Virtual states' have come into existence. Few countries can afford the luxury of sovereignty and an assertively independent foreign policy. All these developments have grave implications for threats and their perception. In many situations, you have threats and their perceptions but you cannot do anything except appeal to the sole super power which controls the UN as well.

Of late, Environmental considerations have been sought to be projected as threats to mankind's existence. But the Americans have refused to sign Kyoto treaty and be part of any international arrangement which places time-bound restrictions to reduce pollution. Even the depletion of Ozone layer does not cause panic. The Club of Rome report is ignored and so are ignored the annual World Watch Institute Reports. Raul Prebisch Report, Michael Manley Report, Brandt Commission Reports met the same fate. Nobody is talking of a New International Economic Order or New Information Order. Transfer of technology ideas are gone and treatment of economic aid as investment for a better common future where every country will be a partner, abandoned. Nobody is asking the developed world to give at least 1 to 1.5 per cent of their GDP as aid to the developing countries. The Western economies are themselves in a mess and ironically PM Manmohan Singh has announced at Rio (2012) a contribution of $ 10 billion to the IMF to help the European banks to tide over their liquidity problems. Neo-conservatism has changed the world beyond recognition. Threats and perceptions have to confront neo-imperialism, neo-colonialism configurations. Either conform or perish. Bilateral and Regional wars soon degenerate into proxy wars as suppliers of costly weapons are located elsewhere. Huntington's West versus the Rest is after all a catchy proposition.

China abandoned Maoism for peace for development and assured neighbours that it has no aggression plans. It wants to be friends with one and all. China's 3000-member National People's Congress has 70 richest delegates who are worth $89.8 billion (to India's 36 richest MPs worth $252 million).[145] A host of trade agreements rule the economic life. Regional economic arrangements are forged. Trade blocs created. No hard enemies exist. Accommodation and trade is the general mood. Not political but economic strategies and partnerships are aimed at. China's relations with Nepal provide a good example.[146]

Cyber Threat has come out of the science fiction genre to become a reality. Recently, Russia developed, in Kaspersky lab, a virus called *flame* that has already been used against Iran by both the US and Israel to snuff out Iran's nuclear and missile programme. Earlier, in mid-2010, President Obama, since his early days of presidency, authorized a wave of crippling cyber attacks aimed at destablising the operation of Iran's key nuclear centrifuges. Publicly, Obama had assured that economic sanctions and negotiations were the only means he was using in the case of Iran. But the US teamed up with Israeli experts to unleash the so-called "Stuxnet" programme on Iran's Natanz uranium enrichment facility. One such series of attacks temporarily took out nearly 1000 of the 5000 centrifuges Iran had spinning at that time. Stuxnet escaped and spread around the world on the Internet. An anxious White House meeting debated the risks involved. Only in May, 2012, it was disclosed that the 20 to 40 times stronger than Stuxnet virus called 'flame' felled the Iranian systems and spreading around the world. Flame is described as an espionage virus that provides blueprint of Natanz's industrial computer control designs. Like Drones, the US never disclosed the use of *Flame* publicly. It means that the US can carry out a cyber war against any country including India which came under pressure over the question of Iran (India voted against Iran in the UN twice : on September 24, 2005 and February 4, 2006).[147] Russia-developed *Flame* virus was put to use almost immediately as the statement of one Israel minister is to be believed. He said on May 29, 2012, that the use of cyber weapons against Iran was "reasonable".[148] Obama ordered accelerated cyber attacks on Iran. Even before him, President Bush ordered such attacks and code-named them "Olympic Games" as detailed in David Sangar's book : *Confront and conceal : Obama's secret wars and surprising use of American Power.* An article in Time provided details of it all.[149] Pakistan, China and other neighbouring countries may take recourse to such techniques and India will have to stay alert on this question. However, right now no such threat exists in a blatant, known form but future is a different cup of tea.

Threats have gone global. Threats from contiguous neighbours are passé. Iran, as pointed out before, is not contiguous to the US nor is Israel. Sanctions can be imposed on any state. Trade and economic considerations also have assumed global dimensions and so have many other threats referred to above. Terrorism, trafficking, smuggling, narcotic trade, piracy, pornography, as threats, defy boundaries.

Energy related threat perceptions are rife. Smooth supply of oil and other energy sources, if threatened, can lead to calamitous situations. All states have become hyper sensitive about smooth supply of energy. Any possibility of disruption is viewed as a threat.

Immigration and multiculturalism are treated as threats by a number of states. Merkel, Camaroon and Sarkozy-all lambasted multiculturalism. Canadians, first to give constitutionally guaranteed status to multiculturalism, and the Australians once sympathetic to multiculturalism, have backed out and declared such a policy impractical and injurious, even a threat.

Threat Perception with Special Reference to India

While being aware that the concept of threat and its perception suffer from many crippling drawbacks as shown in the preceding sections, threat perception nonetheless has to be envisaged for India. What follows is a version of threat perception which is not beyond cavil.

The global scenario represents a mixed baggage. Politically, world remains unipolar with US domination persisting, even though the American economy is not in a good shape. Scholars like Niall Ferguson believe that the alternative to American hegemony is anarchy.[150] We beg to differ. America is hell bent on selling its version of democracy, liberal private enterprise economy, free trade, globalization to the rest of the world, specially to the Muslim world. Even after the Bin Laden's death in 2011, they insist that the spectre of terrorism continues to haunt the world and hence interventions, regime change, pre-emptive strike remain necessary. Some scholars speak of post American or post-Western world, but the domination of both the US and the West persists.[151] War on terror has degenerated into an alibi to interfere in the affairs of the non-Western world. American aggressive predominance, its donning of the mantle of the global cop, with NATO, (even the UN) at its disposal as its extended arms, is a reality India has to face. American repertoire of economic sanctions, blockades, propaganda, subversion remain in operation and the overall American goal of changing the world into its own image stays unchanged. Democracy of late is on the decline.[152] Will it lead to more aggressiveness from the US? Global Progress report says that "war is receding as an instrument of statecraft"[153] but it appears true of only the Western world. Wars are inflicted on the non-Western world with a disturbing regularity. The US wants its foreign policy obsessions/priorities to become the priorities of the rest of the world. If war on terror, isolation of Russia (under Bush), Iran and North Korea (the so-called rogue states), war on terrorism, promotion of globalization and economic integration to a global market, free trade, economic reforms and structural adjustments etc. become the American foreign policy priorities, the rest of the world is forced to emulate those policies. The free flow of goods, information, ideas and values leads to enmeshing of world into a relatively 'open and rule-based liberal order'. The security threats emanate only from failed states and religious (read Islamic only) ideologies.[154] The US-Israel perception of threat has to become the perception of threat for the rest of the world. India has to grapple with this global dispensation when she is calibrating threat perception.

Although India is the largest importer of arms in the world, its threat perceptions in general and with regard to its neighbours in particular, are all muddled. Is India faced with an armed conflict? Is an attack imminent? In May, 2012, only the war on terror was resonating. Can a war on terror cause a hot conflagration of war? Israel-America combine wants India to believe that.[155] As for as India is concerned, two major threat posing countries are Pakistan and China.

Pakistan : Pakistan's threat perceptions are not dealt with here.[156] The focus is on India's point of view. However, the centrality of Kashmir to peace and stability in South Asia is once again underlined by the Chairman, Joint Chiefs of Staff Committee, Gen. Khalid Shameem Wynne as reported on June 17, 2012. He also said : "We seek nothing beyond secure frontiers and pose no threat to any country and will accept no pressure for standing up for our principles."[157] Pakistan's PM Gilani never tires of pleading for improved India-Pakistan relations. Kashmir has long been a festering wound. India is playing a war of attrition in Kashmir, longer it is not solved, better it is for India. For Pakistan, the UN resolutions on Kashmir are important and for India they are obsolescent. The third party mediation is not acceptable to India and quite acceptable to Pakistan. For all the trust building measures, composite dialogue process, summit diplomacy, Tract-II behind the scene diplomacy, the solution of Kashmir problem remains a remote possibility. Lately, the government of India appointed interlocutors who have submitted a report : 'A New Compact With the People of Jammu and Kashmir', made public on May 24, 2012, and the Home Minister Chidambaram has asked for an 'informed debate' on the Report in an all party meeting ana other fora. The Report contains no practical, out of the box, solutions, not even restoring the special autonomous status for Kashmir. Amitabh Matto and Happymon Jacob call the report a farce in three parts.[158] Its main recommendation : to review all the Central Acts, Articles of the Constitution extended to Jammu and Kashmir.[159] In all likelihood, the Centre will dump the reports to gather dust as it does not want to review all the central acts on Jammu and Kashmir.[160] Kashmiri leadership has poured cold water on the Report, some of them threatening not to cooperate with any future interlocutors appointed by the Government of India. *The Hindu* reported on July 10, 2012, that the government India ruled out any troop reduction in Jammu and Kashmir. Wars fought on the question have convinced both the sides that war cannot solve Kashmir problem, more so when both the countries went nuclear in 1998. Extremists elements in Pakistan are jealous of India for its preeminence in the area, break away wound of East Pakistan (now Bangladesh since 1971) (over which Musharraf admittedly cried and called it the saddest day of his life)[161] and the Indian army's atrocities in Kashmir as they see it. They also want to ensure that Muslims in India are not oppressed. While the Pakistan leadership is committed to solve Kashmir issue, they do not want to stay prisoners to it. They are also not in favour of war on the question, although one general boasted to Alastair Cambell, Blair's one time secretary, that Pakistan can nuke India in just 8-seconds.[162] They are willing to go slow on Kashmir improving relations in the meantime. The extremists are in a hurry and the Pakistan government is not. The extremists want to carry out Jihad on the question of Kashmir and the treatment of Muslims in India. The treatment of minorities is a matter of concern for both sides. On May 16, 2012, S.M. Krishna told the Rajya Sabha that he raised with Pakistani authorities the question of maltreatment and oppression of Hindus in Pakistan. He will do so in future as well.[163] The attack on the Indian parliament, Aksherdham temple attack, Red Fort attack, Mumbai 1991 blast and subsequent macabre killing of the innocent people, Delhi High Court attack etc. (the list is long), as reported in our press, may recur. The 1999 Kargil war fizzled out for which Musharraf blames Nawaz Sharif's political ineptitude and his inexplicable haste.[164] As long as the issues between India and Pakistan are not thrown under the carpet, in the name of confidence building measures (CBMs) and the prolonged composite dialogue process under which single-issue focus (i.e. Kashmir) is sought to be avoided, the activities of the extremists will recur causing nuisance. The best thing would be to address these issues on an urgent basis and solve them. These attacks are carried out in the spirit of revenge and not terrorism. One thing is clear: Musharraf said, 'neither side's leadership had an appetite for war.'[165] If that is a correct assessment, then the Indo-Pak journalists meeting in Mumbai on May 27, 2012, were right in calling for cutting defense expenditure by both sides. A kind of disarmament for development logic need to be practiced.[166] More so when the Home Minister, P. Chidambaram believes that terrorism problem has largely been overcome with better equipment now in the hands of the security forces.[167] The presence of criminal elements like Daud Ibrahim and the terrorist training camps in Pakistan are worrisome. So is the presence of Talibans. Can there be a war between India and Pakistan on these issues? Can we persist in being Pakistan-centric? The issues between India and Pakistan have to be noted within the framework of threat perception but in actual fact, the two countries may not go to war on these issues. On the contrary, both the countries are anxious not to become prisoners to the Kashmir issue. A kind of bonhomie prevails where friendship, easing of visa regime (Pakistan finally refused to accept relaxed visa regime)[168] , free movement of people between POK and Kashmir and Indians and Pakistanis in general, is viewed as desirable. Samjhauta Express (which was bombed by the Hindu extremists on February 18, 2012) [169] is to be revived. For all practical purposes, the threat perception may not include a full-fledged war. Besides, both India and Pakistan cannot take hard decisions on the question of war and peace as long as American shadow prevails on both of them almost as its (successor empire to the British one) colonies. Mahmood Sham, a Pakistani columnist, maintains after the 2012 Chicago NATO summit, that the West completely dominates the world and if there is going to be a world government, then NATO will be its police force.[170] We have seen how Nawaz Sharif rushed to meet Clinton in the wake of Kargil war, and how Asif Ali Zardari was anxious to meet Obama (Obama merely shook hands and talked briefly with Zardari)[171] during the May 20-21, 2012, Chicago summit which the latter turned down Zardari's request for a meeting and how India voted against Iran in the UN, skirted oil pipeline that avoided Russia and later Iran under American pressure and recently reduced its oil purchase from Iran after Hillary Clinton's pressurizing visit.[172] Both the countries, for all their nuclear weapons, have never conducted themselves as nuclear powers like throwing their weight around or become more assertive in their foreign policy postures. Their submissiveness to the US is a stark reality. In the post-American withdrawal Afghanistan, India's interests in Afghanistan are undermined by both Pakistan and Taliban who do not want to see India playing any significant role there. But no threat may be caused except that the Talibans may continue their anti-India stance. But Afghan refugees in Delhi remain firmly pro-India and those Afghans who got their education in India will stay pro-India. Women in Afghanistan form a strong pro-India constituency. While the gains for India will be mixed, the threat from Taliban will remain. Moreover, Pakistan has been misruled, misgoverned and mismanaged for so long that its integrity no longer remains beyond cavil. It might end up loosing Baluchistan and a concatenation of disturbing events might ensue that might threaten its integrity. Pakistan's credentials as a sovereign state are bruised beyond repair after the violation of its space by the American air force planes in Abotabad to kill Bill Laden a year ago in 2011 and by the continuing air space violations by American Drone planes that go on killing innocent people unmanly, dastardly, in violation of international law (including 24 Pakistani soldiers that caused great bad blood between the US and Pakistan and the US Defense Secretary has refused to apologize (only in July the US formally did so) and Obama has ruled out any disclosure of information about the Drone attack)[173] despite Pakistan protests. Pakistan PM, Gilani, a great supporter of good relations with India, is now gone. What is described as a 'judicial coup', the Pakistani Supreme Court disqualified Gilani as the Prime Minister and also as a member of parliament on June 19, 2012. His supposed successor Mr. MaKhdoom Shahabuddin is faced with a non-bailable warrant.[174] Raja Parvez Ashraf, the newly elected PM, who is from the same region as the PM of India was born in, has a corruption case pending against him. In this political mess, the rumours about a military coup are doing the rounds. However, Mr. Raja has committed himself to further improve the relations with India.[175]

India's threat perception from without is on par with her internal threat perceptions. Poor economic show (growth down to just 5.3 per cent), political bungling (as in the case of Anna Hazare), weak, indecisive leadership (Time called Manmohan Singh a weak PM and an underachiever in July, 2012), massive all-pervasive corruption culminating in huge scandals involving almost all the politicians, Naxal violence etc. have made politics a dirty word. The faith in the system is sapped making people cynical giving a severe blow to political legitimacy. The former army chief revealed that he was offered bribe of 14 crores (brokers and middlemen galore) that he is sure that our armed forces are not combat ready stacked as they are with obsolete arms. A country plagued with so many internal problems, can go to war? Think tanks in India may make Pakistan-centred threat perception projections but the same will have to take into account the points made above. Pakistan itself is in such a bad shape that it may not survive for long in the shape we see it today. Imran Khan has called Pakistan (which lost 40,000 soldiers fighting America perceived 'terrorism') a borrowed gun to kill American opponents.[176] The *Foreign Policy* magazine gives Pakistan the 13th rank in the failed states index.[177]

China is a different question. Niall Fergusson quotes a Chinese friend : "To understand China you have to think in generations."[178] China, for all its apparent prosperity, is mired in its own internal political and other problems.[179] Corruption, dissidence, regional unrest, peasant, poor and workers unrest and uprisings, power struggle, power projection abroad, over stretch/extension a al Paul Kennedy's thesis etc. The Chinese regime is saddled with a serious legitimacy problems. But the fact remains that it is a huge, world's most populous country which is almost two and half times bigger in size than India, boasts of the second largest economy in the world with a GDP worth $10.9 trillion (to India's $ 4.06), with a literacy rate of 92% (to India's 61%), internet users of 389 million (to India's less than 60 million), great manufacturing prowess leading to exports worth $1.58 trillion (to India' s $ 0.23 trillion), labour force of 815.3 million (to India's 478.3 million), foreign exchange reserves of $2.88 to over $ 3 trillion[180] (to India's $ 0. 29 trillion), military expenditure 4.3 per cent of the GDP (to India's 2.5% of the GDP), inflation down to 3.2% in 2010 (to India's 12.0%).[181] Threats from China are territorial, political and economic. China, with its economic clout as the second largest economy in the world, (more than three times the size of the Indian economy)[182] is the greatest expansionist power. The Chinese now populate the Russian side of the Amur river in Siberia, expanding in the west and south and they are completely in control of Tibet so much so any international dignitary meeting Dalai Lama is objected to by China (although Dalai Lama told *The Hindu,* July 10, 2012, that autonomy for Tibet is the only option available). The latest case is that of David Cameroon who met Dalai Lama recently and as a response a senior Chinese leader cancelled his visit to London.[183] They are in occupation of a large tract of the Indian territory : 90,000 sq. km in the Eastern region, 30,000 sq. km in the western region.[184] China rejects this as wrong and historically unfounded. Interestingly, this is argued by an Indian scholar working in Shanghai Institute of International Studies. Fifteen rounds of talks held so far under 2005 agreement called Political Parameters and Guiding Principles. Article 111 of the agreement states that the boundary settlement, after an agreement is reached, would be, "final covering all sectors (Western, Middle and Eastern) of the India-China boundary."[185] Pakistan claimed 5,300 sq. km which China kept but transferred to Pakistan 1,942 sq. km in the Opening Valley and at the same time dropped claims to another 1,554 sq. km territory. Contrary to what is widely believed in India, China claims that it has ceded territory to Pakistan. The 1963 peace agreement between Pakistan and China, according to the reading by Talor Fravel, an MIT professor, acknowledges a dispute with India in the Western sector of Aksai Chen but recognizes no dispute over its border with Pakistan adjacent to Kashmir. A month after the 15th round of talks held in January, 2012, the Chinese paper *Liberation Daily,* questioned India's claims on Kashmir and argued that the only dispute that remains is that of Arunachal Pradesh.

What is holding back an agreement on border question in general is : (1) India's misperceptions about the McMahon Line left by the British colonialist, (2) India's multiparty system where each party has a different take on the subject, (3) India's mindset that the Chinese side has to make concessions rather than accepting that what is required is mutual accommodation.[186] After 15 rounds of talks, the gulf over border dispute remains as wide as ever. A write up in Party's *Global* Times (June 28th , 2012), reminded India of lesson of 1962 : a "heavy punch" to Nehru to wake up from the influences of USA and USSR. China won but never wanted the Sino-Indian war. China can not be forced to accept an illegal border line created by the colonialists. China will defend its land in future too.[187] Unfortunately, the Brooks-Bhagat report on the 1962 war has not been made public contrary to the assurances given.[188] The Deputy General Secretary information, Ministry of External Affairs of China, Mr. Maja Keishing, reportedly advised (June 27, 2012) India to be patient on the border question and any undue haste would not be helpful.[189] On March 16, 2012, Mr. Mallapally Ramchandran, Minister of State of Home Affairs of India, told Rajya Sabha that there have been 580 border violations from China. The Chinese responded by saying that there have been more than 1000 border violations from the Indian side which China chose to ignore.[190] India believes that Pakistan has cunningly gifted its own occupied territory helping the Chinese to build connecting road to facilitate the movement of trade and troops. The Chinese army is huge and expenditure on it massive, exceeding $ 100 billion (to India's over $ 36 Billion and US's $ 740) which is three times the amount India spends and second largest in the world. China's defense budget is projected to cross $ 238 billion by 2015. The Chinese deny these calculations and suggest that its defense budget in fact declined to 1.28% in 2011 from 1.33% in 2008.[191] The Chinese are said to be involved in stealing American secrets.[192] The Chinese PLAAF's J-10 fighters recently conducted exercises over Tibet. Kinghai-Tibet Plateau is under Chengdu military region. The Indian analysts believe that the use of planes and other activities aimed at defending the disputed territory between India and China.[193] Their designs in Arunachal Pradesh and systematic gobbling up of the Indian territory continues. When A.K. Antony, India Defense Minister, visited Arunachal Pradesh, Beijing took exception saying that India should refrain from steps that serve to complicate border dispute.[194] S.M. Krishna reacted angrily to the Chinese reaction saying that Arunachal Pradesh was an integral part of India which Mr. Anthony had visited before too. India's position would be brought to the notice of the Chinese as and when an opportunity arises.[195] The building of a dam over Brahamaputra, flowing on the Chinese side has environmental implications besides the reduction of water coming to India. At Rio, the Chinese have indicated that they will share river data with India.[196] India's bidding for exploration of oil in the South China Sea is frowned upon by China that led to India withdrawing from the South China Sea oil exploration venture. The Indian

Government's reaction to it all is mute and passive for reasons best known to the Ministry of External Affairs. The Indian businessmen continue to get kidnapped and maltreated. S.M. Krishna sees Sino-Indian relations as "complex but growingly variegated in texture and substance."[197] The Chinese mystique continues. The Indian army chief merely says that China has not settled its border claiming certain parts of our territory. "It has also done a great deal of infrastructural development in Tibet. We need to be prepared till such time as the border remains unsettled." He acknowledges that "the space of conflict remains. After all, wars are an extension of politics." The negotiation process has to be exhausted before any use of force can be thought of.[198] The army chief believes that Maoist problem has become so large because "we have allowed it to grow". "The army should not fight its own people. We don't see Maoists as involved in a secessionist movement. That is why we have not gone to fight them. When Mr. Chidambaram asked me (to fight Maoists), I told him exactly this."[199] On the regional implications, India goes along with the China in saying there is space for both the countries in the area to co-exist and prosper: "India and China have together been prosperous and powerful before and could be so again in the future. There is space for both of us to grow and meet our people's aspirations."[200] But the threat perception from China is of a different proportion. The Chinese leadership successfully lobbied the Indian leadership to play down the threats from China. Even during the Beijing Olympics, the Indian leadership sought no concessions, territorial and other. An oversensitive, vulnerable China plagued by human rights record, at that time, could have made some concessions to India. Large Indian territory is already lost and equally large Indian territory is at risk. Can China and Pakistan join hands to threaten India? While they do constitute anti-India platform, would they be threatening India? For what? Territorial/trade concessions or war? While both Pakistan and China may continue to give some anxious moments to India, war still sounds a remote possibility. Right now (May, 2012), Chinese are a bit cross with Pakistan because they think that the terrorist training camps in Pakistan are producing elements which are playing havoc in the erstwhile East Turkistan. The Uyghurs in Xinjiang province too are said to have links with the Pakistan, although Pakistan has officially condemned all terroristic activities in Xinjiang.[201] In this context, India would do well to establish direct trade links with the Muslim majority area of Xinjiang taking cue from Uighur Vice-President's offer to establish direct trade links with India skirting present Pakistani conduit of Rawalpindi.[202]

Ideological considerations are no longer serious as China is refusing to encourage Maoists abroad. They insist that China needs peace for development and not revolution and destabilization. It is a Commintern like situation under Stalin: Russia dictated what policies to be pursued by other communist parties. The Maoists are faced with a similar situation. When Prachanda in Nepal insisted on calling his faction Moaists, China discouraged him. The Maoists in India are badly divided and occasional Maoist/Naxal violence gets no solid Chinese backing. Mao Xinyu, Major General in People's Liberation Army and Mao's only living grandson and a prolific writer, argued that Mao's ideas are being misused in India and elsewhere. Using violence against the state is wrong. In today's world the relevance of Mao's philosophy is, "to help maintain peace, stability and development." We have to help build up an equitable world order. Mao's ideas of 'people's war' and violent struggles had relevance in the colonial period. He fails to see any connection between Mao's teachings and the Indian Maoists. About 'people's war' ideas, he says, had relevance during the colonial times and no longer relevant in our changed times. Learning Mao's ideas, "can help human development, peace and build a new world order." He stressed five principles of peaceful co-existence.[203] The Indian Maoists, like Nepal's Maoists, have to be on their own. Threat Perception from China in areas other than ideology appears more real and grave. The international community (and not just the US because the US uses the expression 'international community' to mean the US) needs to be sensitized about it.

The other significant dimension to threat from China is trade. The Indian markets are flooded with the Chinese goods. Whether they are legally reaching India is not known but they have captured the Indian markets all the same. The poor quality of the Chinese goods does not diminish their demand. India has to face China in economic and trade matters equally seriously. There are complaints worldwide against China's trade practices. India has to sensitively tackle these issues. The threat China's goods pose to the Indian manufacturers and larger India economy is an area of serious concern. India needs to remember that imported cloth led to the closure of myriad small but prosperous power loom industries in Bhivandi and other areas in Maharashtra rendering thousands of workers unemployed. The situation in sectors other than textile cannot be different. A few Indian traders/businessmen who tried to do business in China are kidnapped and maltreated. The problems have crossed sane limits.[204] So far, the government of India has not proved equal to the task. Treating the Chinese with kid gloves may amount to appeasement but India does not have too many alternatives either. The Chinese penchant of saying something and doing something else persists. The Chinese cunning is that they have played down the Sino-Indian differences on the eve of S.M. Krishna's visit to Beijing on June 6, 2012. They want trust to be established and misgivings tackled. The Chinese are all full of welcoming smiles. The communist party paper, *Global Times,* however, says something with which India may not entirely go along : "Both the countries do not approve of a Europe/US led world and strive to realize multi-polarity. (the Chinese believe that the US power is on the long term decline)[205] Both the countries have similar views in many areas like climate, energy, counter-terrorism, public health, and social security."[206] China and India cannot allow the US-Japan plot to encourage a bitter fight between India and China. "China and India cannot allow this plot to succeed."[207] But nothing is written about the solution to border dispute and other areas of disagreement. Here too, war is not an immediate and feasible possibility for variety of reasons both internal and external. Americans hold some trump cards here too.

On the sidelines of the June 6th, 2012, Shanghai Cooperation Organization meet in Beijing, the Indian Foreign Minister met the emerging new leaders i.e. liberal Vice Premier Li Kequiang (possible successor to Wen Jiabao, who visited India first in 2005 and then met PM Manmohan Singh twice in 2010 in Hanoi and New Delhi) and Vice President Xi Jinping (possible future President).[208] Mr. Krishna told these leaders that India attached "the utmost importance and high priority" to its relations with China. India desired to become full fledged member of the six-member + 5-observer Shanghai Cooperation Organization (observers are : India, Pakistan, Iran, Mongolia and Afghanistan) which is also a security grouping, if not a military bloc like NATO.[209] The Chinese have not resiled from their position on membership calling upon Observers to "work hard" to earn membership. But Mr. Krishna maintained that India is working very hard indeed and had brought prestige to SCO. Strangely enough, security reasons are cited for the Chinese companies not making investments in India. To Mr. Krishna's credit, he mentioned the trade deficit of $ 27 billion in China's favour and pleaded for more balanced trade arrangements. That the South China Sea constitute international waters despite the Chinese objections to India activities in the Sea which he maintained aimed at promoting trade.[210] Yet Chinese concerns about India in the South China Sea persists. The recent American decision to shift its fleets to Asia-Pacific region has quite riled China and pro-America India is not unduly concerned about it. The anti-American bent of the SCO became clear when its Declaration expressed its strong opposition to , (1) armed intervention , (2) forced regime change, (3) unilateral sanctions.[211] 40-minute stock-taking Krishna-Yang Jiechi confabulations included trans-border rivers (to be discussed in detail in July, 2012) on which Jiechi assured that Zangmu project in Tibet was run-of-the river project that aimed at no diversion of Brahamputra waters. Both sides believed that the Sino-Indian relations are going on more 'smoothly' than before. The Chinese want one more consul opened in Chennai where there is growing presence of Chinese companies and India might open one consul in Chengdu where many Indian IT companies are established. The Chinese just assured that the cases of harassed Indian businessmen who were abducted in December, 2011, will find quick solution.[212] All said, no advance was made on the controversial issues bedeviling Sino-Indian relations. The assessment by American geo-strategists writers is America-centric. A good example is Robert D. Kaplan. He argues that India and China are involved inevitably and inexorably in a rivalry and this rivalry is caused by the collapse of distance brought by advanced military technology. India has missiles that can hit Beijing and Shanghai. The Indian satellites can eavesdrop on China. China's expanding reach makes India nervous. India also views with concern the port enhancing activities China is involved in Kenya, Pakistan, Sri Lanka and Myanmar. This makes the rivalry geopolitical. No emotions are involved as is the case with Pakistan or as was the case with USSR and US during the Cold War. Lack of emotional baggage makes the rivalry very terse and calculative. India likes to be compared with China and not with a weak, small and almost failed state like Pakistan. China being stronger, its elite is not obsessed with India as the Indian elite is with China. (On July 10, 2012, *Deccan Chronicle* quoted Ratan Tata's desire to see India closer to China). The rivalry is unequal and as usual the lesser power is obsessed with the stronger. China's fear of its minorities is comparable to India's problems with the bordering smaller states which cause refugee problems and Naxalism and extremism. Besides, China's activities in these countries are a source of great concern to India. The US thinking is that if China can be easy on Tibet, India's role can enhance. India has some long term advantages: relenting on Tibet and Xinjiang, as a consequence of greater democratization in China de-stabilizing the stranglehold of the Communist Party in China (India faces no legitimacy crisis as China faces) will give upper hand to India in this rivalry. America stands to benefit : if an strategic friend like India can get an upper hand in the India-China rivalry in the East, America can better concentrate on the Western front of which it is the leader.[213] But these perceptions are not quite in tune with latest developments. China is immersed in its own economic development and wants for itself and neighbours tranquility and loath to precipitate matters. The East Sea Fleet of the People's Liberation of Army Navy made a friendly call on the Kochi port in India. Joint Naval exercises were held on June 17, 2012. Four Indian ships called on the Chinese ports on June 12 , 2012. Vice-Admiral of the East Sea Fleet Su Zhiquian and Vice Admiral Anil Chopra held friendly talks. This year i.e. 2012 is declared the year of friendship and cooperation.[214] China works hard to play down the differences between the two countries and plays goody goody (as they did on June 18, 2012, at the informal BRICKS leaders meet in Mexico on the eve of Rio+20 UN Conference on Sustainable Development on June 20, 2012)[215] but refuses to solve border problems. On June 15, 2012, a TV report revealed how the Chinese are deeply involved in spreading her spy network in India. The Chinese appear inscrutable with a right kind of surface behavior. For all their pronouncements of friendship, China's People's Liberation Army carried out on June 14, 2012, live fire drills in Tibet apparently to "test their precision strike capability" but, as some analysts believe, in response to India's announcement of deployment of Sukhoi 30 and boost its military in the border areas. The Chinese conducted live fire attack drill in March, 2012, and in October, 2011, air force and army carried out joint drills. These exercises could be signals for India that the Chinese might is impregnable.[216] But their firmness is not changing their position on border and other outstanding issues, refusal to make concessions, persistence in issuing hostile statements periodically is of great concern to India. The Chinese do all this and then embark on the damage control measures. At Las Cabos, Mexico, G-20 summit, (June 20, 2012), the Chinese leaders were all smiles with the Indian PM. The Chinese paper visa issue is a good example. Faced with a Janus faced China, India is condemned to an eternal vigilance.

Bhutan, Nepal, Sri Lanka, Bangladesh may play China card and make some anti-India noises as and when it suits them. But in terms of threat perception, they do not count for much. An embarrassment here and there does not call for serious threat perception analysis with regard to these countries. Nepal is sandwiched between the two giants, "yam between two boulders" – India and China. It has a sizeable chunk of Tibetan population which is well off but infiltrated by Chinese spies. 30-million Nepalese want the Chinese railway link right up to Kathmandu alarming India. If Nepal acts as a bridge between India and China, China stands to benefit more through trade. No wonder, Wen Jiabao on his 4-hour stop over in Nepal (January, 2012), advised Nepalese to build up cordial relations with India. But India feels threatened by Nepal's links to China. China can use Nepal's route to do some mischief. While Bhattarai's party called itself Maoist, China refuses to regard it so. Nepal is prone to play China card against India. However, one million Nepalis work in India and Nepal has open border with India. While India needs to be watchful, no war like threat from Nepal is expected in near future.[217] Nepal is facing serious internal problems right now in 2012. The Constituent Assembly has not produced a constitution and its term expired on the 27th May, 2012, leading to its dissolution on that date.[218] Prime Minister Baburam Bhattatrai sees no alternative to fresh elections.[219] Political uncertainty, ethnic strife and Maoist radicalism is staring the country in the face.[220] Faction wars have broken out in Nepal pushing it to the brink. Bhattarai's coalition is faced with a split. On June 10, 2012, the second biggest party of his coalition has resigned from the coalition. As of today, Nepal is embroiled in serious internal problems of its own.[221]

Bangladesh, right now (July, 2012), is very favourably disposed towards India at the cost of earning the wrath from the internal political opposition.[222] Prime Minister Sheikh Hasina said on May 31st, 2012, that Bangladesh attaches highest importance to its relations with India. But she wants India to move quickly to sort out issues. Teesta water sharing deal is still hanging fire, electricity from the North Eastern States of India for Bangladesh is yet to be tapped, and more business friendly atmosphere has to be created.[223] Occasional border skirmishes and infiltration through porous border resulting in huge Bangladeshis ending up in Delhi and some other places causes some embarrassment and concern. For all of this, Bangladesh is pretty favourably disposed towards India, opposition to it from internal opposition parties notwithstanding.

Sri Lanka's atrocities against Tamils had put India in a difficult situation as the Indian state of Tamil Nadu forced India to vote with the Americans against Sri Lanka. However, India extended $ 300 million for 50,000 displaced Tamils (so that houses could be built for them in Kilinochchi and Jaffna) during the brutal civil war that ended in 2009.

China is not quiet. It now controlled 85% work to expand Colombo's main commercial port. But S.M. Krishna promised that India will not "destabilize or divide a nation"[224] and India stayed away from coup in the Maldives. India allowed Bangladesh's booming garment industry to export 10 million pieces duty free to India. Bangladesh also got a $ 1 billion soft loan from India. Pakistan has gone in for the Most Favoured Nation (MFN) status for India. Sri Lanka is also happy with India right now (July, 2012) where India has opened two more Consulates. Bhutan and Nepal also have one more Indian consulate now. India's largesse and loans, aid and trade with her smaller neighbours will definitely help to an extent but it is the informed, astute, consummate diplomatic skills, its vigilance and finesse that will make a difference in meeting future threats and their perceptions. These goodwill moves and aid is aimed at neutralizing the China's perceived encirclement of India. India's so-called 'near abroad' is also keenly watched by China which is making a string of moves of its own to increase its influence and possibly checkmate India in the area.[225] India-China adversarial syndrome might ultimately take shape although both sides deny any such development. The proxy skirmishes, conceptual or real, are unavoidable but right now do not get translated into credible threats.

Overall, China and Pakistan may be counted among the most important sources of threat and may cause many heart-burning embarrassments in future, short of an all out hot war. In 2012, both Pakistan and China would not prefer war. China is still too preoccupied with Taiwan and South East Asia, its economic development and the US. If fact, the Chinese are more concerned with the US and its moves in the Pacific and the Indian Ocean. South Asia, particularly India, is not a high priority area of foreign policy for China. While Pakistan is not involved in territorial designs (Kashmir is still with India), China is. Apparently, the Chinese wish India and Pakistan to be on friendly terms but in actual fact the Chinese carry Pakistan firmly along with it in a way that is not to India's liking. Pakistan can always be used to cause trouble and embarrassment to India. China and Pakistan are far too close for comfort to India. The only solution for India to have more reliable and effective regional and international allies. G-20, BRICKS and Shanghai Cooperation Organization (SCO) are good moves (although China has openly ruled out membership for India and Pakistan)[226] The June 6-7, 2012, meeting of the SCO saw India asking for larger role in the SCO and an early membership.[227] But the membership will be hard to come by.

Israel and the US have their own pressing concerns and interests to do much in practical terms for India in relation to Pakistan and China. A bigger crisis may leave India alone unless farsighted steps are initiated and pursued. Here, Russia appears more reliable and dependable as in the past. Other individual European states may be cultivated. India is not doing enough with regard to African and Latin American countries. Laying all your eggs in one basket is not a wise policy. The US does not have an enviable record and hence other areas may be tapped making foreign policy more broad based, solid and reliable. A balancing act is very much required.

If one is constrained to prioritize threat perceptions coming from neighbours, then China, Pakistan, Nepal, Sri Lanka (unhappy for India's support to the cause of Tamilians), can be considered in that order. There are extraneous diversions and distortions too. Any explosion in Iran (with which India continues to have oil import arrangement albeit on a reduced scale as disclosed on May 31, 2012)[228] will tax India but Syria might steal the thunder from Iran and India will have to make critical choices in a situation that pits US - EU against Russia and China. Can India meet the situation through defense preparedness ? Perhaps not. War involving India and these states is still a remote possibility. But diplomatic skills will be tested to the utmost on what choices we make. Consequences would follow accordingly. Anticipations in this regard are hard to make. While making choices, the dominant considerations could be: merit and morality (of the cases involved) and the national interest as understood independently of the pressures. For a country of India's size and stature, objectivity and independence of choice cannot be compromised.

ENDNOTES

1. For a review of the debates among the traditionalists and non-traditionalists on the question of security, see Barry Buzan and Lene Hansen. "Beyond the Evolution of International Security Studies", *Security Dialogue*, Vol. 41, No. 6, December, 2010, pp. 659-667. International Security Studies' diverse evolution presupposes a thorough study of history from a realist perspective. Can international security question be studied without "invoking Realism", as an "ontological good and as an intellectual endeavour"? This is touched upon by Nisha Shah, "Security Must Be Defended – Or the Survival of Security", *Security Dialogue*, Vol. 41, No. 6, 2010, p. 637. For a

survey of international security studies and their impact, see Bruce Russett and Taylor Arnold, "Who Talks, and Who's Listening? Networks of International Security Studies", *Security Dialogue*, Vol. 41, No. 6, 2010, pp. 589-598.

2. A good example is the *Report of the Institute for Contemporary Studies, From Weakness to Strength* – Security in the 1980's, (California, 1980), which persuasively pleads for more expenditure on defense. See Chapter 16 and 18.

3. See for example Edward N. Luttwak, *The Grand Strategy of the Soviet Union,* (Weidenfeld, London, 1983).

4. See an interesting article on the subject by Morton A. Kaplan, "Intellectuals and Foreign Policy– from John K. Fairbank to Paul Wolfowitz" in *World & I,* Vol. 19, no. 2 , February, 2004, pp. 1-13

5. For example, see Walter Carlsnaes and Stefano Guzzini, Editors, *Foreign Policy Analysis*, in five volumes, (Sage, Los Angeles, 2011). Similarly one more encyclopedia omits the concept of threat perception. See Stephen Chan and Cerwyn Moore, Editors, *Approaches to International Relations*, (an encyclopedia in four volumes), (Sage, Los Angeles, 2009). Three more encyclopedias do the same. See, Klaus Dodds, Editor, *Geopolitics,* (an encyclopedia in four volumes), (Sage, Los Angeles, 2009), Shaun Bres lin and Richard Higgott, Editors, *International Relations of the Asia – Pacific,* (encyclopedia in four volumes), (Sage, Los Angeles, 2010) and Benedicte Bull and Morten Boas, Editors, *International Development* (encyclopedia in four volumes), (Sage, Los Angeles, 2010). There is no entry of the term threat perception in Martin Griffiths and Terry O' Callaghan, eds., *Key Concepts in International Relations,* (Routledge, London, Chennai, 2004).

6. See Wikipedia, http://en.Wikipedia/Wiki/Security accessed on 2/3/2012.

7. For example, Raymond Cohen writes : "Threat Perception is the decisive intervening variable between action and reaction in international crisis. When threat is not perceived, even in the face of objective evidence, there can be no mobilization of defensive resources. Hence, the phenomenon of surprise. Conversely, threat may be perceived, and countermeasures taken, even when the opponent possesses no malicious intent." See Raynond Cohen, "Threat Perception in International Crisis", http//www.jstor.org/action/show Article Image =images% 2Fpages% 2Fdtc.111. tif.gif&su...

accessed on 1/16/2012.

8. David L. Rousseau and Rocio Garcia-Retamero write : "Realists in international relations realistic conflict theorists in social psychology argue that the perception of threat in intergroup conflict is a function of power asymmetries between groups in contrast, social constructivists and social identity theorists argue that a shared sense of identity can reduce perceptions of inter group threat." See Journal of *Conflict Resolution*, Vol. 51, no. 5, October 2007, p. 744.

9. See Natan Sharansky and Ron Dermer, *The Case for Democracy – The power of Freedom to Overcome Tyranny and Terror*, (Public Affairs, New York, 2004), pp. xx, "We must understand the link between democracy and peace and between human rights and security.", p. xxvi, p. 3, p.271, President Bush argued forcefully that there is an inextricable link between freedom and peace, and between democracy and security. pp. 274, 275, 277-279.

10. See Henry Kissinger, *Does American Need a Foreign Policy – Toward a Diplomacy for the Twenty First Century*, (Free Press, London, 2002), pp. 20-21. The principle of non-interference in the domestic affairs of other states has been abandoned in favour of the concept of universal humanitarian intervention or universal jurisdiction, not only by the US but by many West European countries. At the UN Millennium summit in New York in September, 2000, many states endorsed intervention. In the 1990's the US undertook four such interventions – in Somalia, Haiti, Bosnia and Kosovo. There was intervention in East Timor (led by Australia) and Sierra Leon (led by Great Britain). Except Kosovo, the UN sanction was obtained for all the other interventions.. Ibid, pp. 21-22.

11. See Farrukh Dhondy, "Mr. Blair and the ghost of Iraq War", the *Deccan Chronicle*, Hyderabad English daily, June 2, 2012, p. 10.

12. Leon Panetta's (US Defense Secretary) testimony to the US Congress in February, 2012, that Iran has no nuclear weapon programme. April, 2012, saw the Israel's serving military chief publicly agreeing with Panetta's assessment. Even Ayatollah Khamenei's fatwa that Nuclear weapons are banned in Islam has not prevented the US and the EU from imposing cruel sanctions. They just want regime change. because it does not suit Israelis. For details, see Suvrat Raju, "The Disingenuous Debate on Iran", *The Hindu*, May 23, 2012, p. 13 and on new set of harsher sanctions against Iran by the US that came into force in May, 2012, see an IANS report in *Munsif*, an URDU daily from Hyderabad, Many 13, 2012, p. 5. One IAEA report says that traces of

up to 40% enrichment are found whereas weapon grade requires 90% enrichment. All kinds of lies are cooked up. See a report in the *Deccan Chronicle*, Hyderabad, May 26, 2012, p. 9. Even if Iran reaches 90%, it has the right. It is the Israel which felt threatened by Iraq. It was smashed. Now Israel feels threatened by Iran and it will be dealt with in the similar fashion. Israel has threatened Iran with unilateral action more than once. The US has declared a few days ago (May, 2012) that the all preparations to attack Iran are in place.

13. Arjun Appadurai, "Sovereignty without territoriality ; Notes for a Post National Geography", in Stephen Chan and Cerwyn Moore, eds., *Approaches to International Relations-Encclopeadia in four vols.*, Vol. II, (Sage, London, 2009), pp. 395-408.

14. For a detailed account, see Samuel P. Huntington, *The Third Wave – Democratization in the Late Twentieth Century,* (Adarsh Books, New Delhi, 1993), Chapter I and 4, specially pp. 192-207.

15. In 1973, only 45 of the world's 151 countries were counted as free by the Freedom House but during 1970-2010, the third wave witnessed enormous upsurge. Democracy recession began after late 1990's . See Francis Fukuyama, *The Origins of Political Order- From Pre-human times to the French Revolution,* (Profile Books, London, 2011), pp. 3-4. See also Mohd. Moazzam Ali, "Prospects of Russian Democracy", *Think India Quarterly,* Vol. 8, No. 1, January-March, 2005, pp. 40-51.

16. A plan for an all out war against Islam was sanctioned by the American president, approved by Pentagon, followed by the US intelligence agencies since 1988. The plan includes, inter alia, wiping out of Mecca and Medina. The intelligence and military training programmes carry regular anti-Islam propaganda. For more interesting details, see Saif Ullah Khalid, "Awful plan against the Muslim World was prepared 24 years ago", *Munsif,* May 14, 2012, p. 11.

17. Robert McNamara writes, while the security concerns remain imperative, "...the technological revolution has hurried history forward so rapidly in our own lifetime that we can now grasp more realistically the utter futility of unlimited war." No victory is conceivable in a nuc lear war. See Robert McNamara, *The Essence of Security*, (New York, 1968), p.159.. The developed world will , "reach a point of realism at which it becomes clear that a dollar's worth more of military hardware will buy less of security for themselves than a dollar's worth more of developmental assistance.". "Just as collective Security is the only feasible strategy in a half-free and half–totalitarian world, so collective

developmental assistance is the only sensible economic strategy in a half-fed and half-famished world, collective security and collective development are but two faces of the same coin." See Ibid, p. 162. But no such thing has happened and the developed world is busy imposing sanctions and wars on the less developed world.

18. See Bertrand Russell, *The Basic Writings of Bertrand Russell*, 1903-1959, (Routledge, London, 1999), p. 710.

19. See Martin Wight, *Power Politics*, (Penguin, 1979), p. 23.

20. See Wight, ibid, pp. 23-80.

21. Some of the details in this regard are provided in Harry G. Gelber, *The Dragon and the Froeign Devils – China and the World, 1100 BC to the Present* (Bloomsbury, London, 2008), pp. 423-442.

22. Palestine managed to secure 8 of the Security Council votes. See *Deccan Chronicle*, September 30, 2011, p. 9, Palestine would have become 194th member of the UN, see a report in The *Hindu*, September 22, 2011, p.11

23. See a AFP report in *Munsif*, September 23, 2011, p. 7.

24. See "Iran Gas : US threaten Pak with sanctions", in *Deccan Chronicle*, September 17, 2011, p. 9.

25. See Kenichi Ohmae, *The End of the Nation State – The rise of Regional Economics-How the Engines of Prosperity are Reshaping global markets,* (Harper-Collins, London, 1996), pp. 141-42. "The goal after all is not to legitimize this or that political establishment or power management. It is to improve the quality of life of the people, regular people – no matter where they live. People came first; border came afterwards. It is time for economic policy to remember this simple fact. Just as the current paralysis of nation state now shows them to have been a transitional mode of organization for managing economic affairs, region states may well outlive their usefulness some time in the future.. Nothing is forever. At the moment, however, they are just what the doctor ordered. Given suitable autonomy, region states – by virtue of their unique ability to put global logic first – can provide precisely the kind of change agent the times required – effective engine of prosperity and improved quality of life for the people of the global economy." Ibid, pp. 148-149.

26. See Joseph S. Nye Jr., "Power shifts – As access to the information marketplace eases, nations are losing their ability to control it.", *Time*, May 9, 2011, p. 23. He writes that, "The problems for all states in

today's global information age is that more things are occurring outside the control of even the most powerful states."

27. See Mathew Horsman and Andrew Marshall, *After the Nation-State*, (Harper-Collins, London, 1995), p. 263.

28. See Alfred Adler, *Understanding Human Nature,* (A Premier Book, New York, 1957), pp. 49-50.

29. See Fabio Vighi and Heiko Feldner, "Ideology Critique or Discourse Analysis? Zizek against Foucault", EJPR, *European Journal of Political Theory*, 6 (2), April, 2007, p.141.

30. See Nichola's Humphrey, *A History of the Mind*, (London, 1993), p. 4. "Dualism asserts that the universe contains two very different kinds of stuff, mental stuff (of which subjective feelings are made) and physical stuff (of which brains are made), and they exist semi-independently of one another." "The trouble with dualism is that it explains both too much and too little, and few philosophers have felt comfortable with it." Monism is simpler as it maintains that there exists in reality only one sort of stuff, of which both mind and brains are ultimately made. Ibid.

31. See David Hume, *A Treatise of Human Nature*, Book Two and Three, (Fontana, London, 1978), p. 37.

32. The Empericism, "Developed one side of Aristotle. Its stress on sense data as the primary source of information from which all other knowledge could validly be inducted." See Hack B. Rogers & Forrest Baird, *Introduction to Philosophy – A Case Study Approach*, (Harper and Row, New York, 1981), p. 69.

33. For an account, see "Perception" in A.J. Ayer, *The Problem of Knowledge-An Enquiry into the Main philosophical Problems that Enter into the Theory of Knowledge*, (Pelican, 1957), pp. 84-133.

34. See Thomas Hobbes, *Body, Man, and Citizen –Selections from Hobbes' writings* edited and with an introduction by Richard S. Peters, (Collier books, New York, 1962), p. 188. In fact the whole chapter, pp. 182-188 is full of significant statements made by Hobbes.

35. See Alastair Campbell, *The Blair Years – Extracts from the Alastair Campbell Diaries*, (Hutchinson, London, 2007), p. 556.

36. See H.G. Wells, *The Common sense of war and Peace-World Revolution or War Ending*, (Penguin, 1940, pp 5 and 9. "I despise driven sheep, I despise dogs that fawn upon me, I despise followers

and disciples, I despise simple faith and unquestioning loyalty of human beings who ought, I feel, to think and act for themselves instead of sacrificing the brief opportunities this life affords them of being real.", p. 8

37. Mortimer Adler, *Intellect-Mind over Matter*, (Collier, New York, 1993), p. 92. "Mind and Body" in Nicholas Humphrey, *A History of Mind*, (Vintage, London, 1993), pp.1-8.

38. For a brief but illuminating account, see "Death of Materialism" in Paul Davies and John Gribbin, *The Matter Myth- Beyond Chaos and Complexity*, (Penguin, 1992) p. 423. Mapping of Reality had become more difficult, the faith in Newtonian inert mass of matter and other certainties are gone. Randomness, unpredictability of change is of such an order that Einstein is proved wrong: Nature/God is really playing dice.

39. This is mentioned by J. Robert Oppenheimer, "Physics in the Contemporary World" reproduced in Martin Gardner, Ed., *The Sacred Beetle and other Great Essays in Science*, (A Meridian Book, New York, 1984), p. 214.

40. See a report in the *Deccan Chronicle*, by Robert Evans, July 2, 2012, p. 9.

41. See Richard Wiseman, *Quirkology – The curious Science of Everyday Lives*, (Pan Books, 2007), p. xv.

42. W.H. Auden quoted in Robert Hughes, *Culture of Compliant*, (Oxford University Press, New York, 1993), p. 3. It continues, "feelings in the solar plexus induced by undernourishment, angelic images generated by fever or drugs…every corner boy will congratulate himself : I'm such a sinner that God has come down in person to save me. Every crook will argue, "I like committing crimes. God likes forgiving them. Really the world is admirably arranged." ibid, p. 4.

43. "We think that grass is green, that stones are hard, and snow is cold. But physics assures us that the greenness of grass, the hardness of stones, and the coldness of snow, are not the greenness, hardness, and coldness. The observer, when he seems to himself to be observing a stone, is really, if physics is to believed, observing the effects of the stone upon himself." Russell as quoted by A.J. Ayer, (from Russell's An Enquiry into Meaning and Truth), (Penguin, 1986), p. 82.

44. *Ibid*, p. 87. For a lucid exposition of Outside World as seen by an Idealist, Realist, a Rationalist and Empiric ist and logic and laws of

thought, see C.E.M. Joad, *Guide to Philosophy*, (Victor Gollancz Ltd, London, 1946), Chapter I.

45. Roger Penrose explores the problem of consciousness in a scientific way in his famous book, *Shadows of Mind*, (Vintage, London, 1995).

46. See "Idealism" in Bertrand Russell, *The Problems of Philosophy*, (Oxford, Delhi, 1986), p.19.

47. For an illuminating discussion, see Mortimer J. Adler, *Intellect– Mind Over Matter*, (Collier, New York, 1993), specially chapter I and VIII. Maurice Cornforth, *Dialectical Materialism– An Introductory Course*, (National Book Agency, Calcutta, 1979), Chapters I-4 of volume I and chapters II and III of volume II.

48. See Edward O. Wilson, p. 108.

49. See Edward O. Wilson, *Consilience – The Unity of Knowledge,* (Vintage, New York, 1998), p. 105. The fundamental explanation of mind is in empirical rather than a philosophical or religious quest. p. 106. About the complexity of brain, Wilson writes that Einstein's brain weighed 2.75 while average weight of brain is three pounds. "The human genome database accumulated to 1995 reveals that brain structure is prescribed by at least 3, 195 distinctive genes, 50 per cent more than for any other organ or tissue (the total number of genes in the entire human genome is estimated to be 50,000 to 100,000). The molecular processes that guide the growth of neurons to their assigned places have only begun to be de ciphered. Overall, the human brain is the most complex object known in the universe- known, that is, to itself.", p. 106.

50. Edward O. Wilson, *Consilience, Ibid*, p. 119.

51. Wilson attempts at defining in scientific terms emotions etc., see Ibid, pp.122-126. "The ability of the brain to generate novel scenarios and settle on the most effective among them is called creativity. The persistent production of scenarios lacking reality and survival value is called insanity.", p. 126.

52. Wilson, *Ibid*, p. 120.

53. See Ibid, p. 193. Humphrey argues that there was a time in history when consciousness existed nowhere, and that even today it does not exist everywhere. (The alternative idea, that consciousness has always been inherent in every particle of matter, sometime's called 'panpsychism' is one of those superficially attractive ideas that

crumbles as soon as it is asked to do any sort of explanatory work..). Exactly when and where consciousness first appeared and how far and in what contexts the infection has spread ? The answer lies in the process of evolution. See p. 193. The feasibility of artificial intelligence remains moot.

54. For a brief account of dreams and the theories offered to explain them, see Robert L Van De Castle, Our Dreaming Mind- A Sweeping Explanation of the Role that Dreams have Played in Politics, Art, Religion, and Psychology, from Ancient Civilization to the Present Day, (Ballantine Books, New York, 1994), pp. 109-206.

55. For the impact of 'talk' on society, see Gerard I. Nierenberg and Henry H. Calero, Meta-Talk – Guide to Hidden Meanings in Conversations, (Trident Press, New York, 1973), Chapters I and IV.

56. See Arthur Koestler, The Roots of Coincidence- An Excursion into Parapsychology, (Vintage Books , New York, 1972), chapter I and II.

57. See Roger Penrose, *The Emperor's New Mind – Concerning Computers, Minds, and the Laws of Physics*, (Vintage, London, 1990), p. 575 . In fact he begins to raise fundamental questions like : "what happens to each of our streams of consciousness after we die; where was it before each was born; might we become, or have been, someone else; why do we perceive at all; why are we here ; why is there a universe here at all in which we can actually be? These are puzzles that tend to come with the awakenings of self-awareness in any one of us….", p. 580.

58. See Nicholas Humphrey, *A History of the Mind*, (Vintage, London), p. xvi.

59. See *Ibid*, p. xvi.

60. Roger Penrose records many instances, including that of himself, like Poincare.

61. "it is relatively easy to recognize that sensation is indeed in a different category to perception. Given that the odour of the rose enters my nostrils, my sensation of sweetness is evidently related to what is happening to me"; while given that the odour emanates from the rose, my perception of the rose as sweet is evidently related to 'what is happening out there.' See Nicholas Humphrey, *A History of the Mind*, (Vintage, London, 1993), p. 31.

62. *Ibid*, p. 36. Humphrey makes some eight 'assertions' about sensations

and consciousness. See ibid, pp. 97-98. See also the chapter Five 'characteristics in search of a theory', pp. 112-124. In these pages the question of consciousness is dealt with.

63. For details, see James E. Curtis and John W. Petras, eds., *The Sociology of Knowledge – A Reader*, (Duckworth, London, 1982), pp. 89-96 and Jorg Larrain, The Concept of Ideology, and Will Durant, The Story of Philosophy, (Washington Square Press, New York, 1968), pp. 96-145.

64. Maurice Morleau-Ponty quoted by Ayer. For more details, see A. J. Ayer, *Philosophy in the Twentieth Century,* (Unwin, London, 1984), p. 217.

65. See Maurice Merlea u-Ponty, Phenomenology of Perception, (Rourledge, London, 1962), p. 241. He continues, "There can be no question of describing perception itself as one of the facts thrown up in the world, since we can never fill up , in the picture of the world, that gap that we ourselves are, and by which it comes into existence for someone, since the perception is the 'flaw' in this 'great diamond'.

66. *Ibid*, p. 3.

67. Like all empiricist theories, he continues, "this one describes only blind processes which never be the equivalent of knowledge, because there is, in this mass of sensations and memories nobody who sees nobody who can appreciate falling into line of datum and recollection, on the other hand, no solid object protected by a meaning against the teeming horde of memories. We must then discard this postulate which obscures the whole question. The cleavage between given and remembered, arrived at by way of objective causes, is arbitrary. When we come back to phenomena we find, as a basic layer of experience, a whole already pregnant with an irreducible meaning : not sensations with gaps between them, into which memories may be supposed to slip, but the features, the layout of a landscape or a word, spontaneously in accord with the intentions of the moment, as with earlier experience." Ponty as quoted by A.J. Ayer, *Philosophy in the Twentieth Century,* (Unwin, London, 1984), p. 217.

68. See A.J. Ayer, *Ibid*, p. 218.

69. *Ibid*, p. 218. "it can be countered only by showing how an adequate theory of the perceptible world can be erected on the basis of neural sense-experiences". "Consciousness is in the first place "I think that" but of "I can". Morleau-Popty, cited in Ayer, p. 218. The problem

remains that one does not have the right to ascribe experiences to persons other than oneself. This point is elaborated on pp. 220-222.

70. *Ibid*, p. 225.

71. See Paul Schilder, "Studies Concerning the Psychology and Symtomatology of General Paresis", in David Rapaport, Ed., *Organization and Pathology of Thought- Selected Sources*, (Oxford, IBH, Delhi, 1970, p. 51.

72. See Ibid. Rapaport explains, "Schilder means that the concept sensation implies a quest for a simple psychological "element" (sensation) which would be elicited by a simple enough stimuli (reality-segment), if found. Here Schilder takes the point of view of Gestalt-psychology, and condemns as an idle dream the hope of finding a correspondence between isolated elements of reality and the isolated elements of psyche.", Ibid.

73. *Ibid*, p. 520.

74. A good introduction to Phenomenology and search of essences is given by Maurice Merleau-Ponty in his preface to his *phenomenology of Perception*, n. 64, pp. vii-xxiv.

75. See Charles Taylor, "Interpretation and the Science of Man' in Charles Taylor, *Philosophy and the Human Sciences-Philosophical Papers, 2,* (Cambridge, 1987), p. 19. He dwells on brute data on this page.

76. *Ibid*, p. 19.

77. Writes Einstein, "physical mode of thought and its practical successes which have shaken the confidence in the possibility of understanding things and their relations by means of purely speculative thought. Gradually the conviction gained recognition that all knowledge about things is exclusively a working over of the raw material furnished by the senses." Einstein calls it generally accepted method and points at the, "impossibility of gaining knowledge of reality by means of pure speculation, but rather the fact that the empirical ....procedure alone has shown its capacity to be the source of knowledge. Galileo and Hume first upheld this principle with full clarity and decisiveness.." See Albert Einstein, "Remarks on Bertrand Russell's Theory of Knowledge" in Einstein, *Ideas and Opinions*, (Rupa, New Delhi, 1979), p. 21.

78. All the quotations from Russell are from Bertrand Russell, *Human Knowledge- Its scope and limits*, (Routledge, London, 1997), pp. 220-

221.

79. See Ibid, p. 522.

80. *Ibid*, p. 521.

81. Hobbes' quotations are from *Leviathan*, (Collins/Fontana, Glasgow, 1974), pp. 63-64.

82. See Einstein, n. 76, p. 20.

83. *Ibid*, p. 22.

84. Writes Einstein, "in thinking we use with a certain "right", concepts to which there is no access from the materials of sensory experience, if the situation is viewed from the logical point of view. As a matter of fact, I am convinced that even much more is to be asserted : the concepts which arise in our thought and in our linguistic expressions are all – when viewed logically – the free creation of thought which cannot inductively be gained from sense experiences. This is not so easily noticed only because we have the habit of combining certain concepts and conceptual relations (propositions) so definitely with certain sense experiences that we do not become conscious of the gulf – logically unbridgeable - which separates the world of sensory experiences from the world of concepts and propositions." See Einstein, n. 76, p. 22.

85. See Paul Davies, *God and the New Physics*, (Penguin, 1990), p. 2.

86. *Ibid*, p. 24.

87. See Alex F. Osborn, *Applied Imagination*, (Better Yourself Books, Allahabad, 1980), p. 13.

88. See Ibid, p. Jules Verne also wrote *A Trip to Moon*, 1865, (Neil Armstrong actually did it in 1969), *Twenty Thousand Leagues Under the Sea*, 1870, *Around the World in Eighty Days*, 1872, Master of the World, 1904.

89. See Paul Davies, n. 84., p. 5 and p. 8.

90. See Peter Watson, A Terrible Beauty – The People and Ideas that Shaped the Modern Mind, (Phoenix Press, London, 2000), p. 742. See also pp. 740-41 and 743.

91. See Paul Davies, n. 84, p. vii.

92. See Fritjof Kapra, *The Tao of Physics – An Exploration of the parallels between modern physics and eastern Mysticism*, (Flemingo, London,

1989).

93. See *Ibid*, pp. 220-221.

94. *Ibid*, p. 222.

95. "the mere operation of the imagination- a blind but indispensable function of the soul, without which we should have no cognition whatever, but of the working of which we are seldom even conscious. But to reduce this synthesis to conceptions is a function of the understanding, by means of which we attain to cognition, in the proper meaning of the term." The three step process which brings us to cognition proper is : "The first thing which must be given to us in order to achieve the *a priori* cognition of all objects, is the diversity of pure intuition; the synthesis of this diversity by means of the imagination is the second; but this gives as yet, no cognition. The conceptions which give unity to this pure synthesis.... furnish the third requisite for the cognition of an object, and these conceptions are given by the understanding.." These observations of Kant from his *Critique of Pure Reason* are taken from Slavoj Zizek, *The Ticklish Svbject – The Absent Centre of Political Ontology*, (ABS Publishers, New Delhi, p. 28. Zizek argues that imagination, "enables us to tear the texture of reality apart" and that there is continuity between imagination and understanding. Understanding can heal the wounds inflicted by imagination or can also tear off the unity of imagination. Ibid, p. 32. "When Kant endeavours to move beyond the domain of imagination and to articulate supra-sensible Rational Ideas as what accounts for human dignity, Heidegger interprets this move as a 'retreat ' from the abyss of imagination. Heidegger is right in so far as Kant is in effect try ing to ground imagination in a system of Rational Ideas whose status is noumenal.". *Ibid*, pp. 41-42.

96. See "Phenomenology and Existentialism" in A.J. Ayer, *Philosophy in the Twentieth Century*, (Unwin, London, 1984), p. 214.

97. *Ibid.*

98. *Ibid*, p. 215.

99. See *Ibid.*

100. See *The Hindu,* March 17, 2012, p. 16.

101. See *The Hindu,* March 26, 2012 a report in the *Deccan Chronicle*, September 30, 2011. The total arms sale in the world stood at $40.4 billion.

102. See *The Hindu*, March 26, 2012, p. 1. The report contains information of substandard material supplied to the army.

103. See a report in *The Hindu*, December 8, 2011, p. 1 and 9.

104. See "*Bismarck and Europe*" in AJP Taylor, *Europe: Grandeur and Decline*, (Penguin, 1977), pp. 96-112.

105. For details, see John Toland, *Adolf Hitler*, (Balla ntine Books, New York, 1977) and AJP Tayor, *The Origins of the Second World War*, (Penguin, 1979). Hitler in fact believed that Roosevelt was out to ruin Europe. See Ibid, p. 13. Also AJP Tailor, *The First world War*, (Penguin).

106. For an impressive recapitulation of the Cuban Missile Crisis, see Dino A. Burgioni, *Eyeball to Eyeball – The Inside Story of the Cuban Missile Crisis*, (Random House, New York, 1991).

107. See Tony Blair's autobiography, A Journey, (Arrow books, London, 2011), p. 374.

108. See *Ibid*, pp. 373-375.

109. See *Prem Shakar Jh*a, "When Insanity Rules the World", *The Hindu*, March1, 2012. Jha argues that India should resist the West's brazen efforts to use championship of democracy as a cover for regime change.

110. See Paul Todd, Jonathan Bloch and Patrick Fitzgerald, *Spies, Lies and the War on Terror*, (Zed Books, London, Bangalore, 2009), p. 3.

111. Write Lloyd Pettiford and David Harding, "If war on terrorism means we fight evil with evil, then it is doomed to failure. We begin to create in global society an expectation of violence. As violence becomes the norm, and normalized, society is degraded. If our societies become more secretive, more suspicious, then our democracy will function less well. And if the democratic means of expression are replaced by top-down diktat then we create societies where terrorism one of the few means of expression for excluded people." See *Terrorism – New World War*, (Capella, London, 2003), p. 225.

112. For details, see John Toland, *Adolf Hitler*, (Ballantine Books, New York, 1977), pp. 628-683.

113. See an interesting report on the subject of hit lists with facts in the *Munsif*, June 20, 2012, p. 4.

114. See Jung Chang and Jon Halliday, *Mao – The Unknown Story*, (Vintage Books, London, 2007).

115. See a report in the *Munsif,* Sunday Edition, p. 6.

116. See David Farber, Ed., *What They Think of Us-International Perception of ther United States since 9/11*, (Princeton Un. Pr., 2007).

117. See Pervez Musharraf, *In the Line of Fire*, (Pocket Books, London, 2006), pp. 87-98.

118. See a report in *Deccan Chronicle*, April 15, 2012, p. 1. See also "Musharraf : Man of War, Man for Peace, in Deccan Chronicle, April 15, 2012, p. 8.

119. This is noted in the book From *Weakness to Strength – National Security* in the 1980's, Institute of Contemporary Studies, 1980, p. 481.

120. See Barry Buzan, *People, States and Fear*, (Transasia Publishers, New Delhi, 1987), p. 3.

121. Quoted in Buzan, p. 12.

122. See Buzan, *Ibid*, p. 10.

123. These issues are discussed in Buzan, *Ibid.*

124. See note 6 on p. 15 of Buzan. *Ibid.*

125. Arnold Wolfers as quoted in Buzan, Ibid, p. 4. Buzan believes that Arnold Wolfers' chapter on security, "National Security as an Ambiguous Symbol" in Wolfers' book, *Discord and Collaboration*, (Baltimore, John Hopkins University Press , 1962), Chapter 10, is the best known conceptual piece on security.

126. See Buzan, p. 12.

127. See Konrad Lorenz, *On Aggression*, (Bantam books, New York, 1969, pp. 281-183.

128. In an article in the IHT reproduced in the *Deccan Chronicle*, Hyderabad, Ban Ki-Moon argues that, "so many of today's challenges are global, they demand global response…". He speaks of a new geological epoch and fragile ecosystem. The forthcoming June UN Conference on Sustainable Development, or Rio+20 to be attended by 130 heads of states, 50,000 business leaders. In partnership, they will galvanize global support for a transformative agenda for change. But nothing on global configuration of forces, their oppression of the weak states through sanctions, interventions and other means.

129. See J. Robert Oppenheimer, "War and the Nations", reproduced in

Richard Dawkins, *The Oxford Book of Modern Science Writing*, (Oxford, New York, 2008) pp. 164 and 168.

130. See Lester R. Brown, *State of the World*, (WW Norton & Co., New Hork, 1991). This eighth annual World Watch Institute Report, "attempts first to describe the intricate currents and countercurrents of humanity's interaction with the global environment, and then proceeds to recommend how to shift the currents in other directions.", p. vii. The report sketched, the basic outline of an environmentally sustainable global economy.", p. xiii.

131. See Donella H. Meadows et al, The Limits to Growth, (Pan books, London, 1978). The report sought to, "foster understanding of the varied but interdependent components– economic, political, natural, and social – that make up the global system we live ; to bring that understanding to the policy makers and the public worldwide; and this way to promote new policy initiatives and action." p. 9.

132. Specially the centers of Peace and Conflict Studies in Uppsala and Oslo.

133. See C.L. Wayper, *Political Thought*, (London, 1974), p. 46.

134. Hobbes identified three principal causes of quarrels among men : competition, diffidence and glory. See the introduction of John Plamenatz to Hobbes' *Leviathan*, (Collins/Fontana, Glasgow, 1974), p. 23. Man's, "perpetual fear" led to the imagination about God. See the chapter XII in Leviathan, Ibid, pp. 129-140.

135. See Chester C. Maxey's book on *Western Political Thought*, (1948), p.215.

136. See Buzan, n. 117, p. 65.

137. See Buzan, p. 66.

138. Naomi Klein, *No Logo*, (Piccador, New York, 2002).

139. B uzan, n. 117, p. 69.

140. Some interesting insights are to be found in Vaughn P. Shannon's review article, "Threat Perception and the Psychology of Constructivism", *in International Studies Review*, Vol. 9, issue 2, 2006, pp. 259-261.

141 See Robert McNamara, *The Essence of Security – Reflections in Office*, (Harper & Row, New York, 1968, pp. 141-144. For McNamara, security is development and not just military hardware. Development means

economic, social and political progress. p. 150. It is the duty of the US to provide security to the developing world. p. 151. The US should extend a helping hand to the developmental process in the developing world.p.151. Providing development assistance/economic assistance is a must. P. 153. The US should help develop bridges so that, "We (US) can help gradually to create a community of interest, a community of trust and community of effort." p. 156.

142. For details, see K.J. Holsti, *International Politics – A Framework for Analysis*, (Prentice Hall, New Delhi, 1977), pp. 245-271.

143. See John Perkins, *Confessions of an Economic Hit Man–The shocking inside Story of How America Really Took Over the World,* (Ebury Press, London, 2006).

144. Details are given in Kenichi Ohmae, *The Borderless World – Power and Strategy in the Interlinked Ecnomy*, (Harper Perennial, New York, 1991), Chapter 1 and 11.

145. See Ananth Krishnan, "In China's Parliament, a Long List of Millionares", in The Hindu, March 1, 2012, p. 11.

146. Nepal is crucial to Tibet's stability. Wen Jiabao's half day visit in January, 2012, a year of friendship, was symbolic aiming at boosting trade with Nepal. A dry port at Tatopani, railway lines connecting Tibet, activating Nepal-China Chamber of Commerce and Industry is promoting land trade, Gyirong will have 44.5 km free trade zone for which $ 190 million are spent for infrastructural development, building of highways and rail links, upgrading 318 National Highway called "friendship highway" to Gyirong and Zhangmu where much of the trade takes place, extending Tibet rail line to Nepal to be completed by 2015. The Nepal-China trade is small ($ 1.2 billion) but a flurry of important activities have sprung up. Nepal is home to a large Tibetta population. The Chinese keep an eye on them. Nepal has strategic importance given Indian stakes in Nepal. Nepal can be arm-twisted to support China's Tibet policies. See Anand Krishnan, "China Boosts Trade with Nepal", *The Hindu*, April 3, 2012, p. 13.

147. See a report in The Hindu, June 2, 2012, p. 12.

148. See a report in the *Deccan Chronicle*, May 30, 2012, p. 1, see also p.8.

149. See a report in the *Deccan Chronicle*, June 2, 2012, p. 8.

150. See Niall Ferguson "A World Without Power", *Foreign Policy*, July/ August, 2004, pp. 32-39.

151. See Stephen F. Szabo, "Welcome to the Post-Western World", *Current History*, Security- Global Trends, 2011. Fareed Zakaria wrote a full length book on the subject. See Fareed Zakaria, *The Post-American World*, (Penguin/Viking, New Delhi, 2008). The views expressed are sensational, trendy, premature and lack credibility. A more realistic book is that of Ian Morris, *Why the West Rules – for now – The patterns of History, and What They Reveal About the Future,* (Profile Books, London, 2010).

152. Freedom House reported decline in electoral democracies over the previous year from 119 to 116, the lowest figure since 1995. See Alan Sorensen, "Globalization and the Problem of Evil", (a global progress report, 2011), *Current History*., p. 4.

153. See *Ibid*, p. 5.

154. The quotation is from Ibid. Hence, the Report argues that threat s from extremists hating modernity are found in the Middle East, the political and economic reform in the Middle East remains important. The so-called Islamists will be mollified and become moderates if democracy is established. Everyone has a stake in globalization. The dissemination of knowledge will impel progress. See Ibid. see also the article by Lucian Crowder, "Gazing Across the Divides" in *Ibid*, pp. 6-8.

155. See John J. Mearsheimer and Stephen M. Walt, *The Israel Lobby and US Foreign Policy* (Penguin, 2008). While Michael Sandel, the popular Harvard professor, insists that American is ruined by the brand of capitalism American followed and markets shouldn't be allowed to replace moral judgement, in his book *What Money Can't Buy* (2012). See a review by Michael Fitzgerald in the Newsweek, April 23, 2012, p. 54. Ashley Tellis in his *Non-alignment Redux : Perils of Old Wine in New Skins* (July, 2012), pleads for strong partnership between India and the US in view of inevitable clash with China. See a review by Seema Sirohi in *The Hindu*, July 10, 2012, p. 9.

156. For Pakistan's point of view, see Mohd. Amir Rana's article in Dawn,http://www.dawn.com/2011/10/24/threat-perception. html accessed on 2/21/2012, Arif Ansar, "On Threat Perceptions, Pakistan Today, (online), February 21, 2012, accessed on 2/21/2012.

157. See a report in *The Hindu*, June 17, 2012, p. 9. He also said that: "I must also point out that as long as the regional disputes specially Kashmir, remains unresolved, stability will remain a distant dream, we must therefore continue for a just solution of the Kashmir dispute as it is only fair to all the people who dwell in this region." *Ibid.*

158. See Amitabh Mattoo and Happymon Jacob, "Farce in Three Parts",*The Hindu*, June 4, 2012, p. 10.

159. See a report in *The Hindu*, June 1, 2012, p. 12.

160. See a report in the *Deccan Chronicle*, June 4, 2012, p. 7.

161. See Pervez Musharraf , *In the Line of Fire*, (Pocket Books, London, 2008), p. 54.

162. See a report in the *Deccan Chronicle*, June 16, 2012, p. 9.

163. See a PTI report in *Munsif*, Hyderabad, May 18, 2012, p. 1.

164. According to Musharraf's account, skirmishes on the borders were frequent. Indian defense minister Georg Fernades's 1998 visit to Kargil was taken as a war preparation move by Musharraf. The so called mujahideen had occupied over 500 km of the Indian territory now supported by Pakistan forces. Contrary to Nawaz Sharif's claims, he knew about Kargil as he was briefed by army in January and February, 1999, and in June as well. It was joint effort establishing collective responsibility. Shariff called for a ceasefire and unilateral withdrawal. Kargil did not lead to the brink of nuclear war as Pakistan's nuclear weapons were not operationalized. Unexpected huge Indian losses (600 officially in India but double that number according to Musharraf) caused coffin problem and possible scandal. Musharraf claimed that whatever progress made on the question of Kashmir was due to kargil. See Parwez Musharraf, In the Line of Fire– A Memoir, (Pocket Books, London, 2006), pp. 87-98.

165. See Musharraf, *Ibid*, p. 93.

166. See a PTI report in the *Munsif*, an Urdu daily from Hyderabad, May 28, 2012, p. 1.

167. See a PTI report in the *Munsif*, May 28, 2012, p. 342.

168. See a report in *The Hindu*, May 26, 2012, p. 11.

169. For details, see *The Hindu*, February 13, 2012, p. 1.

170. See Mahmood Sham's column in *Siasat*, an Urdu daily from Hyderabad, May 27, 2012, Sunday Edition, p. 1. It is notable that the US and its 27 allies accepted complete defeat in Afghanistan. American changed its goals/ purposes in Afghanistan : it first said that it is intervening in Afghanistan to apprehend Bin Laden, then finish off Talibbans and establish democracy and political stability, the security of US and Britain was the purpose, to train Afghan soldiers to take

over from the US forces, after Bin Laden's assassination, to prop up Karzai and negotiate peace but actually the Americans want to stay beyond 2014 to perhaps capture its natural resources. In the first place, Bin Laden was not in Afghanistan. The Taliban forces rightly say that US intervened for no sensible reason at all. However, the longest and the most expensive war of the US outside, is costing the US $ 10 billion a month. It has caused the death of hundreds of thousand's of Afghanis, 2854 allied forces, 1827 Americans, 414 Britons. See an article in the Sunday magazine, Asif Jilani, "Acceptance of total defeat in Afghanistan", the *Munsif, Sunday*, May 27, 2012, p. 1. See also Joseph Stiglitz and Linda Bilmes, *The Three Trillion Dollar War* – The True Cost of the Iraq Conflict, (Penguin, 2008) and Ahmed Rashid, *Descent into Chaos – How the war Against Islamic Extremism* is being lost in Pakistan, *Afghanistan and Central Asia,* (Penguin, 2008).

171. See *Deccan Chronicle,* May 23, 2012, p. 9.

172. It is interesting that Robert Blake, Asst. Sec. of State for South Asia, told the US Congress that India reduced oil imports from Iran not under US pressure but because of her financial problems. This came not from India but the US which has been consistently pressurizing India to do so. Americans even explain things on behalf of India as if they are answerable to the world for India and about what India does. See a PTI report in *the Munsif,* May 18, 2012, p. 7.

173. See a Reuter report in *the Munsif,* June 23, 2012, p. 11. For Obama's refusal to reveal the details regarding the Drones under the pretext of national interests, see a report in The *Hindu*, June 23, 2012, p. 15.

174. See a report in *the Deccan Chronicle*, June 22, 2012, p. 8. It is reported that behind Mr. Gilani's disqualification are forces linked to the military. Chief Justice Ifteqar Choudhary's son was found involved in the narcotic business. Many found timeing of the issue of non-bailable warrant against Maqdoom Shahabuddin intriguing. See a report in *The Hindu*, June 23, 2012, p. 13. All this adds to the political mess Pakistan is in and is likely to be in near future.

175. See reports in *The Hindu*, June 23, 2012, p. 1 and *Munsif*, June 23, 2012, p. 1.

176 *See* a PTI report in the Munsif, June 21, 2012, p. 11.

177. Pakistan obtained 101.6 points. Other states include Somalia (114.9 points), Congo (111.2 points), Sudan (109.4 points), Chad (107.6 points), Zimbabwe (106.3), Afghanistan (106 points), Haiti, Yemen,

Iraq, Central African Republic follow Afghanistan. In 2011, Pakistan was ranked 12th and in 2010 and 2009, Pakistan was ranked 10th. See a report in the Deccan Chronicle, June 20, 2012, p. 9.

178. See Niall Ferguson, "China's Great Leap Backward", *Newsweek*, Special double issue, March 26, 2012, p. 10. See a cover article in the magazine, GEO – A New world of *Knowledge*, (Indian Edition), May, 2011, pp. 24-27.

179. See Niall Ferguson, *Newsweek*, February 27, 2012, p. 16 and Newsweek, February 13, pp. 42-43. See Jonathan Mirsky, "Richer but Repressed", Newsweek, special edition, 2012, pp. 14-16, Melinda Liu, "Blind Injustice – The True Story of a dissident's life and daring escape", *Newsweek*, May 14, 2012, pp. 18-21 and Sim Chi Yin, "Waiting for Justice in Beijing", Ibid, pp. 22-26.

180. See Bill Powell, "The Case for China : The Power of Planning" in *Time*, November 21, 2011, p. 44.

181. These figures are taken from a report in Time, November 21, 2011, pp. 40-41.

182. See Michael Schuman, "Will One Economic Model prevail", *Time*, November 21, 2011, p. 42.

183. See a report in *The Hindu*, May 26, 2012, p. 16.

184. For a concentrated treatment of the question, see Zorawar Daulet Singh, Himalayan Stalemate- Understanding th India-China Dispute, (Straight Forward Publishers, New Delhi, 2012).

185. The details of negotiations' mechanism are given by Anand Krishna, "Month after border talks, Chinese paper says Aksai Chen is a closed chapter", *The Hindu*, February 16, 2012, p. 15.

186. See *Ibid.*

187. See a report in the *Deccan Chronicle*, June 29, 2012, p. 9. "Fifty years ago, the Indian government was blinded by selfish interests, and wanted to force the Chinese to accept an illegal border line created by the colonial powers. This was boldly rejected. Today, both countries need to learn from their ancient friendly ties and the lesson from the war. For the Chinese, they love peace but they will also firmly defend their land". Ibid.

188. See A.G. Noorani, "Publish the 1962 war Report Now – The Suppression of the Brook-Bhagat Report on the War with China is a

Betrayal of Nehru's Promise to the Nation", *The Hindu*, July 2, 2012, p. 8.

189. See a UNI report in *Munsif*, June 28, 2012, p. 1. "Althoug difficulties remain", (India should be patient). "As watermelon falls down when it is fully ripe, the border problem will solved in time." Ibid.

190. See a PTI report in *Munsif*, May 19, 2012, p. 11.

191. See a report in the *Hindustan Times*, March 5, 2012, p. 11.

192. See Richard A. Clark, "How China steals American Secrets", *Deccan Chronicle*, April 4, 2012, p. 10.

193. See Anand Krishnan, "China Takes Military Preparedness to a New High", The Hindu, March 23, 2012, p. 16.

194. See a report in *The Hindu*, February 26, 2012, p. 9.

195. For details, see a PTI report in *The Munsif*, February 27, 2012, p. 1.

196. See a report in the *Deccan Chronicle*, June 22, 2012, p. 8.

197. See S.M. Krishna, "India's Foreign Policy Priorities", India Quarterly, Volume 65, No. 4, 2009, p. 347.

198 See Army chief, Mr. V.K. Singh's interview in *The Hindu*, March 26, 2012, p. 11.

199. See *Ibid.*

200. *Ibid.*

201. See a report about Pakistan's condemnation of violence in Xinjiang in Munsif, March 2, 2012.

202. See a PTI report in Munsif, June 6, 2012, p. 1.

203. See Mao Xinyu's interview given to *The Hindu*, March 12, 2012, p. 7

204. See a report in *The Hindu,* May 22, 2012, p. 9.

205. This is the conclusion of a study by Wang Jisi and Kenneth Lieber thal, Brookings Institution in Washington, DC. Wang isi is one of the most influential strategic thinkers, a veteran scholar and the Dean of Peking University's School of International Studies and is on the advisory bodies of the government. Lieberthal is a former member of the National Security Council in the Clinton Administration. They believe that since 2008, China has emerged as the first class global power after weathering financial breakdowns of 1997-98 and 2008-09

plus the success of Beijing Olympics in 2008. The Chinese believe that they can now hold aloft what they perceive as the Chinese Development Model which stands as an alternative to the Western Democratic Model. This gives the Chinese enormous national confidence. The US, on the other hand is a declining power "On the wrong side of history." Financial disorder, alarming deficits and high unemployment rates make the US decline on a long term basis. See a report by Anand Krishnan in *The Hindu*, April 5, 2012, p. 11.

206. See a report in The Hindu, June 5, 2011, p. 14.

207. *Ibid.*

208. See a report in *The Hindu*, June 6, 2012, p. 1.

209. See a report in *The Hinu*, June 8, 2012, p. 14.

210. See a report in *The Hindu*, June 7, 2012, p. 12.

211. See a report in *The Hindu*, June 8, 2012, p. 14.

212. See a report in *The Hindu*, June 8, 2012, p. 14.

213. See an article by Robert D. Kaplan, "*The India-China Rivalry*", *Geopolitics*, (Online), April 25, 2012.

214. See a report in *The Hindu*, June 15, 2012, p. 20.

215. India and China have joined hands before on environmental issues to ward off pressure from the developed world. The Chinese Vice Premier, XI Hangsheng, said : "On the issue of international sustainable development, our two countries have many understandings.... We are under similar pressures and in front of similar challenges." China and India do not favour binding targets and restrictions. They also feel that the developed world need to do a lot to promote sustainable development by moving out of, what the Chinese call, "unsustainable production and consumption pattern" and change to green development and help the developing countries, through financial help and technology, to do the same. The national sensibilities have to be respected too in this regard and there should be no imposition of binding targets. India has similar view on these subjects. See a report in *The Hindu*, June 19, 2012, p. 12.

216. These figures are taken from a report in The Hindu, June 20, 2012, p. 15.

217. The information about Nepal is taken from a report in The *Economist*, (Online), January 18, 2012, accessed on 1/19/2012.

218. See a report in the Deccan Chnonicle, May 28, 2012, p. 9.

219. See his interview in *The Hindu,* June 4, 2012, p. 11.

220. The fundamental divide is on the question of federalism which many parties want identity based comprising 20 or 10 states. In the absence of a constitution, radicalization and ethnic politics will foster political uncertainty. Nepal has moved from monarchy to be a republic, from war to peace and from a Hindu kingdom to be a secular state. What is sure to follow is political uncertainty causing deep political instability. For details, see Prashant Jha, "Amid Uncertainty, Nepal awaits tryst with history – The political class faces its final challenge", *The Hindu*, May 27, 2012, p. 13.

221. See a report in the *Hindustan Times*, June 12, 2012, p. 17.

222. See Haroon Habib, "No alternative to bold steps", The Hindu, May 17, 2012, p. 10.

223. Said Hasina : "India needs to move forward quickly on some pending issues so that the two countries can work to implement the agreed decisions. "India and Bangladesh have already signed many important agreements. For details, see Haroon Habib, "Hasina expresses resolve to work together with India in pending issues", *The Hindu*, June 2, 2012, p. 14.

224. Quoted in *The Economist*, February 18, 2012, p. 22.

225. For details, see *The Economist,* February 18, 2012, pp. 22-23.

226. See a report in *The Hindu*, May 24, 2012, p. 13.

227. See a report in Munsif, May 28, 2012, p. 11.

228. Iran's Minister of External Affairs, Ali Akbar Vilayati, visited India on May 31, 2012, and S.M. Krishna clarified that unilateral sanction imposed on Iran other than the ones by the UN should not come in the way of trade with Iran which is a neighbour with a record of long standing good relations. The non-alignment conference to be held in Tehran in August, 2012, will give an opportunity to Iran and India to interact further. See a PTI report in the *Munsif,* June 1, 2012, p. 7.

References

1. Pick, Otto, Julien Critchley, *Collective Security,* (Macmillan, 1974).

2. Buzan, Barry, Ed., *The International Politics of Deterrence*, (Frances Pinter, London, 1987).

3. Caldicott, Helen, *Missile Envy – The Arms Race and Nuclear War*,

(Bantam, 1986).

4. Berki, R.N., *Security and Society – Reflections on Law and Order and Politics,* (JM Dent, Lonon, 1986).
5. Talbott, Strobe, *End game – The Inside Story of SALT II,* (Kalyani, Delhi, 1979).
6. Levine, Isaac Don, *Eyewitness to History,* (Martin Dale Books, New Work, 1973).
7. Seldes, George, *Wintness to a Century,* (Ballantine Books, New York, 1987).
8. Featherstone, Mike, Ed., *Global Culture – Nationalism, Globalisation and Modernity,* (Sage, London, 1990).
9. West, Nigel, *The Faber Book of Treachery*, (Faber & Faber, London, 1995).
10. Drell, Sidney, *In the Shadow of the Bomb, Physics and Arms Control – An Inside Look at the Rise and Fall of the Nuclear Threat,* (American Institute of Physics, New York, 1993).
11. Friedman, George & Meredith, *The Future of War – Power, Technology and American World Dominance in the 21st Century,* (Crown Publishers, New York, 1996).
12. Girot, Pascal, and Eleonore Korman, Ed., *International Geopolitical Analysis*, (Croom Helm, London, 1987).
13. Kaul, T.N., *Reminiscences – Discreet and Indiscreet,* (Lancers Publishers, 1982).
14. May, Earnest R., Ed., *Knowing One's Enemies – Intelligence Assessment Before the Two world Wars,* (Princeton University Press, New Jersey, 1984).
15. Clarke, Robin, *The Science of War and Peace,* (McGraw Hill Book Co, New York, 1972).

3

Changing Threat Perceptions in A Globalising World

H.E. Ambassador A.P. Venkateswaran

I am honoured to have been invited by Professor Mohammad Moazzam Ali to inaugurate this Seminar on Changing Threat Perceptions in a Globalising World being held by the Department of Political Science in the University of Hyderabad. I am also indebted to Professor Narasimha Rao, whom I have known over the years for persuading me to undertake the travel, which I generally prefer these days to avoid.

I was amused to see from the Concept Paper that the Foreign Policies of countries, drive and are in their turn driven by threat perceptions, resulting from "much meddling, muddling and modeling". I cannot but agree, but would like to add that in this multi-centric[1] world in which we are now, the "muddling" is all the more!

Most important of all threats to a nation's security, is the threat that comes from within. If, India lost her freedom to outside invaders, over a thousand years ago, and came into her own as an Independent, Sovereign Republic, after throwing off the British yoke only in 1947, it was not because she was conquered by outside forces, but because she was shamelessly betrayed from within. (Even though the last colonial power in India boasted that "the sun never set over the British Empire"). India had fallen victim to England due to subversion from inside. In fact, two of the most powerful invaders that the world has ever known, namely, the Greeks under Alexander in the 4th Century BC and later on, the Huns under Toramana in the 6th Century AD, had been forced to retreat from India.

But then, over the Centuries, a subtle decadence had silently set in. The virility of the people began to be sapped. The very prosperity that once arose from the talented accomplishments of the people attracted the jealous attention of others from across the oceans. And those who had less to show for themselves and, therefore had little to lose, set forth to acquire for themselves, by deceit or force, what their cupidity made them to hanker after. Under Britain, the myth of the White Man's Burden was born, which was merely a duplicitous variant of his self-assumed right to rule over others. That phase lasted for many centuries until the final collapse of colonialism under its own weight.

Freedom is invaluable and is the inherent right of all human beings. Nothing can be worse than to deny independence to people, so long as their actions do not impinge negatively upon others. If one had to ascribe one major reason for the conflicts which that one sees around the world, one may say that it is the adoption of double standards. There are few things as unjust in life as to deny to others what one cherishes for oneself. And history is replete with instances where the best relationships, which have lasted a long time, break up due to the practice of double standards by either of the parties.

Security threats come from all directions, and are not military threats only. Hence we speak today of Food Security, Energy Security, Environment Security and so on and so forth. But, it should be clear to anyone that only relatively larger countries can depend on themselves for any kind of security. Hence, it is that the newly independent countries that emerged in large numbers after World War II formed\ the Non-Aligned Movement, which at its peak was constituted of more than a hundred States. Even then, the NAM could function with a degree of independence from the hegemonistic designs of the two Major Alliances, the NATO led by the USA and the Warsaw Pact led by the USSR, respectively, only because these two Major Alliances needed to score points against each other.

However, with the end of the Cold War and the disintegration of the USSR, there was every reason for the NATO Alliance also to disband itself. But that has not happened and not satisfied with the breakup of the Warsaw Pact, the NATO group of countries has not only further strengthened itself militarily, but also set up bases in close proximity to the Russian Federation. This has led to the accentuation of tensions and one may discern a new arms race in the making. The race is now in regard to getting greater access to and control over the world's energy resources. The earlier invasion of Afghanistan by the USA on the pretext of hunting for Osama Bin Laden and the Al Qaeda, was quickly followed by its invasion of Iraq, under totally false pretexts, should awaken everyone to the fact that the world today is an even more dangerous place than at any time in the past. Now, it would appear that the US Administration is looking for any pretext to attack Iran as well!

The discarding of well-known principles of International Law and the brazen use of force by the USA in embarking on these two major adventures, against all canons of International Law, have no doubt sullied the principles of the American Declaration of Independence, but also drawn that country itself into a quagmire from which it will find it very difficult to extricate itself without suffering major damage to its standing in the world and to its own economy. We, in India, should also ponder as to our seeming closeness to such an unprincipled power, for whatever reason. The opposition in India to the US-India Nuclear agreement, which is still in doldrums at present, is in no small measure due to the general revulsion against that country's policies, as it is due to the distrust of Washington's motives in suddenly wooing India after many, many years of a spitefully negative attitude.

Amongst all the Living Civilizations of the world, India's has the unique distinction of being the oldest. Other civilizations like the Egyptian, the Babylonian, the Greek or the Roman have no connection with the people living in those countries now. As for the Chinese civilization, whatever remains has been shattered by centuries of turmoil and the remainder extinguished during the Civil War and thereafter under the iron rule of the Communists who proclaimed that anything belonging to the Past had no value in the Present! So much so, even Confucius's teachings were reviled during the notorious Cultural Revolution spear-headed by Chairman Mao Tse tung, shortly after the proclamation of the Chinese People's Revolution in 1949.

So it was left to India to claim the oldest Civilization as its own, with an unbroken continuity of six thousand years. Any Indian can be justifiably proud that at birth, marriage and death, the same prayers are invoked as they were being done many thousands of years ago. What, indeed, can give a deeper sense of belonging, to any one than this unique sense of identity with the land and civilization?

It has been truly said that of all the Virtues, Courage occupies pride of place. In other words, without Courage, none of the other Virtues can be practiced. I believe all the ills which face our Nation, today, can be traced to the general lack of courage shown by the people, as well as their leaders, to stand up to the challenges which confront them. Merely lamenting our inability to solve the problems we face, hoping that somehow they will vanish, by themselves, and leave us in peace. But that hope does not help!

Whether it be corruption in day to day life, or sycophancy, or the conscious preference to speak a pleasant falsehood instead of the unpleasant truth, which may result in bringing advantage to oneself, the wholesale erosion of societal values has become a pervasive phenomenon. This holds good in private as well as public life. Unless a collective effort is made to connect this negative trend, it may be too late and we shall all go under. Here, the advice given by our ancient Law-Giver Manu is best borne in mind. He advised: "Speak the Truth but not the unpleasant. Speak the pleasant but not the untruth". That way none can go wrong!

Corruption, sycophancy, servility, even betrayal of a cause or treachery to one's own motherland, all these have their roots in a lack of courage. And corruption is not just in terms of money, but extends to other fields, binding down people in all fields, body, mind and soul! It is like a cancer that enters the system and infects all parts of the body which, perhaps, is why our ancients said that the purpose of prayer is not just to prevent present pain, but to prevent the pain that is yet to come!

The old saying that the Lie is the weapon of the weak, no longer holds good and in fact the Lie has earned for itself a permanent place in the armoury of the strong and the powerful. With the explosion of the Electronic Media, Governments seem to have no compunction in using the mass media for furthering their own narrow agendas, whether these are good or bad, right or wrong.

As Henry George has presciently remarked: "Democratic governments in more than name can exist only where wealth is distributed with something like equality ... when the great mass of citizens are personally free and independent, neither fettered by their poverty nor made subject by their wealth .... No chain is stronger than its weakest link and the ultimate condition of any people must be the condition of its lowest class... In the long run, no nation can be freer than its most oppressed, richer than its poorest, wiser than its most ignorant."

It is, indeed, painful to see today that whatever India has stood for during the first forty years of our Freedom, whether it be planning for welfare or for building a just and egalitarian society, instead of dependence on others for what is needed for national sustenance, is being summarily discarded in the name of a blanket globalization! After all, it is we, in India, who had declared in the Rig Veda, thousands of years ago: "Mata Bhoomihi, Putroham Prithivya" or "The Whole World is our Mother Land; we are all Children of Mother Earth", which is the very essence of any Global Outlook. Truly practiced, that is what will bring about peace and amity in this planet of ours. When elsewhere in the world, people were burnt at the stake for thinking differently to the rest, here in India we had given them safe asylum. The early Christians had come to Kerala in 4 AD and found refuge. The Jews came in 70 AD when Jerusalem was put to the fire and sword, and the Parsis in the 7th Century when the Sword of Islam over-ran their land.

Gandhiji taught us, in our own life time, that if Right does not fight Might, then Might will rule alone. The decision of Britain in 1939 to go to war with Germany, despite being much weaker at that time, is an object lesson. We, in India, can seek inspiration from the Mahabharata, which tells us, that if all efforts to achieve an honourable peace do not succeed, waging a just war is preferable to living in dishonour.

Again, to quote Gandhiji, that given the stark choice between Cowardice and Violence, he would choose Violence! In his eyes, there was no justification for Cowardice. In his view Non-violence was the highest form of Courage and could be practiced only by the Strong. He said, unambiguously, in one of the last issues of The Harijan: "It is rather late in my life that I came to realize that many who claim to follow my teachings, do so not because they believe in them, but because they serve as a convenient cloak for their Cowardice!"

In this context, we may turn to the role of Leadership. True Leadership is when a Leader leads from upfront not one who exhorts his followers to go and fight, while he shelters behind others, can lay claim to leadership. Such a negative leadership quality is summed up in a pithy Punjabi Proverb which says: "A thousand Donkeys, led by a Lion, can easily defeat a thousand Lions led by a Donkey!!" We only have to look around us to judge for ourselves the caliber of the leaders we have, and it will become crystal clear why we are in such a grievous situation today. Merely to assert, as New Delhi does frequently, that negotiations have been successful, when in fact we have buckled under to the unreasonable demands of the other side, reflects no credit on oneself. Alas, this is what has become the rule rather than the exception in our dealings with other countries. Anyone can see that as India's Achilles' heel. In our keen desire to be seen as generous, we often surrender our own just rights without getting anything in return!

It is only those in the highest bracket of income, even in the USA who seem relaxed in the economic scenario that has been unfolding in the world. Even that independent US Think Tank, the Pew Institute, confirms this view in its latest analysis of US opinion polls. An economically deprived nation like India, representing one-sixth of the world's population, deserves better than to be side-lined just because of its inability to stand up against stronger counties. Jacques Atalli, the first President of the European Bank for Reconstruction and Development, was absolutely right when he declared, in one of his books, that in the new world dispensation "there will be winners and losers" and added, not surprisingly, that "the losers will far outnumber the winners !"

Fortunately, India's strategic geographical position, astride the Indian Ocean Sea Lanes, and our large and talented population, ensure that we cannot be ignored by any power. If today we are suffering, it is mostly from our own self-inflicted wounds since we are perceived by others as a disunited people with a weak and vacillating government, showing no sense of direction or even a clearly identifiable policy. But this situation need not continue for very long. The very size of our country and its talented population of over one billion people, will see to that, sooner or later. A bucket of water may, perhaps, go stale, but a lake or ocean of water never will, since it perforce regenerates itself.

Nothing has changed the outside perception of India as much as the underground nuclear tests we had carried out in May 1998. After years of restraint and impassioned pleading in the UN and elsewhere for Universal Nuclear Disarmament, a billion people in India had at last come into their own. Not for intimidating others, but for safeguarding their own security from threats of nuclear blackmail from outside. At the same time India has reiterated her readiness to work, with like-minded countries, towards the total elimination of all weapons of mass destruction, on an equal and non-discriminatory basis. It should be very obvious to all that total security for Some, can only lead to total insecurity for all others. The behaviour of the major powers, after the emergence of the current Uni-Polar situation, should convince everyone of this.

There are only a few countries which qualify for being included, similarly, with the requisite area of land, size of population, natural resources and talented people, that can aspire to be in the vanguard of the world. These would be China, India, USA, the Russian Federation and Brazil, to name a few. If one were to be generous, one may also include in the list, collectively, the European Union, the ASEAN and the Latin American Group.

May I end my inaugural speech at this point and wish all the participants a very successful Seminar? I trust that the participants will exercise independence of judgement and properly prioritize things, placing emphasis on what will do the most good to our own interests in this country, without trampling over the rights of others, in any way. I say this because there is a temptation to suffer from a Captive Mind Syndrome, by which I mean a strong tendency to give more weightage to what foreign scholars have to say on a subject, rather than to what our own scholars say, or for that matter what we ourselves have learnt from studying the matter from our own experience and point of view.

Reference

1. The expressions, "muddling, medling and modelling" and 'multicentric world' are origninally used by the doyen of International Relations Studies, Prof. James N.Rosenau-Ed.

4

International Politics, Configuration of Forces at the Global Level, West Asia and Threat Perception

H.E. Ambassador C.R. Gharekhan

When the Berlin Wall was pulled down by the long suffering people of East Berlin on 9th November 1989, few, if any, observers anticipated the consequences of that fateful event. It not only led to the emancipation of Eastern Europe from the stranglehold of the Soviet Union; it caused the dismemberment of the once mighty Soviet empire itself. It unleashed forces which caused an upheaval in the Balkans, the ramifications of which are still being felt today in the form of Kosovo's unilateral declaration of independence. The Socialist Federal Republic of Yugoslavia has ceased to exist and in its place six, possibly seven independent nations have been born. It is still early days to reach definitive conclusion whether the process of fragmentation has fully run its course.

The end of the cold war, which was ushered in with the collapse of the Berlin Wall, and the disappearance of the Soviet Union, led some scholars like Mr. Francis Fukuyama to proclaim, prematurely as it turned out, "the end of history". Fukuyama's thesis was that the triumph of the Western alliance had not only dealt a death blow to Soviet Union and the communist system; it had also demolished, once and for all, the viability of socialism and communism as an alternative to private enterprise and capitalism. The superiority of the western capitalist system could not and would not be challenged, for all time to come. I think it is fair to suggest that democracy as a form of government has certainly come to be acknowledged as the best possible form of government. People quibble about the definition of democracy. There is, however, a broad consensus that democracy implies rule of law, respect for individual human rights, periodic elections, peaceful transfer of power, and so on. The economic argument, however, has not yet been fully settled, as evidenced by the controversy surrounding globalisation.

The end of the Cold War era, which lasted four-and-a-half decades, led the then President Bush to proclaim the emergence, or the beginning of the emergence, of a new world order. The new world order was supposed to be based on respect for international law and an enhanced role for the United Nations in the maintenance of international peace and security. Though the United States did not make it explicit, the post-cold war international order was also expected to lead to the establishment of Pax Americana. Neither of these two developments has taken place. Rules of international law are no more respected since the end of the Cold War than in the preceding period, nor has the United Nations come to occupy a central role in questions of peace and security. There was a period of a few years after 1989 when American supremacy in international affairs appeared to gain ground. This became particularly evident when immediately after September 11, 2001, leaders from all over the world hurried to Washington to pledge support and allegiance to the White House. Today, however, not many even in the United States would claim a position of preeminence and dominating influence in world affairs for their country.

There was a period of some years when it seemed that the United Nations would play the role and command the respect that its founding fathers had envisaged for it. The first major crisis to erupt in the new era was occasioned by Iraq's President Saddam Hussain invading, occupying and annexing Kuwait in the early hours of 2nd August 1990. From the point of view of the United Nations, the timing of Saddam's aggression was fortunate. Here was a case of a blatant attempt by a powerful neighbour to swallow its smaller neighbour, in defiance of the basic rules of international law. Even at the height of the cold war, it would have been extremely difficult, if not impossible, for any friend of Saddam Hussean to come to his political rescue. The Soviet Union of the post-Berlin Wall collapse was anxious to make up with the West, particularly the United States. In the Security Council, the Soviet, and later the Russian representatives at times outdid Western delegates in denouncing Saddam and demanding harshest possible sanctions against his regime. It, therefore, became possible for the permanent members to close their ranks, as had not been possible during the previous 45 years, and join in demanding Iraq's withdrawal from Kuwait, and subsequently in imposing draconian sanctions on Iraq. This unanimity among permanent members was sustained on a few more occasions but came under severe strain during the Balkan crisis of the 1990s.

But not everyone was happy with the advent of the unipolar world. One could hear many delegates in the United Nations lament the disappearance of a countervailing voice, of the lack of balance in international relations. This was particularly true of the Palestinians, who lost an influential supporter and patron for their cause in the Security Council. The Palestinian delegation made no secret of their deep disappointment with the attitude of the Russian diplomats who did not display any embarrassment at diluting and even abandoning their previous stance of total support to the Palestinians. Similarly, when Libya was put in the dock by United States, United Kingdom and France in 1992 in connection with the Lockerbie incident, it failed to evoke Russian support against the move to impose sanctions on it.

It was Iraq which brought the permanent members together in 1991. A dozen years later, it was the same Iraq which fractured that unity. The year 2003 formally ended Pax Americana, if indeed it ever did exist in reality. The fact that the United States managed to obtain barely 25 per cent support in the Security Council – only 4 members out of 15 gave positive indication – in favour of the Anglo-American draft resolution seeking authorization for the use of force against Iraq, was a blow to American prestige and influence. The French Foreign Minister traveled far and wide, lobbying against what he described as the 'hyper power's attempt to go against the international law. Even its closest ally, after Britain, in Europe, namely, Germany, refused to fall in line. When the American troops defeated Saddam Hussain's army in March 2003 within a matter of days, it did not particularly boost the prestige of American military. On the other hand, the fact that after 5 years of occupation, there is no credible prospect of Iraq getting stabilized, at peace with itself and with its neighbours, together with credible reports of torture and other inhumane practices in Abu Ghraib, etc., deeply dented America's moral high ground, creating a negative image of America in the world as well as, and even more damagingly, within the United States. Thus Pax Americana, which seemed a distinct possibility in the early 1990s, has receded from the horizon, for a long-long time to come.

18 months before the US intervention in Iraq, September 11, 2001, had happened. That single event traumatized the American psyche, perhaps more than even the attack on Pearl Harbor in December 1941. 9/11 initiated a process which is still unfolding and will take years, perhaps decades, to play itself out. The immediate consequence was the intervention in Afghanistan which achieved the immediate objective of inflicting severe blows on Al Qaida and the replacement of the Taliban regime by a government which was widely acceptable to the international community. However, as we know, Afghanistan today is far from being stable. Al Qaida has not only survived; its reach and ideology have spread in many parts of the world, including in the West. Taliban is on the rise again and the cultivation of poppy breaks a new record every year.

The intervention in Iraq cannot be directly attributed to 9/11. Enough evidence is available to suggest that the attack on Iraq was thought of well before the events of 9/11. It remains to be seen whether, and how soon, Iraq would stabilize itself. Not so long ago, influential American senators were openly advocating trifurcation of Iraq. Nearly 4000 American men and women soldiers have lost their lives and, according to some estimates, over 1 million Iraqi civilians have been killed. It will take a few generations for Iraq to fully recover from devastation on this scale. We should sincerely hope that the few signs of recovery that are reported, such as increased oil production, comparative quiet in Baghdad, and the somewhat reduced level of violence would be sustained over a long term. Nevertheless, there is no gainsaying the fact that the intervention in Iraq has done nothing to enhance American prestige in the region and in the world. This is particularly true since the reasons, or casus belli on which the intervention was sought to be justified, namely, the existence of weapons of mass destruction and Saddam Hussain's alleged links with Al Qaida, were found to be untrue.

A direct consequence of the March 2003 attack on Iraq was the severe blow to the prestige and credibility of the United Nations. It can be undisputably asserted that the use of force in today's world can be justified only in two situations; with the authorization of the United Nations or in pursuance of the right of self-defence as defined in Article 51 of the UN Charter. For the governments and the peoples everywhere, the fact that the attack was launched without authorization of the UN Security Council rendered it illegal. Even the then Secretary General of the United Nations Mr. Kofi Annan described the intervention as illegal. Media, including in India, wrote obituaries of the world organization. Five years later, the UN has yet to recover from this blow to its credibility. The recent unilateral declaration of independence by Kosovo, in which the United Nations Security Council was scrupulously kept out, will not help in any way in recreating confidence in the global organization.

The net result of the developments of the past 10 years or so is that there is not one single state which can claim preeminence above all other states. No doubt, United States is by far the predominant military power; its defence budget is larger than the combined defence budgets of the next 12 countries. Its share in the world GDP is still the largest. Its R&D infrastructure is probably still the best in the world. But its political and moral influence has declined. In other words, its 'soft power' has diminished. Thus the world remained unipolar for only a few brief years after the end of the Cold War era. We still haven't reached a fully multipolar world, though several poles are emerging. Mr. Henry Kissinger believes that the world consists or will consist of six poles – USA, Europe, Russia, China, Japan and India. On the other hand, there is an interesting paper published in New York Times magazine section on January 27, 2008, entitled "Waving Goodbye to Hegemony". It is authored by a scholar of Indian origin Parag Khanna, who is a Senior Research Fellow in the American Strategy Programme of the New American Foundation. According to Khanna, there will be three genuine superpowers in the 21st century – United States

European Union and China. These three will make their own rules without any one of them dominating. The others will be left to choose their suitors. In various ways, China and Europe will meddle in America's backyard; America and China will compete for the African resources in Europe's southern periphery; and America and Europe will seek to profit from the rapid economic growth of countries within China's growing sphere of influence. The main battlefield for the big three will be what Khanna calls "the second world". The second world countries will be the so-called swing states and are to be distinguished from the third world by their potential. He rules out Russia as a superpower because, in his words, "Russia is disappearing". Its population is declining at half million citizens every year and it will not be much larger than Turkey by about 2025. The important second world countries will be Russia, Turkey, Iran, Saudi Arabia, and a few others. For some reason, Khanna's article contains only one brief reference to India and that too not a flattering one.

Russia, which had become inward looking in the early 1990s, has begun to assert itself on the world stage. Mr. Putin's rhetoric has made him unpopular with the western world. At the same time, his popularity at home has consistently remained high, which goes to show that peoples generally want their governments to project a profile of independence and equality. This is especially true of countries like Russia which exercised considerable influence in world affairs until recently. There is no doubt that Mr. Putin's tough postures have endeared him to many in the developing world also. They feel that some kind of a balance is again being restored in international relations.

The phenomenon of terrorism predates the tragic events of September 11, 2001. We in India know this better than people elsewhere in the world, since we have been the victims of trans-border terrorism for over 20 years. However, it took 9/11 for the so-called "war on terror" to emerge as a major, perhaps the most important issue confronting governments and peoples around the world. The war against terror is not going to be over anytime soon. International community has not even managed to define what constitutes an act of terrorism, though there is wide consensus that intentionally targeting innocent civilians cannot be condoned or justified, no matter what the cause. In the meantime, what this war has done is create a huge wall of suspicion against members of one particular community. This is tragic, dangerous and highly deplorable. Just as terrorism respects no territorial boundaries, it cuts across religious beliefs. Terrorist attacks by some Palestinians are rightly condemned, but no one seems to remember the murderous assault by Baruch Goldstein, a fanatic Jew, in the Holy Mosque of Ibrahim in Hebron in occupied West Bank on February 26, 1994. Let us also not forget that the original suicide bombers came from the ranks of the Tamil Tigers in Sri Lanka.

The campaign against terrorism has to be waged at various levels, not just through the use of force. The danger is that a mishandling of this campaign could cause serious rift in societies and could cause immense harm to communal harmony. It is thus incumbent upon governments to assess the likely impact of foreign policy decisions on domestic situations within their countries. For example, one result, not intended but surely not difficult to anticipate, of the intervention in Iraq is the heightened tensions between Sunni and Shia Muslim communities in West Asia and beyond. Nations with significant Muslim communities have to be conscious of this phenomenon.

At this point, it would be appropriate to examine the situation in West Asia, a region which we in India often describe as part of our extended neighbourhood. It used to be said in the 18th century that whoever ruled Central Europe ruled Europe, and whoever ruled Europe ruled the world. Today, one can say that whoever controls the hydrocarbon resources of West Asia will have a commanding voice in the councils of the world. Happily, it is unlikely that any single power will acquire such control in the entire region. It is in the interest of the international community that the effective sovereignty over their natural resources remains with the countries of the region, undiluted by external factors.

West Asia is highly unstable and volatile today. It has also become one of the two epicenters of terrorism. Besides the Arab-Israeli conflict, the region has been destabilized by the intervention in Iraq and its aftermath.

As for the Israeli-Arab question, anyone who believes that peace can be brought between the Arabs and the Israelis without settling the core issue of Palestine is either daydreaming or refuses to face facts. It may be that some Arab governments are anxious to open official relations with Israel but the public opinion on Arab street will not let them do so. The Arabs for their part have come up with a reasonable and statesmanlike proposal: they are all prepared to recognize Israel in return for Israeli withdrawal from all occupied Arab lands. This constructive proposal deserves a positive response from Israel and others. Indeed, the Prime Minister and other Ministers in Israel government have acknowledged that the Arab Peace Initiative contains positive elements. It is no doubt true that the devil is in the detail. Even if the broad proposition put forward by the Arab side were to be accepted, detailed negotiations would still be necessary in respect of the complex and emotional issues of Jerusalem and refugees. But even these issues can be resolved, given the necessary commitment and political will on both sides. Daniel Gavron, a self-proclaimed Zionist in an article in the New York Times last week, has expressed his astonishment and exasperation at Israel's approach. He believes that since the whole world, including all Arab nations, is ready to accept the existence of the State of Israel in 78% of what used to be the mandated territory of Palestine – a situation which the early Zionists towards the end of the 19th century could not have even dreamt about – Israel does not even realize that it has won. In his words – "for any 'two-state-solution' to work, we would need to conduct a complete withdrawal from the West Bank. Even so, the success of the Zionists enterprise would be astounding."

Without going into the internal situation in Iraq, which is truly tragic, and dangerous, there is no question but that the two biggest beneficiaries of the events in Iraq have been the forces of extremism, and Iran. Extremism and terrorism have already been dealt with earlier in this presentation. As far as Iran is concerned, it has emerged with greatly enhanced clout and influence in the region and beyond. It has acquired almost a decisive voice on the Palestine question through the instrumentality of Hamas. Isn't it ironical that the government of a Shia state should come to acquire such a strong influence on Hamas which is a 100 per cent Sunni movement? This became possible, and was fully anticipatable, the moment Israel and the West decided to boycott Hamas which had come to form the government through perfectly democratic means. Indeed, it is no secret that the Palestinian President Mahmoud Abbas would have preferred to delay the elections of January 2006, but was prevailed upon to holding them by others outside the region.

Iran's association with Hezbollah goes back much longer, commencing with Israel's first Lebanon war of 1982. The 1982 war produced the phenomenon of Hezbollah and the second Lebanon war of 2006 boosted its prestige throughout the Arab world and even to other Muslim countries. Lebanon today is in deep crisis, on the verge of yet another civil war. If that were to happen, it would be truly tragic. The earlier civil war lasted 14 long years. What is even more tragic is that a civil war would not solve Lebanon's problems. Lebanon is crying for and deserves to be left alone.

To come back to Iran. Iran has become the single most important player in Iraq. Iraq cannot become stable unless Iran lets it. This does not necessarily mean that Iran by itself can stabilize Iraq, but its influence is predominant. Thus, Iran has achieved in the short time span of 5 years what perhaps it has aspired for all along, namely, to become a key player in the region. How it chooses to use this leverage will determine in large measure the future of the region.

A few words about the economic situation in the contemporary world before concluding these remarks. In economic terms, the world has truly become a multipolar world. The six names mentioned by Dr. Kissinger, referred to earlier, are indeed or will soon become the principal economic centres in global economy – USA, European Union, Russia, China, Japan and India. The share of the United States in the world GDP was 50 per cent at the conclusion of the Second World War; today it is just over 30 per cent. Correspondingly, the shares of others have risen and will continue to outgrow the rate of growth in American GDP. Let us not forget that China and India, between them, accounted for 50 per cent of world GDP until the middle of the 19th century. These two countries are well set to achieve this target in the coming decades. Historically speaking, therefore, the economic backwardness of China and India for the last 200 years was more like an aberration. The downward slide of the dollar, which some American economists are not perturbed about, does nevertheless reflect the perception and the reality of a decline in American economic strength. The rise in the price of oil in dollar terms has less to do with supply and demand than with the fall in the purchasing power of dollar. The current recession in the United States is bad news not just for American people but for the whole world. United States is a voracious consumption oriented nation. The lifestyles of the American people, with which many might find faults, have in fact supported the export boom in China, India and many other developing countries. Consequently, when Americans curb their shopping sprees, the whole world stands to lose.

Fortunately, some developing countries, especially the BRIC group, namely, Brazil, Russia, India, and China are doing extremely well. India and China, in particular, are growing at a pace which would make it easier for them, as well as for many other nations, to absorb at least a part of the shock which would be felt because of the slowdown in US economy. This redistribution of global wealth will, and must eventually be reflected in the political sphere as well as in multilateral intergovernmental institutions, including the United Nations Security Council.

5

Globalisation, Threats and the Indian Army: A Perspetive

Brig. V.P. Munjal

"*Question: What is the truest definition of Globalization?*

Answer: Princess Diana's death. How : An English princess with an Egyptian boyfriend crashes in a French tunnel, driving a German car with a Dutch engine, driven by a Belgian who was drunk on Scottish whisky, (check the bottle before you change the spelling) followed closely by Italian Paparazzi, on Japanese motorcycles; treated by an American doctor, using Brazilian medicines."

Introduction

1. What exactly is globalization? Globalization is a multi dimensional phenomenon: Information technologies, along with a variety of other Technologies, are developing rapidly and spreading widely. Trade is expanding globally, as is the flow of private capital and investment. Interdependencies are growing in all aspects of our lives. These developments create real possibilities to achieve economic prosperity, spread political freedom, and promote peace. Yet they are also producing powerful forces of social fragmentation, creating critical vulnerabilities, and sowing the seeds of violence and conflict. Economic crises extend across state borders and are producing global hardships.

2. Is globalization a cure to the woes of the world? Simply defined, globalization is the increased international or inter-societal interaction. Above all, it is an idea that no entity in the world, be it a state, nation, society, people or tribe, may exist in complete isolation without interaction and discourse with other world elements. Thus, an important political or social event happening in one state would also affect other states and societies, and therefore likely to elicit a state response. A global free market, international non-state organizations like the United Nations, or International Monetary Fund, can be classified as

features of globalization. Globalization can be regarded as a process, a concept or an existing feature of history such as a war or revolution.

3. All of these are aspects of what is commonly referred to as "globalization," and all have important security implications. Most dangerously, a variety of threats have become global in scope and more serious in their effects as a result of the spread of knowledge, the dispersion of advanced technologies, and the movements of people. These same developments, combined with expanding global economic interactions, contribute to some of the problems and resentments that lie at the root of these security threats. But paradoxically, many of those same aspects of globalization offer new opportunities to achieve economic growth and democracy, thereby ameliorating the threats as well as some of their underlying causes.

4. The dangers were clearly manifested in the September 11th terrorist attacks, which showed how the Al Qaeda organization was able effectively to exploit new communications technologies, global financial networks, and the ease of movements of people. The response by the international community has also benefited from some of globalization's effects, primarily in technological advances in communications and in military weaponry. Many different aspects of globalization now combine to increase the dangers of a variety of transnational threats from weapons proliferation, cyber attacks, ethnic violence, global crime, drug trafficking, environmental degradation, and the spread of infectious diseases. The many dimensions of globalization call for a new way of approaching security in the coming decades. The various transnational threats arising out of different aspects of globalization pose too many risks to be ignored.

5. The model of globalization as given by Micheal Porter uses four components: (1) Investment, (2) Industry or manufacturing (3) Information technology and (4) Individual consumer or marketization. To this a 5th I called international business can be added without which a nation will operate under new trade conditions called autarky.

Globalization and its Implications

6. A key aspect of globalization is the 'globalization' of national economies. As the world becomes, and functions as, a truly borderless global village, every country has become part and parcel of the world economic system.

7. Another facet of it is the formation of world trade system as markets are globalised and companies trade across national boundaries. The establishment of the World Trade Organization (WTO) in 1995 marked the formation of a global multi-lateral trade system.

8. The third manifestation is the global nature of financial systems. As vast Currency movements can be transacted across borders in real time under the world financial system, international investment activities have become worldwide. This development has further enhanced the role of the trans-national corporations.

9. Globalization is being presented as the process of enhancing collective measures to stop international violence and wars, to save globalenvironment, and to eliminate Third World poverty and economic inequality through developed communications, investments, trade, and aid. Globalization implies that "bigger is better".

10. But the central question is: what caused these problems in the first place? Otherwise we end up with the logic of the tragedies caused by drunk driving. More policing, more fines, more punishment, while selling more liquor to the drivers, cannot end drunk driving. The solution lies in going to the root of drunkenness, that is, alcoholism! The root causes for the current global malaise are twofold: firstly, massive and reckless industrialization, and secondly, dehumanization of science, technology, and industry.

11. "Massiveness" means mass production leading to mass surpluses necessitating mass distribution and mass consumption through massive technologicalization, capitalization, monopolization, and governmentalization.

12. "Dehumanization" means total concentration of the industries on commercial profit and economic power to a total exclusion of concerns for human health and happiness in terms of physical, intellectual, and economic well-being.

13. Day one of the technological revolution in industry was also the day one of the revolution in arms manufacture. Every technological improvement was quickly translated into more and more destructive weaponry. This "techno-industrial military complex" also became the powerful vehicle of militarization, world wars, and colonialization.

14. This has been the legacy of globalization of massive industrialization. Now the contemporary advocates of globalization are sloganeering that what is good for the developed West is also good for the poor states. The haunting fact is that the United States, one country out of almost 200 in the world, uses nearly 40 per cent of world resources.

15. The threat is growing that infectious diseases will spread globally and quickly, as a result of increasingly drug-resistant microbes, the lag in development of new antibiotics, poor patterns of land and water use, shifts in climate, the rise of mega-cities with severe health care deficiencies, the ease of movement of peoples across borders, and the growing number of refugees.

U.S. intelligence estimates project only limited gains over the coming 20 years against the overall infectious-disease threat, with virulent diseases, led by HIV/AIDS and tuberculosis, continuing to take a significant toll.

16. Some argue that science-technology and industrialization are not inherently immoral; it is their misuse that causes problems. The criticism is of their massiveness and dehumanization that transform their very purpose.True, the sword by itself does not kill people; people using it kill people. But in the human context, the very purpose for the creation of the sword is to inflict pain or death on human beings. This destructive purpose of the sword will not change until the sword, in Biblical terms, is beaten into ploughshare. When it becomes a ploughshare, then it is not a sword by definition and purpose. Thus ends and means should be integrated, not dichotomized.

17. **Other Transnational Threats**. Information technologies and systems are central features of globalization and have become increasingly important to the functioning of many critical civilian systems—communications, energy, transportation, electrical, water, and banking. The problem is that they now are potentially vulnerable to the threat of cyber attacks and disruption. The dangers arising from environmental degradation, often, cross the state borders. The most publicized danger involves the rising global temperatures that are touching off devastating droughts, floods, and violent storms. Other environmental dangers include air and water pollution, the loss of forests and biodiversity, and the potential introduction of toxic substances into the human food chain.

18. But then, can the answer to globalized militarization and wars, to globalized pollution and ecological disaster, and to globalized exploitation, poverty, and inequality, be less globalization, and its eventual elimination!?

19. It is not that globalization does not have any positive aspects. It has as would be evident from the list given below:

(a) More choice of consumer durables.

(b) Price signals and competition give proper price to the consumer.

(c) With the reduced price of luxury goods, these are affordable by the common man.

(d) The EMI- equal monthly installment - has also encouraged consumerism among every income segment.

(e) Retail marketing has brought to India the very best of world class branded products.

(f) The revolution in mobile telecom has made it hard to imagine a person in India without a cell phone. The number of cell phones has out numbered the land line phones in India.

(g) Balance of trade tilting in favour of India by increased exports.

(h) Improved performance of banking and other financial institutes due to entry of foreign players.

(i) Quantum jump in the economic reforms.

(j) More than two fold increase in India's per capita income.

Implications Toward National Security

20. The spread of globalization far outpaces the ability of societies and their political systems to adjust to the changing global security situation. Until they do, national security will be fragile and vulnerable to backlash from all the "isms" of the post-Cold War world, especially neo-colonialism and neo-interventionism.

21. **Neo-Interventionism**. The borderless world tends to increase the "internationalization" of a nation's domestic issues and thus precipitates the first security impact: Neo-interventionism which poses challenges to the United Nations (UN) principle of territorial integrity and sovereign equality. Globalization has led to an increase in foreign interferences or interventions in a nation's internal affairs, especially by the United States of America (USA) and international Non-Governmental Organizations (NGOs).

22. **Spill-Over Effect of International Issues.** The second impact of globalization is the *spill-over effect* of international issues on national security. The increasing globalization of the world has created a new security environment that enhanced the ability of non-state actors to function beyond territorial borders. In particular, terrorist organizations have become more trans-national in character, operating relatively easily across permeable state boundaries. Globalization has enabled the terrorists to move easily across frontiers; make alliances with other states or other terrorist groups; exploit instant communications and the mass media; and have the potential to gain access to and utilise weapon systems that would have been inconceivable during the Cold War. These products of globalization, more than ever before, allow terrorists to pursue their war against a particular state, community or system on the world stage. The recent terrorists' attacks on USA embassies in Nairobi, Kenya, and Dar Es Salaam, Tanzania and the September 11th 2001, incident have demonstrated the *spill over effect* of the potential threat of unpredictable, strike-anywhere-anytime terrorism and terrorism by proxy.

23. **Economic Sabotage.** The immoral character of the global economy

has exposed national economies to the threat of economic sabotage. Globalization, aided and abetted by the removal of national controls over cross-border financial flows and the computer revolution, has resulted in short term capital entering and exiting markets at lightning speed. Because this capital is as massive as it is volatile, it is capable of wreaking havoc upon an economy which may not have the mechanisms to deal with it. Given the "messy, unreliable and destructive" international financial system, it tends to expose a nation's currency and economy to speculative attacks by currency traders.

24. **Economic Domination.** Another impact and implication of economic and financial globalization is the dominance of those with capitals and the dual faces of North and South. The dominant forms of economic and financial globalization in the context of their concomitant processes of liberalisation and integration are clearly of benefit to those with considerable amounts of accumulated capital or trade in the marketplace. Those without one or both to sell or trade such as the poor and already marginalised in both industrialized and developing countries are clearly being further disempowered and peripheralised by such globalization processes.

25. **The Threat of "Trade-Related Issues".** Another impact and implication of globalization is the threat of "trade-related issues" in trade agreement. The linking of issues to the possibility of sanctions under the clever device of attaching a "trade-related" prefix to the chosen topics has been successfully used in injecting services and investments into GATT/WTO. Northern countries, through their new 'Round' at the WTO, are introducing new issues such as foreign investment regime, trade and labour standards and environment and competition policy. If political leaders and trade officials of the Southern countries do not take note of these developments and actively counter them, they may eventually be pressured to accept new international economic rules that are even more stacked against them than those that already exist.

26. **Control of Information.**The homogenization of consumer culture in place of diversity is another of the major impacts of the globalization process. This is going to become more universal because of the development of Information Technology (IT). The unfortunate thing is that IT industry, and all that will be disseminated through it, will again and be dominated by the big players: the huge corporations owned by the developed countries. As national borders become more porous to information flows and information channels reaching citizens have multiplied into network structures less amenable to centralized control, new threats to national security appear, i.e. the hostile, politically motivated use of information and electronic means by the developed countries.

27. **Trans-national Crime.** Another impact of globalization is the rise of trans-national crime as a serious threat to national security and stability. Globalization, the telecommunications revolution, the opening of international borders, and more, have all contributed to a' business' environment that is just as helpful to the trans-national criminals as it is to a legal trans-national company or the legal entrepreneurial businessman. Growing interdependence between states, improved international transportation links, deregulation within states, and the explosion in information technology are the backbone of the distribution systems that support trans-national business operations. These distribution systems move capital, product, people, currency and information across them at rates that exceed the ability of nation-states to either monitor or control them. This is a case for legal as well as illicit transactions. The drug trade takes centre stage in any discussion of trans-national crime. In recent decades, the trade in illicit drugs has spawned by far the most proficient, widespread and profitable networks of organised crime. The world drug trade is estimated to be worth about US $ 400 billion, of which the drug traffickers take about 90 per cent.

India's Security Concerns

28. India shares land borders with seven countries-including Bangladesh (4096 kms), China (3439 kms), Pakistan (3325 kms) and Myanmar (1643 kms)- and maritime borders with five countries. Given the size of the country and its role in the comity of nations, our security concerns and interests are not limited to our immediate neighborhood. India's area of security interest clearly extends beyond the confines of the conventional geographical definition of SouthAsia.

29. India's security concerns are defined by a dynamic global security environment and the perception that South Asia region is of particular global security interest. The continuing presence of terrorist and fundamentalist forces in its neighborhood has prompted India to maintain a high level of defence vigilance and preparedness to face any challenge to its security.

30. The security challenges facing India are varied and complex. The country faces a series of low intensity conflicts characterized by tribal, ethnic and left wing movements and ideologies as also the proxy war conducted by Pakistan and various radical jehadi outfits through the instrumentality of terrorism. India is also affected by the trafficking in drugs and proliferation of small arms and the fact that it is surrounded by two neighbours with nuclear weapons and missiles and history of past aggressions and war. There is also the ever present possibility of hostile radical fundamentalist elements gaining access to the weapons of mass destruction in Pakistan. The country has experienced four major conventional border wars besides an undeclared war at

Kargil. India's response to these threats and challenges has always been restrained, measured and moderate in keeping with its peaceful outlook and reputation as a peace loving country

National Security Objectives

31. India's national security objectives have evolved against a backdrop of India's core values namely, democracy, secularism and peaceful co-existence and the national goal of social and economic development. These are:-

1. defending the country's borders as defined by law and enshrined in the Constitution;
2. protecting the lives and property of its citizens against war, terrorism, nuclear threats and militant activities;
3. protecting the country from instability and religious and other forms of radicalism and extremism emanating from neighbouring states;
4. securing the country against the use or the threat of use of weapons of mass destruction;
5. development of material, equipment and technologies that have a bearing on India 's security, particularly its defence preparedness through indigenous research, development and production, inter-alia to overcome restrictions on the transfer of such items;
6. promoting further co-operation and understanding with neighbouring countries and implementing mutually agreed confidence-building measures; and
7. pursuing security and strategic dialogues with major powers and key partners

Salient Features of the Security Environment

32. India is strategically located in relation to both continental Asia as well as the Indian Ocean region. India's geographical and topographical diversity, especially on its borders, poses unique challenges to our armed forces in terms of both equipment and training. Its peninsular shape provides India a coastline of about 7600 kms and an exclusive economic zone (EEZ) of over 2 million sq kms. The island territories in the East are 1,300 kms away from the main land, physically much closer to South East Asia. The peninsular India is adjacent to one of the most vital sea-lanes stretching from the Suez Canal and Persian Gulf to the Straits of Malacca through which much of the oil from the Gulf region transits. This is an area which has attracted super power rivalries in the past and continues to be a region of heightened activity by extra regional

navies on account of current global security concerns. India's size, strategic location, trade interests and a security environment that extends from the Persian Gulf in the west to the Straits of Malacca in the east and from the Central Asian Republics in the north to near the equator in the south, underpin India's security response. In view of this strategic spread, it is essential for the country to maintain a credible land, air and maritime force to safeguard its security interests.

The Regional Picture

33. Though there have been positive developments in Afghanistan and Sri Lanka, a closer look at the neighbourhood and the wider region continues to present a disturbing picture. Many of the countries face internal instability threatening their economic progress and peace. However, the single greatest threat to peace and stability in the region is posed by the combination of terrorism nurtured in and by Pakistan for its strategic objectives, and the ingrained adventurism of the Pakistani military motivated by its obsessive and compulsive hostility towards India. Virtually every terrorist act anywhere in the world today has a Pakistani fingerprint somewhere. It is the root and epicentre of international terrorism in the region and beyond.

34. Afghanistan has, with the intervention of the international community, only just emerged from the dark years of a reactionary, medieval and fundamentalist regime essentially created by Pakistan. While the new Government has international legitimacy, the task of reconstruction and rebuilding the institutions is formidable. Pakistan has a vested interest in a weak and unstable. Afghanistan which provides it an opportunity to meddle in the internal affairs of the country in pursuit of its quest for strategic depth vis a vis India and Central Asia. Any revival of jehadi activities supported by Pakistanis of direct security concern to Indiain view of their linkages with terrorism and the proxy war againstIndia. India is also committed to international engagement in Afghanistan so that Pakistan cannot exploit the neglect and inattention of the international community, as it did after the Soviet withdrawal from Afghanistan, to sponsor jehadi politics and training in the region.

Pakistan

35. Pakistan's polity has been repeatedly hijacked by the military that have a vested interest in tension with India as it strengthens their pre-eminence in the Pakistani power structure. India has been on the receiving end of Pakistan's policy of a proxy war against India using terrorism for several decades now, first in the Punjab and then in Jammu & Kashmir and elsewhere. Pakistani provocation reached a dangerous point with the December 13, 2001, attack on the Parliament. A more forceful response became necessary. Additional troops

were moved along the Line of Control (LoC) and the International Boundary in a state of readiness, inter-alia, to prevent further infiltration of terrorists into India.

36. India remains firmly committed to the path of dialogue and reconciliation in keeping with the Shimla Agreement and the Lahore Declaration and has repeatedly called upon Pakistan to end its sponsorship of terrorism in India so that a conducive environment can be created for the resumption of bilateral dialogue. Should Pakistan move purposefully towards eradicating cross border terrorism, India will be prepared to resume bilateral dialogue to address differences and enhance cooperation. It should not be forgotten that the two most bold and meaningful initiatives for dialogue at Lahore and Agra came from India. With this in background, the latest peace initiative of Prime Minister will make worthwhile progress only with end of cross-border terrorism.

China

37. China, India's largest neighbour, is passing through a period of rapid economic growth and modernization with the aim of achieving great power status in the shortest time possible. India's border with China is almost 3,500 km long. China continues to occupy approx. 38,000 sq. km of Indian territory mainly in the Aksai Chin Area, and claims yet another 90,000 sq km in the Eastern Sector. Further, 5,180 sq. km of territory under Pak occupation in Northern Kashmir was illegally ceded to China by Pakistanin 1963. (Whilst several rounds of Border Talks have been held with China, a number of disputed pockets remain).

38. China is rapidly modernising its Armed Forces. In its White Paper on National Defence issued recently, China has stressed the vital importance of maintaining international stability and a global strategic balance, as also a legal regime governing international arms control and disarmament, in order to address an international situation that is undergoing profound changes including a serious disequilibrium in the balance of military power especially between the developed and developing countries.

39. As far as India is concerned, it cannot be ignored that every major Indian city is within reach of Chinese missiles and this capability is being further augmented to include Submarine Launched Ballistic Missiles (SLBMs). The asymmetry in terms of nuclear forces is pronouncedly in favour of China and is likely to get further accentuated as China responds to counter the US missile defence programme. China's close defence relationship with Pakistan takes a particular edge in view of latter's known belligerence and hostility to India and its acquisition of nuclear assets.

40. Notwithstanding these concerns, India continues its endeavour to

seek a long term and stable relationship with China, based on the principles of Panchsheel, mutual sensitivity to each other's concerns and equality and is committed to the process of dialogue to resolve all outstanding differences. Some Confidence Building Measures (CBMs) have been initiated and while these are bearing fruit incrementally, the pace of progress has been less than satisfactory. A number of high level visits have taken place in recent years. These high level visits have improved bilateral relations and understanding of each other's viewpoint thereby contributing to further reduction in tension.

Bangladesh

41. India's relation with Bangladeshis characterized by both affinity and occasional friction. Key security concerns relate to the problem of uncontrolled migration, which Bangladesh refuses to recognize, across the 4,000 kms common boundary, the presence and activities of Indian insurgent groups and leaders from the north-east of India on Bangladeshi soil which it refuses to acknowledge, the rising influence of political parties and organizations of radical Islamic and fundamentalist orientation within and outside the government and border demarcation and border management problems which give rise to ugly incidents from time to time. Border management problems, such as smuggling, illegal immigration, insurgency, trafficking of women and children, and the construction, repair and maintenance of boundary-related structures are addressed through Border Coordination Conferences between the Border Security Force (BSF) and Bangladesh Rifles (BDR) while issues such as exchange of enclaves and adverse possessions are addressed by the Joint Boundary Working Groups (JBWGs) constituted for the purpose. Following the elections, Indiacontinued with its policy of close engagement with its eastern neigh bour discussing all issues in a forthright manner.

Nepal

42. Relations between India and Nepal have consistently been close and extensive, reflecting the historical, geographical, cultural and linguistic links between the two nations. In keeping with this close relationship, several high-level interactions took place between India and Nepal. Defence relations too have been traditionally close. Recently, Nepal has been beset on the one hand by a political and constitutional crisis and on the other, by a growing Maoist insurgency and violence that had spread to almost all the districts of Nepal, with mid-West to Western districts as thrust areas.

43. Another area of growing concern for India's security is the increased activities of Pak ISI and terrorist organizations amongst Nepal's Muslim minority.

Sri Lanka

44. The ethnic conflict in Sri Lanka has, over the years, extracted a severe

political and security cost for India, internally and externally, that goes beyond the assassination of a former Prime Minister through a terrorist act and serious casualties incurred by the Indian Armed Forces in an effort to ameliorate the situation. It has created the possibility for countries hostile or unfriendly to India to establish a foothold there in a manner inimical to India's security interests. The LTTE remains a proscribed terrorist organization in India and its leader, a proclaimed offender under the law.

45. The keystone of the Government of India's policy towards the ethnic conflict in Sri Lanka is a firm commitment to the unity, sovereignty and territorial integrity of Sri Lanka and to the restoration of a lasting peace through a peaceful, negotiated settlement that meets the just aspirations of all elements of Sri Lankan society. On the political front, India continues to support the activities of the Sri Lankan Government towards the Peace Process. The Government of India welcomed the ceasefire agreement stating that it would provide an opportunity to both sides to move forward towards a substantive dialogue for a negotiated political settlement of the ethnic conflict.

Myanmar

46. Myanmar remains an area of security interest for India not only on account of the activities of north-eastern insurgent groups that have set up camps across the Indian border, but also because of the activities of countries working against India's legitimate security concerns and the repercussions of the tussle between the forces of democracy and military government on these interests. India welcomes the greater openness of the Myanmar government in its external relations and steps towards political reconciliation, internally.

Bhutan

47. India shares a relationship based on close friendship, good neighbourliness and mutual trust with Bhutan underpinned by a strong and diverse mutually beneficial partnership in the sphere of economic and social development and a tradition of high-level visits, most recently the visit to New Delhi by King of Bhutan.

48. Traditionally, Bhutan has been sensitive and mindful of India's security concerns. The two countries continue to be in close touch with each other on the issue of presence of ULFA-Bodo militants in Southern Bhutan.

Afghanistan

49. India is closely watching the changing scenario in Afghanistan since it has ramifications on the security scenario of the region and the country,

including in the state of Jammu and Kashmir. India would not like to see Afghanistan once again becoming a breeding ground for terrorism, or a victim of terrorism sponsored from across its borders. India was amongst the first countries to appoint a Defence Attaché in Kabul. India-Afghanistan ties continued to expand and strengthen with time.

Central Asian Republics (CARS)

50. The strategic map of Central Asia has changed almost unrecognisably since the disintegration of the former Soviet Union. Post Cold War, it has become a theatre of a new 'great game' not only because of its strategic location but also its natural resources, notably oil and natural gas. Since 9/11, it has also acquired a new layer of strategic interest because of its vantage point vis-à-vis the central security concerns of the region namely terrorism in its local, regional and global aspects.

51. Central Asia is an area of vital importance to India not only on account of its geographical proximity and India's historical and cultural links with the region, but also because of the common challenge they face from jehadi terrorism. Relations, based on a shared commitment to open and progressive societies, secularism and democracy, have been reinforced by similarity of views in the fight against terrorism. India and countries of Central Asia also share views with regard to checking the menace of drugs trafficking.

Terrorism

52. India has been a victim of terrorism for many decades, much before the West experienced its deadly reality on September 11, 2001. The terrorist menace in Jammu and Kashmir has its roots in Pakistan and is supported financially and materially by the government and institutions of that country. The Indian Armed Forces have dealt with the problem of cross-border terrorism with a multi-pronged strategy that includes psychological warfare, innovative military tactics and counter intelligence methods. These efforts have met with reasonable success but this is a prolonged battle. India's long experience in tackling terrorism can be of valuable help to other countries that are facing similar challenges now.

53. **Infiltration:** Despite the assurances of the Pakistani Government, infiltration continues across the border.

54. For any terrorist movement to be contained, the Government's resolve and the security forces' firmness are a must. India's fight against terrorism has been a long and arduous one and the Indian Armed Forces are fully geared to handle any problem that may arise in future. It is important that the state support for any form of terrorism must cease. Terrorist organisations have

long arms and global reach. The world, therefore, has to fight a united battle by pooling resources in order to remove this scourge from the face of the earth.

India's Nuclear Policy

55. India remains a firm and consistent proponent of general and complete disarmament and attaches the highest priority to global nuclear disarmament. India's policy on disarmament also takes into account changes that have taken place in the world, especially in the 1990s. The nuclear tests of May 1998 do not dilute India's commitment to this long-held objective. As a nuclear weapon State India is even more conscious of its responsibility in this regard and, as in the past, continues to take initiatives in pursuit of global nuclear disarmament both individually and collectively. The steps that were announced after the tests and the initiatives that India has taken since, strengthen this commitment.

56. India's nuclear weapons capability is meant only for self-defence and seeks only to ensure that India's security, independence and integrity are not threatened in the future. India is not interested in a nuclear arms race. This is the rationale behind the two pillars of India's nuclear policy – minimum deterrence and no-first use. The determination of the profile of this deterrent, including accurate and refined delivery systems, is a sovereign responsibility.

Planning Considerations

57. The security environment that has been highlighted above clearly brings out four key elements that are fundamental determinants of our security planning. These are:

(a) The Indian Armed Forces have a two front obligation, which require them safeguard the security of our borders with Pakistan as well as with China;

(b) India is not a member of any military alliance or strategic grouping, nor is this consistent with our policies necessitating a certain independent deterrent capability;

(c) Due to external abetment, India's Armed Forces are involved in internal security functions on a relatively larger scale than is normal requiring a force structure that will be able to cope with it; and

(d) India's interests in the North Indian Ocean, including the security of our EEZ and Island territories, highlight the need for a blue water naval capability commensurate with our responsibilities.

58. Against this backdrop, India remains fully committed to maintaining peace with its neighbours and stability in the region through a combination of

defence-preparedness and unilateral restraint, confidence building and dialogue and expanding bilateral interactions. In the area of defence-preparedness, it has reformed its higher defence management and streamlined procurement procedures. Its defence policy and force postures remain defensive in orientation while its nuclear policy is characterized by a commitment to no-first-use, moratorium on nuclear testing, minimum credible nuclear deterrence, and the rejection of an arms race or concepts and postures from the Cold War era.

Indian Army and Globalization

59. Army's vision is "to be an optimally equipped and weaponised force, with the capability to operate effectively in a joint services environment in the entire spectrum of conflict, in a regional context."

60. Outgoing Chief of Army Staff Gen JJ Singh told *India Strategic* in an interview before laying down the office that the Army is already implementing a long-term Perspective Plan till 2017 to equip its soldiers with new, 21st century weapons and net-centricity to give them instant connectivity to one another and take on an enemy "there and then."

61. There are "specific milestones to induct cutting-edge technologies" to give the best to the war fighter to defend the country. Space-based Information, Surveillance and Reconnaissance capabilities (ISR) are being introduced as well as UAVs, helicopters and particularly night-fighting capabilities.

62. Night-fighting capability was needed by all the three services, particularly the air force. War fighting has changing so fast that there was no option but to have the best of the sensors and target acquisition and destruction capability day and night, 24 x 7, and always, irrespective of the terrain. These night-fighting devices were extensively being put on all the Indian Army's Armoured Fighting Vehicles (AFVs) like tanks and BMPs while the soldiers were being given night vision goggles, handheld image intensifiers and thermal imagers, GPS position locaters and computer connectivity to give still and streaming video pictures of one's own and enemy locations.

63. Lighter weapons, some with laser capabilities, are also being acquired. Even the older tanks like T 55, which are still with the army, are being refurbished with newer weapons and night sensors.

64. The ongoing Revolution in Military Affairs (RMA) meant that technology played "a decisive role" in conflicts and that as future battlefields are likely to be fluid and fast-paced, requiring quicker responses, we are revamping our communication systems to achieve true networking. "Based on

the Joint Doctrine, the Army has already published its doctrine, as have the other two services. All other doctrines, like the one on Sub-Conventional Operations released recently, take into account the imperatives of jointness. The Army is increasingly focusing on the need for increased cooperation while operating in conjunction with the Navy and Air Force." As for tomorrow's soldier, he will look like a "hi-tech man-machine system." "New technologies from sensors to lighter but precision weapons would greatly improve the current capabilities of the soldiers, regardless of their technology and there is no choice but to keep up with them. Our soldier should be able to hit an enemy to effectively neutralize him without losing his own life is that's what we want." "A project, 'Futuristic Infantry Soldier As a System' (FINSAS) has been launched which will provide the infantryman with sensors for night vision, smart electronic displays, lightweight energy absorbing protection with smart surfaces, advanced automated lightweight role, so as to be able to function more efficiently and effectively. The fully integrated 'Infantryman' of tomorrow will be equipped with mission-oriented equipment integrated with his buddy soldier team, the sub-unit, as also the overall C4I2 (Command, Control, Communications Computers, Information and Intelligence) system.

65. Besides the induction of technology, our Infantry, Mechanised Forces, Artillery and Air Defence components are being modernised to retain conventional deterrence against our adversaries. The army is laying special focus on revamping our surveillance and intelligence gathering systems with a view to integrate the same into our decision making process.

66. Modernisation of our Army is an ongoing process, periodically reviewed, to keep in step with operational imperatives that flow from our national security aspirations. The important thing now is that there are rapid advances in weapons, protection against biochemical threats and state-of-the-art light weight communication equipment. It is a major step in our endeavour to make the infantry soldier contemporary, in accordance with the requirements of the modern-day battle environment. As for threats to the security of India, changed security environment, defined by forces of globalisation, terrorism, Revolution in Military Affairs – to name a few – have had a profound effect on the way we perceive threats. Post KARGIL and Operation PARAKRAM, the emerging status of India in regional and global affairs, had accentuated the need for revisiting the doctrinal and operational concepts for the Army. For an emerging modern military power to retain its strategic autonomy, self reliance and indigenisation were also a must. Therefore, considerable emphasis was being laid on encouraging indigenous development of equipment by our Defence Research and Development Organisation (DRDO) independently as well as in partnership with private industry.

Conclusion

67. India is fully committed to maintaining peace and stability with its neighbours, in the region and in the global context too. This is sought to be achieved through a combination of defence preparedness, unilateral restraint, confidence building dialogue, and expanding bilateral and multilateral interaction. Effective diplomacy, backed by credible military power is India's preferred means to meet the multiple threats and growing challenges in the region and globally. The country's military force postures remain defensive in orientation, while its nuclear policy is characterized by a commitment to no-first-use, moratorium on nuclear testing, minimum credible nuclear deterrent and rejection of entering into an arms race. India is fully committed to the twin policies of no territorial ambition, and no export of ideology.

68. The Defence sector in India is marching along at a brisk pace towards self reliance. Increasing security concerns of a rapidly growing economy have driven industry towards giant strides in indigenous manufacture of weaponry, machinery and sophisticated equipments. India's strategic geographical and political positioning provides further impetus to the growth of this sector. The market of export of India's defence technology and products is expanding every year, as are the requirements of its own armed force together, making India an attractive market as well as an investment destination for joint ventures.

REFERENCES

1. Report on *India's Security,* Ministry of Defence.
2. Eric Koo Peng Kuan, *Globalization and its impact on South East Asia.*
3. M.V. Naidu, *Globalization: Threat or Promise?*
4. Supt. Shahbudin Bin Abdul Wahab, *Globalization and its Implications on National Security.*
5. Lyon E Davis , *Globalization's Security Implications.*
6. Sudha Menon, *North East India and Globalization: The Way Ahead.*
7. Interview of Gen (Retd) to *India Strategic.*

6

India and the Computer Technology Revolution: Some Observations

Major General (Rtd.) R.K. Bagga

Introduction

During the previous decades, Information Technology has made tremendous impact in making the world as a global village. In particular, since 1970, computer technology with efficient interface with communication technology has impacted the economy. The new management techniques using large-scale information systems have resulted in improving the productivity of both men and machine. Figure 1 shows the exponential growth of Information Technology from Mainframe era to current agile and wearable computing devices. Availability of broadband internet technology has brought fruits of various techniques to the developing world also.

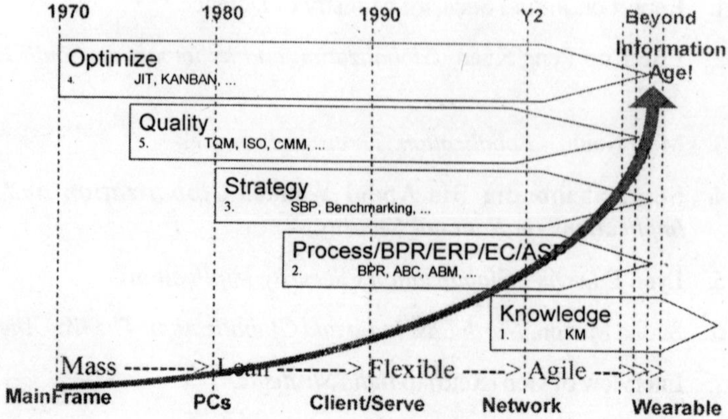

Fig. 1. Information Technology growth in decades.

Information Technology

One of the major thrusts, during Y2K, helped the developing world in strengthening their presence throughout the globe. The meteoric rise of internet based business solutions impacted the world economy by bringing in global competition in different parts of the globe. Figure 2 highlights the effect of globalization on world economy leading to greater customer expectations; thereby bringing in bigger competition in the corporate world. The immediate impact was mergers and acquisitions of a number of major world players.

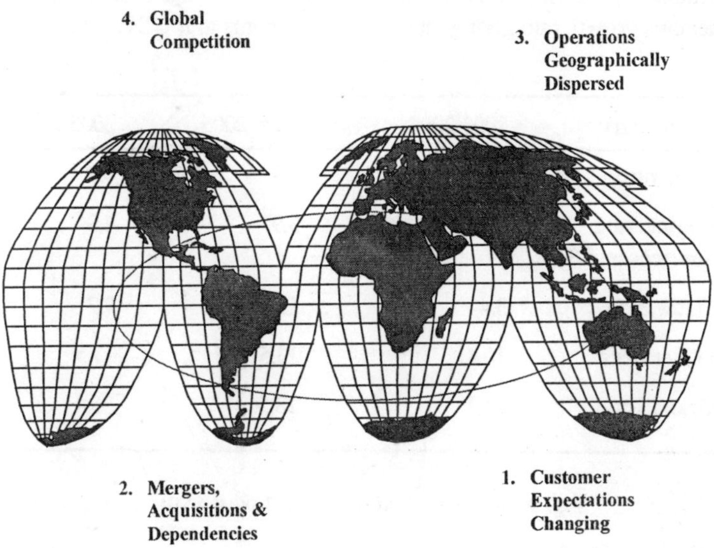

Fig. 2. Impact of Globalisation.

India and Globalisation

India has been fortunate in using Information Technology to train their abundant talented manpower in providing solutions to the world in Information Technology and IT enabled service industry. Fig. 3 and 4 give the summary of NASSCOM strategic report 2008, where in a decade, the software exports have grown to 12 billion USD which was only $ one billion in year 1998. The immediate impact was large manpower being trained by various education institutions found ready market to use their talent to provide turn-key solutions.

This has resulted in bringing in large amount of foreign exchange and growth of national GDP.

	1998	2008
Software exports	1Billion	12 Billion
Domestic IT	NA	8 Billion
ITeS/BPO/KPO	Nil	9 Billion

Indian IT Industry

India's IT industry since liberalization of economy has been galloping at tremendous growth rate giving much needed impetus to it GDP.

	IT Industry	2003-2004	2004-2005	2005-2006
1.	Hardware	5.0	5.9	6.9
2.	Engineering Services and S/w	2.9	3.9	4.8
3.	ITES- BPO	3.4	5.2	7.2
4.	IT Services:	10.4	13.5	17.5
	Grand Total	21.7	28.5	36.4

Fig. 4. Indian IT Industry – 2003-06 (US$B).

Challenges for India

If India has to further strengthen its role in the globalized economy, it must ensure that its products and services meet the following challenges:

1. Reliability
2. Security
3. Transactions
4. Scalability
5. Manageability
6. Accountability
7. Testing

Conclusion

Today technologies in computers and communications have led to the death of time and distance. Computers and networks work extremely fast and technologies can improve anything and everything. Challenges have inspired some very creative responses in our country.

"India only 20 years ago was known as a country of snake charmers, poor people and Mother Teresa. Today the image has been recalibrated; it is also seen a country of *brainy people and computer wizards"*– Thoms L Frieman.

7

Globalisation and its Impact on the Threat Perception of the Indian Navy

Commander Vivek Dahiya

Prior to September 11, 2001, globalisation was viewed exclusively as an economic phenomenon. Evidence pointing towards the economic aspects of globalisation i.e. the rapidly shifting flows of world capital, expansion of overseas markets and investments, the global connections of e-commerce and the Internet were clearly apparent.[1] In fact, by the mid-1990s, the concept of economic globalisation seemed ubiquitous, goading corporate boards and shareholders to thirst after presumably growing international markets, internet junkies to claim their own community sans borders, and anti-globalisation protestors to smash municipal trash cans from Seattle to Paris (to coincide with World Trade Organisation deliberations).

Concurrently, suggestions that globalisation also profoundly impacts upon national security, the threat perception imperatives, is largely confined to debates that are generally considered esoteric by those outside the defence intellectual community; though publicists of contemporary globalisation, such as journalist Thomas L. Friedman, did point to the "hidden fist" of US military power as critical for providing the global security necessary for the flourishing of democracy and free markets. But even his cautionary comments seemed to be drowned out by the exuberant trumpeting of a world, in which geo-economics has replaced geopolitics. Friedman himself put forward the thesis that globalisation had made interstate war almost impossible, or as he argues : No two countries that both had McDonald's had fought a war against each other since each got its McDonald.

Thomas Friedman in his seminal work, *The World is Flat,* describes Globalisation as an historically evolutionary process that can be divided into three distinct phases. Globalisation phase I commenced in 1492 and is linked to the voyages of discovery, opening trade between the Old World and the New world. This phase was all about countries and muscle power. The dynamic force of this era was how much muscle, how much horsepower, how much wind power and later steam power a country had and how creatively it could use these resources. Globalisation phase II was initiated at around the 1800s. The dynamic forces which brought about integration in this phase were : the industrial revolution and the growth of the multinational companies, spearheaded by the British and Dutch joint stock companies (which went global for labour and markets). The last decade of the 20th century saw the emergence of 'convergence' epitomised by the fusion of personal computers, telephone and fax with the fibre optic cable. Convergence, as a phenomenon is enabling, empowering, and enjoining individuals and small groups to go global by providing them a new found ability to collaborate and compete globally.[2]

Globalisation cannot be thought of as an esoteric concept merely for academic debate - Globalisation is not a policy option but a fact to which policymakers must adapt. Globalisation, an intrusive international media, the 'death of distance' and, of course, the end of ideological rivalry epitomised by the end of cold war, have each contributed towards the requirement for nation states to have effective military forces with the capacity to respond to conflicts, that vary in intensity across the spectrum of conflict.

However, whichever description of globalisation that may be adopted, the flux in the existing global order makes it perspicuous that the absolute decline of the Westphalian concept of a nation state as an entity is non-supportable. Nation-states shall remain as key actors in the foreseeable future while many supra-state actors[3] in the globalised international system may be constituted from nations. State, sub-state and supra-state actors will continue to exist alongside non-state, transnational actors of the present era, but, concurrently, a shift in the relevance of military forces, increasing significance of non-traditional security issues and threat perceptions, is apparent.

Therefore, while taking cognisance of the axiom that "future" does not just happen but is an evolutionary process, the *Navy* must decide whether to recognise globalisation as a factor to be assimilated into strategy to help perceive threats and meet challenges emanating from the impact of globalisation; or to see the technology infusion on account of globalisation as providing new capabilities which can then be applied to an unknown, evolving era. Moreover, predicting the future is difficult, that to do so for 30 years hence "is verging on the foolish" and "full of ifs."[4] Therefore, whilst it may not be possible to eliminate "shocks" – good or bad – from international relations or defence, one can strive to provide sufficient flexibility to cope with a number of negative shocks and inspire the necessary contingency planning.

Against this backdrop, the principal aim of the *Navy* is to address whether, given the nature of threat perception, it is possible to develop maritime forces better optimized for high-intensity maritime operations while also relevant across the full range of other tasks expected of it both now, and, as policy and missions change on account of globalization or otherwise, in the future as well. By implication the maritime forces can be "future-proofed" whilst recognising that *if a great sea power is too fearful of losing its precious ships to risk them in battle, save in circumstances so advantageous that any prudent enemy commander must flee from the prospect, then those ships are unlikely to provide the kind of strategic return on investment that the country has a right to expect and may need.* [5]

The idea is to identify the developments and trends in globalisation in order to analyse their implications for the threat perception of the *Navy,* if indeed the 'World is Flat',[6] to highlight the necessity of fully interoperable, balanced, maritime capabilities across the spectrum of conflicts with considerable reach and sustainability. We have also to bring out the enabling concept of 'swing'[7] that is adaptability, configurability, standardisation, simplicity of operations and information superiority and epitomise it as the capability development role to be cherished.

Moreover, defence is principally a function of the relation between political and military aspects of a nation. Therefore, under the impact of Globalisation the *Navy* must seek to clarify the interface between the concepts of security and defence, if it is to understand the role of the military with effective linkages between the 'forces of law and order' and the 'forces of defence'. Consequently, the implications of globalisation (both direct and indirect) ensure that security has become increasingly complex and threat perception multi-faceted encompassing political, economic, military, societal and environmental dimensions of international relations and security[8]. The paper will use this framework as the underlying foundation to aid the analytical process.

The current global security environment has witnessed a quantum increase in non-state and transnational threats (or perception of threats) to national security in the *Societal Sector*. The most obvious of such non-state threats is terrorism including maritime terrorism. However, other threats include global crime, drug and human trafficking, illegal arms transfers, illegal migrations, piracy etc. National borders appear porous to all of these threats, at least to a certain extent. Concurrently, these threats have the potential to destabilise remote regions, with which the global economy is now increasingly linked.

Societal sector security aspects place policing, defence, peace support and conflict prevention responsibilities upon the *Navy.* Management of these activities in collaboration with other agencies, will demand that the technology resulting from globalisation is exploited through innovative design to establish a suitable and robust mechanism for information sharing. The underlying requirement is to develop capability that will help to maximise efficiency and effectiveness of individual units as well as their collective inter-operability so that both stand to gain rather than lose.

Concurrently the public craze for information on the progress of operations and increasing accountability demand rapid and accurate information with effective media integration, if the *Navy* is not to be a victim of the "tyranny of real-time"[9]. Moreover, public pressure towards casualty aversion, on account of the CNN effect[10] – as it progressively develops in the Indian society, will require military capability to achieve effective, rapid and precision strike capability while minimising collateral damage to ensure that damage inflicted is assessed to be just and proportionate.

The National and regional economies, in the present era, are deeply concerned and continuously debating their survivability against successive terrorist shocks. Therefore, trade and economic performance will remain pivotal to security issues in the *Economic Sector* and consequent conflict prevention will continue to generate tasking for the *Navy.* The events of September 11 were identified as deepening the chances of an extended world recession. Therefore, what would happen to the global economy if there were severe attacks against economic infrastructures, such as the Internet and global communication?

Other concerns are related to the increase in maritime traffic and trade in light of threats posed by global terrorism. What about attacks on transportation hubs or utilities? Are the sea-lanes and straits, through which international trade passes, secure? Therefore, maritime operations will have to account for increasing international (particularly maritime) traffic and trade. Since tangible international trade is dependent on maritime transport, an increase in trade due to or as a means of globalisation would naturally result in a corresponding increase in maritime traffic and establishment of a new silk route. Estimates of this increase vary; however, it is accepted that global ocean-borne commerce is expected to grow at an annual rate of 3 to 4% in the foreseeable future. Consequently the increase in maritime traffic raises concerns about the safety of Sea Lanes of Communications (SLOCs), and transit through choke points from a safety of navigation and environmental protection perspective and also from the perspective of national security. Moreover consequent upon the global terrorist threat, the security of the maritime transit lanes as well as the ports servicing international trade has become very serious concerns. Therefore, there are good reasons to see SLOCs and chokepoints as scarce resources requiring increased protection.

Specific concerns include the question of whether we, as a Nation, which spends 1.99% of her GDP on military forces is gaining economic benefit from the current spending on defence, or whether such spending is a dangerous drag on an overburdened economy? Is our environment, including the oceans, being imperilled by economic globalisation? Whether or not these concerns are valid, they have obviously increased due to public perceptions of globalisation and the potential for inequitable benefits.

The relationship of the *Navy* to the Government will be shaped by globalisation; as the role of our nation and new sources of global power continue to evolve in the overall fluidity of the *Political Sector* of Security. "The death of distance"[11] has further exposed the *Navy* and its role as a tool of policy on both the national and international scales. It mandates wide ranging military capability with long legs, reach and sustenance, particularly in a maritime environment which facilitates interregional transportation. However, it is unfair to say that such a military capability is demanded by globalisation or that governmental privilege to prioritise defence commitments is usurped. On the contrary it is clear that a government committed to participation in "interregional flows, networks of activity, interaction and the exercise of power"[12] must be prepared to defend or sacrifice this privilege.

Securitisation of *Environment and consequently viewing it as a tangible security threat to the global community* has resulted in global interest in the oceans as "a barometer of the health of the planet". This development therefore, places administrative and technological responsibilities upon the navy.[13] Consequently, it will place increased ecological demands on the development of maritime propulsion, safety and anti-pollution practice within the *Navy*. The *Navy* will be expected to lead in the application of and adherence to forthcoming environmental standards and will require adaptation of current and future platform design, operation and propulsion. Concurrently, the scarcity of resources, inequality in their distribution across regions and environmental stresses resulting from their exploitation as an inevitable consequence of globalisation will result in resource conflict prevention and policing duties for the *Navy*.

Concurrent to the expansion of security into a more complex concept, the enabling technology of globalisation has provided new types of conflict in the *Military Sector*, with new actors and concomitant effects. Asymmetric threat, perceived or real, and warfare techniques bring forth threats, which are non-traditional in character, and, emanating from new actors which employ a variety of means, orthodox and unorthodox, with new justifications or causes[14]. The reality of the dynamic, globalised battles pace is that, state and non-state actors have the capability to develop new processes and countervailing concepts to counter our traditional superiority in conventional military capabilities. However, "Asymmetry" can be countered in two ways. The first option is available for exploitation when organisational structures adopt the characteristics of asymmetry – like the Taliban government in Afghanistan. This then offers a tangible opponent to counter act upon, thus effectively negating the benefit resulting from the capabilities of a hidden enemy, perceived or real, which employs asymmetric tactics[15]. Secondly, it can be countered through the evolution of advantage by the development of "symmetries" that demand development of alternative "asymmetry"[16].

Concurrently, the interrelationships and dependencies resulting from globalisation of the economy and the society influences and affects nations by conflicts from which they may initially appear isolated. Therefore, considering the spread of investment by the Indian Economic Community, we will inevitably have interests in an increased number of issues and conflicts.[17]

Moreover, the cascading effects of regional conflicts will result in greater likelihood of military presence and intervention in locations not previously considered of interest. UN sanctioned "Intervention to prevent the globalisation of such conflicts" might take the form of peacekeeping, peace enforcement, logistical support for Armed Forces, or direct assault, against regimes whose actions appear as egregious assaults against the international community or their own populace. A prime driver of such "UN mandated Humanitarian Intervention" is the ubiquity of maritime lift and sustenance capability thus mandating a perspicuous role for the *Navy.*

The proliferation of information technologies and high-technology sensors and systems resulting from convergence and globalisation has had a deep and far reaching impact upon the global security environment. Information technology is obviously becoming more and more ubiquitous and much of it has military application—particularly in command and control and battle-management.

Therefore, the consequent "death of distance" and the primacy afforded to time as the fourth dimension implies that the technology of globalisation has the potential to help the *Navy* shape and exploit the maritime battle-space to its advantage. However, the proliferation of commercial technology brings with it new forms of military-applicable sensors as well as intelligence, surveillance and reconnaissance (ISR) techniques. For example, the basic satellite imagery is freely available over the internet while more detailed images can be easily purchased (all that is required is an international credit card). The global positioning system (GPS), originally designed for military navigation, is now the prime commercial global locating system, used to track shipments and direct transportation—both at sea and on land. The European Union has agreed to build a rival to GPS i.e. the Galileo Satellite navigation System, representing a commercial rivalry that, critics charge, may inadvertently make military-quality information available to rogue actors as well. The implications of the information technology explosion go far beyond the commercial effects which characterise economic globalisation. While information technology and advanced sensors may not yet be able to 'lift the fog of war', however, the use of commercial off-the-shelf systems greatly enhances the military capabilities of many potential opponents including global terrorists. The consequent explosion of computing technology allows the global terrorists to create advanced anti-access or area denial systems thus representing the globalisation of high technology military capability (howsoever symbolic it may be). The deployment of such weapons in or in close proximity to the choke points of the Indian Ocean, will have a grave impact on the security environment of the Indian Ocean Region in particular and the world in general. Therefore, there are threats that could come from asymmetrical weapon systems designed to deny passage through maritime chokepoints or impinge on the Indian Navy's ability to conduct operations near land. Therefore, it may not be a mere truism that in the future the *Navy* may not have to face another globalised navy, but may have to face globalised anti-access weapons.

Concurrently, faster and greater (both by volume of bandwidth and quantum of nodes) interconnectivity between systems mandates increased offensive and defensive information operations capabilities for the *Navy*. Information exchange quantum will increase in volume and place manipulation, storage and application strains on systems as well as information users. Moreover, the technological advantage should be employed to project products forward and not to deploy operational centres forward. Concurrently, the requirement to maintain military information superiority and meet the public thirst for knowledge will spur increased use of, and, attack against information systems whilst demanding greater surveillance efforts and coordination. The power of command (including control) and disruption that is available today is in fact beyond the comprehension of many involved in warfare. The pace of change is harrowing and the talk of an electronic Pearl Harbour is no mere exaggeration.[18]

Concurrently, "Technology Turbulence", driven by massive commercial investment, sees the evolution of technology through short life-cycles, in effect very short development to application cycles. Given that the build, trials, acceptance and deployment cycle of ships is greater than 5 years; crew roulement is 2½ -3 years; the *Navy* must review the integration of technology from "concept to doctrine" if it is to compete/operate in a globalising world which demands rapid turn round.

A Doctrine provides guidance of "what to do" not "how to do it" in a particular circumstance and should be considered a handrail; in comparison to dogma which tends to handcuff an individual. The pace of change in systems and technology, under the onslaught of forces unleashed by globalisation, has outstripped the update of doctrine and often practices. The *Navy's* ability to conduct operations in an environment tempered by the effects of globalisation, is premised upon a doctrine that allows it to be flexible and versatile. Therefore, if doctrine is to provide its handrail, then an appropriate culture of understanding, use and timely system of update is essential. Its no mere truism that – *'any preponderant sea power vitally dependent on superiority at sea, whose admirals are unable to provide a contemporary variant of Nelson's "planning attack" invites strategic disaster".*[19]

The hypothesis and arguments thus far clearly bring out that globalisation and its technology will generate additional tasks for and place greater demands upon the resources of the *Navy.* It is imperative for the *Navy* to focus upon the application of developments in the technology of globalisation to identify how best advantage can be gained from technological innovation without compromising its core flexibility. It would be astonishing if, with our knowledge of the 20th century behind us, we concluded that the accelerating technology of the 21st century, and a changed and changing strategic environment, would leave our force structures and ways of operating untouched. Therefore, the *Navy* will function in a new, as yet, unnamed and evolving epoch in which globalisation and the technology of globalisation continue to inspire and facilitate change towards a world where the stakes in international military conflict will be high.

End Notes

1. Tangredi, Sam J. *Globalisation and Maritime Power,* (J Carfax Pishinç, 2003), p. 1.
2. Friedman, Thomas (2006), *The World is Flat – The Globalized World in the 21st Century.* (New Delhi: Penguin Books, 2006)
3. Examples of Supra-state actors are IMF, WTO, World Bank etc.
4. Andrews, David, "Technology, Shipbuilding and Future Combat beyond 2020" in O'Brien, Phillips Payson ed., *Technology and Naval Combat in the Twentieth Century and Beyond,* (Frank Cass Publishers, London, 2001), pp. 248-262.
5. Gray, C S., *The Leverage of Sea Power,* (Free Press, New York, 1992), p. 23.
6. Friedman, Thomas, (2006), n. 2.
7. The ability to configure a force, formation or unit to operate successfully, and cost effectively, across a range of mission types and roles. The components of swing are: Adaptability; Configurability; Standardisation; Simplicity Operation and Information Superiority. (Quoted from the Future Navy document of Royal Navy).

8. Buzan, Barry, Waever Ole, Wilde, Jaap De, *Security: A New Framework for Analysis*, (Lynne Rienner Publishers, London, 1998).

9. Gowing, Nik, "Outfoxed in the Information War", *Time*, November 12, 2001.

10. CNN Effect may be defined as the impact on public opinion resulting from the direct and unfettered beaming, into homes, the images and videos from zones of conflict. The opinion could vary from demands for intervention to stop bloodshed or withdrawal of troops as and when own casualty figures peak to demands for more prudent and humane target selection and engagement to avoid non-combatant collateral damage.

11. Cairncross, Frances, (2001) *The Death of Distance 2.0: How the Communications Revolution Will Change Our Lives,* (Texere Publishing Limited, London, 2001), p. xi.

12. Held, David, McGrew, Anthony, Goldblatt, David and Perraton, Jonathan, (2000) "Rethinking Globalization", in Held, David and McGrew, Anthony, Eds., *The Global Transformation Reader* (Blackwell Publishers Ltd, Oxford), pp. 54-60.

13. Till, Georffrey, "The Royal Navy in a New World, 1990-2020", in O'Brien, Phillips Payson, Eds., *Technology and Naval Comat in the Twentieth Century and Beyond, (Frank Cass Publishers, London, 2001),* p. 220.

14. Development of methods to reduce an enemy's advantage and to exploit perceived vulnerabilities has been crucial throughout history. Colin S Gray has summarised the term asymmetric warfare as the exploitation of orthodoxy through use of unorthodoxy.

15. Taliban government in Afghanistan developed an asymmetric outlook in support of Al Qaeeda thus providing the US led coalition a tangible subject and objective to target.

16. Force Protection.

8

National Security and Media

Nitin Gokhale

Traditionally, national security has always been viewed through the prism of combating external threats and meeting internal challenges. Use of force for protecting the core values of a nation—in India's case it is democracy, secularism and liberty—has been defined as national security.

But of late, the discourse on national security is undergoing a subtle transformation. The scope of national security has been widened. It is no longer confined to counting force levels or just matching military power. Now, experts talk about a multidimensional, multifaceted approach to define National Security. The threats are manifold and before I get into discussing how the Indian media has dealt with and will deal with issue of national security, let me briefly dwell upon what I see as comprehensive national security issues.

In the not-too-distant future, major powers will be focused on the proliferation of weapons of mass destruction, terrorism, narcotics, and organized crime more than conventional armed conflicts.

Information warfare, threats emanating from cyber space and aerospace will consume more national resources than ever before. Rising regional powers like India will have to contend with regional conflicts and developments associated with them: refugee crises, peacekeeping, humanitarian emergencies, environmental problems, global health issues, technological developments, and economic collapse. Issues of demographics, including migration and health; depleting natural resources and degradation of environment will lead to conflicts. (Water resources constitute another security concern). And nations have to be prepared to combat these more than the traditional threats.

According to a CIA trend analysis, by 2015, more than half of the world's population will be urban. The number of people living in megacities—those containing more than 10 million inhabitants—will double to more than 400 million. The explosive growth of cities in developing countries will test the capacity of governments to stimulate the investment required to generate jobs and to provide the services, infrastructure and social supports necessary to sustain livable and stable environments.

Other issues that will take up more time will be:

Health: Disparities in health status between developed and developing countries—particularly in the least developed countries—will persist and widen.

Developing countries are likely to experience a surge in both infectious and noninfectious diseases and, in general, will have inadequate health care capacities and spending.

Natural Resources and Environment

The number of chronically malnourished people in conflict-ridden Sub-Saharan Africa will increase by more than 20 percent over the next 15 years.

Water

By 2015, nearly half the world's population—more than 3 billion people—will live in countries that are 'water-stressed'—having less than 1,700 cubic meters of water per capita per year—mostly in Africa, the Middle East, South Asia, and northern China.

Water shortages occurring in combination with other sources of tension—such as in the West Asia—will be the most worrisome.

Media and National Security

While governments are already looking at these trends and also taking steps to meet the new challenges, it is necessary to take a critical look at the way Indian media has dealt with and treated issues of National security.

In the first 15 years after Independence, the Indian media was generally conformist. Since India was in the nation building phase, media was supportive of the effort as far as possible. So very few anti-establishment views were articulated in that phase. But the debacle the short but brutal war with China in the winter of 1962 was a game changer not only for the establishment but also for the Indian media. The shortcomings and wrong decisions at the policy level were so blatant that the Indian media was forced to sit up and review its pro-establishment stance.

National security gradually occupied centre-stage post-1962.

And by the time the decade of Seventies came, Indian media had started focusing more and more on national security issues, thanks to big international events like the Bangladesh Liberation war of 1971 or the (peaceful ?) atomic explosions at Pokhran in 1974.

Today, it is almost compulsory to have dedicated journalists reporting on various ministries like Defense and Home, traditionally considered the bastions of national security. But even today, we are stuck in covering day to day activities rather than looking at larger issues in these ministries.

There is too much trivia that gets dished out in the name of reporting on these two ministries mainly because there is a lack of skills to handle the relevant issues both among journalists and security personnel in the armed forces and the central police organizations.

While the media needs to train and equip itself to discern, detect and dissect national security issues, the government, the armed forces and even academics who deal in issues of national security, have to understand the way media functions. There is a crying need to have more interaction between these players without the pressure of deadlines. So far, the tendency is to keep away from each other. That does not help either side.

Unless national security becomes the concern of the nation and not just a handful few, we will continue to have a problem of wrong projections. It's time the old policy of keeping the media at an arm's length is jettisoned by the establishment.

9

The Perception of Threat, The Reality of the Ordinary

Prof. Peter Emberley

We live in a time animated by a great sense of danger, anxiety, and the desire to act. Whether our perception of threat has its roots in extreme climate changes, economic swings, political upheavals, crop failures, epidemics, or intellectual and spiritual malaise, a global uneasiness has filtered into every facet of modern life, worldwide. Food production, security, money markets, health, political regime stability, and personal well-being all seem to be at great risk, and the threat to our hopes of continuing flourishing is palpable.

We perceive a threat to our existence, well-being and hopes for a future, despite (or perhaps because of) the formidable technological network we have built worldwide, to shield us from the risks and to subdue the incommodities of everyday life.

The post-world war II era jubiliation, with all its prosperity, expectations of global harmony, confidence in science and technology, and trust in the "other," appears to have progressively dissipated. We are living with, if not quite a distinct threat, certainly a perception of threat, that is filtering into every aspect of human doing. Of course, threat has existed in all human history, but in the past incremental initiatives to patch up what had deteriorated was seen as the appropriate response to the predicaments of existence. Humankind's steady and measured attention to what threatened it built virtues of courage, prudence and fraternity.

Today our expectations about what can be achieved are much higher (and more prone to failure), and our proximity to everyone else in the world (and whose disorders are no longer isolated but are global problems) makes us vastly more susceptible to the woes of others, and the politicization of their grievances. The "have-nots" are sorely aware of what is lacking in their lives, whether what can be had is needed or not, and grievances arise from the pettiest motives, though they are usually moralized into claims of oppression and victimization.

It would, of course, be madness to deny real suffering, and monumental injustice and crime (in Darfour, Rwanda, Somalia, to name a few) and the plausibility of future ramping up of aggression from so-called rogue states (North Korea, Libya, Iran). It is also prudent to anticipate an increase in fractious relations, as the world economy veers from glut to penury, and the poorer and least advantaged slip deeper into debt loads and agricultural failures, while crisis-managing explosive population growth.

But ... prudence counsels one to immediately distinguish "threat" from "threat perception," and analyze carefully whether the perception of threat may be fabricated (and serving diverse economic, social and political interests) or illusory (judged by hyper-perfectionist dreams of perfect order or justice), while elevating the authority of the threat analyst beyond what commonsense and prudence should allow. A balanced assessment of real danger, and the strength of the vast systems of danger-prevention and management we have in place, should lead us to conclude that while extreme contingencies are always possible, our extreme evaluation of the threat to ourselves today arises from a disorder in our expectations, whether they be personal, economic, political, intellectual, or spiritual.

We have been asked to diagnose the prevalence of a heightened perception of threat in the contemporary world. I would identify seven obvious sources:

(a) the pace and saturation of global transformation, which has drawn villages even at the smallest capillaries of the world, into its orbit, inducing what Marshall McLuhan - the first theorist of modern globalization - referred to as a "global village," which like all villages suffers an environment where "everything affects everything all the time," inevitably inducing a primitive terror.

(b) the frisson and anxiety accompanying today's war machines, whose power goes beyond humanly calculable assessments traditionally provided by our political and moral discourses, and which is "ramping up" anxiety of the unexpected to a feverish pitch.

(c) the exaggerated confidence, and inevitable resultant consequence of disillusionment, when the technology to which we are so heavily and excessively indebted is compromised by "unintended consequences," which we no longer know how to control, mostly for having lost traditional moral, intellectual and spiritual, resources to cope with contingency

(d) the over-extension of human desire which brings in its wake envy, greed, rapacity and dependence, thwarting ordinary restraint measures (custom, manners, moral approbation, legal discipline)

(e) the extreme elasticity we are allowing to define the "real," which has dissipated traditional boundaries and limits, and is cynically reducing all motives to self-interest and love of power of the narrowest kind, and

(f) fear of what boredom breeds, once the project of pacifying existence and gratifying desire is complete, and humans no longer (by need or want) have meaningful goals and purposes to pursue.

These are the major catalysts for the widespread anxiety, acute perception of threat, and dramatic swings between paralysis and precipitous action dominating our times. They all seem plausible as long as one ignores or forgets the billions of daily personal, social, political, economic, intellectual and spiritual transactions comprising human relations which stabilize our lives, conferring balance, proportionality, symmetry, and predictability on our lives. And it should go without mentioning that the manufacturing of the perception of dire threat is an industry that is highly lucrative, and conferring great authority and power.

But, there are deeper reasons for the worldwide perception of threat. They emanate, I believe, from the shifting tides of intellectual thought in the west, and specifically the export of these ideas worldwide, under the aegis of globalization which - like a Trojan Horse - contains disruptively more than what its external appearance suggests. For inside are substantive ontological commitments, diagnoses of disorder, significant realignments and *recorso*, - all of which in time play out their unique destiny wherever globalization takes root. We should not be surprised that today's terrorists are often highly educated, conversant with the prevailing intellectual culture (such as post-modernism and deconstructionism, for - to a large degree - their acts of violence are enactments of the intellectual horizon which today prevails, and is broadcast to the minutest capillaries of the globe.

So, if I may be allowed, it becomes necessary to identify some themes which endow globalization with its distinctive texture, and which have had the effect of magnifying and deepening the perception of threat. For, if the pathological elements that came to reside in Western modernity, and are being exported through globalization, are not rooted out, then we risk seeing a widening and deepening of the perception of threat, to the point of severely hobbling the many other important tasks a civilization must undertake, such as fostering liberal education, promoting art and literature, and drawing out opportunities for just and charitable human relations.

In the West, we have been living, at least since the time of the ancient Greeks, with the sense that politics and philosophy are the two activities that essentially humanize us, and keep the forces of disorder and dissolution at bay. There was much to fear in their times - the breakdown of the Greek polis as a meaningful symbol of human order, a disastrous war with Sparta, and an imperial mood which exhibited itself at the low end in a desire to get more and more, with all its accompanying strife and injustice, and at the high end in a desire for conquest, exemplified perhaps most clearly in the figure of Alcibiades - whose passion for glory even Socrates failed to tame.

But neither Plato nor Aristotle allowed the perception of disorder to derail into the conclusion that all is chaos, that all attempts at order must fail, and that only a great revolution that purged to the ground would restore order. In fact, Plato's *Republic* is a deliberate dystopia written to cure the desire for hyper-perfectionist regimes and the dream of total power, by channeling the erotic desire for wholeness into philosophical dialogue and contemplation. And Aristotle, while he realized that the old order had passed, and old compass points could no longer be read, appealed to resourceful prudence and thinking within the grasp of ordinary citizens to repair and reform the polis. His proposal, for example, of how to create a polity out of a corrupt democracy and a corrupt oligarchy, is a masterpiece of realpolitik tied to education and to virtue. Incrementalism, a canny sense of how to mature desires and passions rather than purging them, and a balanced view of how much perfection can realistically be entertained, are the hallmarks of ancient Greek practice.

Priorities shift in the time spanned by Augustine and Hobbes. Now man's will is more intractable to reason, the passions are inclined to break through the political and ethical barriers the ancients had put in place, and the uncertainties of time and the fear of death at the hands of others, makes individuals more wary, more solitary, and less trusting in the ways of the world. In Augustine, man is a fugitive in this life, in, but not of, the political regime, facing contingencies at the hands of others and nature, not to say the incommodities that life in dispersed in time brings. Yet, though man must see through the glass darkly, resources of faith and hope allow for individual consolation, and the virtue of charity creates a worldly activity ecumenic in scope, for which the able administration of the Romans provides the template. The Romans, of course, were, to use Eric Voegelin's felicitous term, "pneumo-pathological," trading in transcendence to God for world conquest, but its success is the sine qua non of Christianity's own universal ambitions of a universal brotherhood under God. The vocation of the Christian, though worldly - and, unlike the Greeks, mostly administrative since the goal of politics is now known - is a life not loved for its own sake, but as a test of will and of the virtues. Still, being in but not of the world, is seeded with the virtues of charity and neighbour love, as signs of the power to remain resolute within the tests of faith. Man may be disengaged from the here and now, and the apocalyptic event lingers at the periphery of everyday life, subduing attention to the world, but the old Jewish injunction "TikkunOlum" (repair the world) sustains meaningful attention to the created order that is the human home, and whose able administration rightly may take a leaf from the book of the Romans. And again, there is no apocalyptic expectation of a great change of the human condition in the here and now, or monumental overturning of the order of being within which it enacts its actuality.

In Hobbes, who supplies much of the text of modern life, the drama is heightened, and the political and intellectual resources which can be brought to bear on political life are lowered. God is unknown or absconded, the theoretical and practical wisdom of the Greeks and Romans remain only hazily, and work in the world loses its ties to cosmic order.

Humankind's natural condition, always the seedy underbelly of conventional life, is one that is "solitary, poor, nasty, brutish and short." It is one where the threat of death at the hands of another is great, and where - as Carl Schmidt points out - the distinction of friends and enemies is foremost in everyone's mind, and where the "decision" - resolute, and indifferent to prudence or institutional sobriety - trumps practical compromise and consensus, not to say truth derived from nature. Are you for us or against us? Decide and act.

Here, man's natural reckonings and desires, even prudence, are insufficient to the task of maintaining order. This is the point, in Western history, where the apocalyptic card is first played at the level of imminent existence. Either the war of each against all, or total subordination to the will of the sovereign; either the sameness of a public personality or arbitrary mischief at the hands of unpredictable others. Either the subordination of all public goods to security and national prosperity, or the disruptions of religious enthusiasms. The decision in favour of liberty under the law, of a life animated primarily through commerce and private rights, may emerge.

From calculative self-regard, but it is a blind decision, in the absence of a substantive order of being within which choices are rationally adopted. There will be friends and enemies, but arising from an act of will, the distinction is not one permeable to reason. To opt for peace, and escape the effects of the false starts of the past, no other option is open. Conventional law, conventional public speech, conventional individual choices and aspirations, and a state religion centred on the sovereign, purge the world and the soul of their uncanny otherness.

Yet, to be sure, Hobbes also gives us the legacy of constitutionalism and legal proceduralism, buoys floating in the sea of commercialism, national chauvinism, and litigiousness which comes to define the modern world. His public world of bureaucracy, commerce, and preparedness for war constitutes an administration still sustained by the palimpsest of ancient prudence.

And as his heirs, Kant and Hegel are the last voices of modernity's attempts to hold together virtue and liberty, in a world seeded with reason and purposiveness, though their political science lends itself dangerously to administrative and bureaucratic procedural-ism, the reduction of citizen to ratifier of plebiscites, and the evacuation of the public realm in favour of pacified social existence. Still, in their writing one continues to find the oldest theme of the West - that the longings of the human soul for freedom, and its capacities for virtue and vice are expressed through a particular ordering of the political and social community. For the ancient Greeks, it was the polis; for medieval Europe, it was the public organizations of the Pope and Emperor. Since the 16th century, it was the national state, and the economic and political institutions at the heart of democratic civilization. This liberal tradition, with its constitutional government, civic virtues, freedoms under the law, and a vocation of commercial industry informed by moral discipline and probity, arose from a sober and balanced judgment of human possibilities and limits, predicated on a philosophical anthropology which held to the middle and to the modest, and which expressed itself through a stable language and the institutionalization of permanent rights and duties, and hence to the promotion of public virtue. Its authority was neither divine nor partisan, but grounded on common sense, and a balanced audit of the human capacity for virtue and vice, predicated on the idea that people cannot be purged of their passions and prejudices, though they can be educated. Liberal modernity is neither grand, nor dramatic, nor profoundly fulfilling, and its liberty is circumscribed by rules and conventions, but it may be the best achievable regime, leaving to private citizens the option of pursuing higher possibilities within circumscribed limits, protected by laws and constitutions, and by judicial and bureaucratic institutions and practices. Its limitations, fully acknowledged by the architects of Western modernity, were to be overcome by liberal education, private religious or spiritual searches, civic and higher friendships, and a sense of humanité. Modest in scope and ambition, but trusting in the natural desire for truth and order, Western modernity left to individuals the task eternal.

In our times the accumulative legacy of prudent discernment of human limits and possibilities is being dispersed, using as tools the very instruments that in the past were employed to build the Western world - reason, will, and probity. Whether it is the search for primordial communities grounded on gender and race, or the hostility to the nation-state, or the wish for a de-subjectivized existence that percolates with what one of my mature students aptly referred to as "zing," we have little patience for the practices that flourish through balance, conciliation and a sense of finality. Indeed, the wish for a de-subjectivized existence, freed from the conditioning of nature, and political and social life, is the most evident sign of the ennui being publicly expressed throughout the West. And that boredom, with the help of science and technology, animates a persistent will to deconstruct and reconstruct the human soul, aiming in the final instance at a new human being, who has overcome the limitations of vice and embodiment, who insists on a life that is non-judgmental, fluid, non-hegemonic and transparent - and especially who is un-erotic. Once this is achieved, the expectation is that the traditional "repressive" virtues of character, and the hegemonic political safety-nets which stabilized human behaviour will no longer be needed.

To this world climate of impatience with incrementalism, prudence, and moderation, has to be added another dangerous trajectory. Intellectuals today have stepped into the breach that is contemporary malaise, diagnosing and prescribing cures, though the verdict must be out whether these cures may be more dangerous than the disease. Singling out merely two acclaimed diagnosticians - Leo Strauss and Rene Girard - offers us a glimpse of the problem. Strauss is renowned commentator on the texts of western philosophy. His students wielded vast influence on the White House throughout the 80s and 90s, especially with the publication of Francis Fukuyama's, book *The End of History and the Last Man.* Strauss was an exegete of classical works of philosophy, whose interpretations were shaped by Muslim and Jewish scholarship, specifically al Farabi and Maimonides. For Strauss the history of the West was a successive movement from the clarity and comprehensiveness of Plato and Aristotle, and then a two-thousand year derailing of their sobriety, epitomized by modern thinkers from Hobbes to Rousseau to Nietzsche. Strauss' daring gambit was to write prudent commentaries which on the surface advocated reading the moderns attentively to find traces in them of ancient moderation which could be disinterred to restore moral and intellectual ballast to America. But esoterically he had embraced the Nietzschean conclusion that the game was up for the modern West. And so - the great dangers of the 20th century notwithstanding - and one must remember the darkness of the 1940's in Europe was descending - Strauss made a daring decision: only by accelerating and radicalizing the process of modern deconstruction by allowing each successive wave to be taken to its inevitable and radical conclusion in Nietzschean nihilism, was it possible to blast a way back to ancient wisdom, where reason was once again the critic of limitless bodily desire, and of the flattened human horizon it validated. Only by playing this apocalyptic card would it be plausible to entertain seriously the restoration of classical rationalism and natural right. The dangerous gambit dismantles Hobbesian and Lockean sobriety and the stable commercial regime and administrative regimes they articulated, disseminates Rousseauean compassion and the solidarity of "the people," and disperses the subjectivized individual which Nietzsche knew must still blush and therefore had to be dispersed. Released into what would more recently be called Derridean 'differance, a free play of signifiers in which no traditional ethical or logical restraint can be allowed to interfere with discourse, it also becomes impossible to know whether one is last man or overman, god or beast. It is as if Strauss has written "*apresmoi le deluge.*"

The second illustration of the thought that is the hallmark of our times is that of Rene Girard, whose work at John Hopkins University and Stanford University has given him international acclaim. Girard aims to uncover what he calls "the things hidden since the creation of the world." Western civilization, he wants to show, did not arise through the serene and immaculate gaze on proportion, balance, and rational order by poets and philosophers in ancient Greece, but from primordial encounters during which desire, jealousy, avarice, and sacrifice were transacted. And the encounter is repeated daily, even when it is ritualized into a more benign form.

Human desire, Girard writes, is not benignly original and spontaneous, but always mediated by the desire of another, and always conflictual. There is no mythic time before competition and political constraint, nothing romantic about the origins of society. Desire, he says, is essentially mimetic - we see another enjoying what they desire, and we desire their desire, not because what they desire is objectively good for us, but because they desire it. In fact, we become so obsessed with our rival's desire that we lose sight of the objects for which we compete and begin to focus angrily on one another. Now, each just wants to prevent the other from obtaining the object they desire, desiring only the prestige that comes from victory over the other. Rivals, formerly different, become mirror images of each other, returning tit-for-tat endlessly. The more intense their mimetic rivalry, the more prone retaliating others are to join in on one side or the other, with an increasing number of individuals polarizing against fewer and fewer enemies, creating an environment of acute danger and anxiety. And then at the apparent height of the contagion of mimetic rivalry, when a society is teetering on the brink of destroying itself, the mimetic contagion suddenly focuses on one person, whose guilt and responsibility for the social violence is universally acknowledged. Scape-goating and the others' death extinguishes their rivalry. The death is a catharsis, triggering memory of the sense of community that generated the violence, and restoring peace and order. More importantly, the scapegoat is a catalyst to a purging of the dark mechanic of desire.

The lesson to be learned from the scapegoat mechanism, for Girard, is not sociological - that individuals must renunciate mimetic desire thus ensuring social unity - but is instead metaphysical. In the classic locus of the scapegoat mechanism, namely Christianity, the God who sacrifices himself to end the mimetic violence, becomes the victim who forgives - evidencing the miracle of transcendent love emerging from immanent collective violence. It speaks too of a redemptive power born in guilt, that gives to choice the ability to refuse mimetic rivalry and instead embrace love. The turn-around is so dramatic and awesome because, where the scapegoat is worshiped as a God, is born the hope that it lies within human possibility to be like god who gives himself freely. While such a God will seem remote from a world enmeshed in mimetic desire, it holds up a model in the sacrificing Christ for a more scrupulous attention to cathartic purification. It affirms what many ordinary individuals have learned in the school of hard knocks: that out of brokenness and despair, indeed at the very bottom where anguish de-creates our worldly being, may open up the absence that is God, and the bond across distance, which triumphs over infinite separation.

Primitive religion, then, according to Girard is the institution that remembers the reviving violence mythologically and ritually reenacts its spellbinding climax. Primitive religion grants one form of violence a moral monopoly, endowing it with enough power and prestige to preempt other forms of violence and restore order. "Religion," he writes, "makes possible ... benefits by bestowing sacred status on a socially tolerable form of violence to which the culture can resort as an alternative to greater and more catastrophic violence."

Girard's analysis is telling because it emanates from a tradition as old as Hegel, if not Augustine, that would fight fire with fire, even if it means going to the edge of total mutual destruction. Now it is true that one conclusion one may draw from Girard is that the portrayal of the West as animated by an appetite for power, wealth and dominion, has to be modified to include equally, the rescuing of innocent victims. The peace and social consensus that conventional cultures could only achieve at the victim's expense, Christianity, and its heir of liberalism, could produce through clogging the gears of the scapegoat mechanism.

But such achievement depends on arousing a violence that fascinates, and then hoping that the scapegoat mechanism necessarily cathartically discharges that fascination, because the violence that fascinates but fails to achieve catharsis leads to imitation. On any account, the practical and incrementalist micro-transactions to which Aristotle made an appeal are worthless in the heightened drama of scapegoat protagonists depicted by Girard. But his is not a lone voice. Informing Hegel, and all the latter-day Hegelians including Sartre, Kojeve, Foucault, and Bataille, one finds ordinary and everyday existence contextualized in threatening environments, where judgment is advised to take its bearing from the emergency situation and the capacity for resolute action.

Strauss' and Girard's thoughts on the fateful paths the modern West is, or must, embark, tear to the point where the soul glistens, where both the poverty and audacity of our being is brutally exposed. It is here that "threat perception" really has its roots - in the judgment on the apparent malaise of modernity, and the hopes for a radical deliverance. The scenario of a life lived at its rawest moment, where even reason coils up against itself and is cancelled out, must be repeated over and over to thwart the recrudescence of atavistic longings. Here everyday life is depleted of its drama and potentialities, and life stands as if at the Göttedamerung - the turbulent chaos of the Gods twilight, where all compromises, concessions, and prudent ironies are disdained and abandoned, and where - as in the thought of Kierkegaard and Barth - the burden of proof comes to rest on the moment of decision. Their demand on us entails navigating a terrain in the soul with great heights and but also fearsome abysses, but for those of us of more timid spirit, it may also be right to ask what the fall-out is of discarding prudent reserve and irony, and for allowing no concession to the fallenness of the world. Their prescription turns away from the idea that the human vocation is to gradually heighten simple existence into a living drama. It demands more than prudent conciliation and consensus building, more than the repair of the artifices and institutions that were historically designed to preempt apocalyptic ruptures and leaps. And, as it has seeped out from the *Ecole Normale Superieure,* it has, even perhaps contrary to intentions, ramped up a lust for apocalyptic transformations of the world, which is to say that one of its legacies is the desire to use force as if it were magic, especially evident in the perhaps too hasty rescinding of the virtue of prudence, and of the political safeguards traditionally designed to hold powerful passions in check and to harness the errant love of the unconditioned.

I have brought these two examples to our attention because this is what is parading as the cutting-edge of political and theological debate in our times. In both cases, the thinking is apocalyptic and prophetic, turning its attention away from ordinary experience and the contours of everyday life. In fact, the pursuit of the ordinary has become a sign of decadence, not of simplicity, ever since Heidegger transformed *phronesis*, practical judgement, into ontology.

While the threat we believe, we face, is uniquely our own, at this time and in this place, we are seeing here a re-play of a seemingly perennial dispute, which first emerged at the beginning of the West when Socrates turned away from the pre-Socratic speculations on nature, and focused on the speeches and deeds of everyday life. The political city provided the framework that held theory and practice together, and which produced a philosophy that transcended, and yet was deeply rooted in, ordinary life. That everyday life was articulated from the activities of the poet, craftsman and statesman, whose speeches and actions testified to an implicit philosophical content to ordinary life. Philosophy, as Socrates teaches, is neither poetry not mathematics, and yet when it departs from the everyday it risks becoming either. And when the political is understood by methods emanating from mathematics and experimental science, it is empty, and inclined to want to master everydayness. As the Greek poet Archilochus writes, "The fox knows many things, but the hedgehog knows one big thing." In our time, we think we know only the one "big thing," and we scorn the many things, not to say the balance that comes from tolerating plurality, difference and otherness.

Perhaps this is a pathology that has hit the West the hardest and deepest. It is highly probably that there lies in the autochthonous intellectual and spiritual resources of India and China, rebuttals and alternatives to this dire portrait of the human condition, and the ramping up of the perception of threat. But as even these great civilizations embrace globalization, and engage in "catch-up" with the West, they are absorbing the cardinal concepts, modes of reasoning, moral re-directions and spiritual temperament of the western pathology, and contributing thereby to the de-stabilization of legal and political institutions, everyday commonsense, and measured reaction to contingency which their civilizations had nurtured for centuries.

If we wish to understand the widespread perception of threat, and the heightened atmosphere of precipitous action and heavy-handed rhetoric, we might want to spend vastly more time re-assessing the intellectual paradigms we enlist in making sense of the world. We might find that the greatest and only genuine threat we face today comes from the schemas within which we bind ourselves, that prevent us from seeing what is often directly in front of our noses.

10

Privatisation - A "Hot Potato" - An Overview of the Privatisation Related Threat Perceptions in India

Katrin Uba

This paper describes how various actors in Indian privatisation process frame their opposition to the policy by using varying constructs of "threat perception". Theoretical framework of the paper combines approaches of threat perception from two fields of political science - international relations and social movement research. It discusses the ways various actors frame the privatisation process as a threat to Indian autonomy, and general public welfare. Empirical examples are derived from the extensive analysis of the Indian privatisation process. This makes use of available newspaper reports, statements of Indian labour movement leaders, prior research on the Indian privatisation process and the proceedings of the parliament. It is shown that frames of "threat" differ across elite and grass-root groups, as well as across economic sector and party affiliation of the claim maker. Opponents of privatisation among elite tend to perceive the process as a threat of conceding to external pressure (World Bank, Multi National Corporations) or of selling public property at too low a price. Grass-root activists are more concerned over threat to Indian labour force, prices and environment. Proponents, on the other hand, see non-privatisation as a threat to Indian economic development. Implications of these various framing processes on Indian privatisation process are discussed in conclusion.

Introduction

A wave of political and economic changes signified the state of the world in the early 1990s. India has not remained unaffected, as the Congress Party-led government announced its "new economic policy" in July 1991. It was not anything radically new, as attempts to initiate privatisation of government owned property or to reform the rules of business-making had also taken place in the 1980s (Kohli, 2006). Still, the scope of this new policy was significantly larger and the clearly pro-liberalisation international market expected radical changes (Naib, 2004). The reforms, however, were slow to come as opponents among political elite and masses, mainly labour movement and grass-root organisations, became involved in the intensive discussion over the positive and negative effects of reforms.

This inherently democratic process forms a ground for this paper. Especially, I will focus on the framing of the liberal economic reforms by various actors in Indian society. While a lot has been written about the economic aspects of privatisation and other reforms of structural adjustment process, we lack a systematic overview of how the arguments in the discussion were framed. As players in the process framed their arguments by emphasising various privatisation related threats, the theoretical framework for the paper combines two types of literatures. It follows the "frame analysis" from social movement research and the analysis of "threat perceptions" from the international relations literature. Thus, I will examine the *discursive controversies* of privatisation process.

Such an analysis is important for better understanding of the general public distrust towards the liberal economic reforms in India. It is well-known that elite and grass-roots mobilisation could affect the formation of public opinion, and the way public discourse frames privatisation related threats or benefits is particularly important here. Moreover, prior studies have demonstrated that not only public or elite approval of economic reforms, but also the perceptions of stake-holders (i.e. employees, managers, trade unions) affect the implementation of the process and its eventual success (Wated, et al. , 2008, Fernandez & Smith, 2006). As there is no scholarly agreement on what groups - labour movement, national elite or international business-groups, dominate the making of economic policy in India (Roychowdhury, 2003), current analysis focuses on the national level actors.

The paper proceeds as follows. First section provides a short overview of Indian privatisation process in order to provide reader with the context of following frame analysis. Second part presents the theoretical framework for examining the threat perceptions in the context of privatisation. The third section gives a brief picture of the empirical data and method. Fourth and fifth sections present then the description of how the elite and labour movement have framed the Indian privatisation process.

1. Background - Indian Privatisation Process

Despite the relatively early start in the context of international pressure and economic crises, reforms in India have been gradual and slow (Naib, 2004). I focus here only on privatisation that narrowly refers to the step-by-step transfer of public assets to private sector and broadly to de-regulate public services or even a part of a "neo-liberal package of structural adjustment programs promoted by the World Bank" (Harris, 2003). It is not surprising that such a process involves conflicting interests and contentious perceptions of accompanying threats and benefits, which in turn prolong the duration of the decision-making process in government and parliament.

This has also been the case of the privatisation process in India, where the incitation and decision-making over privatisation is mainly controlled by the executive power (Government of India) and the implementation by specific government bureaucracies, e.g. Department of Disinvestment. If the government aims to sell the enterprises nationalised by the parliamentary act, it also has to get parliamentary approval. This makes privatisation also a topic of active debates in the lower and upper Houses of the Parliament. Consequently, the Government of India has, up to date, managed to fully privatise only 16 of its enterprises. Some acceleration of the process took place after the 1998, when the Bharatiya Janata Party (BJP)-led coalition government came to power. Then, during 6 subsequent years 10 enterprises were fully privatised and some shares of 47 or 20% of government-owned enterprises were sold (See details in Naib, 2004). These concrete financial transactions have also been complemented with the decline of India's social expenditures during 1991-2000 (Mooij, 2005). The same accounts for the funding of the public health-care and insurance sector (Sinha, 2002).

Privatisation also takes place beyond the central (federal) level and some states, such as Andhra Pradesh (AP), have been even more enthusiastic in restructuring their public sector than the centre (Mishra Kiranmai, 2006). For example, AP had privatised 13 state level public sector undertakings (SPSUs) in 2002, while much larger Uttar Pradesh (UP), had sold only two and West Bengal none of its SPSUs. Often such initiatives could be related to the role of political elite (Chief Minister of State) or to the hope for loan from international financial institutions. The last has been of particular case for the reforms in the electricity sector, which are controlled by the state governments. For example, Orissa and Andhra Pradesh have reformed their energy production with the help of international know-how, while other states lag far behind (Harper, 2003).

Regardless of these changes, it is often stated that the reforms of Indian public sector are much slower than the reforms in Latin American, Eastern European or other Asian countries (Tunc 2005). Partially, this could be related to the prevalent public discourse towards economic reforms in India and this will be discussed further in the following section. Here, suffice it to say that political elite tends to be more uniform in their support to privatisation, while the majority of the mass tends to oppose it (Mitra & Singh, 1999, Yadav, 2004).

Furthermore, the few implemented reforms have resulted in some workforce retrenchment in the public sector (Sharma, 2006). This has, in turn, led to the intensive mobilisation against the process by Indian labour movement (Gupta, 2005, Uba, 2007). Even other civil society groups, such as environmentalist organisations and consumers groups have stated their opposition to the process.

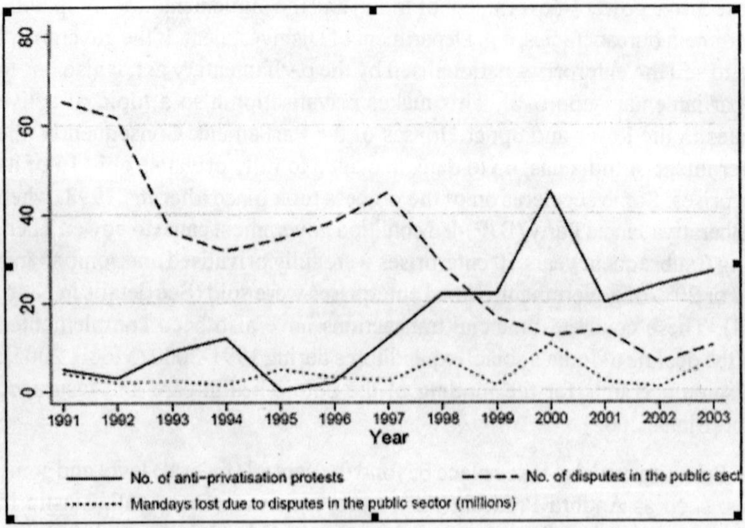

Fig. 1. The trends of labour mobilisation and anti-privatisation protests in India, 1991-2003.

This contention is summarised in the Figure 1, which compares the number of protests mobilised against privatisation and general labour disputes in the public sector (details of the data sources are described in the section "Data and methodology" below). It is clearly shown that protests against privatisation have steadily increased, while the officially recorded statistics show the decline of labour disputes. The explanation of these trends is beyond the scope of this paper, and the trends are shown only for the sake of comparative perspective. Rather, it is important to note that such a protest mobilisation have probably involved intensive framing of privatisation related threats we'll discuss below.

2. Analytical Framework

The analysis of how the participants of the Indian privatisation process frame the discussion on privatisation is based on the theoretical framework, which was initially developed for the analysis of threat perceptions in the field of international relations (Farnham, 2003). Originally, this consisted of three approaches that should aid assessing the level of threat country A faces from country B. These are realist, democratic peace and a norm based approaches (Ibid.).

For applying these frameworks to the context of privatisation, it is important to emphasise that we discuss the *perceived impact* of privatisation or the assessed consequences of transferring the public sector assets or services to private sector (Fernandez & Smith, 2006). Some of these outcomes of privatisation are probably seen as "threatening" for the actors involved in the process, i.e. public sector employees and trade unions. Still, the process could also be framed as leading to negative consequences for general public (consumers) and to a society at large (economic development, environment). On the other hand, proponents of the reforms might assess the outcomes of the process in terms of expected benefits and frame privatisation as something beneficial to everyone. Rather than explaining the differences of various groups, the selected analytical framework allows us studying the reasons why privatisation could be perceived as a threat.

Starting from the *realist perspective*, the privatisation could be assessed as threatening due to the harm-making capabilities of private sector. It can sack workers, impose price hike or lower the environmental standards in production (See the analogue to international relations in Farnham, 2003). Even though the actual outcomes of privatisation in developing countries are highly debated (Megginson & Netter, 2001), the legal protection of employees, as well as consumers and environment might be weaker in the context of private ownership (Philion, 2007). Certainly, the legal protection of workers'rights, price control or environment-friendly production might not be present in the state-owned sector either, but here it is important that such a discourse could be used for enforcing negative opinion regarding privatisation. The notion of capabilities of the other side (private companies or international agencies) does not have to be based on the concrete real-world experience, as one could use some more general "proxies" for negative outcomes of private ownership.

The second approach for discussing privatisation-related threat perceptions refers to ideological arguments. This suggests that the discussion about the negative consequences of privatisation follows the ideological argument. Thus, those active in the framing process suggest that the process means implementation of the right-wing (neo-liberal) ideology. This could be done via the reference to the "class-struggle" or just demonstrating the "principled" rather than pragmatic opposition to the process. Involved actors perceive privatisation as a threat because of their values and norms of state-economy, which in turn leads to different assessment of empirical evidence (Farnham, 2003). We could expect that such frames are mostly used by political parties or organisation that represents the extreme positions of the left-right wing scale of ideology. Note, that ideological frame differs clearly from the realist one, as the first aims to provide empirical reasons for why privatisation is perceived as negative, while the last would mainly focus on ideology - related norms and values.

Finally, the third approach refers to the privatisation related threats by framing it as a violation of the present rules of the game (Ibid.). This is somewhat similar to the first, realist perspective, as it refers to some knowledge of opponents (private company) behaviour, either directly derived from own experience or indirectly via proxies. However, the norm based approach focuses particularly on the perceived damage to generally accepted norms or rights. In contrast to ideological approach, which would mainly use class-based arguments in the framing process, this approach would rather frame privatisation as a threat to human rights in general or some particular social rights.

3. Data and Methodology

In order to examine the framing of the privatisation process with the help of above-mentioned theoretical framework, I use a data-base of anti-privatisation protests in India during 1991-2003 (Uba, 2007). Despite being collected for another research-project, this database consists of a broad set of newspaper reports and therefore highly useful for frame analysis. Still, the use of media as a data-source for frame-analysis could be problematic, as India's mainstream media seems to favour the privatisation process (Gupta, 2005). There presentation of labour movement's opposition to the process is frequently framed by using a disapproving tone, which tries to de-legitimise the group. Still, my analysis makes use of the direct citations of political elite or union representatives and should therefore provide more objective view on the process. The data from news-reports is complemented with the official documents and published materials of various Indian trade unions. In order to provide a picture of elite's frame of privatisation, I use secondary literature on privatisation process and economic reforms (e.g., *Economic and Political Weekly*), as well as the on-line parliamentary proceedings.

The analysis of threat perceptions follows the methodology of "frame analysis", mostly known from the social movement research perspective. This focuses on the process of how social movement activists construct their self-presentations for drawing support from third parties – public opinion, other organisations or political parties (Johnston 2002). One could modify this approach and see framing as the process through which different members of the political elite or grass-root groups interpret and maintain the meaning of their action and their potential supporters, as well as antagonists (See Snow et al. 1986, Benford and Snow 2000). Thus, instead of examining how "collective action frames" mobilise the group, this paper describes how various actors use framing process for affecting public perceptions on privatisation. Hence, following sections describe the statements of elite and non-elite groups, as well as connect their discussion via qualitative discourse analysis to the realist, ideologist and norm based approach of framing threats.

4. Elite perspective – privatisation as a "Hot Potato"

As suggested above, deciding over policies of privatisation in India has not been very smooth. The issue is a delicate one due to the long-time preference for socialist type of economy. Even the term "privatisation" was not widely used in political discourse until the end of 1990s, as political elite favoured talking about "restructuring" and "disinvestment". The last refers to less radical reforms and could be therefore considered as more acceptable to the Indian public (Sarma, 2004). For example, several Ministers of Finance did not promise privatisation, but talked about the "strategic sale" or the need to "open the economy for private sector participation". They just avoided the use of the "p"-word (Ibid.). This is not only the question of public discourse, as the term is also institutionalised. The Government of India set up the Commission of Disinvesœment (1990-1999), the Department of Disinvestment (1999-2001; 2004-), and the Ministry of Disinvestment (2001-2004) (Naib, 2004). One could suggest that this selection of words was a clear result of general negative frame of "privatisation" that had already been developed during the 1980s. The socialist type of economy was probably seen as sign of autonomy and independence, and the word "privatisation" could have been framed by opponents of the reform as something referring to the threat to national pride. Indeed, such ideological approach or framing the privatisation as a threat to national autonomy was used by some radical representatives of right-wing conservative parties (BJP, Shiv Sena). However, this extent was rather small in comparison to Latin American countries (Uba, 2007), probably due to this avoidance of "p-word" in public debates for several years.

The similar tendency of neglecting some concepts from public discussion is notable if one compares the public statements and actual behaviour of Indian political elite. For example, just after announcing the new economic policy in 1991, Prime Minister, Narasimha Rao (Congress Party), promised that the government will not privatise or close down the large loss-making public sector enterprises. He, however, did not mention that Government of India had just approved a World Bank loan that was supposed to ease the closing of sick enterprises. This tendency to avoid public attention has even led to the development of a specific term- "reforms by stealth" (Jenkins, 1999). The reason for such behaviour was probably the prevalent public opposition to privatisation, as well as the numerous protests mobilised by civil society groups (as shown in Figure 1).

Another trend among Indian political elite is the use of pragmatic (realistic) frame of privatisation. Reforms are considered as "*threatening*" only if it might affect them or their power position directly. For example, Ministers of Civil Aviation (SharadYadav from the Janata Dal Party) and of Heavy Industry (Manohar Joshi from the Shiv Sena) agreed with the idea of privatisation as long as it did not involve their own area of responsibility. Indian media even reports about an anonymous politician who told *India Today* (17.07.2000) :

"*As long it is not my ministry and my PSU, I am all for reforms, disinvestment and privatisation. When it comes to my turf I show my real colours.*"

Thus, one could see that privatisation has been treated as a "hot potato" – you want to eat it but have to be very careful about not burning yourself. This resulted in a pragmatic, rather than ideological, framing of privatisation even among the politicians from left-wing parties. Although the members of Communist Parties (CPI-M and CPI) did use the "ideological frame" (a notion to class-struggle, employers' rights, retrenchments) in their opposition to privatisation in the parliament proceedings, their actions in the United Front government (1996-98) proved the opposite (Naib, 2004).

The same tactics were used by the nationalist parties (e.g., BJP). These were concerned over the impact of foreign pressure on India's economic autonomy and opposed privatisation while in opposition. However, while in government (1998-2004), BJP accelerated the Indian privatisation process. This is even better exemplified if one compares the state and federal level policy-making. For example, while privatising at the central level, BJP opposed loudly the Delhi's Congress led city government's initiative to privatise municipal water system. The same was also the case with West Bengal Communist Party state government that initiates reforms at home, but mobilises protests against the reforms at the centre (Sinha, 2004).

All this supports the argument that in India, there is a general political agreement over "the necessity of [economic] reforms" (Mooij, 2005). However, it is not clear whether these reforms were perceived as necessary for a sustainable long-term economic development or for using anopportunity to receive some extra finances to state budget. The last seemed to be case for Andhra Pradesh in 1997, when its Chief Minister Chandrababu Naidu (TDP) argued that the restructuring the power sector should be completed: "*on an urgent basis if the World Bank's offer of credit was to be utilised before others grabbed it.*"

The only clear "privatisation related threat" as proposed by the political elite was the one that referred to an issue of security, particularly a *"threat to national security and to national interest*". For example, Defence Minister, George Fernandes and Petroleum Minister, Ram Naik, opposed the plans of disinvesting the central government owned oil-companies (HPCL, BPCL) by framing the sector as of "national interest" (*The Tribune*, 7.12.2002). This frame has even united the traditional opponents, as the proposal to privatise some parts of the Indian defence industry led to a unified protest by representatives of political elite (right-wing parties) and labour, both from unions affiliated to left-wing parties (CITU and AITUC), as well as to the right wing parties (BMS). Similar security arguments have also been used by those opposing the recent plans for privatising Delhi and Mumbai airports. The last suggests that elite and grass-roots could also use each-others' arguments for framing their opposition to privatisation and this is also shown in the next section.

5. Grass-roots' Perspective – privatisation is a threat

The extensive analysis of privatisation related newspaper articles allowed distinguishing several ways to frame privatisation as a threat, but all these could be covered by a master frame, which demonstrates privatisation as a threat to jobs and employees. The following discussion presents these main frames in a random order.

Threat to "Human Rights"

The assessment of the consequences of privatisation varies across the economic sector and this is best visible on the occasion of normative framing. Privatisation of water, sanitation and electricity sector enterprises has been clearly framed as something important for people in general. The discourse avoids the narrow picture of "consumer's" or "labour's interest, which was more prevalent in the discussions on selling the manufactures or mines. Probably, due to the international context, i.e. the *"War on Water*" in Bolivia (Kohl, 2002), the arguments about water-privatisation in India were also connected to the issues of democracy and threat to "human rights". For example, a well-known activist Vandana Shiva stated in a journal, *Resurgence*, (Issue 219, July-August 2003):

"Privatising water will lead to war.... Privatisation of water is the ultimate human rights violation, the ultimate human wrong."

The last is also closely connected to the perception that the privatisation of water is a threat to the livelihood of "common people" (Hall ja Lobina, 2005). It is not just framed to have negative consequences for the labour movement (i.e. public sector jobs), but also the interests of people in general - consumers, women and environmental organisations. One reason for this perceived negative consequence is the concern over increased corruption or lack of transparency. For example, Andhra Pradesh State Electricity Board (APSEB) Council of Joint Action (JCA) did not oppose the restructuring of the board *per se*, but were against the non-transparent way of planning it.

References to the threat to "common people" or to "human rights" suggest that actors assess the consequences of privatisation on the basis of some existing agreements or norms. Private ownership of a sector is assessed to be violating these rules. It is hard to say weather such a threat is perceived due to the negative examples of private water projects in other parts of the world (South America, Africa) or the lack of trust in Indian regulatory commissions, which are supposed to control the services provided by the private sector. Nevertheless, one could expect that by framing the privatisation as a threat to "human rights" has had stronger effect on public opinion than just discussing the probable loss of jobs.

Threat to the Financial Stability

While the "human rights" frame was mostly used by the traditional grass-root movements, the next set of arguments reflect mainly the discourse of trade unions. These refer to the perceived financial consequences of the privatisation process and depends on whether one discusses the sell-out of a *profit-loss making* enterprise. One could assess whether the government will lose or win financial resources via the privatisation process and how this affects the employees.

The use of this frame presents also the major difference between the "threat perceptions" of Indian labour movement. While the Congress affiliated Indian National Trade Union Congress (INTUC) tends to frame privatisation of loss-making enterprises as something positive, other, mainly left-wing unions follow the ideological framing and oppose all kinds of divestment. INTUC's pragmatic (realistic) argument is based on their assessment that non-privatisation of loss-making units leads to negative budgetary consequences. Such a realistic frame of keeping the financial stability in India was also used for justifying INTUC's non-participation in nation-wide protest campaigns. This frequent non-participation by INTUC, as a second largest trade union of India, is also used by political elite for legitimating their policies. Government officials just neglect the fact that INTUC actually participated in several protest campaigns against the privatisation of *profit* making enterprises (e.g., Modern Foods in 1999 or Neyveli Lignite Corporation in 2006).

This behaviour and framing the privatisation from the perspective of financial stability suggests that labour movements' follow the strategy of realistic rather than ideological or normative framing. They evaluate the capabilities of private sector, as well as the former experiences of privatisation in other countries, and frame their discussion on the basis of this knowledge.

Threat to National Autonomy

Similarly, to the political elite, civil society organisations also emphasise the issue of "autonomy" in the arguments against privatisation. The last is perceived to threaten the political and economic autonomy of India. It is based on the perception that selling the Indian public sector enterprises to non-Indian private enterprises (e.g., Multinational Corporations, MNCs) may have negative consequences. Still, in contrast to the right-wing parties, which were emphasising the aspect of "nationalism", left-wing civil society organisations employ the frame of "capitalist globalization" in their arguments against privatisation. For example, the All India State Government Employees'Federation (AISGE) framed their anti-privatisation campaign in June, 1992, as a fight against the dependence of international financial organisations (e.g., World Bank). On another occasion, the foreign investments into Dabhol power complex in Maharashtra by the U.S.-based electricity company Enron in 1994 were framed as a clear "threat to economic autonomy of India." Similarly, left-wing trade unions opposed the sell-out of several manufactories to MNCs and blamed the negative consequences of privatisation on World Bank and IMF.

This ideological framing is also shown to play a role in the formation of citizens' opinion on economic reforms. Some scholars would even argue that this could explain the failure of BJP in the 2004 parliamentary elections (e.g., Dastidar, Fisman Khanna, 2006). This argument could also be made at the state level in Andhra Pradesh where Telugu Desam Party (TDP) lost its majority in the State Assembly partly due to the citizens' opposition to economic reforms. They protested against high electricity bills, which accompanied the privatisation that in turn was promoted by the World Bank and the UK's Department for International Development.

The more nationalist or right-wing political parties affiliated trade unions, on the other hand, have framed their opposition to privatisation via "threat to Indian unity". For example, Swadeshi Jagran Manch (SJM) and the Bharatiya Mazdoor Sangh (BMS) opposed the opening of Indian bank and insurance sector to [foreign] private investments in 1998 by stating that:

"Allowing foreign participation in the insurance sector, even in a minority stake, was against the national interest. ... *the economic collapse of the Southeast and East Asian nations was because they had allowed* foreign participation *in key sectors of the economy. Under no circumstance must we allow repatriation of funds from India, and foreign participation means just that."*

However, the framing of opposition to privatisation by trade unions has not only been related to specific perceived treats, but it also expresses a complicated game of special interest politics. This could be exemplified with the above mentioned case of West Bengal (WB). Already, in 1993, the Communist Party leader and Chief Minister of WB, Jyoti Basu, promoted foreign investments into the state and even encouraged the sell-out of some manufacturing enterprises (Burnpur steel factory) and tourist services (hotels). In other locations of India, this had led to the protest mobilisation of Communist Party affiliated union –CITU. In WB, however, this was not the case because party leadership suppressed state-targeting protests and instead encouraged the campaigns that targeted the privatisation policies of the federal government. Hence, it seems that the pragmatic rather than ideological framing of opposition to privatisation was prevalent even for labour movement. Only politically, the non-affiliated grass-root groups employed normative framing approach for influencing public opinion.

Conclusion

This paper aimed at providing an overview of how various important players in the Indian privatisation process, that is political elite and civil society representatives, have framed their arguments against privatisation. The study combined the theoretical framework of threat perception analysis of international relations to the analysis of "protest frames" in social movement research.

By analyzing the empirical material from the Indian news-media, as well as labour movement resources on their mobilisation and secondary materials, it was possible to detect one master - and several sub-frames of perceived threats. These were threats to : Indian state unity, economic and political autonomy, jobs' and financial security, national security and human rights.

None of the frames were predominant, but one could say that the pragmatic or realistic approach of framing, that is by referring to probable (negative) capabilities of private owners, was more common for both groups of actors. Although the representatives of political elite, particularly those from ideological extremes, employed the ideology based arguments, this was not very frequent. Similarly, civil society groups, particularly trade unions framed their opposition by combining ideological and pragmatic arguments. Only in a few occasions, while opposing the privatisation of water, the process was framed by following the normative argument – a threat to human rights.

Thus, we have identified various options for framing the opposition to privatisation in India, and one could suggest that this has played an important role for developing the negative public opinion on economic reforms in India. Further, research could identify more clearly the reasons for presenting variations of threat perceptions, as well as relate these variations to the analysis of protest mobilisation against the Indian privatisation process.

References

Benford, Robert D., and David A. Snow (2000), "Framing Process and Social Movements: An Overview and Assessment." *Annual Review of Sociology,* 26: 611-639.

Bhattacherjee, B. (1999) *Organized Labour and Economic Liberalization in India, Past, Present and Future.* ILO Discussion Paper Series No. 105

Bortolotti, Bernardo, and Paolo Pinotti (2006) "Delayed Privatization." *Delayed Privatization.*

Candland, C. & Sil, R. (ed.), (2001), *The Politics of Labor in Global Age: Continuity and Change in Late-industrializing and Post-socialist Economies,* Oxford University Press.

Dastidar, Siddhartha G., Raymond Fisman, and Tarun Khanna (2006), "Limits to Policy Reversal. Privatization in India." *Hitotsubashi University Discussion Paper* 158.

Farnham, Barbara (2003), "The Theory of Democratic Peace and Threat Perception." *International Studies Quarterly,* 47: 395–415.

Fernandez, Sergio, and Craig R. Smith (2006), "Looking for Evidence of Public Employee Opposition to Privatization: An Empirical Study With Implications for Practice, "*Review of Public Personnel Administration,* 26: 356-381.

Johnston, H. & Noakes, J. A. (2002), ed., *Frames of Protest. Social Movements and the Framing Perspective,* Rowman and Littlefield.

Gupta, Nandini (2005), "Partial Privatisation and Firm Performance." *The Journal of Finance,* XL, pp. 987-1015.

Hall, David and Emanuele Lobina (2005), "Public resistance to privatisation in water and energy.", *Development in practice,* 15:286-301.

Harper, Malcolm, "Micro-Privatization in India - success and failure", *Small Enterprise Development,* No. 14

Harris, Richard L, (2003), "Popular Resistance to Globalization and Neoliberalism in Latin America.", *Journal of Developing Societies,* 19:365-426.

Jenkins, Rob, (1999), *Democratic Politics and Reform in India,* Cambridge: Cambridge University Press.

Kohl, Benjamin (2002), "Stabilizing neoliberalism in Bolivia: popular participation and privatization." *Political Geography,* 21:449-472.

Kohli, Atul (2006), "Politics of Economic Growth in India, 1980-2005. Part II: The 1990s and Beyond." *Economic and Political Weekly,* April 8:1361-1370.

Megginson, William and Jeffry M. Netter (2001), "From State to Market: A Survey of Empirical Studies on Privatization.", *Journal of Economic Literature,* 39:321-389.

Mishra, R. K. and J. Kiranmai (2006), "Restructuring of SLPEs in India. A Macroanalysis", *Economic and Political Weekly,* 41: 4170-4177.

Mitra, Subrata and V.B Singh (1999), *Democracy and Social Change in India,* SAGE Publications.

Mooij, Jos (2005), *The Politics of Economic Reforms in India,* Sage Publications.

Naib, Sudhir (2004), *Disinvestment in India. Policies, Procedures, Practices.* Sage Publications

Philion, Stephen (2007),"Workers' Democracy vs. Privatization in China." *Socialism and Democracy,* 21:37-55.

Roychowdhury, Supriya (2003) "Public Sector Restructuring and Democracy: The State, Laour and Trade Unions in India." *The Journal of Development Studies* 39:29-50.

Sarma, E.A.S. (2004) "Disinvestment: What FMs Have Said since 1991." *Economic and Political Weekly,* May 29

Savas, E. S. (2005), *Privatization in the City: Successes, Failures, Lessons.* Washington, DC: CQ Press.

Sharma, Alakh N. (2006) "Flexibility, Employment and Labour Market Reforms in India." *Economic and Political Weekly* 27:2078-2085.

Sinha, Tapen (2002)"Privatization of the Insurance Market in India: From the British Raj to Monopoly Raj to Swaraj," *CRIS Discussion Paper Series* X

Sinha, A. (2004), "Ideas, Interests and Institutions in Policy Change: A Comparison of West Bengal and Gujarat" in Jenkins, R. (ed.), Regional Reflections: Comparing Politics Across India's States, Oxford University Press

Snow, David A., Jr. Rochford, E., Steven K. Worden, and Robert D. Benford (1986), "Frame Alignment Processes, Micromobilization, and Movement Participation." *American Sociological Review* 51:464-481.

Thrall, A. Trevor (2007)," A Bear in the Woods? Threat Framing and the Marketplace of Values," *Security Studies* 16: 452-488.

Tunc, Hakan (2005) "Privatization in Asia and Latin America." *Studies in Comparative International Development* 39: 58-86.

Uba, Katrin (2007) *Do Protests Make a Difference? The impact of anti-privatisation mobilisation in India and Peru,* Uppsala University.

Venkata Ratnam, C.S. (2001), *Globalization and Labour-Management Relations. Dynamics of Change.* Response Books.

Wated, Guillermo, Juan I. Sanchez, and Carolina Gomez (2008). "A Two-Factor Assessment of the Beliefs That Influence Attitudes Toward Privatization," *Group Organization Management,* 33:107-136.

Yadav, Yogendra, "Economic Reforms in the Mirror of Public Opinion." *The Hindu,* 13.06 (2004).

Sources for analysed material (see details in text):

Indian daily newspapers: *The Hindu*, Business Standard, Indian Express, The Times of India.

International news-sources: *The Asian Wall Street Journal, The Guardian, Reuters News.*

11

Globalization as Threat; International Tourism and the Legacy of Romanticism

Peter Smerkel

The modern era has been characterized by ever-intensifying global interconnectedness, and cross-border human interaction and mobility. Since about the mid-1980s "globalization" has been the fashionable term or the technological compression of time and space, boom in reality and in experience. Increasingly touching the lives of people living in all countries of the world, this development is widely debated and contested, often perceived as a threat, rather than an opportunity. This paper argues that the perception of globalization as a threat, like other perceptions of risk and threat in modern society, often has little to do with rational calculations or empirical evidence. Rather, it is shaped by cultural and ideological assumptions about the vulnerability of people and societies, and by sometimes altogether unfounded fears.

This is vividly illustrated by the image of and debate surrounding international tourism, a major manifestation of globalization and an important global industry, which in spite of temporary setbacks, always has been able to recover and break new all-time records. Undeniably, tourism, like most human activities, has its negative aspects. The costs and benefits, however, often cancel each other out. Yet, in contemporary representations of tourism, the negative side of it mostly dominates, and its continuous growth is seen not as a success to be celebrated, but rather as a problem, as something intrinsically undesirable and pernicious, a threat to be concerned about.

This criticism is, moreover, not external to but an integral part of tourism. As a case study of international tourism to a Greek island in the southeastern Aegean revealed the criticism of and the discomfort with tourism can actually be found among holidaymakers themselves. There seem to be at least three explanations for that. First of all mis- 'anti-tourism' has been a part of Western culture ever since the beginnings of modern tourism, and not - as could be imagined - a late and possibly justified reaction against the social and environmental downside of mass travel. Secondly, tourism is a significant arena for the reproduction of 'social distinctions'. 'Anti-tourism' - trying to demonstrate to oneself and others that one is not a 'tourist' by, among other things, overtly criticizing tourism and tourists - is a way of confirming one's self-image as 'non-tourist', and of boosting one's prestige in the eyes of others. Thirdly, any analysis of tourism or 'anti-tourism' will be incomplete without taking into consideration the influence of romanticist ideals, like the rejection of the technologies some of these substantive issues on terroism, which confronts global humanity.

12

China and its Threat Perceptions: An Overview

Prof. Kondapalli Srikanth

Introduction

Threat perceptions, in general, have become an important indicator in a state's foreign and security policies vis-à-vis other states in the international system. This has been a major aspect of the Cold War history, although the idea of threat perception itself has a long past. In the post-Cold War period, there was a debate on expending the security paradigm from purely state-orientation alone and expand it to include individual human beings, groups, nationalities, immigrations issues fuelling social unrest and terrorism, inclusive developmental paradigms, environmental concerns that across boundaries etc. as well. This transformation in the debate expands the scope of threat perceptions from state-oriented point of views to a seemingly broad-based notion encompassing not only the external and domestic dimensions but also from traditional security to the emerging non-traditional security aspects. The state-oriented threat perceptions emphasised only the territorial integrity and sovereignty, building military alliances and blocks for the enhancement of a state's security whereas many other issues, some of them relatively new, like terrorism, impacting upon the security concerns served to enhance the debate on security.

Thus, in the recent period, threat perceptions, expanded to include concerns on energy resources (including the problems pertaining to the nuclear energy) availability, impact of environmental degradation, emerging tensions between different ethnic and religious groups (fuelling debate on the viability or otherwise of multiculturalism) in the society, terrorism, spread of pandemics and diseases across continents, migration of peoples across several countries as refugees and others, illegal financial flows, expanding drug syndicates and smuggling, piracy on high seas, etc.[1]

China's perceptions of the threats that it is facing, likewise, exhibit the above main concerns, and hence, is no exception to the transformation in the discourse. However, there are some differences between China and other states in addressing these challenges, as the former displays utmost sensitivity towards its sovereignty claims and wary of any dilution in the Chinese government's handling of these challenges in the face of outside pressure or intervention. Indeed, if we go back to the historical times as well, the word threat in Chinese language has cultural and etymological connotations.

An old Chinese proverb suggests that a country that has no threats will perish. At least from a 'realpolitik' point of view, this is ingrained in the Chinese thought throughout the long period spanning many centuries. To some extent, the building of the Great Wall over centuries by successive dynasties to ward off restive hordes from north and north east has created an impression in China and outside that threats to the state and society need to be adequately addressed. Also, another historical experience in China had been that several dynasties were replaced successively by peasants and others in various uprisings-thus questioning the political legitimacy of these regimes. This adds a second dimension-that of internal challenges to the regimes. As we come down to the contemporary period, several of these issues remain and pose concerns to the state of China.

Secondly, the word threat in Chinese [*weixian*] connotes both dangers as well as opportunities. This aspect of finding opportunities in challenges is one distinct aspect when we deal with the threat perceptions of China.

This article explores the main threat perceptions as viewed by the Chinese government or its agencies and those that were expressed in open sources. In a sense, then, this article confines itself to the elite perceptions of the threats that China is faced with in the recent period and hence rules out the views of the people or groups whose views may not be in tandem with the official versions. This issue is also concerned with the regime-legitimacy as the guardian of the state.

Traditional Threat Perceptions

China's threat perceptions can be conveniently explored by following the six official white papers released by the government in the last decade, in addition to the Chinese Communist Party (CCP) documents and other sources.[2]

China's threat perceptions over the last five decades have not been constant but evolved. After the People's Republic of China was established in October, 1949, the CCP-led government, despite attempting to initiate dialogue with the United States for a brief period, was critical of the US and its alliance formations in the East and South east Asia.[3] These were perceived as posing threats to China. While the PRC attempted to "lean towards" the then Soviet Union against the US, such united front was over by 1960. Subsequently, China for the next two decades considered both the US and Soviet Union as posing threats.[4]

China perceived four major threats to its security in the 1990s. Jiang Zemin, the then president, while addressing the 14th Chinese Communist Party Congress in October 1992, said that in the post-Cold war period the world would face an outbreak of ethnic, territorial and religious conflicts[5]. Specifically, these threats according to chronological order, are crystallised into the following: the United States attitude on the question of Taiwan in, practising of "power politics and hegemony" in general; Japan on the question of the Diaoyutai [Senkaku] Islands, the recent rise in 'militarism' and the Japan-US renewal of security treaty, in 1997, that enhanced the role of Japanese forces in the Taiwan Straits under 'certain circumstances'; Vietnam and the Philippines on the dispute over the Spratly's Islands and, finally; India on the question of the border dispute, and nuclear explosions, in 1998, that has the effect of tilting the Asian balance of power.[6] The Taiwan Security Enhancement Act proposed by the US Congress in October, 1999, was criticized by China as also the possible inclusion of Taiwan in the Ballistic Missile Defence (BMD) system.[7]

Events in late 1990s further alerted the Chinese leadership to the external threats to its security. The continuous air-strikes against Iraq, Kosovo War and the bombing of the Chinese Embassy in Belgrade in May, 1999, the EP-3 spy-plane incident near Hainan Island in April, 2001, all convinced the Chinese leadership of the NATO forces eastward advance and its possible impact on not only the Taiwan issue but also that of Tibet, Xinjiang and Inner Mongolia.[8]

Of these, the US bombing of the Chinese embassy in Belgrade on the night of May 7, 1999, was considered by China as an attack on its sovereignty. Its foreign ministry spokesman said the next day, "This act by NATO is a gross violation of China's sovereignty and a willful trampling on the Vienna Convention on Diplomatic Relations as well as the basic norms governing international relations. This is rarely seen in the history of diplomacy.... The U.S.-led NATO must bear all responsibilities arising therefrom. The Chinese Government reserves the right to take further actions on the matter". Subsequently, the US embassy compound was attacked by the Chinese students, and others, in what was believed to be backed by the Chinese government or its agencies.

Taiwan

On the specific issue of Taiwan, the People's Republic of China (PRC) does not recognise Republic of China (ROC) or Taiwan after the civil war between the communist and nationalist forces ended in the defeat and flight of the latter to Taiwan in 1949. While ROC retained the United Nations membership till 1971, after the US switch over of diplomatic recognition towards PRC, the independent nature of ROC was questioned by the PRC. Nevertheless, Taiwan is still being recognised by some 23 countries and retains its own political, administrative, judicial and military institutions and conducts direct and free presidential elections from mid-1990s. While the 2000 and 2004 elections brought in a pro-independence-oriented Democratic People's Party, the latest March, 2008, ushered in a pro-unification Kuomintang Party in Taiwan. On this issue, China must be in a more relaxed situation in the coming years.

Nevertheless, to recount China's threat perceptions in the last decade on Taiwan, the white papers issued by China indicate the emerging acrimony. For instance, the 2004 paper depicted the Taiwan Strait situation as "grim" and the events under President Chen Shuibian (viz., referendum, proposed constitutional changes, and arms imports) as "the biggest immediate threat to China's sovereignty and territorial integrity as well as peace and stability on both sides of the Taiwan Strait and the Asia-Pacific region as a whole." These are configured as the first of the several challenges that the country faces. The principal threats facing Chinese security, according to the 2004 paper, are four in number:

- "The vicious rise of the 'Taiwan independence' forces,
- the technological gap resulting from Revolution in Military Affairs,
- the risks and challenges caused by the development of trends toward economic globalization, and
- the prolonged existence of uni-polarity vis-à-vis multi-polarity."

The latest white paper issued in 2006 identified Taiwan as posing serious challenges to China's security. It elaborated thus:

> "The struggle to oppose and contain the separatist forces for "Taiwan independence" and their activities remains a hard one. By pursuing a radical policy for "Taiwan independence," the Taiwan authorities aim at creating "*de jure* Taiwan independence" through "constitutional reform,", thus still posing a grave threat to China's sovereignty and territorial integrity, as well as to peace and stability across the Taiwan Straits and in the Asia-Pacific region as a whole."

Japan

Next to Taiwan, Japan is considered to pose a major challenge to China. Indeed, the first country to have opposed the traditional Middle Kingdom was Japan in 1894-95, besides Vietnam. Chinese hark back to these times when

Japan posed considerable security challenge to it. All the six white papers mentioned Japan, although the 2006 paper is more explicit. While ignoring the October, 2004, incident involving a Han-class submarine in Japanese waters, for which China for the first time reportedly "apologized" to the Japanese government, the December, 2004, White Paper viewed developments in Japan that are leading to the latter's increased strategic role as a potential security challenge to China. The 2006 paper stated "Complex and sensitive historical and current issues in China's surrounding areas still affect its security environment".

To elaborate, these are concerned with growing Japanese military capabilities, frequent visits of high political personalities to the Yasukuni Shrine, revisions of the text books, etc. It appeared that the China-Japan relations, despite the last year's visit of the Japanese Prime Minister and his efforts at normalisation, are poised to be tense, if not in outright conflict. Given the concerted Chinese military modernisation – specifically in power projection capabilities like the medium to long range missiles, naval and air force platforms, Japan is wary of its interests vis-à-vis Senkaku Islands, oil fields in East China Sea, etc. In general, three broad scenarios were visualised by the Japanese Defence Agency, in terms of Chinese attacks on Japan, as follows:

- in the event of a military conflict between China and Taiwan, China may attack parts of Japan to stop U.S. forces based in the country from supporting Taiwan;
- China may use military force to seize the disputed Senkaku Islands;
- China may move to secure its interests in a gas field in the East China Sea.

United States

Continuing its decades-long strategic focus on the US, China has expressed concerns on the role of the US. In the backdrop of the US actions in Iraq, the 2004 paper stated, that, "Tendencies of hegemonism and unilateralism have gained new ground, as struggles for strategic points, strategic resources and strategic dominance crop up from time to time." This is not only reflective of the US neo-conservative agenda of restructuring the West Asian region, but also of the issue of energy security in the West Asia and Central Asia and the strengthening of US-led military alliances in Asia, especially in East Asia with the prospect of ballistic missile defence system deployment.

In general, Sino-US relations, although becoming strategic – in the sense of expanding trade, people-to-people contacts, high-level political and military contacts, expanding coordination and cooperation on the North Korean nuclear issue, maritime trade, arms control and non-proliferation issues, etc. – still remain problematic and a dominant view in China considers the US as posing a challenge which is multi-dimensional.

Sovereignty

The above discussion included China's threat perceptions which could be categorised as a part of the country's minimalist positions. Several of these are related to China's sovereignty concerns such as Taiwan, Tibet, Xinjiang, Inner Mongolia, and the ability to be an independent decision-maker in the international institutions, etc. These are generally considered to be the core concerns of China and can be dubbed as traditional security aspects. In addition, concerns on deployment of BMD in East Asia and the presence of US troops in the region (Japan and South Korea), or the east-ward expansion of NATO or its counter-terrorism networks in Afghanistan and Central Asia are considered to be constraining China's role in the larger region.

To mitigate these challenges, China tried to forge military alliances/ understandings or multilateral cushions. The first such attempt came during the 1950s as a part of a treaty with the then Soviet Union, but it lasted only till August 1960. Subsequently, China concluded a military alliance pact with North Korea which still lasts, albeit without much strategic significance. More successful for China are several multilateral institutions such as Shanghai Cooperation Organisation (SCO), East Asian Summit, Bo Ao Forum for Asia, etc. To some extent these have served to mitigate, to a fairly reasonable extent, the immediate threats to Chinese security.

Emergence of Non-traditional Threat Perceptions

More complicated for China are the new threats that emerged in the 1990s and are in the process of becoming critical in the post-Soviet phase. Foremost of these threats, potentially destabilising, are emerging ethnic tensions in the country's north west, specifically in Xinjiang, Tibet and Inner Mongolia. Some of these were codified by China as a part of the "3 evils", viz., separatism, extremism and splittism. While Taiwanese independence and Uighur unrest are generally clubbed with the phenomenon of separatism, and extremism associated with the militant activities of the Uighurs, Mongols and others, splittism is the code word for the Dalai Lama and Tibetan unrest persistently simmering below the surface which is made use of by both the internal and exterrnal critiques of China fairly regularly. The Chinese literature categorises the Uighur protests as terrorist incidents. Unlike the definitions of the UN, US, Israel, India or other countries, Chinese definitions of terrorism which views it in terms of its impact on national security and "unity of the motherland."

Terrorism

Terrorist incidents in China were triggered with the Uighurs and other ethnic minorities feeling alienated from the mainstream Han-majority domination in their areas of habitation, exploitation of their resources (like energy and mineral resources) to pursue the industrialisation in the eastern parts of the country, and due to rising awareness of their identities and rights, apart from the Chinese short-sighted support to the *Mujahideen* with arms and supplies in Afghanistan during the Soviet occupation in 1979-89 period.

The then Chinese military's deputy chief of staff Xiong Guangkai, who served in Xinjiang during the 1980s, had mentioned in his book that Uighurs have launched more than 260 attacks since 1990 in which about 170 were killed and 440 wounded. He estimated that over 1,000 Uighurs received training from Al-Qaeda.[9]

Eventually, on December 15, 2003, the Chinese Ministry of Public Security publicised a list of terrorist organisations and 11 terrorists to include: East Turkistan Islamic Movement (ETIM), the East Turkistan Liberation Organization, the World Uighur Youth Congress and the East Turkistan Information Centre. The ministry requested other countries to ban these four organisations and their activities, their support base, financial aspects and protection of these organisations. When the head of ETIM, Hasan Mahsum, was killed by the Pakistani army on October 2, 2003, in a joint anti-terrorism raid along the border of Pakistan and Afghanistan, China thanked Pakistan for this operation as Hasan was accused of plotting several incidents in Urůmqi and Hotan of Xinjiang. On January 21, 2002, China released a lengthy article on East Turkestan activities in Xinjiang. It identified six major actions of the "terrorists" in the region including explosions, assassinations, attacks on police and government organs, crimes of poison and arson, secret training bases and plotting and organizing riots and disturbances. These activities continue to the present day, with the last one reported in March, 2008, when certain Uighurs attempted, unsuccessfully, to hijack a plane.

On another front, China's threat perceptions also include Tibet. While China attempted to talk to Dalai Lama's representatives six times, no major progress is visible in resolving the issue. China accuses the Dalai Lama of "splitting" a unit of motherland, while the Dalai Lama suggests that he was only asking for genuine autonomy for the Tibetans. In the light of the recent Olympics torch march and incidents of protests in different parts of the world and within Greater Tibet, China appeared to be concerned about these events. More importantly, on April 10, 2008, the official Chinese news agency Xinhua, carried reports suggesting that Tibet Youth Congress, "is no different from Al-Qaida, Chechnya's armed terrorists, 'East Turkistan's separatists and any other terrorist organization.

Energy Security

China estimates that another critical threat could emanate from its energy dependency. From 1993 onwards, China became a net importer of energy resources, with the obvious in-built vulnerabilities. Its energy dependency has increased with the imports increasing to more than 130 million tonnes. Energy imports are becoming crucial for China if it has to sustain the near-double digit economic growth rates. West Asia is crucial for Chinese oil imports with an estimated 60 per cent originating from this region. It has signed an agreement with Iran for nearly US $ 100 billion with $ 50-100 billion more in the offing for cooperation in exploring oil and pipeline infrastructure. China also signed an energy agreement with Australia to the tune of $40 billion and with India for exploring joint ventures and cooperation in this field.

One of the strategies to mitigate its energy security challenge is through the concept of "string of pearls" in the Indian Ocean and other contiguous areas. China has signed an agreement with Myanmar for constructing a 1,250-kilometer pipeline connecting the deepwater port of Sittwe on the Bay of Bengal coast to Kunming, the capital of Yunnan province. In 2006, China operationalised the pipeline signed in 2004 with Kazakhstan for $ 3.5 billion. China has already laid down nearly 3,000-kilometer long East-West pipeline connecting its oil fields in Xinjiang with its economic hub, Shanghai. China is keen on a 2,400 kilometre long pipeline costing about $2 billion from Russian Lake Baikal to its Daqing oil field. Venezuela has plans to build a pipeline through Columbia for exporting its oil to China. To bridge the transportation links, China also intends to build a 386-kilometer pipeline from Iran connecting to Kazakhstan. Venezuela promised to provide China with 15 mature oil fields. To further its energy security plans, China plans to invest nearly $100 billion in South America in the coming years.

Another area of Chinese concentration is Africa, which accounts for nearly one-fourth of its oil imports. This figure could rise to nearly one-third in the next decade. China has signed agreements or negotiating with several African countries, including with Nigeria, Gabon, Algeria, Central African Republic, Congo, Angola, Niger and Chad. A Chinese company has constructed the Khartoum refinery in Sudan. Sudan provides for nearly 8 per cent of Chinese oil imports.

Economic

Another related non-traditional security challenge that China is facing is economic security. In the year 2000, China joined the World Trade Organisation and agreed to abide by the rules and regulations as a part of this globalisation efforts. In 1997, China escaped the damage caused to the East Asian economies during the financial crisis. Nevertheless, as it integrates with the global economy, China visualises threats in several forms. Foremost is the domestic economic sector, with agriculture, banking, services, etc. now coming under the onslaught of globalisation and opening up to outside competition.

A related aspect is food security that is haunting China. As China graduated into a market economy with emphasis on commercial crops at the cost of food grain production, vulnerabilities are showing up.[10] By the early 1990s, China for the first time in its recent history, became an importer of rice. China is well above the distress levels in terms of grain trade dependence, grain reserves [estimated at 17 to 18 per cent of the safe minimum], changes in grain production and per capita grain consumption. However, unless remedial measures were taken, it is estimated by the Chinese Agricultural Ministry, that there could be food security challenges in the coming decades.[11] Compounding these is the March, 2008, rise in food prices across the world - the highest in 19 years - that led to the increasing concerns in the world, including in China.

Environmental Issues

As with other countries, China is also facing environmental challenges in the recent period. In the debate on development vs. environmental protection, the Chinese are divided, although the state insists on the developmental projects, while making efforts to curb challenges. In the last two decades of economic growth rates also brought in over-exploitation of natural resources to the detriment of ecological balance. It is estimated that although the Chinese GDP increased to nearly $ 3 trillion, environmental degradation is also phenomenal, with nearly $350 billion needed to clean up the environment.

China is concerned with the depleting water resources of the country as it embarks on urbanisation and industrialisation process. In Shandong Province for instance, the Yellow River which joins the sea from its origin in Tibet, large tracts of land is either flooded with sand or ground water tables receded. To mitigate the situation, China is planning to construct dams and divert rivers from southern to northern areas of the country. China today boasts of nearly half of the global dams. On the flip side, this has also created environmental problems. Several people question the viability of the gigantic dams such as Three Gorges.

Due to the fast spread of industrialisation, China's atmospheric pollution rates have increased manifold, with Japan and South Korea accusing it of spreading acid rain. Pollution of the Songhua River in north-east part of the country with chemicals also led to tensions between China and Russia. Some cities such as Beijing are also witnessing "orange" days - a pointer to the dust that swept from far away from Gobi desert.

A related issue is the increase in natural disasters. An assessment report in China indicated that the country has lost nearly US $ 18 billion annually for the devastation caused by the natural calamities from the 1990s. This figure accounts for nearly 6 to 10 per cent of the GDP of the country. It was estimated that since 1949, China experienced three Tsunami-kind of disasters, though of low intensity, in 1969, 1992 and 1994. It was demanded that the Chinese government take measures to establish an efficient and integrated early warning system from the current centralized system that would take nearly 48 hours for relief to be distributed at the local areas when natural disasters strike the country. Other measures include a "protective screen" system of mangroves, coral reefs and coastal forests to minimise the damage during Tsunami attacks. Indeed, the loss of lives and property in Indonesia, Thailand, Sri Lanka and India are traced to the depletion of mangroves due to human exploitation, economic development and pollution. In 1993, China joined the Pacific Tsunami Warning Mechanism and claims to have set up coast-wide early warning system. It has suggested to the ten Tsunami affected countries in 2005 that it would provide meteorological data through its Fengyun satellites.

Drug Trafficking

China is no stranger to drugs. Indeed, the Chinese active involvement with the outside world in 19th century coincided with the export of opium leading to the two Opium Wars in 1842 and 1856. Currently, China is a major destination for drugs in the world and its consumption patterns indicate an upswing. Dwindling narcotics supplies from traditional sources such as Myanmar provided an opportunity for Afghanistan to export drugs to China. According to Jacob Townsend, Afghanistan's drug exports to China increased and by 2004 constituted nearly 20 per cent of total Chinese heroin consumption. While such exports from the Wakhjir Pass between Afghanistan and China border. Are difficult due to terrain and climate factors, other possible routes, according to Townsend, include porous Tajik-China borders, with at least some through Pakistan-China border areas through Karakoram highway. The cultivation of opium is increasing in northern areas (specially in bordering Badakhshan with more than 20 per cent increase) as compared to the traditional southern production provinces, the exports to China also increased from these contiguous areas via Central Asia.[12] Concerned about the drug trafficking and to curb channelizing funds to terrorist organizations, Chinese assistant foreign minister, Li Hui, suggested at the 6th summit meeting of SCO in June, 2006, that the "anti-drug belt" be built around Afghanistan.[13]

Pandemics

During the last one decade, China also witnessed the spread of pandemics. The SARS crisis in 2003 had a debilitating impact on the health condition of the Chinese, in addition to impacting on the economy, specifically in tourism and aviation sectors. Bird Flu, originally believed to have spread from North-western Qinghai province, is today spreading to all parts of the globe.

Refugees

While India has become a major destiny for refugees from neighbourhood like Bangladesh, Pakistan, Nepal, Sri Lanka and Afghanistan, China is relatively free, in its initial years of the republic from the refugee influx. Today, the refugee issue in China has two dimensions: one of the significant Chinese migrations in Siberia of Russia and in Myanmar, while several Chinese are settling down in the Central Asian Republics (mainly for trade). Secondly, the Chinese estimate refugee flow from North Korea and other places in future.

There are several estimates on the influx of the North Korean refugees into China and other countries. While Japan estimates the possible influx of nearly two million refugees in the event of a North Korean regime collapse, the Korean Buddhist group, Good Friends, estimated that such numbers in China around 140,000 to 300,000 in the North-east of China alone. In addition, in the late 1990s and in the last six years, several reports indicated to such refugees attempting to take asylum in several embassies in Beijing and other places.[14]

Also, the domestic churning process in China in the last two decades is posing concerns to the Chinese state. While a household registration system in the 1950s and 1960s constrained major migrations to the cities, currently many Chinese are migrating to the cities. According to some estimates, there are nearly 100 to 200 million people without employment; nearly 200 million people migrate to the cities in China.[15]

Human Security

As several Chinese started venturing abroad recently, specifically in turbulent regions, their safety has become one of the main concerns of the Chinese government. With violent incidents, involving Chinese, were reported from several regions (such as Central Asia, West Asia and Pakistan), pressure is mounting on the Chinese government to tackle this issue through diplomatic means. The Chinese working in Afghanistan are also being targeted by some Afghan groups. On May 10, 2004, for instance, 11 Chinese workers were killed and five injured in terrorist strikes in Jalowgir area 36 km near Kunduz in northern Afghanistan.[16]

Conclusions

As discussed above, China's threat perceptions have increased in the last few decades in terms of their content and spread. There has also been a visible transformation from emphasising on state-oriented threat to acknowledging the presence of varied threats to the state as well as individuals and groups in the society. While previously China was more concerned with traditional security threats such as challenges to its territorial integrity and sovereignty, now, in the post-Cold War period, it is also concerned with non-traditional security threats identified above.

At the level of the state's decision-making process, the emergence of non-traditional security threats calls for a revamping of the actors. For instance, whereas the Ministry of Foreign Affairs appeared to have overall control over the external dimensions of the decision-making, recent spurt in the non-traditional threat perceptions and the effort to mitigate them provide chances for other agencies and institutions to expand their role. More concretely, the role of the public security agencies, military constituents, environmental agencies or energy-related firms etc have witnessed an upward momentum vis-à-vis the foreign ministry and as compared to the previous period. While the foreign ministry had an overwhelming role before, it now has to accommodate other institutions and agencies as a result of this expansion in the threat perceptions.

While there has been a change in the discourse from traditional to non-traditional threat perceptions in China (as with other countries), the difference between China and most other countries is in the former's emphasis on the state's role to mitigate these challenges. In other words, China is sensitive on its sovereignty aspects whenever there is a debate on the transformation in the threat perceptions. Indeed, the Chinese government, despite conceding to the importance of non-traditional security challenges, is still wary of any depletion in its sovereign role in addressing these challenges. Sometimes, however, these appear to take the form of regime stability than the Chinese state *per se*. In the internal political debates of the Chinese Communist Party (CCP) on "peaceful evolution", such concerns become more explicit.

Another relevant aspect of the threat perceptions that became prominent in the recent period is its external dimension. That is, the debate in the world today is whether China constitutes a threat to global security and stability. Several countries in the West and some of China's neighbours sport this concern, albeit in varying degrees and levels. China's rise in the recent period had contributed to this view which is becoming more prominent. Two decades of high economic growth rates coupled with channelizing some of this wealth into building military strength of China, resulted in the view that China may pose a challenge to the established and dominant powers and also to the neighbouring countries.

Endnotes

1. See Barry Buzan, *People, States and Fear: An Agenda for International Security Studies in the Post-Cold War Era* (Colo: Westview Press, Boulder, 1991); and David Mutimer, "Beyond Strategy: Critical Thinking and the New Security Studies" in Craig A. Snyder, Ed., *Contemporary Security and Strategy*, (Macmillan, London, 1999), pp. 77-101.

2. References to all the six white papers issued by China on defense are accessed from the Chinese government website at http://www.china.gov.cn.

3. It was argued that the US Administration had opened secret negotiations with the CCP leadership and, if need be, withdraw support to Taiwan or even contemplated of replacing Chiang Kai-shek by an UN-led trusteeship. Nevertheless, it was noted that China signed the friendship treaty with the USSR that shelved any normalisation of relations between the US and China and thus beginning Cold War in East Asia. See Richard C. Thornton, *Odd Man Out: Truman, Stalin, Mao, and the Origins of the Korean War,* (Brassey's Inc., Washington DC, 2000) and "The Cold War in Asia", *Cold War International History Project Bulletin*, Issues 6-7, Winter 1995/1996.

4. See Li Baojun, Dangdai Zhongguo waijiao gailun (Introduction to *Contemporary Chinese Foreign Policy*), (Beijing: Chinese People's University Publication, Beijing, 1999).

5 See for Jiang Zemin's speech to the 14th Party Congress, Beijing Review, Vol. 35 no.43 October 26-November 1, 1992 p. 26. See also Xu Xiaojun, 'China's Grand Strategy for the 21st Century' in Michael D. Bellows ed., Asia in the 21st Century: Evolving Strategic Priorities, (National Defence University Press, Washington DC, 1994), p. 24.

6. See David Shambaugh, 'The insecurity of security: The PLA's Evolving Doctrine and Threat Perceptions Towards 2000', *Journal of North east Asian Studies*, Vol. XIII no. 1, Spring, 1994, pp. 3-25.

7. See David A. Shlapak et.al *Dire Strait? Military Aspects of the China-Taiwan Confrontation and Options for U.S. Policy,* (RAND Corp, Santa Monica, 2000).

8. See Zhang Wenmu, "Kesuowo zhanzheng yu zhongguo xinshiqi anquan zhanlue" (The Kosovo War and China's New Security Strategy in the Next Century), *Zhanlue yu Guanli*, vol. 3 No. 34 1999; Shen Jiru, "Danji shijie: Beiyue xin zhanlue de shizhi", (Unipolar

World: Essence of NATO's new strategy), *Shijie Zhishi* (World Affairs), (Beijing), No. 10 May 16, 1999, pp.10-13 and Yan Xuetong, "Zhongguo mianlinde zhanlue anquan huanjing", (China's Strategic Security Environment), *Shijie Zhishi*, No. 3 February 1, 2000, pp. 8-10.

9. Xiong Guangkai, *International Strategy and Revolution in Military Affairs*, (Qinghua University Press, Beijing, 2003), pp. 145-46; "PLA Official Xiong Guangkai Outlines China's Anti-Terror Policy at Munich Confab", *Xinhua*, February 9, 2003, in FBIS-CHI-2003-0209, February 10, 2003, and Xue Feng, "International Community Steps up Efforts in Struggle Against Terrorism", *Liberation Army Daily*, July 14, 2003, in FBIS-CHI-2003-0714, July 17, 2003.

10. For the trend setting work on this issue, see Lester R. Brown, *Who Will Feed China? Wake-up Call for a Small Planet*, (WW Norton and Company, New York, 1995) and Thomas M. Kane and Lawrence W. Serewicz, "China's Hunger: The Consequences of a Rising Demand for Food and Energy", *Parameters*, 31, Autumn, 2001, pp. 63-75.

11. This assessment is based on Kang Xiaog uang's estimates as cited in Yu Xiaoqiu, "China" in Paul B Stares, Ed., *The New Security Agenda*, (Japan Centre for International Exchange, Tokyo, 1998), pp. 203-21.

12. See Jacob Townsend, "China and Afghan Opiates: Assessing the Risk", Silk Road Paper, June , 2005, (Central Asia-Caucasus Institute *Silk Road Studies* Program, Uppsala University, Sweden) accessed at <http://www.silkraodstudies.org>.

13. "SCO to build anti-drug belt around Afghanistan", *Xinhua*, June 12, 2006 at <http://news.xinhuanet.com/english/2006-06/12/content_4684603.htm > [accessed on January 24, 2007].

14. See for the relevant report at <http://www.csis.org/pacfor/cc/993Qchina_skorea.html.

15. Guo Nei, "New terror network attacked Chinese workers", *China Daily*, June 14, 2004 at <http://www.chinadaily.com.cn/english/doc/2004-06/14/content_339131.htm > [accessed on September 28, 2007].

References

1. It was argued that the US Administration had opened secret negotiations with the CCP leadership and, if need be, withdraw support to Taiwan or even contemplated of replacing Chiang Kai-shek by an UN-led trusteeship. Nevertheless, it was noted that China signed the friendship treaty with the USSR that shelved any normalisation of

relations between the US and China and thus beginning Cold War in East Asia. See Richard C. Thornton, *Odd Man Out: Truman, Stalin, Mao , and the Origins of the Korean War,* (Brassey's Inc., Washington DC, 2000) and "The Cold War in Asia", *Cold War International History Project Bulletin*, Issues 6-7, Winter 1995/1996.

2. See Li Baojun, Dangdai Zhongguo waijiao gailun *(Introduction to Contemporary Chinese Foreign Policy)*, (Beijing: Chinese People's University Publication, Beijing, 1999).

3. See for Jiang Zemin's speech to the 14th Party Congress, *Beijing Review, Vol.* 35 no. 43 October 26- November 1, 1992 p.26. See also Xu Xiaojun, 'China's Grand Strategy for the 21st Century' in Michael D. Bellows ed., *Asia in the 21st Century: Evolving Strategic Priorities*, (National Defence University Press, Washington DC, 1994), p. 24.

4. See David Shambaugh, 'The insecurity of security: The PLA's Evolving Doctrine and Threat Perceptions Towards 2000', *Journal of North-east Asian Studies,* Vol. XIII no. 1, Spring, 1999, pp. 3-25.

13

India, the US and Emerging Security Challenges

Prof. Chintamani Mohapatra

What is a threat? Does threat exist? Does it remain a threat after it materializes? Or, does it appear and disappear only in the mind? Is it something material or perceptual? Are perceptions real? Is reality only perceptual? Is threat a perceived phenomenon or is it externally generated? Do the strong threaten the weak or can it be the reverse as well?

These are difficult questions. Answers are not easy. Arriving at universally acceptable answers are almost next to impossible. But one thing is clear. Conceptualizing threat is a mind game at practically all levels of analyses-individual, societal or even at international. In other words, as in the case of an individual, so in the case of national security analysis, existential facts can be interpreted as threats or opportunities. Moreover, creation of threats can be a political-diplomatic instrument to protect or promote certain policy. Thus what is considered a threat by one can be interpreted as a defensive reaction by the other. Significantly, threats are a perennial and ubiquitous phenomenon. They have been there in all ages, they have been there all over and they have been there for every one—from an invisible insect to now extinct dinosaurs to the most intelligent of animals called human beings. In the human society, the rich and the poor, the ruled and the ruler and the strong and the weak all have their threat perceptions and all seek to address those threats and seek security in a universe where security is always the goal and insecurity is forever an existential experience.

It is in this background that the current paper will attempt to understand the evolution of Indo-US relations to address each other's threat perceptions and security policies over the decades. The paper begins with a flashback to Indian and American threat perceptions and the resultant respective policy formulations and policy executions and then moves on to the present and then to a brief trend analysis of the future of Indo-US relations.

Divergent Threat Perceptions

When India emerged as a newly independent country in 1947, the United States had already surfaced as a new global superpower. India at this time was a brand new player on the international stage after centuries of foreign rule, where as the US had more than a century and three-quarters of experience as an independent country. Thousands of years of rich civilizational experience, a long series of foreign invasions; centuries of British colonial rule, knowledge and sentiments associated with the freedom struggle and colonial India's assigned role in world affairs; harsh socio-economic realities confronting the country; violent and bloody division of the country along religious lines and several historical and socio-religious concepts, such as truth, non-violence, tolerance, peace and peaceful co-existence among diverse cultural entities shaped the threat perception of Indian political elite.

On the other side, the US threat perceptions were shaped by a relatively a long history of American experience born out of the European wars, American role in the Hemispheric affairs, First and Second World Wars and the perceived destiny of the country influenced by concepts and doctrines, such as Social Darwinism, Manifest Destiny, Monroe Doctrine, Free and Open Trade and a missionary zeal to shape the globe after the American image.

What were the major threats faced by India at the time of its birth and subsequent years? The diverse social geography, uneven economic landscape and a hostile security environment born out of the violent partition of the country made India aspire for an end to imperialism, decolonization at the global scale and creation of an equitable international political and economic order. Such a global environment was considered essential by India to ensure human security at home. In the domestic domain, the Government of India adopted a developmental model that did not discourage private industrial growth but simultaneously emphasized economic regulations, social justice and public welfare measures. Indian development model certainly rejected the US policy of free trade and of markets, while selectively accepting the US-led liberal international economic institutions. The Congress Party-led Government of India also kept at bay the Soviet and Chinese model of developments. But India's foreign policy goal was threatened by the spreading Cold War tension between the US and the USSR. The United States perceived a direct danger to its global interests, economic philosophy and political ideals from the Soviet foreign policy. While there was expectation in Washington that a liberal, democratic country like India, in need of huge economic assistance, would seek closer cooperation with the US, India preferred to stay non-aligned. From the initial years of the evolution of a bipolar global economic and political power structure, India sought an alternative path by employing a non-aligned foreign policy strategy as the best possible insurance policy to acquire strategic autonomy in its foreign policy decisions. Indian foreign policy establishment did not feel threatened by Communist powers, showed no signs of uneasiness over the emergence of Communist China along its borders and saw no benefit in cultivating an alliance relationship with the US. On the other hand, New Delhi expected the US to respect its foreign policy strategy aimed at maintaining strategic autonomy in a divided world. However, as expectations on both sides clashed, divergent threat perceptions prevented New Delhi and Washington to come together on a common platform to take on challenges to their respective security. At a larger systemic level in the realm of global political economy, the two countries advocated and campaigned for two different goals. The US sought to promote liberal commercialism, whereas India fought for the establishment of an equitable international economic order to correct the wide inequity and disparity in income between the industrial North and the developing South. Championing capitalist mode of production and open and free trade, the US had to come to terms with the demand for a new equation in international economic relations by the developing world led by India and a few other countries. The Soviet model was not attractive to the newly developing countries, but the Soviets saw political allies in the developing world against the US-led industrial North.

In the strategic arena, the US pursued a policy of aggressive alliance formation to contain its supposed primary threats, but India espoused non-alignment as the most peaceful alternative to steer clear of Cold War tensions. The US considered communism an evil, but India allowed the Communist Parties to participate in its democratic processes and sought to maintain cordial ties with Communist countries. In other words, the newest and the oldest democracies substantially differed in their world views, systemic preferences and threat perceptions. Secondly, as India struggled to come to terms with its regional threats from a hostile Pakistan and sought to deal with this problem bilaterally first and multilaterally later by approaching the United Nations, the US was not positively disposed towards India. It actually discovered a new potential ally in Pakistan to bolster its Cold War strategy and gave a serious blow to Indian efforts by its diplomacy in the UN and subsequently by providing direct military and economic assistance to Pakistan. Throughout the 1960s, India complained against US arms supply to Pakistan and saw its foreign threats emanating partly from the US arms supply policy. The US policy towards Pakistan was eventually instrumental in impelling India to cultivate defence and security ties with the Soviet Union. From the date of signing of the Indo-Soviet treaty of friendship and cooperation in August 1971, India came to be perceived in Washington as a chummy strategic associate of its foremost antagonist.[2] Thirdly, when the US failed to prevent the Communist Party from winning the civil war in China and became determined to contain the Communist Government in China, India found in the new China a powerful partner that could work with India to redefine the rules of the game at least in Asian affairs, if not the global ones. The Sino-Indian War of 1962 did offer an opportunity to India and the US to develop strategic convergence. But both failed in their objective. The US could not play the India card well in its containment strategy against China and India could not manage its relations with the US to bolster its defence and security capability to prevent future wars or manage existing conflicts. The temporary US support to India during the Chinese invasion of India, in fact, vanished three years later in the wake of the second round of armed conflict between India and Pakistan.

Subsequently, when the US successfully roped in China into its anti-Soviet containment strategy, India found that the US became a close strategic collaborator of its chief challenger. Fifthly, improvement of US relations with China coincided with yet another US-Indian difference over the issue of threats to international peace and security. This was the area of nuclear proliferation. The US led the efforts aimed at drawing the red line and preventing the emergence of further nuclear weapon states in the aftermath of the Chinese entry into the nuclear club. It was instrumental in crafting, negotiating and concluding the Nuclear Non-proliferation Treaty in 1968 and without doubt India was one of the chief targets of the new non-proliferation politics. The US sought to promote non-proliferation and viewed the NPT as an effective method to deal with the threat of nuclear proliferation; while India asserted that the NPT was a partial approach to deal with the nuclear threat to the international community and in addition was a provocation for others to challenge the discriminatory nuclear weapon power structure. As India refused to sign the NPT, conducted a peaceful nuclear explosion in 1974 and kept the nuclear weapon option open, the US erected a series of unilateral, bilateral and multilateral structures that turned the two countries into each other's principal source of threats on the issue of nuclear proliferation.[3]

Partial Convergence of Interests

When the Soviet Union collapsed, the Cold War ended, search for a new world order began; India and the US reappraised each other's bilateral policies.[4] The main American concern vis-a-vis India disappeared with the Soviet disintegration and US policymakers ceased to view India as the most powerful Third World country allied to America's principal global rival. The Soviet troops withdrawal from Afghanistan after the signing of the US-Soviet Afghan Accord, meanwhile, ended the strategic importance of Pakistan. The senior Bush Administration, in addition, cut off all American economic and military assistance to Islamabad under the Pressler Amendment in 1990, on the ground that Pakistan was pursuing a nuclear weapon programme. One of the most serious security concerns of India ended with the closing of the US-Pakistan strategic alliance and the beginning of political confrontation between the erstwhile partners.

In the post-Cold War climate, the US and India re-examined their traditional policy approaches towards each other and found that the oldest and the largest democracies can go beyond rhetoric and come together to address various threats to their respective national security. A mini-economic revolution in India in early 1990s marking the end of the license raj and robust economic growth brought new opportunities for the two countries to forge closer ties. President Bill Clinton, the first occupant of the White House in the post-Soviet global order, took steps to simultaneously build a new partnership with India by improving trade and investment cooperation and by establishing new defence and security linkages. The visit of Treasury Secretary Ronald Brown and Defence Secretary William Perry to Delhi in 1995, signified this new Clinton strategy to engage India. While Brown announced the American desire to set up an economic alliance with India, Perry successfully inked an "Agreed Minutes on Defense Cooperation." It all appeared that a paradigm shift in US-India ties was on the horizon. But it was actually an illusion. The US was of little help to India in its fight against cross-border terrorism in Kashmir. End of the US strategic cooperation with Pakistan in the 1990s also meant end of US security-related attention to the region. While pleased to see the disappearance of its main rival in world affairs, the Clinton Administration turned a blind eye to the consequences of its Afghan policy during the era of Soviet intervention. Its leverage on Pakistan declined with the imposition of the Pressler Amendment, but still the Clinton Administration acted as an uninterested bystander when Islamabad engineered the emergence of the Taliban regime in Kabul and launched a systematic low intensity conflict against India in Jammu and Kashmir. India's appeal to the US to declare Pakistan as a state sponsor of terrorism fell on deaf ears. On the contrary, the Clinton Administration branded terrorism in Kashmir as a domestic terrorism and the US Congress passed resolutions on alleged "human rights violations" in Kashmir.

The clash of Indian and American interests was sharper in the area of nuclear politics. First of all, Pakistan during this time sought to link the Kashmir issue with the nuclear issue and announced that it would abandon its nuclear weapon programme if only the US would help resolve the Kashmir issue. The Clinton Administration teamed up and made noises that Kashmir was a nuclear flash point. Secondly, Pakistan came up with a proposal to declare South Asia as a Nuclear Weapon Free Zone. The Clinton Administration enthusiastically supported this view. Thirdly, when India rejected both these contentions, the Clinton Administration located yet another proposal, considered "outrageous" in India, to "cap, freeze and roll back" the Indian and the Pakistani nuclear programmes.

While economic and broader security concerns led to a convergence of interests between India and the US, issues related to terrorism and nuclear nonproliferation injected fears and apprehensions in the relationship. The partial convergence of interests soon gave way to a temporary rupture in the relationship when India refused to sign the US-backed Comprehensive Nuclear Test Ban Treaty and then went ahead and tested six nuclear devices. The Clinton Administration acted under the US nonproliferation legislations and imposed sanctions against India creating dark clouds over the sky of bourgeoning bilateral economic and political relations.

New Paradigm of Bilateral Contacts

Enter the new millennium and US President Bill Clinton made a path breaking trip to South Asia. He brought with him a new package of proposals to alter the traditional trajectory of US engagement with India. His intention was to end the sanction regime and establish a new strategic partnership with India. Indirectly he indicated that his administration had reconciled with the nuclear fait accompli of the sub continent and that in the absence of a better alternative he would support a fresh set of proposals to build closer security and economic ties with nuclear India. He signed a "Vision Statement" with Indian Prime Minister Atal Behari Vajpayee. It clearly indicated the desire to elevate the bilateral engagements to new heights.

Clinton's new move in South Asia also underlined that the nuclear capable Pakistan was of lesser priority for Washington in comparison to India. His visit to India for five days and to Pakistan for about five hours amplified Washington's new approach. Despite the fact that President Clinton was lame duck, India accorded him a rousing reception. Little apprehension was raised in India that the US presidential election due after a few months could bring the Republican Party candidate to power and Clinton's policy could be reversed or sidelined. India actually celebrated that an American presidential visit could materialize after a gap of about two decades and hoped that President Clinton's novel initiatives to the region would be sustained by the next administration, no matter who came to power.

Clinton's successor George W. Bush turned out to be a president most friendly to India in the entire history of US-Indian relations. As a presidential candidate during the election campaign Bush could not name the Indian Prime Minister, but as the President he entered the White House, according to US Ambassador to India Blackwill, with a new "big idea" about India. By this time the Vajpayee Government, after engaging Clinton's Deputy Secretary of State Strobe Talbot in an unprecedented series of security dialogues, was determined to give new directions to the country's policy towards the United States. The keenness of the Bush Administration and the Vajpayee Government to give further push to bilateral relations was reflected in the Indian response to President Bush's May 2001, speech at the National Defense University outlining his administration's policy on missile defense. The Vajpayee Government hailed Bush's plan to work towards deployment of a missile defense shield as "technological inevitability" and endorsed it in no uncertain terms. The Indian response for a moment dazed the international community in view of its sharp contrast with the customary positions of previous governments in New Delhi to similar issues. Indian response was also in pointed differentiation with that of the Chinese, Russian and European ones. The Russians opposed it; the Chinese criticized it and the European and Asian allies of the US expressed their discomfort based on a fear of outbreak of a missile race.

However, it heralded the arrival of a new phase in US-Indian relations. The terrorist attack on the US by Al Qaeda in September 2001, was the first test of India's new approach to the US on security issues'. Unexpectedly, once again, Prime Minister Vajpayee offered India's unconditional assistance in the efforts that would be necessary to fight back the perpetrators of the 9/11 attacks. Rarely countries give unconditional offer of assistance to other countries. India did that to signal that as a victim for long of terrorist attacks it would not put conditions in tackling this menace that clearly was an emerging major threat to human civilization. It was the US that was hesitant to offer any concrete help to India in its struggle against terrorism. India calculated that the 9/11 incident was sure to alter US understanding of terrorism and thus expressed its desire to extend full support to the US in meeting this common security challenge.

Although the Bush Administration did not take the Indian offer in full, it appreciated the Indian gesture. It was essential to rope in Pakistan in the fight against the Al-Qaeda and the Taliban regime in Kabul and Pakistan's role in Kashmir made it difficult for the US to take India and Pakistan on board at the same time. While Islamabad, under the military regime of General Pervez Musharraf, was coaxed and enticed to join the coalition against the Taliban and Al-Qaeda, the US sought to pressurize Pakistan to end its support to Kashmiri terrorist groups and simultaneously work with India through a working group to strengthen the global war eforts against terrorism. Soon terrorism became a common threat and the two countries began to take several steps to bolster anti-terrorism cooperation. The Bush Administration adopted a healthy diplomatic technique to befriend both India and Pakistan so that this hyphenated relationship would not come on the way of US strategic goals. The US war on terror in South and South west Asia actually created an environment that pushed India and Pakistan to begin and sustain a process of detente in the subcontinent. The composite dialogue initiated by the two leadership and the slow and steady adoption of a series of considence building measures worked to the advantage of India, Pakistan and the US. More signsicantly, the South Asian peace process enabled the US and India to aim at forging a new kind of strategic partnership. There is little doubt that terrorist outfits persisted in their endeavours to create roadblocks. At times, India and Pakistan moved to the threshold of engaging in armed conflict, but the US-India relationship remained strong.

While terrorism, Indo-Pakistan peace process and missile defence cooperation provided the new bases for bolstering US-India security cooperation, the Next Steps in Strategic Partnership (NSSP) was announced by the Bush Administration to elevate further the bilateral relationship with India. The areas of cooperation identified under the NSSP consisted of civilian nuclear, space, dual-use technology and missile defence technology. This initiative was pursued with substantial vigour by both the sides. The change of government in India and replacement of the BJP-led NDA Government by a new coalition called UPA led by the Congress Party did not negatively affect India's innovative steps to forge partnership with the US in ground-breaking and conventionally controversial areas.

Two brand new projects that helped Washington and New Delhi to share common perceptions on security threats and search for solutions were Indo. US defence cooperation and civilian nuclear cooperation. While India did not actively participate in the coalition war against the Taliban and Al Qaeda in Afghanistan by contributing military troops, India extended its support to the Afghan Government and substantially took part in reconstruction activities in that country. And to upgrade its defence cooperation with the Bush Administration in the new milieu of the post-9/11 era established wide ranging military contacts with the United States. This included military-to-military exercises consisting of all branches of the military, joint developments of military doctrines, counter-terrorism exercises, and even defence trade. Indian Navy also escorted US ships through the Malacca Straits against pirates operating in the Indian Ocean and the US Navy extended its support to well-acclaimed Indian Navy's role in tackling Tsunami-related problems in the region.

As military contacts between the two countries expanded and the Pentagon and the Indian Ministry of Defence were able to enhance mutual confidence, the two countries signed a Defence Cooperation Framework Agreement in June 2005. This agreement removed most of the Cold War time mutual apprehensions and proved beyond doubt that the two democracies were no longer averse to defence and security cooperation to meet the emerging security challenges of the post-9/11 world order.

The following month, Prime Minister Man Mohan Singh visited Washington, D.C. and initialed a Joint Statement with President George W

Bush to establish civilian nuclear cooperation between the two countries. It truly heralded a paradigm shift in Indo-US relations. After three decades of political hostility between successive US administrations and a series of Indian governments on the issue of India's nuclear policy, a bold departure from that route was undertaken by President Bush and Prime Minister Man Mohan Singh. India that persistently refused to sign the NPT or the CTBT, conducted a series of nuclear tests in 1998 and declared itself as a nuclear weapon power and aspired to develop and deploy a nuclear triad under its minimum nuclear deterrence doctrine, was offered civilian nuclear technology cooperation by the Bush Administration.[7] It was not easy for President Bush to convince the US Congress and after a long political battle in the Capitol Hill the US legislators passed an enabling legislation—the Hyde Act—for US civilian nuclear cooperation with India.[8]

While it was not easy for President Bush to sell his nuclear deal with India, it was positively a Herculean task for Prime Minister Man Mohan Singh to convince the Indian political parties that the deal would actually bring enormous benefit to India. For three years, the Indo-US nuclear deal was debated in India to an extent all other major and minor foreign policy issues were thoroughly marginalized. The Hyde Act was an enabling legislation for the Bush Administration, but it was perceived in India as a document that could force India to compromise with its national sovereignty. A large number of opposition parties and a few constituents of the ruling UPA Government, particularly the Left Parties, forcefully contended that India would have to play a second iddle to the US under the Hyde Act, if it decided to conclude the 123 Agreement with the US to do civilian nuclear trade. Significantly, the Left Parties withdrew their support to the Government and the Government was bulldozed into facing a no confidence vote in the Indian Parliament. Of course, the UPA Government won the trust vote in the Parliament; the 123 Agreement was finally concluded by the two parties; but the Indian skeptics remained unconvinced. Although there is a change of the administration in the American White House and there may be a new government in place after the forthcoming national elections in India, it is very unlikely any effort would be made to undo the 123 agreement. The extent and scope of actual nuclear trade between the US and India would depend on future negotiations and terms and conditions set by the supplier and the recipient. The Indo-US nuclear deal has already achieved its main purpose – (a) the US Government has allowed its nuclear technology companies to do trade with India under the 1,2,3 Agreement; (b) India has ceased to be a target of the international nonproliferation regime by receiving a waiver from the Nuclear Suppliers Group of nations and signing an agreement related to safeguards with the International Atomic Energy Agency. Thus the American and international legal restrictions imposed on India since 1974 have ended.

Concluding Observations

Threats are endemic and perennial parts of international relations. Nations, large and tiny, affluent and impoverished, muscular and feeble all have their threat perceptions. As part of their endeavours to deal with their respective threats, nation states either form alliances and partnerships or become isolationists and aggressive. During the large part of the Cold War era, the US and India adopted incongruous approaches to deal with their respective security threats, as perceived by their own policy makers. While the Indian and the US policy makers never saw each other as a hostile country, India's global role by leading a large number of developing countries in forums like NAM, G-77 and the UN General Assembly often politically confronted the US interests. Likewise, the US alliance with Pakistan and strategic collaborations with China threatened Indian national security interests.

The post-Cold War global scenario begat new arrangements of relationship among nation states; and India, while not officially discarding the non-alignment foreign policy strategy, ventured to seek out a new kind of relationship with the United States that emerged as the only superpower in the world. The end of the Cold War weakened the realist school of thought and saw the ascendance of the liberal internationalists in influencing foreign policy and national security decision making in many countries, including in the United States and India. The discourse on security threats, earlier dominated by realism, focused on new sources of threats, such as small arms proliferation, spread of HIV AIDS, climate change, international crime syndicates, drugs trafficking and terrorism. It became relatively easy for India and the US to come together to address these new security threats. Although there were differences in nuances and over the details of such threats and the desirable means of tackling them, these were "low politics" area and hence less cumbersome and problematic.

The Indian decision to overtly go nuclear, the unprecedented performance of the Indian economy, and India's responsible and restraint behaviour in the face of provocations, such as the Kargil misadventure by Pakistan, all altered the image of India abroad, particularly in the United States. Democratic President Bill Clinton visited an India that was widely regarded as the next significant emerging power and laid the foundation stone of a new and robust relationship. Republican President George W Bush expressed his desire to assist India's emergence as a global player and his administration persistently pursued policies that would add to India's strength. Washington's modus operandi in handling terrorism, Pakistan, Kashmir issue and the nuclear issue actually created an ambiance to solidify Indo-US bilateral relations to the point of making them two "strategic partners". It was nonetheless clear that "partnership" was quite different from "alliance". Both Washington and New

Delhi time and again sought to dispel interpretations that the two countries were marching on a road to establish an alliance relationship. India's refusal to send troops to Iraq, the US rejection of the idea of declaring Pakistan as a state sponsor of terrorism, Indian rebuff against the suggestion to end Iran-Pakistan-India gas pipeline project, and the American move to declare Pakistan as a major non-NATO member are but a few examples that insinuate that there is no alliance relationship in making between India and the US. In years to come, the US will most likely experience decline of its global influence and India will most probably extend further its already growing weight in international affairs. The American economic crisis, the Afghan imbroglio, the uncertainties in the Middle East all indicate that the abilities of the hyper power are already waning. India's economic resilience, growing military clout and rising diplomatic profile are crystal clear. What will be the nature of Indo-US engagement in the future? It will most probably grow more cordial, intense and expansive than India's relations with any other major powers of the globe today.

Endnotes

1. For a detailed account of Indo-US relations during the Cold War years, see *The Hope and the Reality: U.S.-Indian Relations From Roosevelt to Reagan*, (Boulder, Westview Press, 1992).

2. The Soviet intervention in Afghanistan met with stiff resistance from the United States. Washington turned Pakistan into a frontline state to wage an unconventional war against the Soviet troops by using the mujaheedin groups. India did not condemn the Soviet action in harsh words, but New Delhi's discomfort against foreign military intervention by friend or foe was not hidden. The US actually began an attempt to befriend India to wean it away from the Soviet Union. See a paper written by Teresa Lynn Dillon, "India and the United States: A Need for Improved Relations", (Defense Intelligence College, 1985). This can be found in the American Library, New Delhi. Another must read is H.W. Brands, *India and the United States : The Cold Peace,* (Boston, MA:Twayne, 1990).

3. An excellent research work on the nuclear issue related to India is George Perkovich, *India's Nuclear Bomb: The Impact on Global Proliferation,* (New Delhi, Oxford University Press, 2000).

4. Many think tanks in the US began to make quick assessment on the emerging India in the aftermath of the Soviet collapse and recommended improved ties with India. See, for example, "India and America after the Cold War: Report of the Carnegie Endowment Study Group on U.S.-India Relations in a Changing International Environment", 1993.

5. The performance of the Indian economy since the institution of economic reforms in 1991, India's decisive nuclear policy reflected in 1998 nuclear tests and India's handling of issues, such as the Kargil War had generated changes in the traditional image of India in the United States. See, Stephen P. Cohen, *India: Emerging Power,* (Washington, D.C., Brookings Institution Press, 2001).

6. India never conducted any military exercises with the former Soviet Union, despite signing the 1971 Treaty of Friendship and Cooperation. It began modest naval exercises with the US Navy in Indian Ocean after the end of the Cold War. But slowly the quality and number of exercises involving the navy, air force, army and special forces became more sophisticated and numerous. India also sent its air force personnel to Alaska to conduct joint exercises and its navy to the Pacific to conduct exersies with a multinational naval force, including the American Navy.

7. The Bush White House lobbied in the US Congress in favour of the nuclear deal and sought to convince the legislators that this deal would strengthen US relations with an emerging power and serve the cause of global environment as well.

8. Documents and short articles covering the debate on the Indo-US nuclear deal can be found in *India's Nuclear Debate: Indo-US Civil Nuclear Cooperation Agreement*, compiled by *World Focus*, (New Delhi, Academic Excellence, 2008).

14

India's Interests and Threat Perception in Indian Ocean: Navy as an Instrument of Foreign Policy

Prof. P.V. Rao

India's foreign and security policies were thoroughly revised following the breakdown of the bipolar system. In a world of rapidly altered geo-political scenario, India was compelled to rewrite her foreign policy objectives which emphasized a clear and conscious preference for a version of pragmatism preferred by the political leadership. Foreign policy discourse had departed from the Nehruvian paradigm which underlined a certain degree of professed idealism and dislike for *realpolitik* approach to conducting foreign relations. Early years of the Cold War breakdown had seriously engaged the Indian policy elite to give new directions to country's engagement with the rapidly changing global environment. As a result, the decade of 1990's marked changes in the "conceptual bases on which Indian diplomacy had been founded. If Nehru defined a unique foreign policy for independent India in search of its manifest destiny, the Indian leaders of the 1990s had to break out of the strait jacket to which Nehru's foreign policy ideas had been reduced." (Raja Mohan, p. xvii)

Fall of the Cold War system and its impact on Asia carried serious geo-political implications for India. India lost her close and dependable friend, the Soviet Union, while India's relations with the sole super power, the United States, were never warm, as also with the Asian powers like China, Japan and the ASEAN countries.

Broadly, India's post-cold war foreign policy was transformed to address the following objectives. Firstly, to engage the country with the Asia-Pacific region which was witnessing the shift of global political and economic power from the Euro-Atlantic to the Asia-Pacific. Secondly, India's market-driven economic strategies worked out after 1991, demanded that the country build close trade and investment synergies with those growth poles centred in the

Asia-Pacific. Thirdly, India's growing economy required regular and uninterrupted oil supplies. About 70 per cent of energy requirements are imported from foreign countries, especially the gulf. Ensuring adequate supplies of oil should be the major goal of national security planning. Energy security has become a key objective of the country's revised foreign policy objectives. Fourthly, considering that over ninety per cent of India's global trade is seaborne, ensuring the safety of sea lanes of communication (SLOCs) in the Indian Ocean was crucial to the country's maritime trade.

India's 'extended neighbourhood', a post-cold war strategic concept, devised the comprehensive framework of engaging the regions to her east and west. Regions which hitherto figured least in the country's external priorities such as Central Asia, South-east and East Asia had assumed greater and even urgent priority in the larger canvass of India's foreign policy. Extended Neighbourhood is not just an operational concept of enlarged involvement of India in new areas, but this concept had rather superceded the foreign policy values of the Nehruvian and post-Nehruvian era. A new set of values, ambitions, power equations, regions and countries became integral to the extended neighbourhood. It carved out a vision of power play and projection for 21st century India.

To accommodate foreign policy to the above objectives, India had decided to build her strategic image in Asia. India's strategic aspiration is to emerge as an Asian power and play active role in the Asian power balance. Accordingly, India is upgrading her military capabilities and projecting power in Asia. She is adopting a dual strategy which aims at bolstering the hard military power and at the same time cultivating close political, economic, energy and cultural synergies with the Asian countries. A number of bilateral and multilateral agreements are signed with the Asian countries, so much so, today there is hardly an Asian regional group in which India is not represented.

The Indian Navy (IN) has come to be regarded as an important instrument of enforcing India's interests and influence in the extended neighbourhood. It is a highly visible and vibrant military force around the Indian Ocean, a role hitherto was denied to her, given the limited involvement of the country in regional affairs. Indian Navy today is the symbol of India's power and prestige abroad, the sentinel of her maritime security interests and emissary of goodwill missions. To play such combined roles, the navy's military capabilities are heavily augmented and fire power is well oiled.

This paper will examine the varying roles assigned to the Indian Navy and the strategies it is employing in pursuit of India's foreign and security objectives in the Indian Ocean Region.

India's Maritime Objectives

India's geographical location at the centre of east-west highway across the Indian Ocean – maritime Asia-Pacific linkage with the Europe-Atlantic – imposes greater security burdens on her. Large number of military cargo and oil vessels crisscross the sea lanes of the Indian Ocean. Several regional and extra-regional powers who depend on oil and resources of the Indian Ocean Region, have regular military presence in this third largest ocean of the world. Hence India has reason to be concerned with such military developments and regional conflicts like the Iraq and Afghan wars on her security.

Several policy documents published by the Ministry of Defense (MOD) in recent years have clearly chartered the maritime dimensions of India's security and the strategies required to underwrite the military and diplomatic roles. The Indian Navy (IN), as implied above, is not just seen as a sheer military service tasked to display India's power abroad but to help promote India's image as a friendly and benign power among the Indian Ocean Region/Littorals (IOR). The three major policy documents which elaborately defined and updated the role, rationale, strategies and employment of maritime power by the Indian Navy are: *Indian Maritime Doctrine* (2004); *Freedom to Use the Seas: India's Maritime Military Strategy* (2007); *Indian Maritime Doctrine (2009)*. These public documents charter the vision and policy-framework for IN's growth, maritime political and diplomatic role, strategic plans and the challenges which the naval forces should be prepared to encounter. Explaining the IN's role, Admiral Suresh Mehta, former chief of the IN said :

"The Indian Navy is the primary maritime means by which the state ensures the use of sea for its own purposes, while at the same time ensuring that others do not use it in a manner prejudicial to its interests. The Indian Navy by virtue of its capability, strategic presence and robust presence in the Indian Ocean Region (IOR), can be the catalyst for peace, tranquility and stability in the IOR. It can be used to engage other maritime nations and extend our hand of friendship and co-operation. Also it can act as a strong deterrent to prevent conflict, or to respond, should it become inevitable." (Freedom to Use Seas, p. iv).

The above statement combines various tasks the IN is expected to undertake in defence of the country's overall maritime objectives. It has to act as the instrument of India's foreign policy interests overseas, deter hostile countries and forces threatening the country's security by projecting its military power, play a pro-active role in ensuring the freedom of navigation or what the naval people would like to call good order at sea. At the same time the IN has to cultivate friendly relations with other coastal states of the Indian Ocean through naval diplomatic means and help them in times of maritime disaster.

Successive policy documents and statements by responsible naval personnel have been emphasizing the multitude of activities the country's naval forces are designated to undertake. This kind of functional approach is a departure from the conventional responsibilities which meant that the IN, like any other navy, is concerned with ensuring the country's maritime security from military threat or attack from an adversary.

But, the nature of maritime threats that a littoral country in the Indian Ocean Region (IOR) is encountering today is far more complex compared to the previous decades. The sheer complexity of combat and non-combat forces – terrorism, piracy, drug-trafficking, arms trade, illegal migration - that endanger the security of a coastal state has grown so much in their frequency and intensity that on a comparative level contemporary IOR state is more threatened by non-combat or non-state forces than the state actors. No single coastal state and its naval forces can effectively counter these non-conventional threats to their maritime order and peace. In other words, non-combatant and benign (peaceful) utilities of naval power are in greater evidence today than in previous centuries. (P.V. Rao, "India's Naval Diplomacy")

Recognising such combat and non-combat security scenarios, the IN's missions of activity are broadly enumerated as follows. *Military missions* which include conventional and strategic nuclear deterrence against regional states; deter extra-regional powers against India's security interests; exercise sea control in Arabian Sea and Bay of Bengal as well as at the entry/exit points of the IOR ; provide security to country's coastlines and offshore assets. *Diplomatic missions*: using navy as an effective instrument of India's foreign policy; develop maritime partnerships to gain confidence of IOR littorals ; contribute to UN peacekeeping forces. *Constabulary* such as regular surveillance of the country's maritime zones and extended neighbourhood; and lastly, *Benign missions* which include providing humanitarian aid, disaster relief and hydrographic services to littoral states. (*Indian Maritime Doctrine* 2004, pp.100-103)

India's Maritime Strategy

Maritime strategy is the coastal state's perspectives of the ocean, its plans to use and conserve maritime resources and its preparedness to face military threats from the sea. Though maritime strategy is generally understood as the military plans of a littoral power to counter threats to its national security objectives, the concept also suggests a more broader and long-term approach of a country to harness the resources of the ocean to the economic, energy, scientific and technological purposes. In fact, maritime strategy is a dynamic one hinged on the changes in maritime environment, neighbourhood relations, power balance on the seas and progress in the exploration and exploitation of ocean resources. The third UN Law of Sea (UNCLOS), for example, has significantly changed the peacetime strategy of a country's maritime strategy as the new sea law regime added large ocean spaces to the maritime sovereign jurisdiction of a coastal state. In political sense, the sudden collapse of the Soviet Union and its subsequent withdrawal from the Indian Ocean geo-politics had demanded a thorough reorientation of the maritime strategies of the Indian Ocean countries including those of Indian.

Maritime strategy, in military sense, is a county's blueprint for extension of its naval activities on the seas around and away from its littoral domain. It is the coastal state's assessment and expression of its response to the maritime environment around it, its threat perceptions and plans to meet such threats. As well summed up by Geoffrey Till, a renowned maritime scholar, maritime strategy involves, "a set of ideas and beliefs about the importance of power at sea, about what nations have to do in order to increase and defend it, and what happens when they lose it."

Maritime strategy also reflects a country's nature of aspirations and level of naval deployment on high seas. It defines a coastal state's planned extension of its naval arm in pursuit of its political objectives, employment of naval force in peace and war times, their operational tasks and regions of deployment. India has chosen a time span of fifteen years to draw her maritime strategy in the Indian Ocean.

Above mentioned official documents have periodically defined and updated India's naval strategic perspectives and operational doctrines. They have clearly articulated the political imperatives of India's extended naval presence throughout the IOR and the need for an expanded naval power. Following is one such statement underlining the political rationale of India's maritime strategy for the next decade and so.

"The maritime strategy recognized that the major task of the Indian Navy during the 21st Century will be to use warships to support national foreign policy. During the long years of peace, we need to project power and show presence; catalyze partnerships through our maritime capability; build trust and inter-operability through joint/combined operations and international maritime assistance. The strategy also highlights the Indian Navy's role in helping to maintain peace and tranquility in the IOR and in meeting the expectations of our friends when needed." (*Freedom to Use the Sea,* p. 10)

Almost in literal sense, IN today is thoroughly engaged in advancing the country's political objectives, sea power projection and naval partnerships. The geo-political rationale for employing the national naval forces is explained in terms of "the shift in global maritime focus from the Atlantic-Pacific combine to the Pacific–Indian Ocean region," and, geo-economically too the centre of gravity "is shifting from the North-America–Western Europe axis to the North America-Asia Pacific rim, with Japan, China and the Asian Tigers looming large in global economic deliberations." Such global shifts in political and economic power hence provide India, located centrally in the IOR and rising economically, with enough logic to stake her legitimate role in the region's power dynamics. And the IN is mandated to carry the responsibility of demonstrating the country's intent and power through its maritime diplomacy.

Moreover, India is worried about the rapidly growing maritime threats to freedom of seas in the IOR and the increase in the presence of extra-regional powers in the region. Since all the major sea-based threats are located in the Indian Ocean – terrorism, piracy, WMD proliferation, etc. the region has become the obvious foci of naval military deployments by the concerned states, in particular by the extra-regional powers, to ensure the safety of Sea Lines of Communications (SLOCs). Such maritime presence in the Indian Ocean has far surpassed the deployment of foreign naval forces during the cold war years. The series of threats to peace, beginning with the first gulf war, their growth in frequency and violence ever since and Western strategic responses to counter these threats, had drawn in the maritime combat forces of highest sophistication into the region which had given "extra regional navies an unparalleled situational awareness and an ability to influence operations in the Indian Ocean Region (IOR.)" (*Freedom to Use the Seas*, p. 41) India therefore has strong reason to be worried about such disturbing scenario and draw necessary naval plans to face threats to her national interests.

Unlike in the past decades, IN has declared that the country's "maritime vision for the 21st century must look at the arc from the Persian gulf to the straits of Malacca as a legitimate area of interest." (*Indian Maritime Doctrine*, 2004). Accordingly, IN has brought under its strategic penumbra, the IOR west encompassing the Persian Gulf, Arabian Sea, Red Sea; eastern and southern African rim; central Indian Ocean basin including its islands and the Southern Ocean skirting the Antarctica; to the east areas beyond the Malacca straits stretching up to the Philippines and South China Sea. Plainly speaking, IN's pervasive presence across the Indian Ocean Region symbolizes India's new strategic vision and ambition. The pronouncement of extended strategic interests in Asia is meaningless unless supported by a matching and mobile instrument of state power. The IN fits the task.

The IN today is receiving unprecedented budgetary support to meet its force modernization programmes. IN's augmented military strength includes 140 war ships, 1 aircraft carrier, and 16 submarines. The proposed Ship Building Programme plans 185 ships for IN by 2017. Another aircraft carrier, in addition to the present *Vikrant* bought from Russia called *Adm. Gorshkov*, renamed as *Vikramaditya*, is being refitted to suit Indian requirements and is expected to enter the IN's formidable fleet soon. The navy's military doctrines have been substantially revised to bolster its sea power and reach in the Indian Ocean. The IN was criticized during eighties for being one of the "few major navies which first acquire hardware and then thinks about how to use it." It meant that the country's naval force lacked a doctrine and strategy (Adm. Arun Prakash, *From the Crow's Nest*, p. 97) Hence the current effort to provide it with a clear military vision and strategy. IN's redefined conventional and nuclear deterrence are the primary strategies of denial and punishment, capable of convincing a potential enemy of unbearable costs if a military or nuclear attack is contemplated against India. *The Indian Nuclear Doctrine*, which was worked out following the 1998 nuclear tests, is a composite doctrine designed to provide nuclear deterrent capacity to the country's three defense forces, Army, Air force and Navy. The "primary military objective for the IN is to deter any military adventurism against the country, including intervention in India's affairs and subversive strategies against our national interests.....The ways and means of deterrence by the IN would include developing a sea-based second-strike capability." (*Indian Military Doctrine,* 2009, p. 92) The imperative need to equip the IN with a credible deterrent military capability to counter the other naval powers and maintain naval power balance in the Asia-Pacific is the recurring theme in the Indian naval military discourse today. Of course, the Maritime Doctrine, as spelt out in 2004, also did not fail to invite a few dissenting reflections like the one from a formal admiral who thinks that the Doctrine "would have made better sense if its formulation had flowed from an overarching national or defense perspectives," and moreover, "it does not specify how specific operations will be conducted but rather, what operational activities will be necessary and must be catered for." (Premvir Das, p. 87)

It may be pertinent here to recall that much before the end of the Cold War, IN had been thoroughly modernizing its conventional capabilities by adding the latest available military hardware to its armory. In fact, "it had been the Navy's overriding priority to be as contemporary as possible in technology. Between 1976-1990, the growth of the IN was "extraordinary," and though it received lesser budgetary allocation compared to its counterparts, army and air force, the IN "was able to stay abreast of other navies in naval propulsion, weapon, sensor and computer technology." Naval military acquisitions during this period almost matched those of the navies of supplier countries. (Hiranandani, *Transition to Eminence, the Indian Navy 1976-90*, Lancer, 2004, p. xx). The main reason for such expansion was the Indian government's decision to strengthen the country's sea power following the US gunboat diplomacy against India in support of its loosing ally Pakistan in the December, 1971, Bangladesh liberation war. What distinguishes this phase from the current post Cold War era is in giving a well-defined strategic vision to the naval forces by endowing them with conventional and nuclear deterrent capability.

In augmenting its military capabilities, IN has been procuring naval combat vessels and equipment from conventional sources like Russia, which had been the largest supplier during Cold War years and continues to be so and the United States, whose strategic partnership with India mandates as the second largest provider of naval armory, and other countries including France and United Kingdom. While outsourcing its requirements from foreign countries, IN has also greatly increased the domestic base to produce military capabilities to attain self-reliance so much so that it is "one of the largest and most significant indigenous production capabilities in the developing world." Thus, the IN's major modernization and up-gradation programmes which have enormously increased its fire and fleet strength have ranked it as the fifth largest navy in the world and, "barring a war against a major power, India appears capable of securing its national interests and responding to its traditional threats through its blue water strategy." (Hiranandani)

Naval Diplomacy

In consonance with India's new range of strategic ambitions, country's naval forces are actively engaged in peacetime diplomacy. It involves projecting India's sea power by showing her flag around the IOR, gaining littoral friendship and confidence through naval goodwill missions, offering disaster relief and sharing the country's naval expertise with the other coastal states. Naval diplomacy, simply speaking, is "concerned with the management of foreign policy short of the actual employment of forces." (Ken Booth, *Navies and Foreign Policy*) Naval diplomacy is a combined display of the country's hard and soft power endowments overseas in national interest. While hard power accounts for the navy's military capabilities including its deterrent capacity, nuclear power, warship mobility, submarine arm and naval military exercises, soft power is the use and sharing of naval skills and technologies with willing littorals to build friendly bridges.

Major Asian powers today are actively encouraging their soft power skills to gain regional confidence and friendship. China has excelled in invoking this skill in the Asia-Pacific and Africa by offering soft loans, credit lines, trade concessions, technical know-how and many such concessions. Though India has realized the importance of soft power in her diplomacy, she is lagging behind much despite sufficient potentialities in this regard. In maritime parlance, soft power means offering military training to the naval personnel of other maritime powers, giving naval aid, sharing naval military technologies, building maritime infrastructure, helping in hydrographic surveys, rescue and relief assistance to countries and ships in distress, etc. Indian Navy today is offering all these peacetime services to the IOR littorals. Geoffery Till has captured rightly the IN's current strategy of building synergies with other navies in the following words:

"(This) maritime consensus-building can be developed by ship visits, fleet reviews, joint procurement and combined exercises. India is well along this track in this 'age of engagement' and its 'look east policy' ... has conducted a series of important exercises with locals and outsiders and has also participated in patrols in the waters off Southeast Asia." (Geoffery Till, p. 208).

IN had chosen naval peacetime goodwill missions to the South-east Asian countries immediately after the end of the cold war. Primarily the IN carried the strategic message of engaging itself in the void left by the withdrawing Soviet Union, and also counter the growing Chinese involvement in the region. In fact, India's Look East policy, which aimed at closely engaging the country strategically and economically with the dynamic Asia-Pacific region, chose the navy as its instrument. Beginning with early nineties, defence and naval cooperation agreements were signed with Malaysia, Thailand, Singapore, Vietnam and others in the region. Cold war suspicions by Southeastern neighbours about an 'expansionist Indian navy' were relaxed and a demonstrated willingness to accord the IN a positive role in the region was displayed by them. A well-informed South-east Asian scholar, GVC Naidu, claimed that the IN was responsible for opening the initial channels of communication with the Southeast Asian countries and that its Confidence Building Measures (CBM) formed the basis of India's Look East policy. (G.V.C. Naidu, p. 7).

The IN had also initiated the multinational naval exercises, beginning with the *Milan* in 1995. This biennial naval conclave in the Andaman & Nicobar islands (AN) was a true naval initiative, without a precedent. *Milan* is not just an Indian initiative, but it is the first Indian Ocean attempt to assemble the regional navies on a common platform. For India it is a notable diplomatic success in the sense that the participating countries, increasing in their number, had displayed confidence in Indian regional maritime role and leadership. India's strategic objective of expanding her influence into the Asia-Pacific cherished by the Look East policy has borne results. And the Indian Navy can rightfully take the credit for this positive diplomatic outcome. The *Milan* tradition was extended to gather a wider fora of international naval forces. Thus the International Fleet Review (IFR) hosted by the IN in 2001, off the Bombay coast, included almost all the navies of the IOR.

A maritime power possessing strong naval and oceanic capabilities can employ them for diplomatic purposes by lending relevant maritime services to other littorals. IN has been lending maritime services such as conducting hydrographic surveys to Indonesia and Oman; disaster relief to the 2004 tsunami victims of Sri Lanka, Indonesia and Maldives; and naval training programmes to personnel from Singapore, Maldives, and some African countries. IN has also deployed its forces to offer security to the US high value cargo in the Malacca Straits and offered security to the OAS summit in Mozambique in 2004. These peacetime services are the currency of gaining influence and prestige overseas and the IN is exploiting its soft power tactics to the hilt. Justifying the diplomatic motives behind IN's immediate response to the tsunami-affected countries, unnamed Indian naval officials were heard saying that "we have proved that navy can be used as a diplomatic instrument in support of our political and geo-strategic objectives." (David Scott, p. 15)

IN recently had set up a Directorate of Foreign Cooperation (DFO) at naval headquarters with the objective of promoting goodwill and coordination of peacetime relations with the littoral countries. DFO hosted at Delhi, the Indian Ocean Naval Symposium (IONS), participated by the naval chiefs of twenty six coastal powers in 2008. Pakistan, though invited, did not attend, while China though interested, was not invited. IONS was a unique exercise with no such previous initiative by any other regional country in the past. There hardly had been a forum so far which brought the naval leadership of the IOR countries on a single platform with a view to debate issues of common maritime security concern to the region. IONS had accomplished such a task, in an atmosphere of comeradari and consensus. It was not intended to be a onetime event but a 'movement' periodically to be making rounds around the IO littoral countries. In fact, the second IONS was held in 2010 in one of the Arab littorals. Implicitly the IONS initiative was a recognition of Indian Navy's leadership role which demonstrated its sheer ability to mobile regional navies, not known for security consensus, toward a cooperative ideal. It was a bold effort in constructively engaging the regional navies in cooperative security. Undoubtedly, IONS also added to the growing stature and prestige of the IN, a fact which the participating as well non-participating countries like Pakistan could not fail to take note of. "Successful naval diplomacy depends not only on ships at sea," in Ken Booth's words, "but also on the skill of the country's diplomats and businessmen onshore." IONS symbolized this.

Naval Strategic Partnerships

While maritime strategy is to provide a broader framework of a country's naval engagement in a given maritime region and environment, naval strategies are the more specific plans of defining the navy's activities, its operational doctrines, nature of building relationships with foreign navies to advance the country's overall foreign policy interests. Naval strategies lay down patterns of relationships the country's naval forces should build with others to serve the specified strategic interests. As mentioned above, the IN since the nineties, has been actively building strategic relations with several Asian maritime powers both in the east and west. Such partnerships have extended into the eastern hemisphere with countries like Japan and South Korea. But the most significant of the IN's strategic relationship is with the United States Navy

(USN) which is part of the broader Indo-US cooperation in Asia. In fact, Indo-US maritime strategic partnership has added a newer dimension to the Asian security framework and both have been working together to draw more Asian powers like Australia, Japan, Singapore and Vietnam to give a multilateral basis to such framework.

China is at the core of the Indo-US naval partnership as both share the common perception that rising China and her increasing presence in the Indian Ocean is a challenge to the Indian and American interests in the region. The Chinese People's Liberation Army Navy (PLAN) has been actively moving around the Indian Ocean littoral countries ranging from South-east Asia to the gulf region and Africa in west Indian Ocean. A series of naval facilities, though not bases like the USN, have been obtained by the PLAN from some of the IOR countries. In other words, China is allegedly building a 'string of pearls,' a strategic euphemism for the Chinese drive to encircle India through closer political and military ties with India's neighbours. Such Chinese strategic behaviour of active involvement in the IOR is offered as the chief justification for closer Indo-US strategic comraderie to counter the rising Asian giant. The need to balance Chinese power is the major narrative in the Indian strategic discourse. Working with the US is seen as a compelling reason which serves the interests of both in any case. *The US Maritime Strategy*, 2007, postures combined role for the IN and USN not only in the Indian Ocean but western Pacific too. (USN, 2007). Both navies have been regularly conducting war games nicknamed *Malabar exercises* around the Indian peninsula in the Arabian Sea and Bay of Bengal.

Conclusion

There is no doubt that the Indian Navy has emerged as an important interlocutor of India's foreign policy objectives in the Indian Ocean. It has succeeded in sending clear message to the regional and extra-regional powers that the country should no more be seen as reactive to the regional geo-political developments as was its practice during Cold War years, but that it had chartered a definite political agenda of playing active role in Asia's security. India's Look East policy, unveiled almost soon after the advent of the post-Soviet era, testifies to such doctrinaire approach to India's blueprint of active engagement with the Asia-Pacific region. As the maritime representative of India's enlarged role in Asia the IN to a larger extent had so far fulfilled satisfactorily the country's expectations about its role. Its, "confident, competent and visible maritime presence has served to build stronger relations and demonstrate an 'abundance of empathy' to the many nations which it has come into contact. Its emphasis on international cooperation has significantly contributed to its overall political objectives...." (Daniel Rahn, p. 39)

Among the IN's major diplomatic achievements since the waning years of the previous century are its commendable job in shedding the fears of Southeast Asian countries of Indian 'naval expansionism,' entertained by them in Cold War years. Countries like Malaysia, Indonesia and even far off Pacific power, Australia, shared the apprehension about a rising Indian Navy capable of threatening the Asian regional security order. Fortunately, such misperception dissipated out of the Asian mind not long after the Cold War break. Thus, as early as in the first years of nineties, Malaysian prime minister Mahathir Mohammed could confidently assert that the region had no reason to be worried about the Indian Navy. Further, gradually, the regional powers represented by the ASEAN and its security forum ARF (ASEAN Regional Forum) which included the Pacific powers also preferred the IN's regional presence, as they saw it, as a balancing force against the Chinese in the South China Sea. Hence all these powers along with the Australian, Japanese and even the South Korean maritime forces are regularly interacting with the Indian naval forces. In other words, in the contemporary Asia-Pacific regional security environment, IN is well regarded as a consensual maritime force worth its role and presence.

India's maritime strategy in this period had also departed from the Cold War tradition. That bygone era marked by super power competition in the Indian Ocean, India's foreign policy emphasized opposition to extra-regional presence and building naval bases in the region as the US did at Diego Garcia. The country's naval forces, operating in a limited geo-political framework, were not involved in working with any other regional or extra-regional navy. Of course, such a non-participatory naval policy did not prevent the IN involving, on a lease basis, the Russian nuclear-powered submarine *Charlie* though returned later to Moscow. Nor the IN exercised with as many foreign naval forces as it is involved today as part of a broader strategy. Implicitly, through her public pronouncements against extra-regional involvement in Indian Ocean affairs, India preferred the region to be left to her own naval influence and management. Hence, one could notice the Indian naval involvement in regional crises such as Maldives, Sri Lanka and Seychelles.

But today, Indian naval strategy has reversed its Cold War approach and mandates the IN to enter into a network of strategic partnerships with regional and extra-regional navies. This policy reversal is surely in tune with the Indian decision to extend her influence form Red Sea to South China Sea and the navy is ordered to shoulder the task of building partnerships. In the process, it has emerged as one of the most visible and mobile naval forces in the Indian Ocean symbolizing India's power and prestige.

IN's initiatives in bringing the Indian Ocean navies on a common platform under its 'foreign cooperation' banner are well received. The In sponsored

Milan regional naval exercises in the Bay of Bengal, International Fleet Reviews off the Mumbai and Vishakapatnam coasts and the IONS – all these multilateral exercises, along with the many bilateral exercises, are symbolic of cooperative diplomacy, a strategy gaining wider regional attraction for its peace dividend. No other regional maritime power in the Indian Ocean in the past had managed to assemble regional naval leaders and their forces into a common assembly as the IN did. Such naval diplomatic initiatives have certainly served to convey the message that the IN is a major as well as a responsible naval force in the region. Concurrently it also enhanced India's image as a growing and responsible power.

REFERENCES

C. Raja Mohan, *Crossing the Rubicon, The Shaping of India's New Foreign Policy*, (Viking, New Delhi, 2003).

Indian Maritime Doctrine (2004), Integrated Headquarters, Ministry of Defence (Navy), New Delhi.

Indian Maritime Doctrine (2009), (Integrated Headquarters, Ministry of Defence (Navy), New Delhi).

Freedom to Use the Seas: India's Maritime Military Strategy, (Integrated Headquarters, Ministry of Defence (Navy), New Delhi, 2007).

P.V. Rao, "India's Naval Diplomacy", *CNW Annual Journal*, College of Naval Warfare, Mumbai, 2008.

"*International* maritime trends and Indian Ocean in 21st century," *Journal of Indian Ocean Studies*, August 2001.

Admiral ArunPrakash, *From the Crow's Nest*, (Lancer, New Delhi, 2007).

Admiral Premvir Das, "India's Maritime Doctrine: the good news and the bad news," *Indian Ocean Survey*, Vol. 2, no.1, 2006.

Ken Booth, *Navies and Foreign Policy*, (Holmes & MEIER Publishers, New York, 1979).

Vice Admiral GM Hiranandani, *Transition to Eminence, the Indian Navy 1976-90*, (Lancer, New Delhi, 2004).

G.V.C. Naidu, "India and South-east Asia," *World Focus,* Vol. *25,* no.9, September 2007.

David Scott, "Indian 'footprints' in the Indian Ocean: Power Projection for the 21st Century," *Indian Ocean Survey*, Vol. 2, no.2, July-December 2006.

Daniel Rahn, *Unlocking Indian Maritime Strategy*, (Naval Postgraduate College, California, 2006).

15

India's Changing Threat Perception from West Asia

Prof. A.K. Pasha

Jawaharlal Nehru was one of the first major Asian leaders who identified the implications of European imperialism and set about to work for Asian identity, development and cooperation. It is in this context one should see Nehru's initiative to organize the first Asian Relations Conference in Delhi at Indian Council of World Affairs, Sapru House, in March, 1947, in which, during the inaugural speech, he fervently pleaded for Asian unity, cooperation, solidarity and identity. Nehru pinpointed the strategic role of Asia in global politics in, what he called, the 'atomic age'. The idea of 'Asiatic Federation' was necessary. He "announced the arrival of Asia on the world stage." Later, Nehru declared, "…the world is something bigger than Europe… Asia counts in World Affairs. Tomorrow it will count much more than today."[1] Nehru opposed the western backed military alliance systems. He was opposed to aggression against Egypt by Israel by England and France in 1956 and assured Naser of India's full support. He was opposed to the US Secretary of State John Foster Dulles's strategy of Collective Security through military pacts. He proposed the concept of collective peace. He proposed the Panchshila or five principles of peaceful coexistence. The 1955 Bandung Conference was a milestone.

New Directions in India's West Asia Relations

The Bangladesh crisis and the Indo-Pak war in 1971 had a major impact on India's ties with West Asia, as Pakistan sought to get closer to the Arab States. With great skill, India managed to convince Saudi Arabia and other Arab and Muslim leaders about its desire to live in peace with Pakistan and respect its territorial integrity. The 1972 Shimla agreement and the release of Pakistani POWs helped the atmosphere as Saudi Arabia's concern for Pakistan's integrity had become a major issue. Moreover, the new Egyptian President Anwar Sadat's preoccupation with the liberation of Sinai from Israeli occupation and his growing friendship with Riyadh, as also mounting differences with

Moscow, constrained him to follow a policy of "neutrality" and "passive posture" towards India on the issue. Egypt's posture during the 1971 crisis in the sub-continent brought home to India the harsh reality of little to choose between the so called progressive and conservative Arabs in their stand towards such a crucial issue affecting Indian security.[2] In the light of new regional developments, India had to reorient its policy from one of heavy reliance on Cairo to other power centers which had emerged in the region particularly Iraq, Algeria, Libya, Iran and the Arab Gulf monarchies. Iran continued to give diplomatic and political support to Pakistan after the latter's defeat and division in the Indo-Pak war of 1971. The dismemberment of Pakistan was perceived by the Shah as part of a larger conspiracy aimed at Iran. Subsequent developments like Soviet-Iraqi friendship treaty signed in April, 1972, the overthrow of the monarchy in Afghanistan (of Zahir Shah) in July, 1973, and the secessionist movements in Baluchistan and Sind provinces of Pakistan confirmed the Shah's fears about Soviet attempts to encircle Iran. It must be mentioned that notwithstanding Iran's resistance to Pakistan's pressure to activate the CENTO and provide a legal and institutional basis for its clandestine assistance, revealed Iran's desire to keep contacts with India. Moreover, Iran refused a Pakistani request for US made planes on the premise that Pakistan could not provide sufficient logistical support[3].

Israel's refusal to withdraw from occupied Arab lands compelled Egypt and Syria to launch a surprise military attack on Israel on October 6, 1973. They crossed the Suez Canal and the Golan Heights respectively. The October war came as a rude shock to the US. Coupled with this was the oil embargo by OPEC members on US and its allies who supported Israel. Soon, Dr. Henry A. Kissinger threatened the Arabs of a US military occupation of the oil rich Gulf region if they tried to "strangulate" western economies. At the same time, he embarked on the shuttle diplomacy and brought about temporary peace between Israel, Egypt and Syria. India supported the Arab military initiative. India declared that the cause of tension in the area "is due to Israeli aggression and refusal to vacate territories occupied by armed force. This intransigence on the part of Israel is clearly the basic cause leading to the present outbreak of hostilities. Our sympathies are entirely with the Arabs whose sufferings have long reached a point of explosion". India refused to call the Arab action as aggression. Justifying India's support to the Arab cause, it further said that the Arab cause was based on justice and demanded "immediate implementation" by Israel of UN Security Council Resolution 242 for peaceful solution of the Arab-Israeli Conflict [AIC]. Moreover, India's traditionally close ties with the Arabs required India to "stand by its friends in the time of their travail". The Arab states due to India's unequivocal support for the Arab and Palestinian causes assured New Delhi of uninterrupted supply of oil and treated India as a "friend". But, after the 1973 AIC, India's economic and political contacts widened especially with the oil rich Gulf States. This partly alleviated India's balance of payment situation caused by the increase in oil prices[4].

The Primacy of Gulf

The 1970's and the 1980's saw India's ties growing with Gulf states as India began to import its oil requirements from them, growing remittances to India from Indian workers, as also exports and investments became important. All these issues brought India and the GCC States closer. For India, the Gulf region in particular is important for a number of reasons. First, nearly 70 per cent of India's oil [increasingly gas as well] is imported and the bulk of it comes from the Gulf region and the demand for oil is growing at an estimated 6-8 per cent annually with domestic oil production gradually declining. India annually imported oil and oil based products to the tune of over Rs. One Lakh crores. Any disruption of oil supplies or increase in oil prices due to uncertain situation in the Gulf region has and will adversely affect Indian economy both in the short and long term. Secondly, nearly 40 lakh Indians were gainfully employed in the GCC states sent over $ 12 billion dollars as remittances annually. Not only this foreign exchange was significant but the safety and security of the workers was of prime importance to India. Thirdly, the region is important in terms of trade especially exports (about 16 percent of India's total) which fetch us valuable foreign exchange. Besides these factors, investments from the region both official and private are significant for the Indian economy. Numerous Indian companies [public and increasingly private] are engaged in lucrative joint ventures and in building various projects and are making huge profits. Finally, security and stability in the region is also significant[5].

The emergence of Janata party in 1977 had raised the question of a review in India's Arab policy. This was mainly due to A.B. Vajpayee of the Jan Sangh becoming the Minister of External Affairs, who had been a vocal critic of India's support to the "Arabs and who advocated close ties with Israel". It was during this period that Israeli leader Mosha Dayan paid a secret visit to India in August, 1977. Unfortunately for Israel, Dayan achieved nothing concrete as Prime Minister Morarji Desai refused to establish diplomatic ties with Israel unless the latter withdrew from all Arab lands. He told Dayan that if he established ties, his government would collapse. To the surprise of Israelis, A.B. Vajpayee reiterated India's traditional policy towards Arabs when he said: "there is no change in India's stand. Israel must vacate all occupied Arab territories and the legitimate rights of the Palestinian people must be restored". Since then, up to 1992, the successive Indian governments highlighted the absence of ties with Israel as an indication of support to the Arabs. West Asia's old trouble spot- Palestine-under Israeli occupation since 1967, AIC had seen the largest Arab state, Egypt, sign a Peace treaty with Israel in 1979. Soon after, in 1982 Israel invaded Lebanon to evict PLO and in the process committed atrocities against civilians and Palestinians in particular. The Palestinian Intifada broke out in later 1986 in occupied territories which led to escalation of violence from both sides. Hezbollah, Hamas, Islamic Jihad and many other Palestinian groups resorted to violence against Israel in response to Israeli repression and state terrorism. In order to neutralize this and the Intifada, the US organised the Madrid peace conference in October, 1991, and soon after saw the Oslo Peace process inaugurated in September, 1993, between Israel and the Palestinians, under which, at the end of 1998, the Palestinians were to have an independent state of their own after Israeli withdrawal under UN Security Council Resolution 242.[6]

The out break of war between two major NAM members Iran and Iraq (in September, 1980) was a cause of deep concern to India. Of particular significance to India was the fact that both were New Delhi's major suppliers of crude oil. India, as the Chairman of the NAM did try hard to find a solution of the Iran-Iraq war but without success. Non-involvement in internal or intra-regional disputes had been an integral part of India's Arab policy and it applied to Iran-Iraq as well, although, both sought India's support against the adversary which India found hard to provide. The foreign presence in the Indian Ocean area and the Gulf area increased and in seas surrounding India which assumed greater significance in the wake of the 1990-91 Iraq-Kuwait crisis.[7] This was a matter of concern.

India and Arab-Israeli Peace

The Soviet withdrawal from Afghanistan and the disintegration of USSR together with the end of the Cold War initiated a gradual but necessary change in India's policy towards the Arab world. It can be said that it was now much more realistic as well as practical in terms of its objectives. In the wake of the 1990-91 Kuwait crisis and the Madrid Peace Conference which was held in October, 1991 India decided to establish diplomatic ties with Israel on January 29, 1992, under the Congress government led by PV. Narashima Rao. Things changed dramatically after 1991 when both the Arabs and Israelis decided to sit down and negotiate their problems. Israel, over the years, emerged as a major supplier of arms to India. Egypt and the Palestinians wanted India to go slow on Israel. The Arab Israeli Peace Process suffered due to the assassination of the Israeli PM, Yitzhak Rabin. The US President, Bill Clinton, tried to salvage the situation at the Camp David Summit in July, 2000, but failed. The result was the second Intifada. This was not in India's interest as it will fuel terrorism leading to wider regional instability. This had undoubtedly allowed Islamic groups, especially Hamas, Hezbollah, Islamic Jihad and others to grow which led to use of the Israeli-Palestinian issue to resort to violence and terrorism. The assassination of Israeli PM, Rabin, on November 4, 1995, and the emergence of Likud leaders like Benjamin Netanyahu and Ariel Sharon, led to the collapse of peace with Israel. The US invasion of Iraq took place in March, 2003. Israel had bombed Iraqi nuclear reactor in May 1981 and since then Israeli policy had been to destroy Baathist Iraq which was perceived as a threat to Israeli security. The death (some call it assassination.) of Arafat in November, 2004, led to the election of Mahmoud Abbas as PLA President by Israel on January 9, 2005. Israel's refusal to withdraw from occupied Arab lands as per UN Security Council Resolutions 242 and 338 and the non-resolution of the Arab-Israeli Conflict [AIC], and Israel's opposition to the establishment of an independent Palestinian state in West Bank and Gaza was not in India's interest as it had fueled terrorism leading to wider regional instability. The time had come for India to vigorously support the creation of an independent sovereign state of Palestine at the earliest and strongly impress upon Israel to implement the innumerable UN Resolutions and peace accords signed in this connection.[8]

The continued denial of their basic right in the face of universal support and growing concern for the sad plight of the Palestinian people, was an issue, which India had to address on a priority basis. If this issue is resolved to the mutual satisfaction of both the parties, one of the root causes for the growth and spread of violence and terrorism in West Asia would have been addressed. Any delay in the resolution of the Arab-Israeli conflict had the potential to adversely affect peace, security and stability in the region with the consequent implications for India. But could India expect anything from Israel which had become the second-largest supplier of arms to India after Russia. There also existed close military, intelligence and security cooperation between the two countries?[9]

The Iran-Iraq factor

After the 1979 Iranian revolution, there was fear that it may affect a section of India's minority population especially after the inflammatory speeches were made by the Iranian leaders, and their support to Kashmiri militants but since there was no repetition of the Iranian revolution elsewhere in the region except for minor events like the Kaaba [Saudi Arabia] Mosque takeover in 1979 and the *coup* attempt in Bahrain [1981], and as the Sunni Arab governments took effective steps to check Iran, the impact on India was marginal. The Saudis gradually realized that their close ties with Pakistan need not come in the way of establishing good ties with India. Under these circumstances, King Fahd invited Mrs. Indira Gandhi to Saudi Arabia in 1982. In an interesting development in early April 1981, Mr. Eric Gonsalves, Secretary in the Indian Ministry of External Affairs, in an interview published in *The Washington Post* said, among other things, that the sale of US arms to Saudi Arabia and other Gulf States could provide these states with a false sense of security that could lead to their royal families being toppled as the Shah of

Iran. He gave the interview on the eve of Saudi Foreign Minister's visit to India. This created a ripple in India's ties with Arab Gulf monarchies.[10]

Although the Iran-Iraq war came to an end in July, 1988, the Indian government partly shared the fear of the West, in particular, the US, that Saddam Hussain would control thirty per cent of the world's oil reserves, if he were not pushed out of Kuwait. No wonder, India allowed (initially) the refueling of US military planes and went along with the sole superpower (US) at the UN.[11] Despite the Iraqi expulsion from Kuwait, defeat at the hands of US and acceptance of UNSC Resolutions, the uneasiness persisted. [12]

India's geographical proximity to the Gulf region and especially the location of Muslim countries on its borders (East-West) compels New Delhi to view its security in encouraging secular governments in the area which incidentally were under mounting pressure from a growing number of Islamic groups. It must also be noted that US-Israeli policies in the region were principally responsible for creating instability and opposition groups–secular and religious groups are increasingly using violence and terror-groups were growing. The US domination of the area through its military and naval presence, as also the control of oil resources and blind support to Israel's aggressive policies is being opposed by most Arabs. In all GCC states, pro-US policies are encouraging religious extremism and many groups are embracing violence. Such groups may resort to greater violence and terror in future not only against the US-West and Israel but also against US friends in the area. Since bulk of the Indians live and work in GCC states, some Indians are likely to be influenced due to mounting extremism preached by the Islamic groups. The large scale purchase of arms by the Gulf states would not only lead to pressure on India's defense budget but also may lead to presence of foreign military advisers especially from Pakistan in these states and probable transfer of weapons to states hostile to India. According to a recent US report, there has been a shift of focus for terrorism from West Asia to South Asia. The September 11, 1991, events in the US have strengthened the hands of Israel under the garb of combating international terrorism as it has become clear that the US has almost given a free hand to Israel to do what it wishes in Palestine especially the military occupation of West Bank and use of IDF (Israel Defense Forces) including US weapons to suppress Palestinians. Most secular Arab regimes are on the defensive due to internal challenges and India has been supporting the GCC conservative Arab regimes lately than the secular Arab regimes. For New Delhi, the fight against terrorism in Kashmir and other parts of India and in the larger context of South Asia, it needs cooperation from the Gulf States especially UAE, Saudi Arabia and Oman. In this connection, India has signed extradition treaties with the GCC States. One can argue that India cannot make much of a difference so far as the Arab-Israeli Peace equation is concerned but upgrading of ties with Israel, since 1992, has undoubtedly led to greater Indo-Israeli military and political cooperation especially under the enthusiastic support of the BJP led NDA. Muslim and other groups and parties in the region have adversely reacted to this development especially since India has traditionally maintained close ties with the Arab states. Both privately, until recently, and now publicly, growing number of political leaders in the Arab/Islamic World have also expressed concern and apprehensions about the direction of New Delhi's domestic and foreign policies: increasing–religious extremism [anti-Muslim Hindutva groups] at home and closer identification with Israel–and undue emphasis on fight against global terrorism. The BJP's [including Shiv Sena's and the larger Sangh Parivar's] communally biased policies against the Muslims [pogroms, whipping up anti-Muslim hatred and inciting violence against Muslims as in Gujarat, Maharastra and elsewhere] have led to the internal turmoil and economic disruption which has, by and large, affected the entire country. This is having an adverse impact on India's interaction with the Gulf States as political contacts, with some exceptions, [Saudi Arabia's King Abdullah and Kuwaiti Amir visited India in 2006] are declining and may isolate greatly. Moreover, Pakistan continues to paint India in dark colours at international fora, particularly the UN and the OIC, for the violation of human rights and killings in Kashmir, treatment of Indian Muslims and of India being hegemonic in South Asian affairs. The NDA government in New Delhi and its support to the BJP government in Gujarat and their short sighted policy towards minorities especially the killings of Muslims and Christians (elsewhere as well) has provided a handle for outsiders to meddle in India's internal affairs. Only a sound, secular domestic policy and vigorous support to secular forces in the Gulf region and opposition to mounting outside military interventions may prevent the spread of terrorism to India. It has also become clear that placing undue emphasis on Israeli collaboration for fighting terrorism in India is unwise, as it would send a wrong message domestically and regionally.[13]

As seen before, India has vital interests in the Gulf region, and US military adventure against Iraq would have implications both for India's domestic and foreign policies. India's support to Nasser against London, Paris and Israeli invasions of Egypt during the 1956 Suez crisis is still fondly recalled by Arabs all over the region. At the moment one gets the impression that the US wants to redraw the map of the region in order to keep the beleaguered state of Israel as a predominant unchallenged state and bring Iraqi oil under US influence. It also wants to divert American public attention from the troubled US economy. India can and should, if wiser counsel prevails, be with the people of the region and support their just aspirations for greater participation in the decision making process and on the broader issue of democratic reforms and also support their desire to see an end to Israeli-US military presence. US domination of the region is slowly elbowing India out from the strategic region as witnessed by sanctions on Iraq, [and now chaos, civil war and clear threat of disintegration] and Iran [earlier on Libya and Sudan] which has led to reduced trade, winding up of joint ventures, return of Indian workers and declining investments from these countries for sometime now. India could work with the secular and democratic forces in the region, as also some of the major world powers which have vast stakes in the region, to maintain security and stability so very essential to protect our vital interests and also to prevent the spread of violence and terrorism from this volatile region to India in future. Hence India needs to enhance its interaction with the countries to seek greater role in to enhance our energy security. As briefly mentioned earlier, India could actively encourage the process of political change and modernization because once the Arab [Gulf] regimes become democratic and responsive to popular demands, not only their legitimacy would be enhanced but more significantly their dependence on outside states especially the US would come down and this may lead to reduction in outside military and political intervention which has periodically undermined peace, security and stability in the region. Genuine political reforms would give the politically oppressed people a stake in the running of the political system as also much needed political stability and smooth transition of political power. The abundant oil resources could then be used to advance economic development so as to engage the Arab people in the process of political and economic progress. Undoubtedly for India the threat of religious extremism and terrorism from the region would be contained if this democratic process takes shape early. Along with the steps towards democratic transformation, steps to resolve the thorny AIC would also be debated, discussed, at all forums thereby allowing Arab leaders to take initiatives for meaningful steps along with serious US-Israeli steps (which are very essential). Both these steps would reinforce the momentum for change and India could then look forward to greater peace, security and stability in the Gulf region in future. If democratic reforms are not initiated in the Arab world, instability, religious extremism and terrorism could then spill over into South Asia as security and stability in both the regions are mutually interlinked through a number of factors. The most credible option to tackle this twin menaces posing a new challenge to India's composite culture, liberal democratic structures and also national security, is to adopt a political course that prevents alienation of any segment of the population–especially religious minorities-so that they do not take recourse to unlawful activities or violence. In India, certainly, the rising tide of Hindu radicalism has led to the emergence of certain Muslim radical groups as had happened in Sri Lanka in which Israel also had a hand.[14]

As briefly seen before, US-Israeli policies in West Asia are undermining peace, security and stability leading to periodic threats of military intervention or wars or to proping up threatened fragile regimes against their own population who are demanding political participation. Another issue which is impacting India's foreign policy in the region is the US invasion and occupation of Iraq and instability [also fear of split] in many parts of Iraq, in addition to US accusations of Iranian interference in Iraqi affairs used by the US to put pressure on Iran to cease "its ideas and programms". This has also put pressure on Indo-Iranian ties. India did a wise thing by not sending troops to Iraq at US request. The anti-US sentiments sweeping the Islamic world are likely to intensify in the coming years due to US war against some Muslim states and groups. The US-Israeli policies are spreading hatred and extremism and this is the prime reason for spreading of violence and terrorism. India with the GCC states and Iraq and other like-minded states in West Asia, should work for speedy end to US occupation of Iraq which will put an end to the atrocities committed by US occupation forces.[15]

From the Indian perspective, increasing bilateral ties with Gulf States is not only important due to trade, oil and gas, but also due to the unique proximity of these states to events in the wider West Asian region. The common political and strategic concerns of India and these Gulf states will reinforce and strengthen mutual cooperation. Given the close GCC-US relations as also growing Indo-US ties, if India in cooperation with the US and others, vitally interested in Gulf security, works out a harmonious approach which reassures the Gulf states of the need to work for peace, security and stability in the region, the outside interference could be contained, which many perceive to be the root cause of most of the problems which India and the GCC states face. The1990s saw the reassertion of regional identities in the face of external interference. The critical space is widening and it is in this context that India and GCC can create opportunities for mutual benefit and jointly prepare to meet emerging domestic and external challenges in the Gulf region.[16]

There is no need for India to place undue emphasis on bilateral relations between India and Israel as the NDA did. The United Progressive Alliance (UPA) government's common minimum program stated that "it will maintain the independence of India's foreign policy stance on all regional and global issues even as it pursues closer strategic and economic engagement with the US". But the reality is that in the context of the Gulf, US policy is actually affecting India. The American policies in the Gulf have serious implications for India. US influence over Gulf oil may in the future affect India's quest for energy security. All of this calls on India for new initiatives, dynamism and recognition of the traditionally close historical relationship with the Gulf States. India's economic ties are unlikely to suffer with these states in the immediate future, but one needs to be cautious in developing closer ties with Israel until the process of reconciliation gets under way between the Arabs, especially Palestinians and Israelis. The UPA coalition may attempt to balance the traditionally close ties with the GCC states with Israel. Security and stability in the region is linked with early resolution of the Iraq crisis, (withdrawal of US forces) establishment of a viable Palestinian state and encouraging political reforms and genuine democratization which alone can contain the growing slide towards religious resurgence, violence and terrorism leading to instability in the region.[17]

The US Nuclear Policy Review identified seven countries against which nuclear weapons may be used in the US national interest in certain cases. These are Asian countries – China, Iran, Syria Iraq and North Korea. Russia a Eurasian power is the sixth. The doctrine of the war on terror is primarily focused in Asia - from West Asia –Gulf region to East Asia which is seen as the 'theatre of war'. The US policies are formenting terrorism which India has to face. The US invasion and occupation of Iraq and Afghanistan has given new boost to Islamic groups who are resorting to violence. Shia-Sunni- Kurdish sectarianism has led to the civil war in Iraq with fears of its disintegration. Now the US is threatening Syria via Lebanon and Iran on the nuclear issue. Regime change which was applied in Afghanistan and Iraq is being threatened in Iran and Syria. This had led to greater violence in Iraq as both Syria and Iran support the Iraqi resistance which is fighting US occupation. Religious groups from Hamas, Hezbollah, Islamic Jihad, Al Qaeda and many more have emerged preaching violence to counter US – Israeli hegemony. [18]

Under the US pressure, India voted twice against Iran at the IAEA on September 24, 2005, and February 4, 2006, although the Indian PM said: "our relations with Iran, we relish a great deal. We have civilizational links. We are in the same region as Iran. And our concern with regard to Iran is that Iran is a signatory to the NPT. Iran must, therefore, have all the rights—which go with its being a member of NPT. But it has also certain obligations, which it has voluntarily taken". [19] India has also been saying that it was not in India's interest to have another nuclear weapons state in its neighbourhood but Tehran had the right to peaceful uses of nuclear energy subject to its international obligations. The announcement that the Iranian President Mahmud Ahmadinejad will be visiting India on April 29, 2008, is a very positive development. Among the bilateral issues to be discussed are the IPI (Iran-Pakistan-India) gas pipeline and the LNG (Liquified Natural Gas) contract. What the NSA (National Security Advisor), Mr. M.K. Narayanan said is most interesting: He said: "There is a great deal happening between India and Iran which is not in the public realm: what we have avoided is getting involved in any conflict diplomacy. We believe that we understand Iran better. India and Iran have civilisational and economic ties. Iran is a big country and you need to deal with them diplomatically and with erudition. Any mishandling will impact negatively on us. We have capabilities and capacities." Of course, he was referring to India's own sizeable Shia population which gave a certain vantage point to engage with Iran as our immediate neighbor with a large Shia population. India's Foreign Secretary, Mr. Shiv Shankar Menon, meanwhile criticized the idea that the US and its allies could find a solution to the Iran issue without talking to Tehran. He said: "Ultimately, you need to have in place a system in which Iran is a party to whatever you agree on her own program. Otherwise, whatever you do, any of the alternatives or the other options - sanctions, military action - none of them is a lasting solution. In fact, it is only likely to exacerbate the problem." Meanwhile, the former US Ambassador to India, Robert Blackwell, acknowledged that Iran had the potential to be a divisive issue in Indo-US relations in the second half of 2009 as the next administration moved to mount pressure on Tehran over its nuclear energy program. He said; "It is my impression that although India very much wants Iran not to acquire nuclear weapons, if it faces a binary choice of either that or an American attack on Iran it would choose to try to deal with a nuclear Iran, without the attack. But [that] is not the view that is now dominant in Washington."[20] Under the circumstances, should India watch the unfolding events in Iran like it did when the US invaded Iraq in 2003, which led to the overthrow of a secular regime. As things are today in Iraq, it has become a hotbed of religious fanaticism much worse than Afghanistan, with violence and terrorism spreading to the neighboring areas fast. Will India remains immune from all of this? Will Indian workers be safe in the GCC states? Is India's oil and gas supply from the Gulf region secure? The time has come for the Indian government to play an active role to defend its interests as also to restrain the US from repeating in Iran what it did in Iraq. Can we prevent another tragedy in our neighbourhood? From Palestine to Iraq to Afghanistan and now to Iran, the fire is getting closer to India. Not only the US role has brought uncertainties to the gas pipeline from Iran to India but also the future of India's energy security might be in jeopardy. A confrontation is most likely between the US and Iran in future as also due to the Israeli factor.[21]

There are nearly ten million migrant workers from over 100 countries in the GCC states alone in the Gulf region. More than 4 million are from India alone residing in these countries. The safety and security of these workers is a matter of utmost concern to several governments. More over, due to growing anti-Americanism in the region in the wake of Afghan, Iraqi and other developments, religious groups have become very active. This is also due to absence of democratic structures and authoritarian rule by family based systems. In future, the migrant workers may be targeted by these groups leading to problems of security and stability in the entire Gulf region. Related to this is the growing concern over the safety of oil installations especially the security of oil pipelines which criss-cross the entire Gulf region and the innumerable oil terminals all of which are high value targets for extremist groups.

We have seen how resistance groups in Iraq have been blowing up oil pipelines and terminals with huge success thereby affecting Iraqi oil exports and pushing up world oil prices. In future such groups could target oil installations in the GCC states where there is a growing resentment against local rulers for their pro-US policies in the region. This could not only affect oil production but will push oil prices higher than what they are today thereby affecting the economies of many countries. There could also be attacks on the western installations and facilities in the Gulf region by the extremist groups. US pressure on the Gulf rulers to normalize ties with Israel is also under attack by anti-normalization groups in most of these states.

As Lord Curzon once said whichever states dominates the Arab world it will be in a position to influence India appears to be coming true. Pax Americana and Israeli domination of the region should be a wake up call for India to devise new policies to prevent fragmentation, violence, wars, instability and terrorism which is spreading fast in the Arab world and whose impact will be surely felt in India as well.[22]

The ultimate goal is to contain China, Russia and India. The Indian government has been working to establish closer ties with US in this backdrop. India has core interests in the Gulf region. Security and stability in the Gulf region is of utmost concern to the Indian government. The challenge from terrorism, religious and ethnic extremism from the Gulf region is growing. India has been striving to maintain good ties with GCC states and it is in this connection one has to see Indo-Iranian ties including the visit of Mohammed Khatami as Republic Day Guest in 2003, and the recent invitation extended to King Abdullah of Saudi Arabia to be the Chief Guest for the Republic Day celebrations in 2006. In a situation where even powerful countries like China, Russia and even France and Germany cannot oppose the US, India instead has quietly decided to work with the sole super power in many areas including the Gulf region. Although many in India are aware of the US policies leading to periodic upheavals and turmoil in the Gulf region, but due to US-Pakistani ties, Kashmir, nuclear and other issues, India has to work with the US but, at the same time, maintain its autonomy as manifested by its refusal to send troops to Iraq and its determination to maintain the viability of oil pipeline with Iran, despite overt US objections and pressures. The short sighted US policies are undoubtedly generating tremendous tensions in the Gulf region but our diplomatic efforts should engage the US, Arabs, Iranians, Israeli's as well as the Turks and Kurds.

Conclusion

Until 1973, India's policy towards the West Asian region was mostly Cairo-centric and it was premised on the support to Arab nationalism,

Palestinian cause, support to Arab secular regimes as also the need to contain Pakistan's attempt to isolate India in the region as also western attempts to enlist Arab states in a western sponsored military alliance. Since the 1979 Iranian revolution, India became cautious about Islamic fundamentalism, fallout from Afghanistan and also growing Saudi-Pakistani cooperation. The prolonged Iran-Iraq war, accumulation of sophisticated weapons and rise in oil prices were areas of concern in 1980's. The 1990 Kuwait crisis and growing US military especially naval presence in the Gulf region became a matter of concern for India. The emergence of US as the pre-eminent power after the end of Cold War and the disintegration of USSR and India's own domestic economic and political problems in the period 1990-1991 made India vulnerable to US pressure. The result was India's decision to establish diplomatic ties with Israel and establishment of close ties with US. The Kashmir militancy, the demolition of the Babri Masjid and the ensuing crisis, Mumbai bombings and the killings of Muslims in communal riots - all added to complications in Indo-West Asian ties. After 1998 nuclear tests, although India's image improved in the region, it soon came to be balanced by the Pakistani tests as "Muslims feel more secure from any Israeli threats under the Pakistani nuclear umbrella". The 9/11 events brought home the issue of terrorism and violence closer to India via Pakistan's support to the Kashmir militants. India sought to invest quite a lot through ONGC (VL) to ensure its energy security, as the dependency on Gulf oil was seen as dangerous as also due to growing Indo-Israeli and US ties. Israel was also perceived as an important player to develop closer ties with the US. Although India opposed the US invasion of Iraq but it could hardly do anything to prevent this blatant aggression in clear violation of UN Charter and international law and international public opinion. Due to massive opposition from the Indian public, left, Congress and other parties, the BJP led NDA government was forced not to send Indian troops to Iraq at the behest of the US. India did achieve some "strategic autonomy" by this bold decision. Also India additionally had to confront the issue of Iranian quest for nuclear technology. But more than ever, it has become imperative to keep our lines of communications wide open and following a wise and judicious policy at home and strive to reduce the number of flash points in the Gulf region, where accumulation of sophisticated arms, lack of democracy, growth of religious extremism and availability of oil/gas and enormous wealth drew the global attention to our extended neighborhood. Ever since India's decision to establish diplomatic ties with Israel in 1992, Indo-Israeli ties of course have improved quite rapidly, especially during the BJP led NDA when there was a talk of a strategic alliance with the Jewish state. Moreover, Israeli PM Ariel Sharon visited India on September 9, 2003, and talked about his determination to act against terror and called for greater Indian support to Israel in UN and NAM fora. Although India was keen to join the Arab-Israeli peace process after the

Madrid Peace Conference (1991) but this did not survive for long. India, more recently, was also excluded from the 2003 Road Map of the Quartet. Mahmoud Abbas visited India in May, 2005, and India promised Rs. 65 crore in aid for infra-structure projects in West Bank and Gaza including the building of a library-cum-activity center at the Palestinian Technical College at Deir al Balah and one at the Al Azhar University in Gaza. India has been offering scholarships to Palestinian students for studies in Indian universities through the ICCR as well as giving training in security to Palestinian police officers. Medicine and other humanitarian aid has also been going regularly to the Palestinians. India has reiterated its support to the Palestinian struggle for self-determination and also called for an end to violence. Fully aware that the UPA government led by the Congress Party is as keen as the NDA to consolidate its ties with Israel, PLO President Mahmoud Abbas confirmed that India's ties with Israel were its own bilateral affair. Of course, the visit of Abbas could have been used to expose Israeli policies against Palestinians and a firm call to end Israeli occupation in a time bound schedule. But there is no doubt that the Palestine issue remains fairly popular in India with overwhelming support from all sections of Indians for an early end to the misery and sufferings of the Palestinians. Many Indians see the continuing violence in Palestine mainly due to inflexible Israeli policies. Although India is keen to join the Arab-Israeli peace process but it has become imperative to coordinate its efforts with Russia, China and the regional states like Egypt, Turkey, Saudi Arabia and others. But with India taking a "less strident position against Israel in the UN forums much to the chagrin of the Palestinians" and having "made considerable attempts to moderate anti-Israeli resolutions" at the NAM meetings in Durban and elsewhere, it is obvious that the expectations of many, especially in the West Asian region, that the UPA government would restore the balance it had pursued in its policy towards West Asia earlier remains largely elusive. Any contention that Israel is a major arms supplier to India and hence the government should soft pedal any firm stand against Israel will obviously affect India's credibility in the West Asian region where bulk of India's interests lie. India must continue to support wholeheartedly the Palestine cause and ensure that justice is given to the Palestinians and other Arabs struggling for freedom. Suicide bombings, lack of democracy, dependency syndrome, growing clout of religious groups especially non-state actors, narco-terrorism, maritime security, WMDs, arms race and mounting outside military interventions are matters of growing concern to India, as threats from all of these factors are bound to increase in future.

Endnotes

1. Sharma, R.R., Ed, *India and Emerging Asia* (Sage, New Delhi, 2005), pp. 12-79; See also Mahavir Singh, Ed., *Building a New Asia* (Shipra, New Delhi, 2005); Agwani, M.S., "Nehru and the Arab World", *Secular Democracy*, Nehru Number,

1976, p. 171; Agwani, M.S., "India and the Arab World" in B. R. Nanda, Ed., *India Foreign Policy : The Nehru Years,* (New Delhi , 1976), pp. 72-73, Chhabra, Hari Sharan, *Nehru and Resurgent Africa*, (Africa Publications, New Delhi, 1989); Pasha, A.K., "Asian Security: Flash Points in the Gulf Region", *World Focus*, Vol. 26, nos. 10-12, October-December, 2005, pp. 25-33; A.K. Pasha, "India and West Asia", *World Focus*, vol. 25, October-December, 2004, pp. 41-46; M.S. Agwani, "India and the Arab World", in B.R. Nanda, Ed., *Indian Foreign Policy : The Nehru Years* (New Delhi : 1976), pp. 72-3; A.K. Pasha, "Tipu's Sultan's Diplomacy in the Gulf Region", *Gulf Studies Program*, Working Paper No. 10, February 1997, CWAAS, SIS, JNU, New Delhi; A.K. Pasha, "South India and the Gulf: Trade and Diplomacy during the late 18th Century", in N.N. Vohra, ed., *History, Culture and Society in India and West Asia,* (Shipra, New Delhi,11C, 2003), pp. 237-49; A.K. Pasha, "India's Cultural Diplomacy in West Asia" in M.H. Ilias and PJ Vincent eds., *India-West Asia Relations: Understanding Cultural Interplay's* (New Century Publications, New Delhi, 2007), pp. 39-58; A.K. Pasha, "Nehru and the Crises in West Asia", *Détente*, (New Delhi), Vol. 9, no.1, May-June, 1990, pp. 4-9; "Indo-Egyptian Ties: Retrospect and Prospects", *Third World Impact,* Vol. 2, no. 20/23, November, 1991, pp. 23-27; A.K. Pasha, "Tipu's Relations with the Ottoman Empire", *Détente*, Vol. 10, nos. 4-5, January-April, 1992, pp. 6-11; A.K. Pasha, "Tipu and the Ottoman Empire", in B. Sheik Ali, ed., *Tipu Sultan: A Great Martyr,* (Prasaranga, Bangalore University, 1993), pp. 219-32.

2. G. Pant, AK Pasha and P.C. Jain, Eds, *Contemporary Iran and Emerging Indo-Iranian Relations,* (Neelkanth Publishers, New Delhi, 1996) ; See also A.K. Pasha, Ed, *India, Iran and the GCC States: Political Strategy and Foreign Policy*, (Manas, New Delhi, 2000); Bruno Tertrais, "The Iranian Nuclear Crisis: Prospects and Scenarios", in *Gulf Research Center, Year Book, 2006-07,* (Dubai), pp.271-177; A.A.A. Fayzee, *Introducing the Middle East,* (Mysore, 1970); A. K. Pasha, "Indo-Egyptian Cultural Relations: Retrospect and Prospects", in Zohurul Bari, Ed, *Modern Egypt : Culture, Religion and Politics,* (Shipra Publications, New Delhi, 2003), pp.199; see also Saryu Doshi, Ed., *India and Egypt: Influences and Interactions,* (Garg Publications, ICCR, New Delhi, 1993).

3. Riyaz Punjabi and A.K. Pasha Ed., *India and the Islamic World,* (Radiant Publishers, New Delhi, 1998); See also A.K. Pasha,*India and OIC: Strategy and Diplomacy* (Center for Peace Studies, New Delhi, 1995); "Russian Policy and the Iranian Dossier" and Anoush Ehteshami, "Iran Post-Détente?, *in Gulf Research Center, Year Book, 2006-07,* (Dubai), pp. 219-87; and 407-415; According to J.N. Dixit, the 1979 Iranian Revolution, while restoring some normalcy in bilateral ties, did not result in any substantive improvement mainly because of religious intensities and more important concerns of the Iranian Revolutionary Government. He also says India evidently did not fully comprehend the abrasive and involuted psyche of Iraq's Saddam Hussein or the passionate determination of the Iranians in his book, *India's Foreign Policy, 1947-2003*, (Picus Books, New Delhi, 2003), p. 158.

4. Bhabhani Sen Gupta, Ed., *The Persian Gulf and South Asia: Prospects and Problems of Inter-Regional Cooperation*, (South Asian Publishers, New Delhi, 1987); AK Pasha, *India and West Asia: Continuity and Change,* (Gyan Sager, New Delhi,

1999); See also A.K. Pasha, "India and the Gulf: An Overview", in Second *Netaji Subhas Commemorative Souvenir, INA Trust*, (New Delhi, 2008), pp.11-27.

5. A.K. Pasha, Ed., *Perspectives on India and the Gulf States* (Détente Publications, New Delhi, 1999); A.K. Pasha, *Egypt's Relations with Soviet Union: The Nasser and Sadat Period,* (CWAS AMU, Aligarh, 1986); A.K. Pasha, *Egypt's Quest for Peace,* (National Publishing House, New Delhi, 1994); A.K. Pasha, "Indo-Egyptian Relations: Retrospect and Prospect,' *Third Word Impact*, Vol. 11, no. 23, November, 1991, pp. 23-27; See also Achin Vanaik, Ed., *Masks of Empire,* (Tulika Books, New Delhi, 2007).

6. According to J.N. Dixit, there has been much ado about India diluting its non-aligned and neutral position by having allowed [refueling] facility to the US. One has to analyze this decision in terms of India's interests and compulsions. Indian planes over fly Gulf. If India had refused refueling facilities to the US planes involved in Kuwait operations, which technically were UN operations and which had full endorsement of the GCC states, these states could have withdrawn facilities being extended to Indian planes in terms of over flying their airspace and providing technical and refueling stopovers. This would have been apart from jeopardizing the large-scale economic and commercial interests which India had in GCC states. See Dixit, n. 3, p. 366; See also A.K. Pasha, Ed., *India and Kuwait: Strategic, Economic and Political Developments* (Gyan Sagar, New Delhi, 1999); and A.K. Pasha, *Kuwait: Strategies of Survival,* (Har Anand Publications, New Delhi, 1995).

7. A.K. Pasha, "India and Israel: Growing Cooperation", *World Focus*, Vol.14, no. 8, August, 1993, pp. 19-2; A.K. Pasha, Ed, *Contemporary Gulf: State, Society, Economy and Foreign Policy,* (Détente Publications, New Delhi, 1999); Is Iraq another 'Vietnam'?, Analytical Monthly Review, June 2004, Vol. 2, no. 3, pp. 1-10; *A.K. Pasha, Iraq: Sanctions and Wars* (Sterling Publications, New Delhi, 2003); Mohammed Jawad Ali, "Developments in Iraq", in *Gulf Research Center, Year Book, 2006-07,* (Dubai), pp. 429-445; But J.N. Dixit says, "at the UN India took a vacillating and ambiguous stand till the unanimity of international opinion persuaded us to go along with the UNSC Resolution. Indian policies fell short of moral principles and political adroitness in dealing with this crucial development", Dixit, n. 3, p. 366.

8. P. R. Mudiam, *India and the Middle East,* (British Academic Press, London, 1994), p. 56; K R Singh, "India and WANA", in Bimal Prasad, Ed; *India's Foreign Policy: Studies in Continuity and Change,* (Vikas, New Delhi, 1979), pp. 247-59.; A.K. Pasha, *Arab-Israeli Peace Process: An Indian Perspective* (Manas Publications, New Delhi, 2000); J.N. Dixit says: "There was even an extraordinary unrealistic assessment from our mission in Baghdad that Saddam Hussein should be treated with kid gloves because he was not likely to be defeated by the combined forces of the international community under the UN umbrella led by the US", Dixit, n. 3, p. 213; *The Hindu*, 14-04-2008.

9. A.K. Pasha, "India and West Asia: Continuity and Change," in, Nalini Kant Jha, ed., *India's Foreign Policy in a Changing World: Essays in Honor ofProfessor Bimal Prasad,* (South Asian Publishers, New Delhi, 2000) pp. 240-69; *The Hindu*, 6-12-2005; Pasha, n. 7, p. 139-40; Marc Lynch,"Iraq and the Arab Street: Iraq and the Arab Public

Sphere", *Politics and Society*, vol.31, no.1, March, 2003, pp. 55-91; Naveed S. Sheikh, *The New Politics oflslam : Pan–Islamic Foreign Polity in a World of States,* (Routledge Curzon, London, 2003), p. 60, p. 8. In May, 2004, the Lancet report found that about 100,000 additional Iraqi deaths had taken place sine the US invasion in March, 2003. A team from Johns Hopkins University identified more than 12,000 family members and tracked those who had died since the invasion- an estimated 650,000 additional Iraqi civilian casualties. Most of these deaths have been of men aged 15-44.

10. Richard Horton, "The death toll in Iraq", *The Hindu*, October 13, 2006; Amin Saikal, *Islam and the West: Conflict or Cooperation,* (Palgrave, Macmillan, London, 2003), p.130; A.K. Pasha, "The US Invasion of Iraq and the Muslim World", in V.D. Chopra, ed., *Genesis and Fall out of US-UK Military Action in Iraq,* (Kalpaz, Delhi, 2004), pp. 207-226.

11. See also A.K. Pasha, "Arafat, Palestinians and the Future", *Mainstream*, Vol. XLII no.50, December 4, 2004, pp. 7-10; Zafar Imam, *Iraq-2003: The Return of Imperialism,* (Aakar Books, New Delhi, 2004); A.K. Pasha, "Significance of Indo-Russian Strategic Partnership: Its Impact on Arab World", in V.D. Chopra, ed., *Global Significance of Indo-Russian Strategic Partnership*, (Kalpaz Publications, New Delhi, 2005), pp. 135- 172.

12. *The Hindu,* June 23, 2005; See also Toby Dodge, "Iraq's Future: The Aftermath of Regime Change", *Adelphi Paper 372,* (Routledge, London, 2005); see alsoToby Dodge and S. Simon, eds., "Iraq at the Cross Roads: State and Society in the Shadow of Regime Change", Adelphi Paper 354, IISS,(Oxford, OUP, 2003), *pp. 77-92;* Seymour M. Hersh, *Chain of Command: The Road from 9/11 to Abu Ghraib*, (Harper Collins, New York, 2004); *Frontline,* August 25, 2006, pp.18-22. According to J.N. Dixit, on 31-1-1998, I.K. Gujral (IKG) made a statement that the Government of India will not "tolerate" any military action against Iraq and that India had cautioned the US by means of a letter to President Clinton. IKG stressed that India's concern was that such an attack would result in regional tension and create danger for Indians in GCC states. Dixit, n. 3, p. 376.

13. Richard J. Kozicki, "India and the Arab World after Indira Gandhi: Continuity in Foreign Policy", Arab-American Affairs, Fall, 1985, no. 14, pp.1-17; A.K. Pasha, Ed., *India, Bahrain and Qatar: Political, Economic and Strategic Dimensions,* (Gyan Sagar, Delhi, 1999); See also A.K. Pasha, Ed., *India and Oman: History, State, Economy and Foreign Policy,* (Gyan Sagar, Delhi, 1999).

14. A.K. Pasha, "India the Gulf States: Challenges Opportunities", RajenHarshe and K.M. Seethi Eds., *Engaging with the World: Critical Reflectionson India's Foreign Policy,* (Orient Longmans, New Delhi, 2005), p. 389-424; A.K. Pasha, "Pax Americana in the Gulf Region: Implications for India's Quest for Energy Security", in S.N. Malakar, edited: *India's Energy Security and the Gulf*, (Academic Excellence, Delhi, 2006), pp. 116-122; A.K. Pasha, "Post-Arafat Palestine", *World Focus*, vol. 26, no. 5, (305) May, 2005, pp. 7-10

15. Boutros Ghali, *Egypt's Road to Jerusalem : A Diplomat's Story of the Strugglefor Peace in the Middle East,* (Random House, New York, 1997), pp. 80-81;

120, 214, 257, 278; Salim Mohd. El Sayed, Ed., *Egypt and India in the Post-Cold War World : Comparative Paradigms* (CAS, Cairo University, Cairo, 1996); A.K. Pasha, "India's Policy towards the Arab World in the 21st Century" in V. D. Chopra, ed., *India's Foreign Policy in the 21st Century*, (Kalpaz Publications, Delhi, 2006) pp. 215-250; Bansidhar Pradhan, "Changing Dynamics of India's West Asia Policy", *International Studies*, vol. 41, no.1, 2004, p.51; "Why the US promotes India's great power ambitions", *Analytical Monthly Review*, Vol. 3, no. 12, March, 2006, pp. 15-30; A. K. Pasha, "Egypt's Search for food security", *Détente*, Vol. 7, no. 5, January, 1989, pp. 10-15; A. K. Pasha, *Egypt in a Changing World* (National Publishing House, New Delhi, 2003), pp. 242-260; P. R. K. Swamy, "Mubarak is busy, please mail the Nehru award", *Asian Tribune*, 7-7-2007.

16. A.K. Pasha, "India's Cultural Diplomacy in West Asia and North Africa", in Anwar Allam ed., *India and West Asia in an Era of Globalization*, (New Century Publications, New Delhi, 2008); During 2007-08, India paid almost $50 billion for oil and related products imports; A.K. Pasha, "Rediscovering Old Bond with Egypt", *The Pioneer*, 23 December, 1991; A.K. Pasha, "A Great Leap Forward Taken by India and Israel", *India Abroad* , (New York), January 17, 1997, pp. 2-3; A.K. Pasha, "India-Saudi Relations: Past and Emerging Challenges", in G Dietl, G. Pant, AK Pasha and PC Jain Eds, *Contemporary Saudi Arabia and the Emerging Indo-Saudi Relations,* (Manas Publications, New Delhi, 2007), pp. 143-166; A.K. Pasha, "Safety and Security Aspects of Hajj", *The Pioneer*, May 24, 1997; A.K. Pasha, "India's Cultural Diplomacy in West Asia", in A.K. Sinha and A.K. Singh, eds., *NewHorizons in History, Classics and Inter-Cultural Studies,* (Amanika Publications, New Delhi, 2007), pp. 295-310.

17. Mustafa Alani, Dhafer Al Ani and MahmoodSariolghalam, "Developments in Iraq and Iran", in *Gulf Research Center, Year Book, 2004*, (Dubai), pp. 249- 272; A.K. Pasha, "India's West Asia Policy: Continuity and Change", *Strategic Analysis*, Vol. XVI, no.6, September, 1992, pp. 783-804; A.K. Pasha, "India and West Asia: Past and Future", in N.S. Sisodia and Ashok K Behuria, eds., *West Asia in Turmoil: Implications for Global Security,* (Academic Foundation, New Delhi, 2007), pp.441-470; A.K. Pasha, "Yemen-Saudi Security Relations: Implications for India", *Third Concept*, vol. 8, no. 87, May, 1994, pp. 33-36; DilipHiro, *Blood of the Earth: The Battle for the World's Vanishing Oil Resources*, (Penguin Books, New Delhi, 2008); A.K. Pasha, "Indo-OIC Relations: Perspective and Trends", *Journal of Peace Studies*, Vol. 1, no. 3-4, March-June, 1994, pp. 22-50; A.K. Pasha, "The Recent Gulf Crisis: India's Options", *Strategic Analysis*, vol. XVII, no. 10, January, 1995, pp. 127-86; Mustafa Alani, "The Curse of oil and the disintegration of Iraq," *Gulf Monitor, GRC*, Vol. no. 4, June, 2007, p. 8-9.

18. Christian Koch, "Iran, the National Intelligence Estimate and the Gulf Security", *Gulf Monitor, GRC,* Vol. 2, no.1, January, 2008, pp. 4-7. See also A.K. Pasha, "India, Iran and the GCC States: Common Political and Strategic Concerns", *Encounter,* March-April, 1998, pp. 66-74; A.K. Pasha, "India and the GCC States: Challenges and Opportunities", *World Focus*, vol. 24, no. 2, (278) February, 2003 pp. 9-15.

19. TalmizAhmed, "The Iran-Pakistan-India gas pipeline", *Seminar*, no.584, April, 2008, pp. 48-51; A.K. Pasha, "India's Cultural Diplomacy with the Arab World", *Arab League Special Issue* (New Delhi), 60th Anniversary, 2006, pp. 42-45; A.K. Pasha, "50

Years of India's Ties with West Asia", *The Pioneer*, August 19, 1997; Mohammed Abdel Salam, "Civilian Nuclear Program in Arab Countries", *Security and Terrorism, Research Bulletin*, Nuclearization of the Gulf, *Gulf Research Center*, Issue, no.7, December, 2007, pp. 28-30; *The Hindu*, 21 April, 2008; Anna Rulska and David Jackson. "At the Crossroads of Foreign Policy Decisions: India and the Middle East", in Jack Covarrubias and Tom Lansford Ed, *Strategic Interests in the Middle East: Opposition and Support for US Foreign Policy*, (Burlington: Ashgate, 2007), pp.109-120.

20. *The Hindu*, 21 April, 2008; A.K. Pasha, "India-Saudi Ties Ready for a new Dawn", *GCC-India Research Bulletin*, (Dubai, UAE), Issue no.1, January, 2006, pp. 6-7; A.K. Pasha, "Relations to a New Dawn", *Arab News* (Jeddah), 26 January, 2006, (with N Janardhan); A.K. Pasha, "Indo-Saudi Arabian Summit is long over due", *The Pioneer*, August 3, 1992; K Natwar Singh, "Whither Foreign Policy and Diplomacy", *Seminar*, no. 584, April, 2008, pp. 70-71; A.K. Pasha, "India-Oman: Emerging Security Partnership", *GCC-India ResearchBulletin*, Issue no. 2, June, 2006, pp. 10-11; A.K. Pasha, "India and Persian Gulf: An Overview", *World Focus*, Issue on New Dynamics in Persian Gulf, Vol. XXVIII, no. 2, [326], February, 2007, pp. 39-45; *The Hindu*, 23-2-2008.

21. Anoushiravan Ehteshami, "The Year of Crisis in Iran" (2005), in *Gulf Research Center, Year Book, 2005-06* (Dubai) , pp. 349- 355; A.K. Pasha, "Indian Perceptions on Persian Gulf ", *World Focus*, Vol. XXVIII, Nos. 11-12, Nov-Dec, 2007, pp. 446-457; A.K. Pasha, "Recent Developments in the Gulf Region: An Overview", *World Focus* issue on Persian Gulf, Vol. 39, no. 2 (338). February 2008, pp. 43-47.

22. Rajesh Kumar Mishra, "Nuclear Proliferation Challenges and India's response", *Strategic Analysis,* Vol. 31, no. 5, Sept., 2007, pp. 791-814; See also A.K. Pasha, "Iraq and its Future: An Overview", *World Focus*, Vol. 26, no. 2 (302), February, 2005, Issue on Iraq and its Future: Doubts and Fears, pp. 3-6; A.K. Pasha, "Iran and Iraq: Are they Becoming Friends?" *South Asia Politics*, Vol. 4, no. 5, September, 2005, pp. 29-34.

16

Neighbourhood Concerns in the Era of Globalization

Prof. P.L. Dash

Introduction

When the debate about turning the world has revolved around "Global Village", there are peripheral concerns that affect integrative process in many countries of the rising Asia. All countries are certainly not rising; few of them are indeed sinking. The brutal killing of Benazir Bhutto in Rawalpindi on 27 December, 2007, highlights the fact that India's immediate neighbourhood is in political ferment. With each passing day, terrorism is proving to be intractable, unpredictable and fathomlessly intriguing. It is a phenomenon that has affected the body polity of most of India's neighbours, from Srilanka in the south to Nepal in the north and from Bangladesh in the east to Pakistan in the west. A cursory look at the extended neighbourhood of India in the West Asian and Central Asian directions provides us with equal or more gruesome pictures. The fighters against terror are working hand in gloves with the terrorists. Or else, how does one prove Musharraf welcoming openly the released terrorists Masood Azhar and others from Indian jail on demand by the IC 814 hijackers to Kandhar, one of whom subsequently killed the American journalist Daniel Pearl. Or for that matter Taliban ambassador to Pakistan, Mullah Omar, openly defying the US on television in support of the Taliban regime in the immediate aftermath of 9/11, or for that matter shielding nuclear proliferators A.Q. Khan?

The southern neighbourhood of the erstwhile Soviet Union, spanning from the east of the Black Sea to the east of the Tien Shan mountains suddenly assumed importance because all littoral countries of the Caspian Sea were endowed with enormous energy resources. All Central Asian countries also assumed importance in view of their geographic locale in the heartland of Asia and the natural, mineral and energy resources they possessed. Meanwhile, the region continued to remain politically unstable, economically volatile and socially fragile, thereby precipitating numerous concerns to face impending challenges. While the region passed through unprecedented transformations in all spheres of life, making efforts at building a new polity and economic system, the emergence of fifteen sovereign countries on the debris of the Soviet Union and five countries on the Yugoslav territory further accentuated apprehensions about other multiethnic countries soon following suit. Fortunately, however, physical vivisection has bypassed other countries. What has come to help is their understanding about the imperatives of economic cooperation for the nation they wish to build, the gloomy regional security scenario they desire to avoid, particularly after the fall of the Taliban in Afghanistan and ouster of Saddam Hussain in Iraq. All these developments taken together present a worrisome security scenario in India's neighborhood that policy makers and the governments in the region have to grapple with. Meanwhile, 9/11 episode dramatically altered the prevailing equations in international relations. The resultant American military entanglement in Afghanistan since 7th October, 2001, had further complicated the regional security scenario. For India, the Soviet disunion had vertically shifted the country's security frontier from across the northern boundaries of Jammu and Kashmir to far beyond the northern borders of Kazakhstan. The American involvement in Afghanistan and subsequently in Iraq had horizontally widened this security frontier from Mesopotamia to the eastern region of the Black Sea through Caucasus, Caspian, Central Asia and the Tien Shan mountain ranges right up to Xing Xiang in China. India must look ahead to this extended security frontier in its neighbourhood in terms of her internal stability. This article makes an attempts to focus on issues that fundamentally influence and affect India's concerns in general vis-à-vis the region under focus.

Looking Beyond Kashmir

Far too long the Kashmir problem has been the prime security preoccupation for India across the north. The withdrawal of Soviet forces from Afghanistan suddenly altered the salutary effects of India's years of negotiations with Pakistan. Insurgencies once again forked their ugly heads in the Kashmir valley. The government has had no control over the shifting theatres of terrorist activities. Yet, elections in Jammu and Kashmir in September-October, 2002, were evidence of the faith people of that state had reposed on Indian democracy. The declaration of the Indian government on 16 October, 2002, about partial withdrawal of troops from the Indo-Pak borders was further a testimony of the flexibility of Indian polity. These two internal developments do not, however, alter the gloomy scenario on cross-border infiltration of terrorists. The logic remains bluntly simple: Pakistan did not wish to settle the Mujaheedin terrorists it once nurtured and trained within the country for fighting the Soviets in Afghanistan. It had effectively diverted them in two directions: in the west to the volatile Pak-Afghan borders across the Durand Line, and in the east to the Pakistan occupied Kashmir. Pakistan had fairly succeeded in its endeavour, so that within Pakistan, these trained, hard core terrorists did not pose a menace to Musharraf. The subsequent increase in terrorist acts across India, whether it was the attack on Indian Parliament or 7/11 Mumbai train blasts, or Akshardham temple in Gujarat, the pointer was only in one direction at Pakistan.

Things look promiscuously different on the geopolitical map. The American, physical military presence in Pakistan, Afghanistan, Iraq, in Uzbekistan, Kyrgyzstan, Tajikistan and its oil and gas interests in Kazakhstan and Turkmenistan have been positing that great power against Islamic Iran in what Zbigniew Brzezinsky called wider "chess board" of geopolitics.

Within the framework of existing conventional security system that was shaped to face the Cold War challenges and the energy security system that was devised in response to the 1973 Arab oil embargo, there has to be paradigm shift in the mindsets of regional and global actors to accommodate the rising aspirations of China and India, the two giant economies that have begun demanding their share in the available energy market worldwide. As of December 2, 2006, India's ONGC Videsh has been engaged in 15 different countries worldwide in its quest for energy. It has welcomed the first arrival of Sakhalin-I oil in Mangalore on this very day. Similarly, China which was an exporter of energy to South East Asian countries in the early 1980s, has turned in 25 years later as a net importer of oil. Since two of every sixth world citizens live in these two countries, their share in energy consumption ought to correspond to size of population and the economy they pilot. Since there is an incredible asymmetry, a new framework is bound to be worked out in which the suppliers and the recipients of energy would accommodate the rising demands of India and China. And this is likely to happen in the periphery of India - the world's oil and gas reserves are concentrated in the periphery of India – in the Persian Gulf, in the Caspian Sea region and in the Russian Federation.

Centrality of Central Asia

Over the past fifteen years, post-Soviet Central Asia has assumed a significant place in international relations. From relative obscurity of Soviet years, it has come a long way to the limelight. Countries from far and wide have been vying to gain a foothold in the region with a view to accessing the region's resources. India looks at luscious Central Asia with a lurking sympathy primarily for three reasons: as a single geo-cultural space with which it has had centuries of affinity, as a geopolitical space with which it has shared commonalities and as a geo-economic space that occupies in recent years a primary place in shape of things to come in the realm of India's energy security. Age-old contacts through the Silk Routes have engaged the area as a compact region over centuries that has assimilated itself into multicultural ethos of world civilizations. Supplemented by commonness of history and cemented by geographical proximity, Central Asia as a geo-political entity, has provided meeting points and battle grounds to many conquerors from east and west alike. In the post-Cold war scenario, Central Asia has become an arena of intense competition among many interested powers for its geo-economic prowess.

The abundance of natural and mineral resources and the colossal deposits of natural gas and oil in Caspian basin have been central not only to Central Asia, but to other actor attracted to the region. However, each country pursues its interests in its own way: Turkey for a common cultural space, Russia for not allowing the region to slip in to the sphere of influence of other countries, China to vigorously pursue economic and strategic objectives, Japan to procure raw materials and make an energy bridge with Central Asia, the USA to balance out Russia and China in the region, and project its own objectives of democracy building, Pakistan to buffet a wave of Islamic renaissance and so on. The evolving relationship of each of these countries with Central Asia was voluminous and deserves special scholarly treatment. However, what remained of utmost importance to us for a variety of reasons was how Central Asia was central to India; and this requires a brief analysis. Synoptically factored out below are a dozen of important parameters that tell us what Central Asia literally means to India and why the territory is significant for India's geo-political pursuits.

Firstly, Central Asia was central to India for strategic reasons. The Soviet break-up had as much altered the security scenario in the region as it did in India's north. Need arose to gauge the strategic depth of Central Asia in the changing context of post-Soviet developments. It is in this backdrop that India began assessing her pursuits. For India, the appearance of five independent countries in her northern neighbourhood dramatically altered the existing equations. The political and ethnic volatility prevailing in Central Asia through the 1990s, enhanced India's security concerns and evidently these concerns included the tenuous and still emerging relationship with the new states. India felt that its security horizon was bound to widen to include the Central Asian countries.

Secondly, the geographic location of Central Asia is central to India. It is from this area that conquests were undertaken by invaders in the past. An unstable neighbourhood is an unwelcome proposition, and the area in constant ferment, may threaten national interests of all countries in the region. The sheer geographical vastness of countries such as Russia, China and India located in the proximity of each other to Central Asia and their weighty economic and demographic role dictated upon Central Asia to be free from volatility, but unfortunately the region is entrapped in a cobweb of conflicts of various kinds.

Thirdly, political development in the surrounding neighbourhood was central to India. Development in Afghanistan and Pakistan was of sinister import. An Indian airplane was hijacked to Kabul that led to the release of a hard core terrorist from Indian prison, and the released terrorist drove down from Kabul to Pakistan in full view of the world public. The whole event was politically unpalatable and diplomatically unprecedented. It cast a morose shadow on the morale of Indian security forces and such incidents threatened to spill over to Central Asia. Subsequent to 9/11, the developments in Afghanistan have remained bewildering, albeit not worrisome.

Fourthly, the resource potential of the Central Asian countries was central to India. Rich in oil and gas, gold and other minerals, the Central Asian countries were an alluring area of emerging commerce. They kindled crimson hopes for future, and India being one of the major countries in the neighborhood, was naturally interested in expanding commercial ties with Central Asia.

Fifthly, Central Asia's sixty million people are central to Indian business community. They provide a sizeable market for Indian export. As traditional gift items were popular from the Soviet era, India was expected to harvest yield from further commercial transactions. Everyone celebrates birthday, and should occasion arise for sixty million people to buy one item each to gift on birthdays, and that too an Indian item, the magnitude of sale would be expectedly high.

Sixthly, the secular ethos of these new states was central to India. The neighbouring countries were aflame with radical Islam and apprehensions abound that fundamentalist Islam was on the rebound in Central Asia. India and Central Asian states espoused together secular values.

Seventhly, Central Asia's response to globalization is central to India. It was a closed economy in the Soviet era and has not eschewed state control completely. In a complementary sense, the marketizing economy and democratizing polity in Central Asian countries may like to learn the Indian experience in reforming their economy.

Eighthly, viable regimes that could ensure political stability in Central Asia are central to India. Although the degree and level of democratic reforms have varied from one country to another in the region, by and large, the same regimes have been continuing in power in Central Asia for the past 15 years; and that itself is not a platitude of democracy, although attitudinal approach of the leadership has remained invariably warm, positive and friendly toward India, providing a fecund ground for bilateral ties to prosper.

Ninthly, in the aftermath of 9/11, the demonstrative interest of the USA in Central Asian military bases is central to India. The Manas airbase in Kyrgyzstan is leased to the USA, where varying reports say that some 800 to 3000 troops are stationed. Similarly at the Khanabad airbase in Uzbekistan, some 1700 US troops were located. Given that Russia has leased out a base from Kyrgyzstan, some 180 kilometers away from Bishkek and Russian troops are there in Tajikistan, the regional juxtaposition of these troops seems relevant in the changing geo-political context. Further added to this picture is the sizeable US military involvement in Afghanistan, Pakistan and Iraq that enhances the worry, making Central Asia central to all, and particularly, to India. Further, central to India is the role Central Asian countries are likely to play as bridge between Russia and India in bilateral and trilateral trade, commerce and security relations. The paradigm shift the region has followed in the past decade in embracing those countries traditionally inimical to Russia tells us a tale of probable military rivalry in future. The form of rivalry may be different, but the content would remain the same and that would not only affect India exclusively, but also other countries too. It would remain central to India's diplomatic interest how smaller countries in Central Asia, with definite pattern of internal turbulence and political volatility, evolve their foreign and security policies in order to accommodate interests of bigger countries such as Russia, China, India, the USA and others in the years to come.

The eleventh factor central to India is the nascent Central Asian national armies. Inevitable for their own defense in each country, the genesis and growth of these armies have been slow, lopsidedly dependent on Russia and varied in their degree of preparedness in each country. India has been training officer cadres for some of these countries at the National Defence Academy in Khadakvasla and may pursue a proactive policy of helping Central Asia build national defense systems. The setting up of the Aini base in Tajikistan is a telling example of military cooperation.

The twelfth factor of centrality of the region to India remains inherent in the two magnificent corridors of communication linkages being worked out. The North-South corridor and Eurasian Continental Bridge would be the line of surface communication linkages of the future. However, keeping aside, what the future would entail, the existing cross-country road network along the Old Silk Route could easily be harnessed, should there be only political commitment to peaceable communication between Pakistan and India. The related moorings of all these twelve dimensions of centrality of Central Asia's location in the very neighbourhood of India put the region on a high pedestal of cross-country competition. Big and small countries alike are afield in one game. Competing powers evince their interest in Central Asia and this itself puts the region into limelight and centrality.

Factors of Instability

The sudden Soviet sunset in 1991 had downsized the Slavic influence along the Russian southern underbelly. A rising population across the post-Soviet space, conjoined with the population of West Asia and Middle East and elsewhere constituted a sizeable demographic configuration of 1.3 billion Muslims or a quarter of the world's population. This population lived in an area rich with natural endowment of energy, the oil rich region of the world and threatened the energy security of the world. The gruesome events of 9/11 and Osama bin Laden factor further compounded the scenario as never before. The US war against global terrorism severely accentuated by physical military involvement in Afghanistan and Iraq is a picture never seen before in recent memory. Further the US threats to Iran and Syria denoted a selfish twist against the region, too much in favour of US dominance. The Russian acquiescence to the unfolding complexity in the regional scenario and her policy of shrinkage from an area it was once dominating made the region perennially unstable, straddling an area between Kosovo and Kashmir, Palestine and Pushtunland and between Chechnya and Xingjiang.

All three Asias have been facing a problematic time. An interrelated sets of five active factors are coming into interplay at the crossroads of the millennium in a regional and global scale. These inter-linkages are entwined with the national interests of the countries involved and coming into frequent interplay in regional politics. An individual treatment of each of these factors is essential for understanding the complexities of the burning regional issues. These factors are:

- Muslims/oil/Multinationals/pipelines in and around the Caspian.
- Muslims/terrorism/Mafia and their nefarious activities.
- Islam/governance/ and a shaky local elite.
- Muslims/narcotic trade, arms trade/social services, Madressas.
- Muslims/national identity/ideology/nation building.

One the most profitable aspects is the oil wealth. But the rising disparity strikingly clashes with the aspirations of the people who endeavour to occupy a certain political space in the emerging ethos of new governance. When the new political space is denied to them by the rulers, whether kings or dictators or authoritarian presidents or a demand to occupy such a space is crushed ruthlessly, a void in aspiration is created. In recent years Western democracy has rushed to fill this void disregarding the fact that ten years of Soviet experiment in Afghanistan to supplant a regime alien to the native had ended in futility. If supplanting western liberal democracy to traditional Islamic societies fails to achieve the desired goal, it is likely to create a fertile ground for unending hostility between the natives and western non-natives. The changing face of Jeehadi movement in Afghanistan, Pakistan or anywhere, where the failed state is the entity, assumes the subject of notoriety in a real sense of nation state building. The assumption creates an imbalance between the native aspirations and western interests and to strike a balance between the two one must search answer in two areas: how more effectively to assimilate native ethos of governance with modern ethos of western democracy. Democracy must evolve from within the country and must not be supplanted by a big brother.

An Aberration or Role Model

Pakistan has neither ensured democracy, nor viable dictatorship, nor permanent military rule. 9/11 had truly revealed the dilemmatic nature of the Pakistani regime. It may be headed towards use of force or probably military dictatorship. Pakistan's quest for democracy and peace will be successful not by the army at the helm. Participatory democracy mandates grassroots input to governance not through exiled leaders, but leaders who could really provide the country with a civil society protected by elected representatives and governed by constitution through efficient bureaucracy. The inadequacy or lack of all these elements of governance in Pakistan makes it a state deep in trouble waters, threatening it with possible vivisection and maybe possible demise. Border disputes with neighbours, falling economic standard, rising Jeehadi culture, autonomy demands within the country, and incapacity of the rulers to handle these problems are Pakistan's roadblocks to peace. With a dangerous military culture laden with a nuclear bomb, Pakistan poses precisely that incredible threat which illiterate mass in that country cannot realize. But the western countries realise the potentials of a nuclear danger to the neighbourhood of South and West Asia. Spillover effects are being felt. Proliferation apprehensions have already pointed at Pakistan that its scientists had supplied Iran, Libya and North Korea with nuclear know-how.

Oil-MNC Linkage

There are two clear directions in which world oil supplies are carried out. The two most oil rich regions are the Russian reserves and the Persian Gulf reserves. After the Soviet collapse most of the politico- diplomatic activities are conducted across the interloping region between these two oil rich areas. Russia's loss of glory has facilitated America's influence in the Persian Gulf region. For over a decade now, the region is agog with pipeline politics of incredible proportion along areas which were once even inaccessible in imagination. Unfortunately the ongoing pipeline saga to harness the Caspian oil reserves and the hydro-carbon resources are being carried out.

There are five directions via which these new pipelines are proposed: (1) from Azerbaijan, Kazakhstan and Turkmenistan to Europe through the existing Russian pipeline structure. This is the easiest way, when national pipeline structure of the given countries could join with existing Russian infrastructure;

(2) From the Caspian littoral countries through the existing national pipeline structures of Islamic republic of Iran; (3) From Azerbaijani capital, Baku to Turkish Mediterranean port of Ceyhan; (4) From Daulatabad gas field in Turkmenistan and Iran through Afghanistan, Pakistan and India and (5) From Tengiz oil field in Kazakhstan Western Turkmen gas fields two pipelines, one of gas and the other of oil, to mainland China. Thus we obtain a complicated picture of cross country pipelines, entirely in consonance with the ongoing globalization process, but very much in disharmony with the existing state of political bickering among states. It is time states of the region must bury their hatchets, adapt flexibility to the emerging ethos, allow economy to prevail over politics and resolve mutual disputes amicably. Multinational corporations have invested their fortune in a risky zone of oil economy.

Concerns of the Periphery

Some areas in the region that have occupied considerable attention of countries, governments, NGOs and the societies across the cockpit of Asia are on the rebound with perennial problems of intricate significance. One of them is narcotic trafficking. There is no way one could stop it or escape from the pernicious impact of it. In the periphery of India, Afghanistan alone exports $30 billion worth of narcotics to the world every year. Narcotic circulation within Afghanistan is pegged at $2.5 billion annually. The farther the drug marches from the centre of production toward the market destinations across Europe and the US, its volume decreases, while its cost increases significantly. The profit from the trade is used largely for recruiting terrorists and acquiring arms from the open international markets to use it for terrorist or subversive activities. So far no interdiction measures have succeeded in curbing this lucrative narcotic trade, let alone combating it. Since India is geographically located between the Golden Triangle and Golden Crescent of narcotic trafficking in Asia between Myanmar and Afghanistan, its northern territories are vulnerably sandwiched between illicit narcotic trade and related crimes. The foreign policy implications of narcotic trade and trafficking is pervasively enormous for the region in general and for each individual country in particular.

The periphery of India is also a proven region of nuclear proliferation. The menace is evidenced by the fact no other region is so crowned with nuclear materials as is Asia. The shoddy episodes of proliferation by the A.Q. Khan network is famous across Asia from North Korea to Iran and beyond. While India's proliferation records in the past decades as a non-signatory to the NPT has been exemplary, Pakistani record has been equally abominable. The impacts of these clandestine proliferation have enormous negative consequences on confidence building measures among nations as well as on the pattern of evolving foreign policy. The concentration of nuclear weapons in the hands of Asian nuclear powers such as Israel, Pakistan, India, China, Russia and Kazakhstan in a single geo-cultural space is a dangerous phenomenon sans demonstrative responsibility. Among all these nations, all but Pakistan have evinced their highly responsible conduct. However, it is alone Pakistan that endangers the Indian periphery with its nuclear irresponsibility. And the situation cannot be reversed. India's special role as a non-proliferater has been sidestepped and largely overlooked to camouflage support for Pakistan. And this has largely impacted upon the pattern of evolving foreign policy postulates in India in the years to come. The peripheral impact of Pakistani nuclear irresponsibility on the region is enormous; so enormous that its future implications are too early to unravel.

Widespread prevalence of poverty and human rights violations unconnected with areas of ethnic bickering is a paramount concern that countries of the region grapple with. In the neighbourhood of India, all countries have a more or less dismal human rights record. While the haves get away with the law of the land, it is the have-nots who pay the price because they are poor; and there is none to protect them. The correct evaluation of lawlessness in each given country from Georgia to Uzbekistan and on each incident from Chechnya, Beslan, Nalchik to Kashmir tells the Amnesty International sad commentaries on human sufferings. And the situation remains irreversible because poverty is not easy to eradicate, and human sufferings and their rights violation have been intrinsically linked to social status predicament. The poorer you are the more you suffer. Widespread sufferings mirror on the image of a country in the international arena. The sum total of all these intricately interwoven developments impact upon the foreign policy of a country like India because foreign policy cannot be seen in isolation from the overall regional picture of development.

Another area of concern for Indian policy makers is the rising extremist fervor across Asia and its apparent linkage to terrorist activities. From the hijacking of the Indian Airlines plane to Kandahar to the massacre of Kashmir pundits at Nandigram, the involved people belonging to a particular religion. From the Taliban fight against the northern alliance in Afghanistan to the hostage taking by Dzuma Namangani in Uzbekistan, the involved people are all Muslims. From the mercenary Jeehadis in Chechnya to Hizb-Ut-Tahrir in Central Asia to separatist movements in Xing Xiang, the involved Jeehadis are all Muslims. Although India remains one of the countries with largest Muslim population, efforts are made to downsize her stature and connotations are attached lopsidedly to a particular religion although other religions are equally important. The challenge before Indian foreign policy is to face this rising extremist fervour.

References

1. At The Crossroads, A Survey of Central Asia, *The Economist*, 26 July, 2003, pp. 1-16 (Special Report).

2. Alec Rasizade, Entering the Old Great Game in central Asia, *Orbis*, Vol. 7, No.1, Winter, 2003, pp. 41-58.

3. Unfamiliar Questions in the Arab Air, Special Report: *Arab World*, Iraq and al- Qaeda, pp. 48-50.

4. Daniel Yergin, Ensuring Energy Security, *Foreign Affairs*, March-April, 2006, pp. 69-82.

5. Mark Gould, Understanding Zihad, *Policy Review*, February-March, 2005, pp. 15-31.

6. Zbigniew Brzezinsky, Hegemonic Quicksand, *The National Interest*, Winter 2003-2004, pp. 5-16.

7. Charles Fairbanks, Andrew J Bacevich, Base Debate, America in Central Asia, *The National Interest*, Summer, 2002, pp. 39-53.

8. Mark N. Katz, "Less than Great Expectations: The Pakistani-Russian Rapprochement", *Current History*, March, 2005, pp.137-141.

9. "Today's Nuclear Equation", *Foreign Policy Agenda*, E-Journal USA, March, 2005, pp. 30-33.

17

Energy Security: A Study of Changing Thrust in India's Foreign Policy

Prof. R.S. Yadav

The end of Cold War has not only led to many unique and not so unique transformations in the international system, but the concept of security is no longer looked upon in the same way as before. During the Cold War era, security was perceived mainly as a territorial and military oriented, whereas in the present, it is variously called comprehensive security, human security, non-military security, non traditional security etc. not restricted to military affairs but incorporating political, social, economic and environmental issues.[1] As a result, threat to security has not only been limited to territorial sovereignty but also include poverty, oppression, social injustice and ecological degradation. Therefore, objective of security goes beyond achieving an absence of war to encompass the attainment of democracy, sustainable economic development, social justice and protection of environment. Hence, energy security became one of the major components of security by the state. This became all the more important in case of India with the adoption of structural reform process since 1991. In the current process of globalization India has projected 8 to 9 per cent growth target of its GDP in the next decade. This is likely to involve large scale progress both in its infrastructural and industrial developments. For this consumption of huge energy is not only required to meet this demand, but will be an area of prime concern for the policy makers in the country. Consequently, due to the above twin developments, energy security has acquired important place in India's foreign policy orientations in the post-cold war era. Besides, its importance also lies with the fact that "unlike other non-military aspects of security, energy security has had the most direct connection with the narrow, military concept of security."[2] Thus due to the growing demand for energy for the economic development of the country, as well as, the competitive-influence- building policies of the powers to capture the economic resource rich areas have made it a matter of serious concern for the policy makers in India. That is why, in this paper, a modest attempt has been made to analyze and evaluate India's energy security policy vis-à-vis its comparative position with other Key players. Simultaneously, an effort is made to examine how India's foreign policy is going to project its energy interests in this unequalitarian order not only by fulfilling its own needs but also to prolong the development by preserving the environmental concerns of humanity.

Economic development is the core objective of any country's foreign policy after territorial security. In this context, energy security acquires prominence. In broad sense, it is the assurance of continuous flow of resources to meet the energy needs of the country. It be sustained by developing the available sources in the country, as well as, getting the deficit obtained from outside. It involves all types of activities like exploration, production, import, acquisition of acreages, strategic resources etc. for the perennial flow of energy. Thus, energy security has been well defined by European Commission as "the ability to ensure that future essential energy needs can be met, both by means of adequate domestic resources worked under economically acceptable conditions or maintained as strategic reserves, and by calling upon accessible and stable external sources supplemented where appropriate by strategic stocks."[3]

Before a detailed analysis of India's energy security policy is made, at the outset, it has be categorically made clear that: (i) India's energy security issue be understood in the over all context of global availability of various resources and the competitive-influence-building activities of the major powers; (ii) availability of these natural resources be looked into the context of demand for sustainable development; and (iii) the exploration and development of resources be linked to global concerns for environment.

The common sources of India's energy are coal, oil, natural gas, nuclear, thermal, solar, wind, geothermal, tidal and hydroelectric. But major source which have foreign policy linkages are oil, natural gas and nuclear. Hence the present paper is limited to exploring these three issues and their likely fallouts on India's foreign policy in general and energy security in particular.

(a) ***Domestic Production*** - India had 5.6 billion barrels of proven oil reserves as of January 2007, the second largest amount in Asia-Pacific region (behind China). Much of its crude oil reserves are located off the Western Coast (Bombay High) and in the North east (Assam) of the country, although substantial undeveloped reserves are located in the offshore Bay of Bangal and Rajasthan. But with the impressive growth rate during last few years, India is also becoming a significant consumer of energy resources. Presently, it is the fifth largest consumer of oil in the world. Its annual oil production is about 32 to 33 million tons, while its consumption is approximately 135 to 140 million tons. Hence, the gap between its production and consumption is very large and tremendously increasing annually which is evident from following Figure.

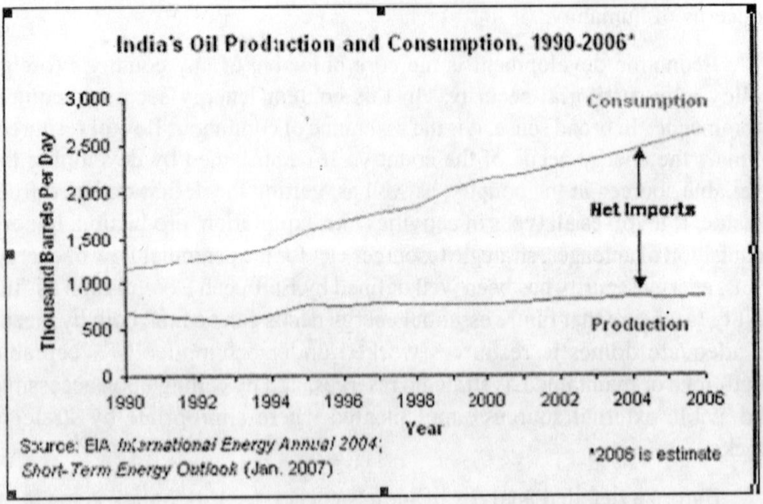

Fig. I[4]

The above gap is being filled up from the import of oil from outside. Hence, India imports 70 per cent of its crude needs mainly from the Gulf States and it is being projected that by 2020 India's dependence on oil imports is likely to be around 91per cent. This huge imports has serious bearing for its economy as it is likely to have tremendous increase in the import bill, which is manifest from the table I[5].

Table-I[5]

		The Rising Import Bill
Year	*Quantity (mmt)*	*Value (Rs.crore)*
1996-97	33.9	18,337
1997-98	34.4	15,872
1998-99	39.8	19,907
1999-2k	57.8	40,028

2000-01	74.1	65,932
2001-02	84.9	80,116
2002-03	90.0	85,042
2003-04	95.0	93,159
2004-05	100.5 (estimated)	1,30,000

To meet the deficit, India has involved private companies in domestic explorations and overseas exploration and production. However at domestic level, except for Reliance, most of the production remained in the hands of Indian Oil Cooperation. This scenario has not changed much.

(b) Oil Exploration and Import- At external level, Approach Paper to Ninth Five-Year Plan (1997-2002) recommended the acquisition of acreage in other countries.[6] As a result, by January 2007, ONGC Videsh Ltd. (OVL) has acquired 25 oil and natural gas projects in 17 countries spanning Africa, Asia and Latin America. Consequently, India is making an annual investment of US $ 1 billion in Sudan, Russia, Libya, Vietnam, Iran, Syria, Lebanon, Kazakhstan, Indonesia, Iraq, Myanmar, Bangladesh and Sri Lanka. India's major equity shares are :-

1. India invested US $ 750 million to acquire 25 percent equity in Sudan's Greater Nile Petroleum Operating Company (GNPOC) in 2003. The GNPOC acreage in Sudan holds proved crude oil reserve of more than one million barrels, and current production levels from the 8 main GNPOC fields exceeds 3 lac bbl/d. This company also operates a 935-mile crude oil pipeline that pumps oil to Port Sudan for export. India has its largest investment in this region and already four shipments have been received by now.

2. India's OVL has obtained a 20 per cent stake in Sakhalin-I in Russia at a cost of US $ 1.7 billion and the field became operational since 2005 and reached a production of 2,50,000 bbl/d till 2007. India is involved in the project through a consortium arrangement with Exxon-Mobil, Sodeco and the Russian Companies R N Astra and SMNG. Exxon Mobil is the operator. India's share in the first six or seven years is about 5 million tons a year, which included Russia's share as part of the repayment for a loan to the Russia government. After the loan is paid, India's share tappers off to 2.5 million tons a year. Gas production in this region also started in 2008.

3. In Kazakhstan, OVL has submitted a bid for minority stake in Kurmangazy oil field which is being shared by Russia and Kazakhstan.

This venture is likely to give India a toehold of recoverable reserves. It is also considering acquisition of a 15 percent stake in Alibekmola, a discovered field, currently controlled by the Canadian firm Nelson Resources. To support energy security interests in Central Asia, India has already stationed troops in Tajikistan, provided it with US $40 million aid package and undertook to refurbish an air base near Tajik capital Dushanbe.

4. Other state in Africa from where India is importing around 15 million tonnes of oil annually is Nigeria. Since August, 2000, the contract with Nigeria is being renewed annually.[8] With Angola, it tried hard to enter into agreements but failed. It has also had agreements with Ivory Coast and Ghana on oil explorations.

Despite its explorations elsewhere, West Asia continues to be its greatest source of energy needs as it continues to import at least 65% of its oil from this region. Saudi Arabia, Iran and Iraq continue to be its biggest sources despite turbulences in that area.

Strategic Petroleum Reserve: India is also planning a strategic petroleum reserve and for this construction of storage tanks with 36.7 million barrels of crude oil has been approved. Mangalore, on the eastern coast, has been considered as site for this purpose. About the actual quantity of reserve and when to fill up such tanks are yet to be decided by the government. It is being handled by a state owned organization Indian Strategic Petroleum Reserve Cooperation Limited.

Natural Gas

(a) Domestic Scenario—As on January 2007, the proven natural gas reserves of India have reached 38 trillion cubic feet (tcf). The bulk of India's production comes from Bombay High, Assam, Andhra Pradesh and Gujarat. If 2004 statistics are taken into account, India has produced 996 billion cubic feet (bcf) and consumed 1089 billion cubic feet (bcf). India is making explorations in offshore Bay of Bangal, Krishna-Godavari basin and Mahanadi Basin. Though government-owned companies are doing the main task, yet partnership of private sector is also being invoked by involving Reliance Company in the Krishna-Godavari basin. BG International and Reliance are also jointly working to expand production at the Tapti, Panna and Mukti fields in Bombay High. Through various exploration activities, it is expected that by 2009 India is going to double its production of natural gas. Despite the large gas explorations, however, most observers feel that India's demand is likely to outstrip its production soon. During the last five years, its consumption of natural gas is increasing very fast.

(b) Gas Imports— India imports natural gas from abroad to meet its current needs. In this context, it is seriously working on imports through pipelines. Though pipelines are generally the most economic mode of transportation, yet it involve the problem of route security, huge investments and serious political implications.[9] At present, discussions on the construction of three pipelines are going on and final decisions have not been arrived at. One such project is to build a Iran-Pakistan-India pipeline to the length of 1700 miles to run from South Pars fields in Iran to the Indian state of Gujarat. The discussions are going on since 1994 but variety of political and economic issues, involving both global and regional politics are preventing the finalization of such process.[10] Since February 2006, India is also making efforts to join Turkmenistan-Afghanistan-Pakistan 1050 Mile pipeline originating from Turkmenistan's Dauletabad-Donmext natural gas fields. But the security threats emanating from instability and terrorism from Afghanistan and Pakistan are major irritants in this project. Besides, availability of adequate quantity of gas from Turkmenistan is also preventing the finalization of such deal. In March 2006, India has signed a deal with Myanmar, but specifics about pipelines, whether through Bangladesh or through its eastern border to Tripura, is yet to be finalized. Import of small amount of natural gas from Bangladesh is also feasible, but internal politics in that country is preventing its decision in favour of New Delhi.

(c) Import of LNG— Currently India is also involved in the purchase of Liquefied Natural Gas (LNG) from abroad and building of terminals to receive such imports. Since 2004, it is importing LNG from Oman and Qatar to its Dahej terminal in Gujarat. This facility is being owned and operated by Petromet LNG, a consortium of state-owned Indian Companies and international investors. Its second terminal, which became operational in 2005, is again in Gujarat near Surat, It is being operated by Hazira LNG, a joint venture of Shell and Total. India is also building another such terminal at Kochi, which is likely to be completed by the year 2009.

Nuclear Energy

India launched its nuclear programme, under the leadership of Homi dehangerBhabha for nation's security and self-reliance in its energy needs. As a result, its nuclear power programme commenced in 1969 with the building of Tarapur Atomic Power Stations (TAPS-I & II) employing Boiling Water Reactors (BWRs) with American assistance. Later, Rajasthan Atomic Power Stations (RAPS-I & II), based on Pressurized Heavy Water Reactors (PHWRs), were established with the help of Canada. At present, India has 15 operating nuclear power reactors and 8 more under various stages of construction or commissioning.[11] Through these reactors India has planned to attain 10,000 mw nuclear power by 2010 ; 20,000 mw by the year 2020; and, 50,000 mw by the year 2050. But presently it is just producing 8,400 mws from its 12 reactors with a capacity of 700 mwe each. In the given scenario, at the very conservative estimates, India requires at least 1000 mw from each reactor in addition to its existing capacities. Despite all these, India's meeting of energy target has been very low to the tune of, approximately, 3 per cent, whereas the US nuclear share of electricity generation is about 19% and France utilizes nearly 78% and the over all electricity generation by nuclear power in the world is 17 per cent.[12]

But the main problem for India, to enhance its nuclear energy use, the shortage of nuclear fuel in the form of uranium. It is because the known uranium resources in Jaduguda mines are depleting fast and Department of Atomic Energy (DAE) is unable to start fresh mining in Domiasiat in the Northeast and Nalagonda in Andhra Pradesh due to local opposition to uranium mining. Besides, Indian natural uranium ores are of very low grade. Finally, the uranium produced in India is roughly six to seven times more costly as compared to the prices available in the international market.[13]

Consequently, India has been in desperate need for nuclear fuel to meet its future energy needs. Most important priority, at this stage, is to give attention to three important issues- (a) procuring natural uranium fuel for its PHWRs to consolidate the indigenous three-stage nuclear power programme envisaged by Bhabha; (b) continuity of enriched uranium fuel supply for Tarapur reactors at least for the next 10 years; and (c) to seek US assistance in facilitating nuclear supplier groups (NSC's) clearance for opening of the way to imports of nuclear fuel.[14] In the light of these requirements, India started making efforts to collaborate with the USA in the area of nuclear programmes. In the post-Pokhran-II era, USA was also interested in engaging India in the nuclear non-proliferation activities, not insisting on signing of NPT or CTBT.[15]

As a result, during Prime Minister Manmohan Singh's Visit to the USA on 18th July, 2005, both India and America agreed to cooperate in the area of "peaceful nuclear energy related initiatives".[16] Later, on 2 March 2006, during the visit of President George Bush to India, both countries agreed to proceed further by agreeing to separate India's civil and military nuclear programmes. India agreed that, by 2014, it will separate these twin reactors and 65 per cent of them, put in civilian category, will be placed under the inspection of IAEA.[17] Later on, due to some compulsions of domestic politics, 'Henry J. Hyde, US-India peaceful Atomic Energy Cooperation Act of 2006' was passed on 18th December, 2006, which placed certain restrictions on India. As a result, it provoked serious criticism by different strata of society in India.[18] But continuous diplomatic efforts on both sides did not allow the process to derail and on 1st August, 2007, both signed a draft agreement for cooperation in the peaceful uses of nuclear energy between the two countries.[19] But in India, Left parties, the coalition partners of the UPA government, made serious criticisms, not allowing the ruling party to enter into such agreement.[20]

But if objectively analyzed, India's military alignment with the USA has not been due to the current 123 agreement, rather it evolved due to its military-to-military cooperation started from the Kickleighter proposal; ten-years defence agreement in 1995; incident of 9/11; formation of High Technology Cooperation Group (HTCG); development of Next Step in Strategic Partnership (NSSP); and finally defence framework cooperation agreement of June 2005.[21] Thus, civil nuclear cooperation with the USA is the urgent need for India, to make its opening with the NSG for its nuclear fuel requirement. Besides, India's large nuclear infrastructure is not weapon-oriented, rather designed to meet its civilian needs.

Coal

Coal is the predominant energy source for power production in India, generating approximately 70 per cent of its total domestic electricity needs. Visualizing the energy demands of the future, coal, along with oil and natural gas, is going to remain an important source of power generation. Current production of coal in India is 290 million tones per year, but its demand is going to be more than double by the year 2010. Major coal fields are found in Bihar, West Bengal and Madhya Pradesh. The Indian government controls almost all coal production, which has been plagued by low productivity, distribution problems, and an increasing loss of domestic market share to higher quality, less expensive imports. Nearly all of India's 390 mines are under Coal India Limited (CIL), which accounts for about 90 per cent of the country's coal production.[22] Though, in terms of use of coal in power production, India is going to remain self sufficient in the next 100 years, yet, because of higher ash content and the peculiar chemical and combustion properties of Indian coal, substantial modification of the technologies available with foreign companies to suit India fuel resources will have to be made.[23] To this limited extent, foreign policy outlook of India will be affected in the context of development of energy through coal.

II

Policy Options for India

Now questions arise: what are the strategies needed for the Indian policy makers? What are the initiatives required, at this juncture, to meat the energy security requirements of the country? How India is making re-orientation in its foreign policy in the changed context? This is a fact that, presently, Indian foreign policy is making efforts to adjust itself in the changed regional and global milieu. It is also making efforts to realise its changed priorities in the contemporary world order. To attain its core objectives in an appropriate manner, India's policy makers need to adopt multi-pronged strategies, making new permutations and combinations visualizing changes both at region and global power structure. In the realm of energy security, the following options seem pertinent for its policy makers :

(i) Changed scenario reveals that, presently, most of the energy sources are located in Asia and Africa. The new regions in Africa, Central Asia and states in Southeast Asia are emerging as new centers of natural gas and oil, besides the already existing West Asian Oil. In this context, new India-China partnership could serve as the foundation for an Asian energy union, as both are not only emerging as fast growing economies, but also are competing for oil exploration and production in these states. By signing an agreement on 12 January, 2006, between ONGC Videsh Limited and CNPC, for joint bidding of oil exploration projects, at the time of visit of the then Indian Minister of Petroleum and Natural Gas to Beijing, both have made a good beginning. Such an agreement may open the new vistas for energy cooperation in the form of recovery technologies for aging oil field and basin evaluation and drilling rigs by China and IT-enabled exploration and production services of India. Both can also help each other in transport mechanism including pipeline and use of backhaul cargoes in very large crude carriers. Ultimately these cooperation may facilitate the growth of Asian market. Though role of the Western powers and their border problems may work as irritants, yet the larger economic interests may overcome such hurdles.

(ii) Developments in the last few years show that Russia under Putin is emerging as world's biggest single producer of hydrocarbons. It is also positioning itself for the role of the main motor and coordinator of new global strategy for energy security. In this context, it is eager to link itself with the Asian countries by offering to help guarantee the energy security and its readiness to provide long term and stable supplies of energy resources. It is also eager to join with them in joint projects of exploration of oil and natural gas fields in the Russia and third countries. It is keen on evolving joint ventures for the construction of pipelines for transportation of oil and gas. India being a close friend of Russia, can explore these possibilities in a very positive manner. As explained earlier, it has already invested US $ 1.7 billion for the exploration of Sakhalin-I and reaping the fruits of such cooperation since 2005. Emerging India-China and India-Russia Cooperation, along with their commonalities of interests in Central Asian Republics, can work as a cementing force to strengthen their energy ties.

(iii) Availability of oil surrounding Caspian Sea has brought Central Asia to the forefront of global oil diplomacy.[24] Competitive-influence-building efforts for power had begun in Central Asian Republics (CARs) due to the availability of natural resources in the form of oil and gas. Multinational companies of Italy, Britain, USA, along with Russia's Gazprom started fighting for their influence. Even the states surrounding Caspian Sea are fighting for their sovereign rights and pipelines issue. The USA is also making efforts in devising pipelines in a way to avoid Russian hold. But developments in last few years have consolidated the Russian hold more than anybody else's. Even in the regional forum like SCO, Russian predominance is clearly manifest. China through building pipelines and rail road linkages has established its hold with some of the republics. Here China is also collaborating with Russia in its anti-Western outlook in the SCO. India is making efforts by collaborating with some of the republics and also joining the SCO as an 'observer' country. But it has to do a lot more to take benefit of this region's oil and gas resources. It has to give clear support to pipeline construction from this region to South Asia, despite USA's opposition to such activities.

(iv) India's ONGC Videsh Limited is making huge investment in 17 countries abroad for exploration and production of oil and gas. But geography plays a very important role in creating impediments to utilize such resources. Even if that is overcome costs rise to prohibitive level. Therefore, there is need that India's energy security be ineluctably linked to its neighbourhood. This reality should not be ignored by the policy makers. Fortunately India is ringed by gas rich neighbourhood- Myanmar, Bangladesh, Turkmenistan and Iran. Concentration on these neighbours, on the one hand, will make the easy availability of oil and gas at cheap rates, and on the other hand, the goodwill with them will ensure supply through pipeline from far off land in non-interruptive and continuous manner. The promise of collateral gains from the 'peace pipeline' indeed too alluring to be ignored by any one of them. Hence, in a world that is decisively gravitating towards regional coalitions and groupings based on economic cooperation, India's linking of its energy security benefits with its neighbours stands out to be beneficial to all.

(v) In the given scenario, nuclear energy can work as very important component for India's energy security. It is because India's nuclear programme since its inception has major focus on its civilian use. However, there is scarcity of availability of fuel for indigenous energy production. In this context, stalling the signing of Indo-US nuclear civil energy deal seems to be based on ignorance[25] and misperception among people and officials.[26] Even the objections by the left parties, as discussed earlier, some consider this deal against India's strategic national interest. This apprehension also does not seem to be tenable. Many experts are of the view that these apprehensions are baseless.[27] Visualizing this as very important for the pursuit of nuclear technologies for the benefit of the nation, even prominent nuclear scientists made an open appeal to parliamentarians to clear this deal.[28] Besides, without an agreement with the NSG, the running of the nuclear programme on a large scale is not possible. Even opening up to the IAEA inspections, need not affect our security and secrecy, as six reactors are already working under such inspection. Moreover, this deal is permitting the nuclear fuel to India without signing the NPT and in no way restrict India's options to the US alone. Rather the majority of reactors in India are PHWRs type for which US does not have expertise. Thus, by leaving India outside the international regime is not going to resolve its energy needs.[29]

III

But exercising the above mentioned options is not problem-free. Numerous geo-political and geo-economic issues are going to affect future course of energy security of India. Following factors are likely to work as major irritants in this process:

(i) For its energy needs India is mainly dependent on import of oil from West Asia. This region, due to its geo-strategic location and geological resources, is highly politicized and threat prone. Inter-state and intra-state rivalries and warfare, including the interventions by the major powers, has been routine in this area. Even embargoes on the production and supply of oil have been very frequent. Consequently, continuous political instabilities and turmoil are not ruled out. Political stability works as an important ingredient in oil production and price stability. Prices are also affected by the scarcity of availability of these resources in future. Both these factors have raised the price to an exorbitant level of more than US $ 100 from nearly US $ 20 a decade ago. Therefore, the growing instability in the region and souring prices of oil may create problem of availability and financial difficulties for India.

(ii) The region of West Asia is criss-crossed with the oil pipelines and dotted by oil and gas fields, handling facilities and export terminals. Presently, India is also planning to import oil and natural gas from

West Asia and Central Asia through pipelines. But most of the pipelines have to pass through the turmoil prone countries of Afghanistan and Pakistan. The presence of terrorism in these states has made the task more difficult. Sometimes even politics and the need of huge financial investments are also creating problems. Even natural gas from Myanmar, being off shore, it can be accessed only after laying a pipeline undersea or overland through Bangladesh. But whether Bangladesh would be willing to allow the pipeline to be routed through its territory and the security of such a pipeline would be paramount concerns which would decide the pace of the acquisition of this available gas.

(iii) Use of piped gas or liquified natural gas (LNG) will be dependent upon the associated infrastructure (LNG regassification facilities or pipelines) and the piece of the gas. Though India is importing huge LNG from Oman and Qatar but is much costlier as compared to the cost of natural gas. This also requires construction of LNG terminals which pose serious security risks and are attractive targets for terrorists. In terms of price, India follows dual producer pricing formula. While international oil companies (IOC) producing gas in India are paid a price that is linked to an index of fuel oils, the domestic gas producer (ONGC) is paid a cost plus price. Besides, ONGC absorbs the difference between the price paid to IOCs and the price charged to domestic consumers. But, as share of IOC gas in the total domestic gas production goes up, and LNG imports increase, it would be difficult to maintain dual pricing system.[30] This increase in price may create problem in Indian market, as well as, it may make the cost of electricity generation though gas a prohibitive option.

(iv) Despite possession of substantial amount of energy reserves in the form of coal and availability of huge import of oil from West Asia, a country of India's size and economy, a prudent mix of energy resource policy, to meet out its burgeoning electricity requirement, is needed. In this context, enhanced use of nuclear energy is best possible alternative.[31]But availability of nuclear fuel is a serious problem in this direction. Present government is making efforts to get rid off NSC's restriction, regarding supplying of nuclear fuel, by entering into nuclear civil deal with the USA. But the compulsions of domestic politics are preventing it to pursue such course. Future of such collaboration will be dependent upon how changes take place in India's polity and perceptions of the parties in power at a particular time. Only the emergence of consensus on this issue will facilitate the country to make use of this source. Hence, resolution of this dilemma is very essential for the future nuclear energy use.

Above mentioned problems can be resolved by taking steps in the directions of policy improvement and domestic reorientations. At policy level, formulation of Hydro-Carbon vision 2025 is good beginning but a lot needs to be done to formulate an integrated and comprehensive energy security policy. A full desk dealing with oil diplomacy on regular basis is set up in the MEA to coordinate such activities of different concerned ministries. Such policy should focus on the activities like developing relations with energy resource countries, ensuring uninterrupted supplies of oil and gas, making strategies to deal with oil organization regimes etc. It should also make effort to evolve collective thinking for sustainable development of energy resources. It should also try to create a balance between nuclear technologies and fuel dominant group led by the USA and the emerging hydrocarbon suppliers' states of Russia and China. As India is in need of both nuclear, as well as, oil and natural gas for its energy requirements, a delicate balance between them is not only essential, but imperative.

Simultaneously, policy initiatives are also required at domestic level. Its present dependence on imported oil is reduced by the use of renewable energy sources available in the country. Utilisation of clean coal technologies need to be encouraged. Shift may be made towards next generation fuels from bio-mass technologies. To make improvement in the production of domestic oil and gas, efforts are also needed to enhance energy efficiency mechanisms at various levels. Through various fiscal, legal and regulatory methods, an attractive environment for FDI and joint ventures could be created. Improvement in the overall basic infrastructure, suited to the new global business culture, needs to be established. Thus, efforts at both the levels are pre-requisites for the growth of healthy, long term, and smooth energy security policy.

IV

Form the above facts, it may be concluded that the end of cold war has led to redefining the concept of security and beginning of the process of globalization. Now, considering security as holistic concept, energy security became its important component. Impressive growth of the Indian economy, as a result of globalization, has further boosted its energy needs. These changes have led to the reorientation in India's domestic and foreign policy outlook. Issue of energy security became very important in the context of its increased need for oil, natural gas and nuclear fuel, which resulted in shift in India's foreign policy. Among the three segments, oil will continue to affect its foreign policy decisions in the times to come. Hence its foreign relations with the countries of West Asia and Central Asian Republics will continue to remain warm. This thrust will also consolidate its ties with Russia and China to a great extent. Even its regional cooperation through forums like SCO and consolidation with Asian energy groups are likely to strengthen. The need for energy will also work as compulsions to take policy initiative toward the improvement of relations with neighbouring states in the West (Afghanistan and Pakistan) and East (Myanmar and Bangladesh). Simultaneously, its thrust to fulfill its nuclear fuel requirements will likely to consolidate its ties with the USA. Though efforts may be made at domestic level toward the growth of alternative fuel and renewable source of energy, yet for some more time its focus will continue to remain attracted to above three core areas. Accordingly its foreign policy options will be utilized to suit the changing energy security needs.

Notes and References

1. For details see, Kanti Bajpai, "The Idea of Human Security", *International Studies*, 40(3), 2003; Dipankar Banerjee, "Towards Comprehensive and Cooperative Security in South Asia", *South Asian Survey*, 6 (2), 1999; and Takashi Inoguchi, "Political Security: Towards a Broader Conceptualization", *International Studies*, 40 (2), 2003.

2. Gulshan Dietl, "New Threats to Oil and Gas in West Asia: Issues in India's Energy Security", *Strategic Analysis*, 28 (3), July-September 2004, p. 374.

3. Cited in Gawdat Bahgat, "Central Asia and Energy Security", *Asian Affairs,* 37 (1), March 2006, p. 1.

4. Source: Energy Information Administration, *International Energy Annua*l, 2004 (Washington, 2005).

5. Source: Govt. of India, *Ministry of Petroleum and Natural Gas,* Annual *Repor*t, 2005 (New Delhi, 2005).

6. Govt. of India, Planning Commission, *Approach Paper to the Ninth Five Year Pla*n, 1997-2002 (New Delhi, 1997).

7. This equity was purchased from Candian Talesman Energy Inc. which had to whithdraw from Sudan on pressure from Human Rights Group in their country. Other stock holder in that company are China National Petroleum Company (CNPC-40%), Petrones (30%) and Sudan National Oil Company (Sudapet- 5%).

8. India's detailed imports from Nigeria from 1999 to 2005 are given below.

India' Oil Import from Nigeria*

Year	*Quantity (mmt)*	*Value (US $ mn.)*
1999-2000	15.450	2595.7
2000-2001	12.570	2140.4
2001-2002	11.320	2001.9
2002-2003	11.578	2389.0
2003-2004	11.074	2393.0
2004-2005	15.081	N.A.

* *Source*: Ruchita Beri, "Africa's Energy Potential: Prospects for India".

Strategic Analysis, 29 (3), July-September 2005, p. 381.

9. For details see, S D Muni and Girjesh Pant, *India Search for Energy Security,* (New Delhi, Rupa, 2003); Kuldip Singh, "Iran-Pak-India Gas Pipeline and Energy Security", *Punjab Journal of Politics*, 30(1), 2006; and Rahul Roy Chowdhary, "An Energy Security Policy for India: The Case of Oil and Gas", *Strategic Analysis*, 21 (II) February 1998.

10. For details see, Singh, Ibid, pp. 1-20, Also see, Bhagyashree Pande, "US Threatens Sanctions Over Indo-Iran Gas Pipelines", The Pioneer, 22 May 2005; and, Seema Sudhir, "Iran-India Pipeline: One Step Forward, To Steps Back", *Mainstream*, XLIII (30), 3 September 2005.

11. Details of the Indian power reactors is as under:

(i) Pressurised Heavy Water Reactors (PHWRs) 18(Canadaand Indigenous)

(ii) Boiling Water Reactors (BWRs) (USA)

(iii) Pressurised Water Reactors (PWRs) (USSR)

(iv) Prototype Fast Breeder Reactors (PFBRs) (Indigenous)

(A. Gopalakrishnan, "Indo-US Nuclear Cooperation: A Non-Starter?", *Economic and Political Weekely*, 2 July 2005, p. 2935).

12. "N-Power Generates 17% of World's Electricity", *Times of India*, 25 July 2005.

13. Gapalakrishnan, n. 11, p. 2936.

14. *Ibid,* p. 2937.

15. This is very much evident from 14 rounds of talks held between

Jaswant Singh, then the External Affairs Minister of India, and Strobe Talbott, the then US Deputy Secretary of State of the USA, during 1999 to 2001. For detail see, Strobe Talbott, *Engaging India:Diplomacy, Democracy and the Bomb,* (New York: Brookings Institution Press, 2004).

16. For details see, "Prime Minister Manmohan Singh's Visit to the US", *Strategic Digest*, 35 (8), August 2005; and, http://meaindia.nic.in/treatesagreconent/2005/18ta 1807200507.tm

17. For details see, Venkateshwaran, "Indo-US Relations: Recent Developments", IPCS Special Report no. 19, May 2006, www.ipcs.org/countspecialreport. Also see AjeyLele, "Nuclear Indulgence to India: Will US Congress Relent?", *www.ipcs.org.*article no. 1975, 22 March 2006; and, Manish Dabhade, "Indo-US Nuclear Deal: New Realism", *www.Ipcs.org.*article no. 1958, 7 March 2006.

18. For details on Left Parties Statement on the Indo-US Bilateral Nuclear Deal, see, *www.mainstreamweekly.net/article 277. html.*

19. "Agreement for Cooperation Between the Government of India and the Government of the United States of America Concerning Peaceful Uses of Nuclear Energy", *http://wwwhindu.com/nic/123agreement.pdf.*

20. Communist Parties feel that this arrangement is likely to make India an ally of the US hegemonic design of power expansion in the post-cold war era. For details see, Suresh Srivastava, Agreement 123: Bharat Ke Gale Ki Fance, New Delhi, *Confluence International*, 2007.

21. For details see, Kanti Bajpai, "India-US Relations: Where Are India and the US Heading?" *Economic and Political Weekly*, 6 August 2005, pp. 3577-3581; Achin Vainaik, "Significance of Framework Agreement on Defence", *Economic and Political Weekly*, 6 August 2005, pp. 3581-3585; Verghese Koithara, "India-US Defence Cooperation: Expectation and Prospects", *Economic and PoliticalWeekly*, 6 August 2005, pp. 3585-3589; and ,SukumarMuralidharan, "Partnership and its Discontents", *Economic and Political Weekly*, 6 August 2005. pp. 3589-3591.

22. "Economic Recovery Propels India's Engery Demand", *Energy Today*, 1 (1), March-April 2005, p. 54.

23. A. Gopalakrishnan, "India and the US: For Synergy in Energy", *Frontline*, 31 March 2000, p. 82.

24. For details see, R.S.Yadav and Suresh Dhanda, "Oil Politics of Caspian Sea and Central Asia: policy Options for India", *Contemporary Central Asia,* X (2), August 2006.

25. O.P. Sabharwal, "Nuclear Ignorance: M Ps Must update their knowledge", *The Tribune*, 8 November 2007.

26. Inder Malhotra, "Stalled Nuclear Deal: Gap Between Official and Private reaction", *The Tribune*, 2 November 2007.

27. VP Malik, "Strategic Aspect of N-Deal: India Must be Guided by National Interest", *The Tribune*, 7 November 2007; and, Arundhati Ghose, "The 123 Agreement: No Threat to India's Strategic Interests", *The Tribune*, 12 November 2007.

28. These scientists were: H.N. Sethna, M.R. Srinivasan, P.K. Iyengar, A. Goptalakrishanan, S.L. Kati, A.N. Prasad, Y.S.R. Parsad, Placid Rodriquez. "Appeal To Parliamentarians on Nuclear Deal", *The Hindu*, 15 August 2006.

29. M.R. Srinivasan, "Can the Impasse on the Nuclear Deal be Broken?", *The Hindu*, 26th December 2007.

30. Sudha Mahalingam, "Energy and Security in a Changing World", *Strategic Analysis*, 28 (2), April-June 2004, pp. 267-268.

31. For details see, Shebonti Ray Dhadwal, "India's Energy Security Policy: A Case for Nuclear Power", *Strategic Analysis*, 23 (8), November 1999, pp. 1289-1303.

18

Trafficking in Persons Perceived as Threat : A Study of its Impact on the Safety and Security of States in South Asia

Prof. M.J.Vinod

Trafficking in human beings is a global problem, with an estimated 800,000 to 900,000 people trafficked across international borders each year and a phenomenal number trafficked within their own countries. Of the 900,000 trafficked across borders, approximately 80 per cent of the transnational victims are women and girls, and up to 50 per cent are minors. Nationalities of people trafficked are as diverse as world cultures. Research into trafficking in human persons in any country is a very challenging exercise. At any given point of time, the International Labor Organisation (ILO) estimates, that 12.3 million people are in forced labor, bonded labor, forced child labor and sexual servitude. About 2 million children are exploited in the global child sex tourism. UNICEF estimates that approximately 300,000 children under 18 years of age are currently exploited in more than thirty armed conflicts worldwide. Trafficking in persons is a brutal abuse of human rights that affects nearly every country in the world. The Congressional Research Service and the U.S. State Department estimate that between one to two million people are trafficked each year worldwide with the majority originating in Asia - over 150,000 from South Asia and 225,000 from South East Asia.

Trafficking in persons is complex and multifaceted, simultaneously a development and a criminal justice problem. Victims may be deceived by false promises of legitimate work, defrauded, tricked, threatened with force, coerced, abducted or even sold by their parents. Women are often more vulnerable to traffickers because of lack of education or access to work near their homes, or because of the prevalence of gender-based abuse and violence. Victims are exploited for sexual purposes, such as prostitution or pornography, or for labour without compensation in homes, farms, factories or other businesses. Those who are sexually exploited may become infected with HIV or other sexually transmitted infections (Trafficking in Persons, USAID's Response: 2004).

Human trafficking is a form of modern day slavery. One may define trafficking as "the recruitment, transportation, harbouring or receipt of persons, by means of the threat or use of force or other forms of coercion, of abduction, of fraud, of deception, of the abuse of power or of a position of vulnerability, or of the giving, receiving or payments of benefits to achieve the consent of a person having control over another person, for the purpose of exploitation (Article 3 of the United Nations Protocol). Exploitation shall include, at a minimum, the exploitation of the prostitution of others or other forms of sexual exploitation, forced labor or services, slavery or practices similar to slavery, servitude or the removal of organs". By definition 'trafficking' involves 'force fraud and coercion which typically involves 'confinement' and 'physical' and 'psychological' 'abuse.'

This paper will revolve around the following hypotheses:

- Human trafficking undermines the health, safety and security of the South Asian states.
- Human trafficking has serious public health implications as it involves physical and psychological traumas.
- Trafficking in human persons is a major threat to the human rights of individuals, as well as a major national security threat.
- Globalization of markets and labor forces and relaxation of trade barriers have spawned new trafficking routes and scenarios.
- Internal trafficking takes place within each country, typically bringing rural women and children to cities in order to work as prostitutes, domestic servants and forced labourers.

The United States' State Department categorizes trafficking into three 'tiers', based on individual countries' efforts to combat the scourge. These include :

- Tier 1 groups of countries that are in compliance with the minimum standards of the Trafficking Victims Protection Act of 2000 (TVPA). The TVPA is the most comprehensive anti-trafficking legislation passed in the U.S. It focuses on US involvement in prevention measures by increasing assistance to victims, and by enhancing penalties for perpetrators. The TVPA focuses on the 'three P's approach' viz., 'prevention', 'protection' and 'prosecution'.
- Tier 2 includes countries that do not fully comply with the TVPA minimum standards, though they are making efforts to comply.

- Tier 3 groups countries that are not making significant efforts to combat the problem.

The State Department prepares the annual *Trafficking in Persons Report* in response to a congressional mandate.

Strategies used by Traffickers

Traffickers take advantage of the following strategies to lure potential victims: One, traffickers *take advantage of the poverty levels* of many women and children in recruiting and luring victims into the traffic industry. For instance, women may enter voluntarily but be deceived as to the conditions under which they would be forced to work. Some are forced to work twenty four hours a day receiving little pay, not being able to leave, and being forced to endure physical abuse. The ILO Convention Number 182 of 1999, Article 3 (Worst Forms of Child Labor) declares that "all forms of slavery or practices similar to slavery, such as the sale and trafficking of children, debt bondage, serfdom and forced or compulsory labour, including forced or compulsory recruitment of children for use in armed conflict represent a set of practices prohibited by the ILO Convention of 1999. [Stopping Forced Labour, A Global Report, the International Labour Conference, 89 Session 2001 Report I (B), International Labour Office, Geneva, ISBN 92-2-111948-3].

Two, women may be recruited through *debt bondage*. Parents, friends, or other close acquaintances may sell a child or a woman for employment in return for cash.

Third, women and children are *lured, deceived, kidnapped, or tricked* in other ways into prostitution. Women and children are deceived by recruiters who gain their trust and promise a higher paying job somewhere else. The fact is they are lured and deceived.

Major Push and Pull Factors in South Asia that Abets Trafficking in Persons:

The following are some of the major 'push' and 'pull' factors that sustain and complicate the problem of trafficking of persons in South Asia:

- Poverty
- Lack of employment opportunities.
- The commercial sex industry.
- Violence against women and children.
- Demand for prostituted women, boys and girls.

- Discrimination against women.
- Corruption.
- Various forms of armed conflict.

Very often traffickers pose themselves as 'employment agents'. Parents are induced to part with their children into prostitution and domestic servitude as a commercial enterprise. Victims are exploited for sexual purposes, such as prostitution or pornography, or for labour without compensation in homes, farms, factories or other businesses. Markets for sex and cheap labour in destination countries and the growing sex tourism industry fuel the demand. Weak rule of law, porous borders and widespread official corruption provide the context that allows human traffickers to operate with impunity.

UNICEF reports that, in the last 30 years, trafficking in women and children for sexual exploitation alone has victimized more than 30 million people in Asia. The International Organization for Migration (IOM) estimates that 200,000 to 250,000 women and children are trafficked every year in Asia. The US Department of State suggests that 150,000 South Asians are trafficked every year. The IOM estimates that nearly one-third of the global trafficking trade in women and children are trafficked from South-East Asia. About 50,000 women and children were trafficked annually to the United States from other countries. Of this, approximately 60 per cent originate from South Asia.

In South Asia, Bangladesh and Nepal are the main countries of origin for human trafficking. There is an estimate by the Global Alliance against Trafficking in Women (GAATW) that 300,000 Bangladeshi women have been trafficked to India and 200,000 to Pakistan, and over 200,000 Nepalese sex workers are reported to work in India, one fifth of whom are supposedly under the age of sixteen years (Sanghera Jyoti, in GAATW Newsletter, January 6-8, 1999).

The South Asian Scenario: An Overall Perspective

India is a 'source', 'destination' and 'transit' country. In India trafficking largely takes place for two reasons:

- One, for 'forced labour' and;
- Two, for 'commercial sex exploitation'.

The Ministry of Home Affairs in India estimates that 90 per cent of India's sex industry is for purposes of 'commercial sex exploitation' and 'forced marriage'. Children are often subject to various forms of 'involuntary servitude'. The Parliament of India however had passed a law, in 2006, banning the employment of children in domestic work. The USAID Mission in India is working with the United Nations Development Fund for Women (UNIFEM) and a number of Indian NGOs active in anti-trafficking throughout the country. Activities include information centers and shelters, psychological counseling, and educational and vocational opportu-nities, including for children of prostitutes in order to prevent them from falling victim to traffickers. Training helps communities advocate against trafficking and reach at-risk groups with prevention efforts. USAID also supports information-sharing networks among NGOs and local law enforcement, and training for judiciary and law enforcement officials on the causes, nature and magnitude of trafficking. Awareness campaigns are under way at state and national levels using a variety of media (Trafficking in Persons, USAID's Report: 2004).

Trafficking in women also takes place across the India-Bangladesh and the India-Nepal borders. India has not been able to effectively guard its long and porous borders with both these countries. The Government of India prohibits various forms of trafficking. The Immoral Trafficking Prevention Act penalties range from seven years to life imprisonment. Various acts like the 'Bonded Labour Abolition Act', the 'Child Labour Act' and the 'Juvenile Justice Act' are other important Acts passed by the Parliament of India.

Pakistan

Pakistan is a 'source', 'destination' and 'transit' country. At one level, trafficking takes place from countries like Afghanistan, Sri Lanka, Myanmar, India, Nepal, Central Asian states for purposes of 'commercial sexual exploitation' and for various forms of 'involuntary servitude'. At another level women are trafficked to Pakistan from countries like Sri Lanka, Nepal and Myanmar. Many Pakistani boys trafficked to the Middle East serve as camel jockeys, sex work and dancing. Internal trafficking also takes place within Pakistan, whereby rural women and children are brought to cities to work as prostitutes, domestic servants and forced laborers.

Pakistan has increased trafficking-related prosecutions and convictions, strengthened implementation of its 2002 Prevention and Control of Human Trafficking Ordinance, established an Anti-Trafficking Unit within the Federal Investigation Agency, and co-sponsored several public awareness campaigns.

Sri Lanka

Sri Lanka is a 'source' and 'destination' country for the following reasons:

- Different forms of 'involuntary servitude' – when an individual is faced with restrictions on movement, threats, physical or sexual abuse and debt bondage.
- Commercial sex exploitation; and

- Child soldiers being recruited by the Liberation Tigers of Tamil Eelam (LTTE).

The US State Department has placed Sri Lanka in Tier 2 Watch List in its June 2007 'Trafficking in Persons Report'. The report contends that this is due to Sri Lanka's "failure to provide evidence of increasing efforts to address trafficking in the previous year (2006) especially in its efforts to punish trafficking for involuntary servitude". The report says that Sri Lanka needs to improve its record of prosecution and conviction of sex and labour trafficking crimes, and need to institute a formal procedure to identify victims of trafficking among vulnerable groups, such as women arrested for prostitution, to ensure that they are not punished'. Though In April, 2006, Sri Lanka amended the 'Penal Code' prohibiting all forms of trafficking, yet many loopholes remain in the implementation of the code. However, over the years, there has been a marked improvement in Sri Lanka's trafficking prevention efforts.

Bangladesh

Bangladesh is basically a 'source' and 'transit' country for 'commercial sexual exploitation' and various forms of 'forced labour'. In Bangladesh women and children are falling victim to trafficking mainly for the purpose of prostitution, sexual abuse, forced labour, camel jockeying, cheap labor, bonded labor, domestic servitude, selling of organs and marriage. In case of women and girls, the destination is usually the sex-market both within the country and outside. In the case of boys, the destination is usually Middle Eastern countries where they are engaged as camel jockeys. In most cases the girls, who are trafficked abroad, are trafficked to India. In case of the boys, India is usually treated as a country of transit to the Middle East. On the other hand, within the country, an alarming number of boys and girls are forcefully engaged in prostitution. The girls are engaged both in brothels and the street sex-market, while the boys are almost exclusively engaged in the street sex market. (A.K.M. Masud Ali: 2004).

The Bangladesh National Women Lawyers' Association (BNWLA) has established 13 watchdog sites to monitor trafficking cases and provide legal assistance to victims. It repatriates victims from other countries, facilitates the release of those trafficked within Bangladesh and reintegrates them into community life. In 2003 for example, BNWLA repatriated 29 women, children and men from various countries, effected the release of 32 women and children from internal trafficking and provided information that led police to arrest 76 traffickers. In the same period, 16 traffickers received convictions (Trafficking in Persons, USAID's Report: 2004).

Bangladesh established an inter-ministerial anti-trafficking committee to oversee its national efforts to combat trafficking, created a national anti-trafficking police monitoring unit with presence in all 64 districts. However, Bangladesh continues to have difficulty confronting the trafficking problem due to generalized corruption of public officials who in many cases are complicit in the human trade. The 'Repression of women and Children Act 2000' was amended in 2003. Besides many safeguards, the Act also prohibits the buying and selling of minors for prostitution.

Afghanistan

Based on specific cases and trends and employing the legal framework of the 2000 Protocol to Prevent, Suppress and Punish Trafficking in Persons, Especially Women and Children, which supplements the UN Convention against Transnational Organised Crime, the International Organisation for Migration (IOM) believes that the following forms of trafficking are taking place in Afghanistan.

Exploitation of Prostitution (forced prostitution and prostitution of minors);

- Forced Labour;
- Slavery and Practices similar to Slavery - abductions for forced marriage, marriage for debt relief, and exchange of women for dispute settlement.
- Servitude - sexual servitude and domestic servitude; and
- For removal of Organs.

Afghan trafficking victims are drawn from the most vulnerable communities. Displaced, destitute, and indebted persons and families, young people seeking economic opportunity abroad, and rural women are all targets for trafficking crimes. Afghanistan's chronic insecurity, massive displacement, and poverty born of conflict and drought contribute to making many people vulnerable to this kind of exploitation. The role of women and girls as objects for dispute resolution, the power of local assemblies which often apply customary rather than constitutional (or Islamic) law, and the limited autonomy of women in marriage decisions, are additional factors that contribute to trafficking and make it difficult to combat. The problem of trafficking in Afghanistan is deeply intertwined with the country's other problems as it emerges from decades of lawlessness. The IOM recommends action in the following action plan to deal with trafficking:

- To create a legal framework ranging from a constitutional prohibition on slavery to laws enforcing the various international agreements to which Afghanistan is a signatory to laws protecting women from the most extreme versions of customary justice.

- To manage education and outreach regarding trafficking in persons to target Government officials, traditional leaders and members of the community, paying special attention to decreasing the stigmatization of victims.
- To ensure that programs to reduce economic insecurity, including training and education, micro-credit, and food security take into account trafficking risk factors in selecting beneficiaries.
- To include trafficking issues in security sector reform programmes such as the Afghan New Beginnings Programme.
- To strengthen and sensitize the police and courts to address all forms of trafficking and sexual violence.
- To re-examine cases in which persons now held in jail may in fact be the victims of trafficking.
- To work with traditional leaders to provide culturally appropriate support mechanisms for victims.
- To provide a mechanism to file complaints about past violations. (Tristan Burnett: 2004).

Nepal

Nepal is primarily a 'source' country for commercial sexual exploitation and involuntary servitude mainly to India and the Middle East. Nepal has a National Plan of Action to combat trafficking, and a National Rapporteur on trafficking. Women police cells have been established in many districts. In spite of safeguards like the 'Human Trafficking Control Act, 1986', there have been cases of corrupt government officials facilitating trafficking along the India-Nepal border.

The Nepalese government's law enforcement effort works side-by-side with nongovernmental organizations (NGOs) to provide protection and assistance for the victims. The government has established anti-trafficking "vigilance committees" in high-priority districts, conducts mandatory "safe migration" orientation sessions for workers traveling abroad, and carries out national public awareness campaigns.

Observations

Today in a globalised world trafficking is facilitated by the following factors:

- Sex tourism.

- Child pornography; and
- The global demand for cheap, vulnerable and illegal labour.

Of these, sex tourism and child pornography have become world-wide industries and totally commercialized. Child sex tourism is the dark side of globalization, and this is fuelled in South Asia by weak law enforcement, poverty, corruption, besides the role of technology in the form of internet and digital cameras. The link between child sex tourism and child pornography is also very strong.

Jyoti Sanghera aptly summarises the scenario in South Asia as follows:

"In the contemporary reality of South Asia women and increasingly young girls are the new migrants, the new movers and shakers. Traditional as well as on-going male out-migration for employment, together with an increasing insecurity of funds and sustainable livelihoods, act to push women and girls into assuming new roles for their families. Limited access to the public world and safe channels for mobility, as well as the lack of recourse to measures of legal and social protection intensify for women and minors vulnerability during the process of migration." (Joyti Sanghera: 2000)

In South Asia, the number of victims of severe forms of trafficking is increasing significantly. South Asian countries are trying to cope with the problem of trafficking internationally in the framework of the South Asian Association for Regional Cooperation (SAARC), which adopted the Convention against the Trafficking of Women at its 11th Summit in Kathmandu in 2002. Many countries in the Asian region have legislation that criminalizes trafficking, but in most cases the existing legal frame-work does not offer adequate controls. Implementation of current laws is limited, and law enforcement officials lack adequate training. Prosecution is increasing, but, given the magnitude of the problem, much more needs to be done. Most Asian governments are stepping up public awareness and victim assistance programs on their own and in conjunction with NGOs and international organizations. These programs often are very modest due to resource constraints. Several states are beginning to collaborate on investigations and have signed cross-border agreements to regularise the return of victims. However, the need for coordination and information sharing among the countries of the region remains great (Trafficking in Persons: USAID's Response: 2004).

Many NGOs in the South Asian region are working in the areas of prevention, rescue, care and support either as a principal activity or as an important aspect of a broader social development project. Activities to improve local conditions for women and children that also incorporate messages to reduce vulnerability to trafficking are being implemented by NGOs throughout

South Asia, with varying levels of government support. A number of NGOs in Nepal, India and Bangladesh are conducting women's leadership training courses, family life education, livelihoods skill building programs for adolescent girls and the formation of women's cooperatives (for group savings and credit activities). These programmes seek to improve conditions that have often been identified as being the underlying causes of trafficking. NGOs in the region are also implementing programmes that directly address the vulnerability of persons to trafficking. Awareness-raising activities directed at the general public (through street theatres, rallies and community meetings) and community leaders are common elements in many of the prevention programmes (Anti-Trafficking Programmes in South Asia: 2001).

Human trafficking is a 'human rights' and 'national security' issue, and hence needs to be seriously addressed by the South Asian states both individually and collectively. Perhaps the time has come to strike a balance between the two. There is the need for greater coordination of the 'law enforcement' efforts to 'investigate' and 'arrest'. Repatriation measures also need to be improved and streamlined. This is necessary to prevent victims from being 're-trafficked' and from being 'further victimized'. The South Asian states need to enhance cooperation between the 'source' and 'destination' states. Moreover efforts need to be made to 'investigate', 'prosecute', 'convict' and 'sentence' public officials who participate or facilitate various forms of trafficking.

The causes, magnitude and inter-linkages of trafficking are very complex. Both 'state' and 'society' need to comply with the minimum standards to prevent human trafficking. The time has come to bring together representatives from various segments of state and society to address the problem more holistically and effectively. 'Government', 'law enforcement', 'civil society' 'academia', 'media', 'film industry' and 'industry' have to all come together to effectively deal with the problem of human trafficking.

REFERENCES

1. *Trafficking in Persons Report*, (US Department of State Publication, Office of the Under Secretary for Democracy and Global Affairs and Bureau of Public Affairs, June, 2007).

2. *Trafficking in Persons USAID's Response*, (Office of Women in Development, Washington: 2004).

3. Ali, A.K.M. Masud, "Trafficking in Persons: Towards an Inclusive Paradigm", (paper presented at the Seventh Sustainable Development Conference, 8-10 December, Islamabad, 2004).

4. Burnett, Tristan, "Trafficking in Persons: An Analysis of Afghanistan",

(paper presented at the Seventh Sustainable Development Conference, 8-10 December, Islamabad, 2004).

5. Trafficking in Persons: USAID's Response, n. 2.

6. "Trafficking in Persons, the USAID Strategy for Response," USAID, February, 2003.

7. "Anti-Trafficking Programmes in South Asia: Appropriate Activities, Indicators and Evaluation Methodologies", (Summary Report of a Technical Consultative Meeting, September 11-13, 2001, Kathmandu, Nepal).

8. Brown, Louisie, *Sex Slaves: The Trafficking of Women in Asia 2000* (Virago Press, 2001).

9. "Stopping Forced Labour, A Global Report", (The International Labour Conference, 89 Session, 2001 Report I (B), International Labour Office, Geneva, ISBN 92-2-111948-3).

10. Sanghera, Jyoti, "Towards the Construction of an Empowered Subject: A Human Rights Analysis of Anti-Trafficking Legal Interventions and Trends in South Asia", (Paper presented at a seminar on Anti Trafficking Programmes in South Asia, Kathmandu: 2001).

11. Snaghera, Jyoti, "Sexually Abused and Sexually Exploited Children and Youth in South Asia: A Qualitative Assessment of their Health Needs and Available Services", (GAATW *Newsletter, ESCAP, January 6-8, 1999,* Bangkok: 2000).

12. Lam, Lin Lean, *The Sex sector,* (International Labour Organisation: 1998).

13. http://www.saarc-sec.org/brief.html.

14. http://www.unicef.org/programme/cprotation/focus/trafficking/issue.html.

19

The Significance of Indo-Russian Relations in Combating Threat Perceptions

Dr. Niranjan Mohapatra

India and Russia shared common approaches to various important international problems and issues. During the last fifty years they have worked in close cooperation towards establishing greater peace and stability in Asia as well as in the world. The former Prime Minister of India, Jawaharlal Nehru emphasized that India's foreign policy was based on the principle of united Asia and one world of which India and Soviet Union were two important and integral parts.[1] Global events brought India and Russia together in the 1950s-1980s when the Cold War dominated international relations.

Both India and Russia have been considerably influenced by the major developments in international relations after the Cold War. After the disintegration of the USSR and emergence of the Central Asian states, India and Russia have been cooperating on various issues pertaining to the security and stability of the world such as Central Asia issues, Afghanistan crisis, international terrorism, development of multipolar world, international peace and stability, Iran and Iraq issues, West Asia crisis, Korean issues, role of the UNO and many more.

Dr. Manmohan Singh, the Prime Minister of India, said that, "there is a need to anticipate what measures we need to take to meet new and emerging opportunities for further strengthening of our strategic partnership, in meeting our respective national priorities as well as in pooling our efforts in sharing global responsibilities".[2] Prime Minister Mr. Vladimir Putin affirmed in New Delhi that "our two countries share common views on the key issues in global politics and we are jointly fighting international terrorism which has challenged our civilization.[3] He also maintained that:

"We are ready to coordinate in promoting human rights, global and regional stability and sustainable development".[4] If strategic partnership between India and Russia is understood as normal partnership for peace and against proliferation of weapons of mass destructions, then the two countries can play a very positive role in international politics.[5]

International Terrorism

On the issue of terrorism both the countries reaffirmed their resolve to tackle the menace. Intelligence-sharing, coordination of strategies etc. are taking place between the two countries. Both Russia and India are major players in the global fight against terrorism. The Memorandum on Mutual Understanding and Cooperation in combating terrorism signed between Russia and India in 2003 showed their commitment to fight against this global evil jointly and relentlessly.[6] It has endorsed and reinforced the view and principles stated in the Moscow Declaration on International Terrorism released in November, 2001, during the visit of former Indian Prime Minister A.B.Vajpayee to Russia. This Memorandum envisages accelerating efforts and enhancing cooperation in this field by setting up a Joint Working Group on Terrorism at the Foreign Office level. Russia and India showed their determination to continue to work together for promoting India's draft Comprehensive Convention on Combating International Terrorism and Russia's draft Convention on Combating for the Suppression of Acts of Nuclear Terrorism in the United Nations, and closely cooperate within the framework of the Joint Working Group on Terrorism through consultations between the Security Council and collaboration between intelligence services. Bilateral cooperation in the fight against international terrorism has become a tangible embodiment of the strategic partnership; it is one of the many areas where Moscow and New Delhi stand as old and time-tested allies.[7]

The 9/11 (September, 2001,) terrorist attacks in New York and Washington changed the whole international perception towards terrorism. Both India and Russia treated the attack as a major security threat and as an opportunity to use the issue of terrorism to reshape international politics. In his televised message to the Russian people after the attack, former Russian President Putin affirmed that "today's event once again underscore the urgency of Russia's proposal to unite the effort of the international community in the fight against terror, the plague of the 21st century".[8] Similarly, former Indian Prime Minister A.B. Vajpayee in his address to the nation on 14th September, 2001, affirmed the Indian stand that the international community must come forward in a concerted effort against the evil. He proposed for a Comprehensive Convention against Terrorism under the auspices of the United Nations to tackle the menace.[9]

The Russian position was further reinforced in the joint statement on 3rd, February, 2002, in which both the countries gave the call for a comprehensive, long-term, multi-dimensional cooperation among the members of the international community to fight against the existence of extensive ties between the terrorist outfits active in Afghanistan like the AL-Qaeda and Taliban with other terrorist organisations active in other parts of the world, including Chechnya and the Central Asian Republics. A Memorandum of Understanding (MoU) signed in December, 2002, between India and Russia gave rise to India –Russia Joint Working Group on Combating International Terrorism.[10] In its second meeting held in April, 2004 in New Delhi, both the sides agreed to strengthen their counter terrorism cooperation through particular means such as:

1. Exchange of information and sharing of experience in their fight against international terrorism,
2. Strengthen cooperation in curbing trafficking in narcotics,
3. Continuing support and cooperation to address the threat of terrorist financing,
4. Extending support for the full and effective implementation of the UN Security Council resolution 1373 which deals with anti-terrorist mechanisms and the work of the Security Council's Counter Terrorism Committee,
5. Continuing consultations on the Comprehensive Convention on Terrorism, and
6. Convention against Acts of Nuclear Terrorism with a view to their finalization.

India and Russia opposed Washington's tendency to concentrate on the 'global campaign against terror' solely on manifestations of what concerned it. They insisted that the campaign against terror should be uniform, comprehensive, continuous and multi-faceted.[11] They urged that confidence be built among members of the anti-terror coalition by giving due consideration to the interests of each of them.

The fourth meeting of the India-Russia Joint Working Group on Combating International Terrorism was held in New Delhi on October 24, 2006. The negotiations were held in the atmosphere of trust, frankness and mutual understanding. The two sides shared concern on cross border terrorism and emphasised the importance of actions by all States to deny safe heaven to terrorists. They stressed the necessity to take more efficient measures on preventing the propagation of terrorism, including in the Cyberspace. The importance of broader dialogue among cultures and civilizations to counter divisiveness, on which terrorists thrive, was underlined. In this context the two sides called for unconditional implementation of the United Nations

Security Council (UNSC) Resolution 1624 on fighting incitement to terrorism.[12] The Russian and Indian delegations reiterated that cooperation in combating terrorism constitutes an important part of strategic partnership between the two countries.[13] They unequivocally condemned terrorism in all its forms and manifestations and reiterated their commitment to further strengthen counter-terrorism cooperation. The two sides agreed to enhance cooperation in the international fora, especially in suppressing Weapons of Mass Destruction (WMD) and terrorism.[14] They noted that early entry into force of the International Convention on Suppression of Acts of Nuclear Terrorism (ICSANT) would facilitate this objective. They stressed the need to further improve the legal framework for the fight against terrorism. The two sides also urged the early finalization of the Comprehensive Convention on International Terrorism (CCIT) at the United Nations (UN) during this meeting.[15] Issues of regional anti-terrorist cooperation were reviewed. It was noted that India-Russia partnership within the Shanghai Cooperation Organization (SCO) and ASEAN Regional Forum must be enhanced, including eliminating new threats and challenges in Central, South and South-East Asia. At the same time, both sides also discussed the emerging threat to oil and gas installations from terrorists and agreed to exchange experiences to counter it, underscoring energy security as a vital component of national and international counter-terrorism strategies.

Afghanistan Issue

The situation in the common neighbours-Afghanistan and Central Asia-is of vital security interest to both Russia and India. Their cooperation on Afghanistan has been quite durable. They underscored the need for the international community to remain engaged in the effort to ensure the revival of Afghanistan as a sovereign and independent state, free from terrorism, drugs and external interference.[16]

The successful cooperation of India and Russia through the Joint Working Group on Afghanistan led to the creation of Joint Working Group on Global challenges. Its first meeting was held in New Delhi on 13-14 October 2003.[17] Both countries said they were concerned about the "continuing deterioration" of the situation in Afghanistan and the growing terrorist threat posed by the Taliban and other extremist forces.[18] The Joint statement further held that India and Russia were interested in strengthening Afghanistan's statehood.

Emergence of Multipolar World

The declaration of strategic partnership, in 2003, between Russia and India emphasized that it is necessary to build a multipolar global structure based on sovereign equality of all states and people, democratic values and justice and recognized their special responsibility by virtue of being among the largest multi ethnic, multilingual and multi religious states, inspired by the desire to jointly contribute to the strengthening of international relations as well to the promotion and the establishment of a just and stable world order.[19] The strategic partnership of the declaration provides for joint initiatives on key international issues, and informing each other of planned foreign policy initiatives in the international arena. Both the countries expressed their conviction of the necessity to build a multipolar global structure based on sovereignty and equality of all states and peoples.[20] During former Indian Prime Minister Vajpayee's visit to Moscow, on 12 November, 2003, a joint declaration on Global Challenges and Threats to International Security and Stability was signed which emphasized on multipolarity against unilateralism in world affairs.[21] Both India and Russia have time and again reiterated their commitment to the evolution of a multipolar world order. The Foreign Ministers of India and Russia during their bilateral discussion at the Kazakh capital Almaty, on 21 October, 2004, decided to strengthen a collective approach to world affairs and reaffirmed their commitment to fight terrorism and drug trafficking.[22]

Whether it is the issue of Iraq or Afghanistan or the Middle East peace process both the countries have emphasized on multilateralism.[23] India and the Russian Federation affirm that the future international order based on multipolarity should be determined by collective and multilateral processes rather than unilateral ones.[24]

International Peace and Stability

The India and Russia, as strategic partners, agreed to coordinate their positions on key global issues by issuing the Declaration on Global Challenges and Threats to World Security and Stability.[25] India and Russia have agreed on the importance of maintaining global strategic stability, and in this context, India supports all nuclear disarmament measures which would rectify the irrationalities of the Cold War.

Former Indian Prime Minister, A.B. Vajpayee, highly praised Indo-Russian ties as a "shining example of relation between the two friendly countries-to be followed everywhere if world peace is to be achieved.[26]" Our ties have not lost their historical mileage and have not shrunk to realpolitik pragmatism. Together we advocate the ideas of equality and non-violence, supremacy of international law amidst the central role of the United Nations, we jointly fight on the anti-terror front and react to world crises, searching for ways of responding to new challenges and threats and closely cooperate with the United Nations and other international organizations".[27] The former Russian President said, "we are determined to strengthen and enrich our strategic partnership which today is the optimal long-term model of interaction and foreign policy coordination between Russia and India. Our task today is to maintain and develop the potential of this partnership for the good of the two nations, for the sake of international peace and stability.[28]

India-Russia Joint Working Group Summit on Global Challenges held its first meeting in New Delhi in October, 2003. Both countries agreed to coordinate their position on various regional and international issues. Mr. Vajpayee, the former Prime Minister of India, said: "My discussions with President Putin and other representatives of the Russian leadership will also cover major global and regional political developments".[29] The Russian PM Vladimir Putin said that both the countries have convergent global interests and share common responsibility for maintaining international security and stability.[30]

National Missile Development, Disarmament, Non-Weaponisation of Space

Moscow and New Delhi continue to share excellent understanding on important global issues such as disarmament, NMD and non-weaponization of space. New Delhi's welcome to the NMD proposals was a surprise for Moscow as it was for the rest of the international community, but the war on terrorism has put the NMD issue on the back burner. In a joint statement issued during former Indian Prime Minister Vajpayee's visit to Russia, India and Russia expressed their support to preserving the existing arms control and disarmament agreements, including the ABM treaty of 1972.[31]

Another crucial and relevant dimension on which India and Russia share a close concern is the dangerous linkage between terrorism and Weapons of Mass Destruction (WMD). Both the countries reiterated their commitment towards strengthening non-proliferation and disarmament goals.[32] In this respect the Delhi Declaration very clearly pointed out that India and Russia are convinced that the promotion of the disarmament process, including reduction and eventual elimination of nuclear weapons, is one of the most important components of security both in Asia and in the world at large.[33] The space based weapons would make the situation even more dangerous.[34]

The subject that has secured an important place in the recent political declarations between India and Russia is the central role of the UN in meeting the common global challenges and threats. There is regular consultation and cooperation between the two countries in the UN and other international fora on important international issues. The Joint Political Document of the two countries reaffirms their shared conviction of the centrality of the UN and the need to further strengthen it.

Central Asia Issues

Russia and India have vital interests in maintaining security, stability and a secular order in the Central Asian region. India as well as Russia considers Central Asia to be an important region with vital geo-strategic interests. The geo-strategic importance of Central Asia draws the interest of India and Russia together in this region. Both are keen on maintaining peace and stability in this region. Both stand for:

1. establishing stability and peace in this region.
2. working against the spread of terrorist networks.
3. working for the greater regional cooperation.
4. controlling drug trafficking in the region.

Building a viable security order and stability in central Asia and Afghanistan continues to be the prime concern of the international community. For regional stability it is important to ensure that Central Asia does not become the next Afghanistan.[35]

Iran and Iraq Issue

Both India and Russia want the Iranian peaceful nuclear programme to be operationalised at the earliest, (But India remains loath to the emergence of another nuclear weapon possessing state in her vicinity) and have expressed the hope that the issue would be resolved at the level of International Atomic Energy Agency. Both have agreed that the international community should rely on consultation rather than confrontation in sorting out doubts over Iran's nuclear ambitions.[36] The two countries prefer to rely on dialogue and diplomacy to avert confrontation in this matter.[37] The two countries were "convinced" that an effective solution to the Iranian nuclear issue would best be found through political and diplomatic efforts.[38] "They agreed that implementation of [U.N. Security Council] Resolution [1737 on Iran] should facilitate resumption of negotiations for a long-term comprehensive agreement.[39] In a declaration signed by the former Indian Prime Minister, Atal Bihari Vajpayee, and the former Russian President, Vladimir Putin, the two countries had agreed that a "concrete and time-bound" action plan under the aegis of the United Nations should be adopted for the "earliest restoration" of Iraq's sovereignty.[40] Expressing concern at the "continuing deterioration" of the situation in Iraq, India and Russia declared that these developments indicated the need for "collective international efforts" toward restoring early normality in the West Asian nations.[41]

Stability in Eurasia

India and Russia underscored the need to ensure stability in Eurasia and the world and favoured creation of a just and fair world order based on international law and principles of mutual respect. Both sides also stressed that all issues should be addressed through dialogue without any interference or show of authority.[42]

West Asia Issues

On the Israeli-Palestinian conflict, the two countries called for the "prevention of the failure of the roadmap" to settle the problems.[43] Any failure of the roadmap, backed by Russia, the United States, the United Nations and the European Union, may result in worsening of the situation in Israel and Palestine, as also in the entire West Asia, spiraling beyond control.

Korean Issues

Both nations have favoured the efforts of the "countries concerned" and the international community for a peaceful settlement of the nuclear issue on the Korean peninsula and for maintaining its non-nuclear status.[44]

Conclusion

The strategic partnership between India and Russia had not only served the long-term national interests of the two countries, but has also contributed to the stability and security of Asia and the world at large. The overall India-Russia political dialogue process focuses on a large complex of leading substantive international issues-political, economic, social, cultural, humanitarian, including security, disarmament, international terrorism and its close nexus with drug trafficking and illicit arms transfer, the international terrorism WMD connection, sovereignty, role of the UN, globalisation, sustainable development and the environment, the international economic order, issues of public health, technology transfer, cultural cooperation etc., as well as leading regional developments currently in West Asia and the Far East. While these issues have been preoccupying the international community for decades, they have acquired social profile following the end of Cold War. These issues are largely cumulative products of accelerated technological and economic progress and the voluntary policies and actions of statesand non-state actors. Coming to terms with them means essentially updating the strategic and political framework in which the international community has dealt with them- i.e., establishing a rational world order, in relation to security development and the welfare of nations. India and Russia are deeply affected by these issues and perhaps more so than other countries because of their size and pluralistic nature of their societies.

It can, therefore, be concluded that there is a great scope for Indo-Russian relations not only with regard to improving the socio-economic conditions of their people but also to play an important role in shaping the future world order. The unipolar world order headed by the United States of America which came into existence after the collapse of the Soviet Union in 1991, and can be replaced by the multipolar world order if the Asian powers in general and India and Russia in particular come closer to each other to form an Eastern Alliance against the growing influence of one single super power. The European Union in general and old Europe in particular also emerges as powerful grouping to counter the Anglo American hegemony in shaping the future world order. The Huntington's clash of civilisation thesis needs to be replaced by a dialogue among the major power blocs for sharing the global resources in an equitable and sustainable manner that would eventually lead to peace and stability in the world. In this context, it can be rightly said that the Indo-Russian economic, strategic and cultural partnership has and can continue to play a significant role in shaping the 21st century world order. The global presence of India and Russia and their tremendous power, influence, and willingness to remain engaged in countering global threat perceptions can be a key factor affecting the future shape of the international security environment.

Endnotes

1. See G.M. Shah, "New Themes in Indo-Russian Relations-A Futuristic Study" in V.D Chopra B.ed., *New Trends in Indo-Russian Relations,* (Kalpaz Publications, Delhi, 2003), p.179.

2. See Jyostna Bakshi, "Prime Minister's Moscow Visit", *Strategic Analysis*, Vol. 29, No. 4, October-December 2005, p.732.

3. See V.P. Dutt, "Putin's Russia and India: Over View", in V.D. Chopra, ed., *New Trends in Indo-Russian Relations,* (Kalpaz Publications, Delhi, 2003), p.25

4. *Ibid.*

5. See Ravim Bakaya, "Looking Beyond Indo-Russian Military-Strategic Partnership", *Mainstream*, Vol. XLII, No.12, March 13, 2004, p. 22.

6. See Alexander M. Kadakin, "Indo-Russian Relations: Problems and Prospects" in Mahavir Singh and Victor Krassilchtchikov, eds., *Eurasian Vision*, (Anamika Publishers and Distributors (P) Ltd., New Delhi, 2003), p. 110.

7. *Ibid*, p.111.

8. See Debidatta Aurobindo Mahapatra, "Russia's Policy Towards the

Kashmir Issue in the Changing World Order", *International Studies*, Vol. 41, No.1, January-March 2004, p.130.

9. *Ibid*, p.139.

10. See Biju Thomas, "Putin's India Policy: Mutual Gains For Future", *India Quarterly-Journal of International Affairs*, Vol. LXIII, No. 2, April-June 2007, p. 131.

11. See Rouben Azizian, "Russia-India Relations: Stability Amidst Strategic Uncertainty", *Asia Pacific Center for Security Studies*, Special Assessment, October 2004, p. 5.

12. See http://www.meaindia.nic.in/.

13. *Ibid.*

14. *Ibid.*

15. *Ibid.*

16. See Rouben Azizian, "Russia-India Relations: Stability Amidst Strategic Uncertainty", *Asia Pacific Center for Security Studies*, Special Assessment, October 2004, p. 5.

17. See *The Hindu*, 13 November, 2003.

18. See *The Hindu*, 26 January, 2007.

19. See Biju Thomas, "Putin's India Policy: Mutual Gains For Future", *India Quarterly-Journal of International Affairs*, Vol. LXIII, No. 2, April-June 2007, p.136.

20. See Debidatta Aurobindo Mahapatra, "Russia's Policy Towards the Kashmir Issue in the Changing World Order", *International Studies*, Vol. 41, No.1, January-March 2004, p.139.

21. See Biju Thomas, "Putin's India Policy: Mutual Gains For Future", *India Quarterly-Journal of International Affairs*, Vol. LXIII, No. 2, April-June 2007, p.137.

22. See Debidatta Aurobindo Mahapatra, "Expectations From The Putin's Visit", *Mainstream*, Vol. XLII, No. 49, 27 November 2004, p. 28.

23. See http://www.indianembassy.ru/doc-htm/en/en_03_03_to 12. htm.

24. See *The Hindu*, 13 November, 2003.

25. *Ibid.*

26. See Alexander M. Kadakin, "Indo-Russian Relations: Problems and

Prospects" in Mahavir Singh & Victor Krassilchtchikov, eds., *Eurasian Vision*, (Anamika Publishers and Distributors (P) Ltd., New Delhi, 2003), p. 109.

27. *Ibid.*

28. *Ibid*, p.110.

29. See *The Hindu*, 12 November, 2003.

30. See *The Hindu*, 12 December, 2007.

31. See John Cherian "Firming Up A Friendship", *Frontline*, Vol.18, Issue 24, November 24, December 07, 2001.

32. See Meena Singh Roy, "Commonalities of Indian and Russian Interests in Central Asia", in V.D. Chopra ed., *New Trends in Indo-Russian Relations,*, (Kalpaz Publications, Delhi, 2003), p. 216.

33. *Ibid.*

34. *Ibid.*

35. *Ibid*, p. 210.

36. See *The Hindu*, 17 September, 2005.

37. See *The Hindu*, 18 November, 2006.

38. See *The Hindu*, 26 January, 2007.

39. *Ibid.*

40. See *The Hindu*, 13 November, 2003.

41. See *The Hindu*, 26 January, 2007.

42. See *The Hindu*, 25 May, 2005.

43. See *The Hindu*, 13 November, 2003.

44. *Ibid.*

20

Terrorism Islamic Fundamentalism and its Implications for Democracy and Human Rights

Dr. Sujit Lahiry

Discourses on strategic and security studies invariably focuses on terrorism, whether it may be local or global Terrorism, like war, is a historical condition. The global terror networks using the modern communications technology, other communication means and dispersed operative cells is actually a two-decade old phenomenon. However, terrorism became a global problem and a threat for the majority of nations after the unfolding of events of 9/11, which quite seriously questioned the very basis of US unipolarity.

The rise of Islamic fundamentalism, as represented by Al Qaeda and Taliban has, also propelled the growth of global terrorism. Though the menace of terrorism existed earlier also, but it has assumed a global dimension, leading to the evolution of new forms of "globalized" terrorism after the events of 9/11. Terrorism whether it is local or global violates human rights and endangers human security. What kind of counter-terrorism measures have been and can be taken by a state to offset local or global terrorism? This paper makes a modest attempt to explore some of these substantive issues on terrorism, which confronts humanity. This paper accordingly has been divided into four sections.

I

Meaning and Dimensions of Terrorism

'Terrorism' is now widely discussed in the discourses on freedom, liberal democracy and human rights. A very asymmetrical relationship usually exists between terrorism and liberal democracies, as the two cannot exist in conjunction with each other. In the contemporary world, terrorism has become an ideology in itself, essentially connoting to 'rule by terror'. Terrorism has not only re-defined regional, state and national politics, but is also trying to re-define the geopolitical landscape of the contemporary world.

Terrorism, in itself, reflects what I believe is a 'movement of resistance'. This resistance can be against an individual, a group, a region, state or even the global community. It thus essentially produces an 'other', with which it continues its politics of resistance in the form of violence, attack on neutrals, primarily to realise their own parochial and narrow political objectives. Terrorism, per se, does not have any objective definition, since one man's terrorist is another man's freedom fighter. The concept of terrorism is therefore all subjective. It will however, be a good exercise to elaborate some of the prevailing definitions of terrorism. The *Oxford English Dictionary* defines terrorism as "the state of being terrified and greatly frightened: intense fear, fright or dead, the action or quality of causing dread". Terrorism thus has a tendency to use violent, aggressive and coercive measures. As Jenny Tiechman argues, terrorism : consists of violent actions carried out for political or other social purposes, including some large scale mercenary purpose, by individual or groups, having an aim, which might be either good or bad, but carried out by means of either or both of the following:

(1) attacks on innocent or neutral or randomly chosen people, or

(2) using means which involve atrocities, e.g., torture, cruel killings, or mutilation of the living or the dead, committed against randomly or non-randomly chosen people who may be innocent or not.[2]

The *Penguin Dictionary of Politics* defines terrorism as "the use of violence politically as a means of pressurizing a government and/or society into accepting a radical political or social change".[3] The genesis of the word terrorism is usually traced from the Latin word 'terrere', which means tremble' or 'to frighten from'.[4] It came into popular usage after the 'Reign of Roberspierre' or 'Reign of Terror', in the French Revolution in the late 18th Century. Terrorism itself does not have any quantifiable meaning. It has to be understood in the context in which it is used. As the history of international politics will reveal that the Roman Empire, Czarist Russia, France, nationalist movements in various parts of Asia, Africa and Latin America all have experienced or even used terrorism, or what I call 'terror polities' at some or the other point of time. Therefore, it is very difficult to define terrorism.

Terrorism needs to be understood in the specific socio-economic and political set-up of the country. Various factors that give rise to terrorism are usually the class-structure of the society and the internal contradictions within the society, socio-economic deprivation, poverty, marginalisation and alienation of the marginalised and deprived sections of the society, ideology, nationalism, sub-nationalism and ethno-nationalism, autonomy and secessionist movements, weak state and even hegemonic aspirations of a strong state; fundamentalism; Weapons of Mass Destruction (WMDs) including nuclear, chemical and biological weapons, role of Information

Technology including the news media, satellite channels, etc.[5]

Terrorism essentially induces fear, ruthlessness on the victim and has no regard for established humanitarian values. It usually resorts to methods like kidnapping, hijacking, indiscriminate shootings, bombings, assassinations and mass murders.

Terrorism, per se, has an inbuilt mechanism of moving in various dimensions. For example, individual and group terrorism is usually distinguished from state terrorism. Whereas, the former refers to the politics of violence being used by an individual or group for achieving their own political or other objectives, the latter refers to the politics of terror being unleashed by the state in order to maintain political control or law and order. Similarly, there are revolutionary terrorists, who essentially advocate a class-struggle approach (for example, Naxalites). However, the revolutionary terrorists have much in common with political or ideological terrorists, who essentially espouse their ideological struggle as a manifestation of terrorist struggle, like Naxalites, ULFA (United Liberation Front of Assam) in Assam, the Bodo National Front, the Tamil militants, the JKLF (Jammu and Kashmir Liberation Front), Hamas in Palestine, etc.[6]

Then there is 'Cross Border Terrorism', the prime example here will be terrorism emanating from Pakistan against India. Another quite significant dimension is 'nationalist separatist terrorism', which takes place when nationalist separatist organisations do not have any say in "public decision processes as a result of state coercion or pluralistic competition"[7] (like say, Irish Republican Army in Northern Ireland, LTTE in Sri Lanka). Then, there is 'fundamentalist terrorism' born out of religious extremism (like Islamic fundamentalism).

Sometimes, one can also usually talk about 'suicide terrorism', as can be discerned from the use of suicide bombings as a method of terror by radical extremist groups, like Hamas and Palestinian Islamic Jehad in Palestine. Now, even the PLO (Palestinian Liberation Organisation) - affiliated groups like the Fatah, Fatah-Tanzim, the Popular Front for the Liberation of Palestine, al-Aqsa Brigade have increasingly resorted to suicide bombings. However, groups like Hamas and the LTTE essentially have nationalist aspirations.

It becomes pertinent here to identify one shared characteristic among all forms the acts of terrorism take. For example, targeting of civilian population as opposed to state forces and with an aim to coerce behavioural change through the instrument of fear is one prime manifestation of all forms of terrorism. Also, it is important to distinguish common crime from terrorism - while, terrorism is politically informed, common crime is not. Further, one needs to understand that where terrorists are embedded insurgencies, such as Al Qaeda and the Taliban, the seriousness of their threat to the state's existence is real. It is the insurgencies, not terrorism per se, which pose potential threat of destabilisation of the existing order.

Thus, even though there are myriad manifestations of terrorism in different parts of the world, it is now 'global terrorism' which poses a serious threat to the entire humanity. It has been primarily catapulted by September 11, 2001, attacks on the World Trade Centre in the US.

Before 9/11, the US did not take due cognizance of this all-pervasive problem. The 7/7 (July 7, 2005) terrorist attack on the United Kingdom further reinforced the need for a grand coalition in the US war against terrorism.

II

Global Terrorism and the Rise of Islamic Fundamentalism

While the phenomenon of terrorism became a global problem ever since the events of 9/11, but the genesis of terrorism in more recent times can be traced to the 18th Century. It was in Russia that modern terrorism first made its appearance and then subsequently spread to Western Europe, Asia and the Balkans. The first wave of modern terrorism, which was primarily being developed by the Anarchists, continued for one generation. The primary strategy of the Anarchists was to develop 'assassination camps against prominent officials', and this strategy of the Anarchists was used by groups having nationalist aims elsewhere also, like in India and the Balkans.[9]

As David C. Rapport argues, one can discern four waves of modern terrorism :

The Anarchist wave was the first global or truly international terrorist experience in history; three similar, consecutive and overlapping expressions followed. The "anti-colonial wave" began in the 1920s and lasted about forty years. Then came the "New Left Wave", which diminished greatly as the twentieth century closed, leaving only few groups still active today in Nepal, Spain, the United Kingdom, Peru and Colombia. In 1979, a "religious wave" emerged; if the pattern of its three predecessors is relevant it could disappear by 2025, at which time a new wave might emerge. The uniqueness and persistence of the wave experience indicates that terror is deeply rooted in modern culture.[10]

It is the fourth "religious wave", which in the contemporary period has given birth to religious fundamentalism, and has produced the most virulent form of terrorism. Religion always has been a dominant factor in modern terrorism. Religious elements can be seen in the various struggles in Macedonia, Armenia, Ireland, Israel and Palestine - though the primary objective of these struggles was to create a secular state. However, religious extremism in the contemporary period has radically different objectives. As David C. Rapport points out, "Today, religion has a vastly different significance, supplying justifications and organizing principles for a state. The religious wave has produced an occasional secular group - a reaction to excessive secular zeal. Buddhists in Sri Lanka tried to transform the country, and a terrorist response among the largely Hindu Tamils aims at creating a separate secular state".[11]

The fourth wave of modern terrorism has been catapulted by three events in the Islamic world. These were the Iranian Revolution of 1979, beginning of a new Islamic Century and most important, the Soviet invasion of Afghanistan in 1979.

The Iranian Revolution of 1979 was the first turning point in the emergence of Islamic fundamentalism. The Shah of Iran was overthrown and Ayatollah Khomeini came to power, thus making Iran a major adversary of America. As David C. Rapport observes:

Most immediately, the Iranians inspired and assisted the Shiite terror movements outside of Iran, particularly in Iraq, Saudi Arabia, Kuwait and Lebanon. In Lebanon, Shiites - influenced by the self-martyrdom tactic of the medieval Assassins - introduced suicide bombing, with surprising results, ousting American and other foreign troops that had entered the country on a peace mission after the 1982 Israeli invasion.[13]

The Soviet invasion of Afghanistan was the second major turning factor for the rise of Islamic fundamentalism. With the Soviet invasion of Afghanistan in 1979, the US became hyper-active and started finding ways and means of countering the threat of spread of communism and establish its hegemony in the form of *'Pax-Americana'*, that the US started the policy of mixing fundamentalism and terrorism together. This has now evolved in the form of Islamic fundamentalism. The Afghan mujahideen (or holy warriors) were essentially armed, trained and financed by CIA of US and ISI of Pakistan in order to drive the Soviets out of Afghanistan. And, this well-coordinated enterprise was given the name of 'Jihad' or to be specific, an 'Islamic Jihad'.[14] In this process, the US enlisted the support of its key allies, namely Israel and Pakistan. These Afghan mujahideen have over the years created a major Islamic fundamentalist group, i.e., the Taliban and Al Qaeda, headed by Osama bin Laden. The Taliban garnered sufficient strength to capture power in Kabul in 1996, notwithstanding the rebellion of Tajiks, Hazaras and Uzbeks. Consequently, while the US succeeded in throwing out Soviet Union from Afghanistan, Islamic fundamentalism in the form of Taliban and Al Qaeda stayed back, which now posed as a major force to reckon with in the post-Soviet world.

In the contemporary world, Islamic fundamentalism seeks to restore the pure, true and original Islam through the mechanisms of terror, coercion and violence. And, one of the prime manifestation of this Islamic extremism has evolved in the form of Al Qaeda. The evolution of Al Qaeda as a dominant Islamic fundamentalist group has been well explained by Fred Halliday: "The perceived failure of secular nationalism.......to create viable and equitable states, to develop economies, or to confront the enemies of the Islamic world, and not least, to liberate Palestine, provided, in the 1980s and 1990s, the context for the reassertion of fundamentalism."[15]

Jonathan Stevenson has pointed out three specific objectives of Al Qaeda. These are reproduced below:

> First, al-Qaeda seeks to overthrow Arab regimes — in particular Egypt's and Saudi Arabia's, whose close relationships with the United States render them 'apostate' and thus inimical to true Islam. These are the 'near enemies'. Second, it wants to debilitate the US - al Qaeda's prime 'far enemy' - as a superpower and purge Muslim states of all American and Western political, economic and cultural influences. Third, and less centrally, al Qaeda would like to eliminate the state of Israel (another 'far enemy') and liberate the Palestinian people. None of these aims are realistically negotiable, and al Qaeda's broader- but equally decipherable - goal of an apocalyptic 'clash of civilsations' between Islam and the Judeo-Christian West enroute to a pan-Islamic Caliphate merely underlies its implacability.[16]

Al Qaeda as an umbrella terrorist organisation in the contemporary times has forged alliances with major Islamist group.[17] The space occupied by the Islamic Umma is "Dar-al-Islam, the 'Abode of Islam', the metaphysical space defined by religious and universal truths found in the Koran. Set against is Dar-al-Harb, the 'Abode of War', the site of conflict and infidelity, the area in which Islamic law is not yet observed."[18] As Elena Pavlova points out:

> In restoring the Muslim umma (community of believers) to the original sources of its faith — the Qu'ran and the Sunna (example of the Prophet) - radical Islam attempts to bridge the conceptual gap between modernity and religion by re-interpreting historical events in religious terms. As such, political Islam combines the quest for religious authenticity with the need for social and political revolution, focusing on the state as the instrument of social transformation.[19]

Pavlova further continues this argument thus:

> According to radical Islamists, modern societies have returned to a condition of pre-Islamic ignorance *(Jahiliyya)*. The secularist

> tendencies of the modern state have effectively obliterated God's sovereignty on earth *(hakimiyya)*. By abrogating the Islamic legal code *(Sharia)* and substituting it with faulty man-made laws, the ruling elites have deviated from the straight path of Islam, bringing upon themselves the status of unbelievers *(kuffar)*.[20]

'Global jihad' has also flourished because of Al Qaeda's use of the global Information Technology revolution that has swept the world. Al Qaeda now not only post pro-cause *fatwas* and Islamic books on the internet, but also makes use of cassettes, propaganda videotapes, coloured photographs, chat rooms, internet discussion groups as well as the widespread use of websites like http://www.al-neda.com, and http://www.drasat.com in order to spread its ideology as well as the message of 'global jihad'.[21] In their crusade for 'global jihad', the Taliban committed large-scale atrocities against "women, children, ethnic-religious minorities and political opponents, thereby deepening the internal divide in Afghanistan, besides violating the basic human rights of Afghans."[22]

However, the rise of this Islamic fundamentalism and terrorism was not confined, to, Afghanistan. alone, but soon spread to Pakistan and Bangladesh as well. This has resulted in the growth of a large number of religious mercenaries in Pakistan, and consequently, the Indian state of Jammu and Kashmir has always been in a state of turmoil and upheaval as a result of Pakistan's policy of promoting cross-border terrorism in Kashmir ever since 1989.

Pakistan-sponsored terrorist groups like Lashkar-e-Toiba, Hizb-ul-Mujahideen and Jaish-e-Muhammad, which owed their allegiance to the *Jamiat-ul-Ulema-i-Islam; Jamaat-i-Islami* and *Ahle Hadith* openly ignited the youth in Kashmir. The *Pan-Islamism* based on the concept of Umma (or Millat) not only united the Kasmiri Islamic insurgents and the Afghan mujahideen, but also created turmoil and violence in Kashmir. At the same time, it also led to ethno-religious cleansing of Kashmiri Pandits from the Kashmir valley. They thus clearly threatened the pluralist and multi-ethnic secular democracy of India.[23]

As Syed Ali Shah Geelani of the Jammat-e-Islami of Kashmir once pointed out, "The Muslims (of Kashmir) were part of Millat........This very feeling of being part of Millat attracts Mujahideen from Afghanistan, Saudi Arabia, Sudan, etc. to Kashmir."[24] Thus one can easily discern two major trends of religious fundamentalism, i.e., Islamisation of politics and politicisation of Islam. The Islamisation of state can be seen in the fact that the Federal Ministry of Religious Affairs and the Council of Islamic Ideology in Pakistan openly "justified the destruction of the Bamiyan Buddhas by the Taliban, saying that there was nothing wrong in destroying them.[25]

The *Task Force on Terrorism and Unconventional Warfare* set up by the US House Republican Research Committee in a report called the "New Islamist International" (February 1, 1993) has well documented the growth of religious fundamentalism and the growing inter-linkages between Islamic fundamentalism and terrorism.[26]

III

9/11 and the US War on Terror

The September 11, 2001, terrorist attack by the Taliban and Al Qaeda was therefore fallout of the deep hatred of Taliban towards US policy of promoting imperialism and establish its hegemony. The Islamic fundamentalists realised that in order to establish an Islamic Caliphate and Umma as well as to stop US from establishing its hegemony in the form of *Pax-Americana,* the US needs to be punished and targeted, which ultimately culminated in the events of 9/11. The precursor to 9/11 can be located in the bombing of the World Trade Centre basement in New York by the Taliban in 1993. Tracing the historicity of this deep hatred of the Taliban towards the US, Andreas Behnke points out, 'It is precisely the presence of American soldiers on the Arabian peninsula that provided the initial rationale for Osama bin Laden's terror campaign against the USA. Having failed to stabilise the regimes in Egypt and Saudi Arabia through a number of attacks, al Qaeda's strategy as of 1996 was to open a second front against the United States, or "King of Sattan", the temporal power that facilitated the rule of "false" (jahiliyya) Muslim regimes".[27]

The Taliban attack on the World Trade Centre and the Pentagon, Washington D.C. in the US gave a serious setback to the economic and military might of the US. Consequently, the US started its counter-offensive measure in the form of 'War on Terror', also referred to as *'Operation Enduring Freedom',* and also enlisted its support from major European countries as well as countries like India, Pakistan and Israel. The US strategy essentially seeks to "target the military and financial assets of Al Qaeda.[28]

In its war against terrorism, the US President, Bush jr. directed his attention primarily against those states, which constituted the 'Axis of Evil', like, Iraq, Iran and North Korea and those states, which it describes as *rogue states,* i.e., where democracy is non-existent. The wider US objective inter alia was certainly to control Iraq's oil. The "9/11 Commission Report, released in July 2004, found no institutional or planning - level links between al - Qaeda and Saddam Hussein's regime.[29]

The execution of Saddam Hussein in Iraq on December 30, 2006, who was captured in December 2003, has been hailed by President Bush Jr. as a landmark victory of the US in its war against terrorism. Saddam was executed for committing crimes against humanity in the 1982 killings of 148 persons in a single town of Dujail. However, the manner in which the execution was carried out has been deplored as barbaric, even by the Amnesty International. Saddam's execution is likely to trigger much more turmoil, bloodshed and anarchy in Iraq, as sectarian violence between Shias and Sunnis are likely to escalate. While the Shias are rejoicing over the end of a tyrannical Sunni domination in Iraq, the Sunnis are angry and have proclaimed Saddam as a martyr. The execution has not only left the Arabs divided, but is also likely to increase the anti-US sentiment and also the likely possibilities of the growth of fundamentalism and terrorism.

Moreover, President Bush has not accepted the recommendations of the 10-member Iraq Study Group, headed by James Baker, which has called for phased withdrawal of US troops from Iraq. and initiate reconstruction process.[30] On the contrary, President Bush has decided to send about 20,000 troops to Iraq, thus ignoring the core thrust of the Iraq Study Group, as well as flouting the advice of Democrats in the US and Prime Minister Nuri Kamal Al Maliki of Iraq.

Quite similar to Iraq, in Afghanistan, the US-led coalition very conveniently removed the Taliban away from power and installed in its place a puppet government (essentially being controlled by the US) under the leadership of Hamid Karzai. But in the post - 9/11 period, Al Qaeda has not only survived, but also continues to carry out its Islamic jihad with renewed vigour. While, some of its terrorist activities have been successful, in others, Al Qaeda has quite blatantly faced defeat as Rohan Gunaratna points out.[31]

Al Qaeda has quite vociferously continued with its Islamic Jihad by continuing to attack and launch terrorist operations, including the planned kidnapping and murder of the well-known journalist of *Wall Street Journal,* Daniel Pearl; the bombing of a church in Islamabad, killing a US diplomat's wife and a daughter, two abetted attempts to assassinate Afghanistan President, Hamid Karzai and his cabinet ministers. In this regard, one can definitely foresee the revival and resurgence of Taliban and Al Qaeda. The Taliban-Al Qaeda relationship is so fused and forged that while Taliban operates as a guerrilla force, Al Qaeda is essentially a terrorist group.[32] Together, they try to establish a Pan-Islamic Caliphate. The resurgence of Taliban-Al Qaeda can be seen in the fact that the leader of the Taliban, and the former head of the Islamic Emirate of Afghanistan, Mullah Omar and Al Qaeda's deputy leader, Dr. Ayman Al Zawahari now plays a substantial and pro-active role in fighting the US-led coalition forces in Afghanistan. Moreover, the fresh recruitment of various rungs of leaders by Al Qaeda along with Lashkar-e-Omar (which will conduct low-intensity campaign in Afghanistan), as well as by inspiring terrorist groups in Pakistan, like Harkat-ul-Mujahideen, Lashkar-e-Toiba, and Jaish-e-

Muhammad, Al Qaeda is actually trying to revive and rejuvenate itself in the post 9/11 period.

Bruce Hoffman has actually portrayed a typology of four distinct, but mutually exclusive dimensions of contemporary *Al Quaida*..[33]

IV

Terrorism, Democracy and Human Rights: Understanding the Interfaces

The myriad manifestations of 'terrorism' and 'global terrorism' thus not only violates human rights and endangers human security, but also greatly undermines democracy, and especially liberal democracy. What kind of interfaces therefore we can actually locate between terrorism, democracy and human rights? Terrorism essentially instils fear, intimidation and coercion on the victim. The victim can be an individual, a group or a state. And, the basic unit of analysis in both human rights and human security is the individual, his life, their well-being, safety and dignity.[34] At the same time, democracy essentially espouses freedom of speech and expression without any kind of threat to the life of an individual. Freedom of choice and voicing of dissent are integral to democracy. Terrorism, by suppressing freedom of choice and expression is essentially creating the need for 'freedom from fear', which forms an integral part of the discourses on human security. It is thereby not only violating human rights, but is also seriously questioning human security as well.

Serious consideration also merits to the fact that the US has either in the name of 'imparting or implanting democracy', in the name of humanitarian intervention[35], or in its drive against 'War on Terror', or in guise of search for WMDs, the US is interfering in the internal affairs of sovereign states, long ago ensured by the Westphalian state system.[36] This has greatly undermined the basic principles of liberal democracy in a fundamental way, as the US has become the world's sole policeman in the post-Soviet world. The US is thus constantly trying to homogenise and hegemonise the world power structure and the global space and thereby impose its *imperial sovereignty* over the developing and the underdeveloped countries, which constitutes the periphery.

The neo-conservatives who have the dominant say in the US administration and foreign policy have been primarily guided by the neo-liberal theory of 'democratic peace', elaborated by Michael Doyle. One of the fundamental premises of this theory is that democratic states do not go to war against each other. It is this neo-conservative thinking and neo-liberal thinking, which led President Bush to describe Iraq, Iran and North Korea as an 'axis of evil'. This has led President Bush junior to eliminate all those 'rogue states', which supports terrorism, both overt and covert, and implant democracy through various means, whether it be forcible intervention in the internal affairs of a country, or even more clandestinely by the US doctrine of *'pre-emption.* The US argued that terrorism cannot thrive, if democracy exists: and democracy alone can protect human rights as well as the wider notion of human security. Democracy for the US simply meant in a narrow, simplistic manner as electoral democracy, which also however, is subject to president Bush's final approval of that elected government.

Democracy also implies that government ensures 'Good Governance', i.e., everybody has access to food, shelter, clothing, etc. But in most liberal democracies, including India, what is actually visible is that there is rampant poverty, unemployment, illiteracy, malnutrition, growing rural-urban divide, increasing socio-economic deprivation and marginalisation of the deprived. All these may be referred to as structural factors in establishing the linkages between terrorism, democracy and human rights.

Thus, the war against terrorism was juxtaposed to the protection of human rights and success of democracy. The US identified Taliban and Al Qaeda as the major harbingers of terrorism, which have made gross human rights violations. In *State of the Union Address* in November 2001, the Bush administration made explicit its stand on human rights:

> America will always stand firm for the non-negotiable demands of human dignity: the rule of law, limits on the power of the state; respect for women; private property, free speech, equal justice; and religious tolerance.......we have a greater objective than eliminating threats and containing resentment. We seek a just and peaceful world beyond the war on terror.[37]

In a major counter-terrorism operation unleashed by the US 'War on Terror', President Bush junior designated Pakistan and Uzbekistan as frontline states, Indonesia and Malaysia as second-front states and China as one third front country. Consequently, the US Congress within six weeks of 9/11, had passed a US Patriot Act on 26th October, 2001, which gave vast new powers to the US governmental agencies, primarily in the areas of intelligence, surveillance, immigration and detention. The Bush administration also rewarded these five frontline states with economic aid, directly or through International Financial Institutions (IFIs). Along with the Patriot Act, the US established the US Formal Homeland Security Advisory System in March 2002, for assessing threats, enforcing laws and managing diverse types of risks. However, the results of these US counter-terrorism measures have proved to be dismal on the human rights front. As Rosemary Foot points out[38]:

> Since 11 September, there are many examples that can be drawn upon to suggest that the US has compromised its stance in the sphere of human-rights promotion, as it searches for military bases, intelligence cooperation and political support in the struggle against terrorism. The US has moved closer to governments with poor human rights record which it once shunned, has reversed or modified policies that were introduced in order to signal displeasure with a country's human rights record, and has downgraded attention to human rights conditions in some other nations[39]. US national security officials have also been reported as using techniques outlawed under the 1984 Convention against Torture and Other Cruel, Inhuman or Degrading Treatment or Punishment, which the US signed in 1994, in their interrogation of al-Qaeda suspects. US authorities have also returned or sent a number of prisoners for further interrogation to countries where there are strong grounds to suspect that they will suffer torture. Moreover, these compromises have run in parallel with a serious curtailment of fundamental civil liberties at home, including the detention of an estimated 5,000 or more non-US citizens on alleged but unproven terrorist grounds. These trends have undermined the international authority of the US stance in this issue area and imply that there has been a trade-off between the imperatives of security in the 'age of terror' and human rights protection.[40]

Similarly, the US has committed blatant violation of human rights of the prisoners of war in Afghanistan. About 625 prisoners (approximately) have been held captive at the US naval base at Guantanamo Bay, Cuba, as a result of the US War on Terror in Afghanistan. Though, none of the prisoners have been charged, but they neither have been accorded the status of prisoner-of-war, nor the principles of Third Geneva Convention were applied to them. Moreover, to add insult to injury, the photographs of these prisoners in orange overalls crouching before US marine commanders, blindfolded and shackled were distributed around the world. There have been also reports that those prisoners who were held at the US-occupied Bagram air base in Afghanistan in December, 2002, have either been sent to third countries for further interrogation, where they were repeatedly tortured, or have been tortured while they were in US custody.[41] Thus, secret detention and torture, imprisonment, atrocities on prisoners, arbitrary and illegal kidnapping usually referred to as 'extraordinary rendition' are being routinely practised by the US forces, thus leading to serious erosion of civil liberties and human rights by the US.

The implications of this global terrorism also have some repercussions in India, as can be witnessed in the increased intensity of cross-border terrorism by Pakistan in Kashmir. But the Indian state has also promoted terror by invoking extra-constitutional measures, like 'encounters', 'disappearances', 'extra-judicial killings'. Along with these extra-constitutional measures, the Indian state has also invoked various draconian laws, like the *Maintenance of Internal Security Act* (MISA, which was repealed in 1977 by the Janata Party government); *Armed Forces Special Powers Act (AFSPA) and Disturbed Areas Act* (both of which exists in Jammu and Kashmir, Assam , Nagaland, Manipur and parts of Tripura), *National Security Act* (NSA); *Terrorist and Disruptive Activities Prevention Act (TADA),* which expired in 1995 and was replaced by the *Prevention of Terrorism Act* (2002). In December 2004, the UPA government replaced POTA by *Unlawful Activities Prevention Act* (in which, some of the provisions of POTA were retained through amendment). All these measures and laws have led to serious violations of human rights. This has generated a wide-ranging debate about individual rights vis-a-vis the need for public security. While, the state needs to provide security and maintain law and order, but should it be at the cost of individual rights and liberty? This essentially is a normative question, which needs to be seriously addressed.

The *US Department of State's Country Report on Human Rights,* 2005, provides ample clue of how serious violation of human rights and individual personal liberty have taken place at the hands of the oppressive Indian state. The Report observes :

> The Home Ministry reported that security forces killed 927 insurgents and terrorists during the year. The ministry also reported that insurgent and terrorist attacks in Jammu and Kashmir declined in 2004 with 733 civilians (including 92 women, 32 children, and 62 political workers), 330 security force members, and 976 insurgents killed. Security forces often used staged encounter killings to cover up the murder of captured non-Kashmiri insurgents and terrorists from Pakistan or other countries, often after torturing them. Human rights groups accused security forces of targeting suspected terrorists, militants and their suspected supporters. There were no widely accepted data on the magnitude of extra-judicial killings in Jammu and Kashmir, with estimates or reports depending on the political orientation of the source. In 2003, the Jammu and Kashmir state human rights commission received 15 complaints relating to custodial deaths and 27 complaints relating to disappearances. Human rights organizations sought to clarify these cases by submitting numerous requests to Jammu and Kashmir authorities, but they received inadequate and unsatisfactory responses. According to human rights activists, press reports and anecdotal accounts, the bodies of persons suspected of terrorism and detained by security forces in Jammu and Kashmir often had

> bullet wounds and/or marks of torture The South Asian Human Rights Documentation Center (SAHRDC) reported that the number of such custodial deaths decreased slightly during the year, most likely due to overall increase in infiltrations, as well as new emphasis by the government on reducing human rights violations. Custodial deaths however, remained a serious problem.[42]

Justifying the above contention, the Report further observes:

> The Asian Center for Human Rights (ACHR) reported that the Jammu and Kashmir government ordered 54 inquiries into alleged extra-judicial killings and other human rights violations in 2004 and completed only one. The Home Ministry reported in December that custodial deaths decreased from 183 in 2002-03 to 136 for the 2004 calendar year.[43]

Regarding custodial torture, the Report specifically observes:

> The ACHR alleged that deaths in custody were a severe problem and that police regularly used torture. Because many alleged torture victims died in custody, and other victims were afraid to speak out, there were few first hand accounts. Marks of torture, however, were often found on the bodies of deceased detainees.......Police and jailers typically assaulted new prisoners for money and personal articles. In addition, police commonly tortured detainees during custodial interrogation. Although police officers were subject to prosecution for such offences, the government often foiled to hold them accountable. According to Amnesty International (AI), torture usually took place during criminal investigations and following unlawful and arbitrary arrests.[44]

The above discussion clearly reveals how civil liberties and human rights have been violated in a blatant repressive manner by the democratic Indian state in the name of curbing terrorism. This is the reason why Manoranjan Mohanty points out to the duality of state structures in India, whereby in the Indian polity, democratic strands coexist along with a tendency towards authoritarianism.[45]

V

Counter-Terrorism Measures: The Way Out

In the foregoing discussion in the preceding pages, I have broadly analysed how the rise of Islamic fundamentalism has given rise to global terrorism and how consequently terrorism became a global problem leading to the evolution of global terrorism or globalisation of terrorism. I have also analysed how terrorism results in large scale human rights violations, especially the rights of the civilians, prisoners of war, etc., and endangers human security as well. The most obvious and pertinent question which arises now is, can terrorism be countered by counter-terrorism? What kind of counter-terrorism measures have been adopted by US and Europe? And, lastly, what kind of additional counter-terrorism measures should be adopted not only for countering terrorism, but also for maintaining international peace and security? I will now dwell on some of these substantive questions.

There is no one approach to curb global terrorism. As Jonathan Stevenson observes:

> There is only a pragmatic approach, inextricably involving both 'hard' counter-terrorism and 'transformative' counter-terrorism. These functions are non-optical and complementary. Hard counter-terrorism, along fairly clear operational parameters, is indispensable, and, in light of the difficulty of determining victory over terrorists, needs to be sustained even when a downturn in terrorist attacks leads to budgetary pressures on counter-terrorism measures. Transformative counter-terrorism, while essential for 'victory' and no less mandatory, will be highly contingent on emerging circumstances and subject to trial-and-error.[46]

Since the US started the 'War on Terrorism' five years ago, the US counter-terrorism strategy has proved to be grossly inadequate. The US essentially has adopted a *"vulnerability-based approach* that stresses risk minimisation."[47] The US counter-terrorism strategy have been primarily military in nature, as it has relied on targeting some of the talented planners and operational leaders of Al Qaeda, and destroyed some of the Al Qaeda bases and operational capabilities. As Brian Michael Jenkins has pointed out:

> The United States has understandably focused its efforts on disrupting terrorist planning and operations, but what's needed is a strategy that disrupts the entire jihadist cycle. The cycle begins with proselytizing, radicalization, indoctrination and recruitment. It breaks the surface with planning, preparing and executing terrorist operations. And it ends in the death or captivity of the holy warrior.[48]

While, the US definitely has taken some measures for self-defence to counter terrorism, like the US Homeland Security System and anti-terrorist laws etc., the US has failed in combating the continued resonance and reinvigoration of Al Qaeda's ideological appeal. Al Qaeda has not only been able to continually resonate their message, but has also been successful in replenishing their ranks by making new recruits and thereby Al Qaeda has been successful in regenerating and renewing itself through new and innovative mechanisms. Until and unless the US addresses these core issues of Al Qaeda's strategy systematically, the US will not be successful in disrupting Al Qaeda's ideological appeal, and also disrupt the highly dispersed and broad-ranging trans-national network of Islamic terrorism.[49]

On the other hand, European counter-terrorism strategy, as Jonathan Stevenson points out, is essentially "a risk-management problem to be handled with a threat-based security system, whereby specific emergent risks are assessed and minimised."[50] Stevenson elaborates the major strategies of British counter-terrorism also.[51]

Lawrence Freedman has articulated a 'norms-based deterrence by denial strategy' as an effective counter-terrorism policy. This strategy will appeal to the international community, especially the wider, non-radical Islam to reject principles that promote terrorism. Freedman points out that "all political groups, however apparently fanatical in their ideology, adjust to shifting power relationships and act with some thought to the consequences."[52]

Bruce Hoffman emphasises the need to develop a 'Global Counterinsurgency' (GCOIN) operation instead of the 'Global War on Terrorism'. Hoffman then elaborates that in order to be successful and effective, the GCOIN should take into account the following factors :

1. Separating the enemy from the populace that provides support and sustenance.

   This, in turn, entails three basic missions:

   (a) Denial of enemy sanctuary

   (b) Elimination of enemy freedom of movement

   (c) Denial of enemy resources and support;
2. Identification and neutralization of the enemy;
3. Creation of a secure environment — progressing from local to regional to global;
4. Ongoing and effective neutralization of enemy propaganda through the planning and execution of a comprehensive and integrated information operations and holistic civil affairs campaign in harmony with the first four tasks; and
5. Interagency efforts to build effective and responsible civil governance mechanisms that eliminate the fundamental causes of terrorism and insurgency.[53]

However, my contention is that along with these measures, every state must try to win the heart and mind of its people, or the civilian population, which will ensure both state security and human security.[54] Every state should try to address the legitimate demands of the people and ensure that everybody has access to food, shelter, clothing, education, etc. They should also ensure that socio-economic disparities are minimal and people do not suffer from abject poverty, illiteracy, unemployment, exploitation, malnutrition, etc. These measures will reduce terrorism to a certain extent. For example, in Kashmir, large number of unemployed youth takes easily take to terrorism.

Along with these steps, in India, the bureaucracy, the police force and the judiciary - all need to be educated about the proper ways of carrying out their functions keeping in view the requirements of human rights. It is only education that can literate the mind from the thraldom of obscurantism and bigotry, nurture democratic values and promote social transformation.[55]

Extremist politics should not be promoted. The US has a primary role in this regard. The US should not only unnecessarily interfere in the internal affairs of sovereign states, as it violates the basic principles of the Westphalian state system (1648), and promotes the breeding ground for terrorist movements. It should also properly carry out its rehabilitation and reform projects, especially in Iraq and Afghanistan. It becomes categorically imperative that violation of civil liberties, basic human rights and fundamental rights promotes terrorist activities.

Since some terrorist movements are ideological in nature, they can be countered only by offering an alternative ideology of democracy, peace and universal brotherhood. These movements cannot be fought in the battlefield and it is essential to have tolerance, and adopt a more reconciliatory and pacifist approach.[56] In carrying out all these measures in a step-by-step approach, the state should work in tandem with civil society.

End Notes

1. *The Oxford English Dictionary,* Vol. XI, Oxford University Press, London, 1961, p. 216.

2. This argument of Jenny Tiechman has been cited in Rakesh Gupta, "Changing Conceptions of Terrorism", *Strategic Analysis,* 25 (9), 2001, p. 1010.

3. David Robertson, *The Penguin Dictionary of Politics,* Penguin Books, London, 1993, p. 458.

4. This argument of Mark Jurgensmeyer has been cited in Rakesh Gupta, "Changing Conceptions of Terrorism", *Strategic Analysis,* 25 (9), 2001, p. 1006. For details, see Mark Jurgensmeyer, *Terror in the Mind of God: The Global Rise of Religious Violence,* Berkley, University of California Press, 2000, pp. 4-5.

5. Tore Bjorgo, "Introduction", in Tore Bjorgo (ed.), *Root Causes of Terrorism: Myths, reality and ways forward,* London, Routledge, 2005, pp. 3-5.

6. Dilbar Kaur Bajwa, "Terrorism: Its Dimensions and Preventive Measures", Paper presented at the *Seminar on Politics in North-West India: Emerging Trends and Changing Patterns,* Department of Correspondence Courses, Punjabi University, Patiala, 2006, p. 4.

7. Tore Bjorgo, no. 5, p. 9.

8. Dipak K. Gupta, "Exploring roots of terrorism", in Tore Bjorgo (ed.), no. 5, pp. 3-5.

9. David C. Rapport, "The four waves of modern terrorism", in David C. Rapport (ed.), *Terrorism :Critical Concepts in Political Science, Vol. IV, The Fourth or Religious Wave,* London, Routledge, 2006, pp. 3-4.

10. *Ibid.*, p.4.

11. *Ibid.*, p. 17.

12. *Ibid.*, p. 18.

13. *Ibid.*, p.18.

14. M.S. Agwani, "Global War on Terrorism: A Reappraisal", *Mainstream,* 44 (6), February 2, 2006, p. 14.

15. Fred Halliday quoted in Andreas Behnke, "Terrorisng the Political: 9/11 Within the Context of the Globalisation of Violence", *Millennium: Journal of International Studies,* 33 (2), 2004, p. 307. For details, see Fred Halliday, "Politics of the *Umma",* 36.

16. Jonathan Stevenson, "Counter-terrorism: Containment and Beyond", *Adelphi Paper 367, International Institute for Strategic Studies (IISS),* New York, Oxford University Press, 2004, p. 10.

17. Rohan Gunaratna, "The al Qaeda Threat and the International Response", in David Martin Jones (ed.), *Globalisation and the New Terror: The Asia-Pacific Dimension,* UK, Edward Elgar Publishing Limited, 2004, p. 51.

18. Andreas Behnke, "Terrorising the Political: 9/11 Within the Context of the Globalisation of Violence", *Millennium: Journal of International Studies,* 33 (2), 2004, pp. 305-306.

19. Elena Pavlova, "An Ideological Response to Islamist Terrorism: Theoretical and Operational Overview", in Rohan Gunaratna (ed.), *Terrorism in the Asia-Pacific: Threat and Response,* Singapore, Eastern Universities Press, 2003, p. 32.

20. *Ibid.*, p. 32.

21. *Ibid.*,pp. 35, 40-41.

22. K. Warikko, "Islamist Extremism: Challenge to Security in South Asia", *Strategic Analysis,* 30 (1), Jan-March 2006, p. 31.

23. *Ibid.*, p.35.

24. Riyaz Punjabi cited in K. Warikko, "Islamist Extremism: Challenge to Security in South Asia", *Strategic Analysis,* 30 (1), Jan-March 2006, p. 35. For details, see Riyaz Punjabi, "The Concept of an Islamic Caliphate: The Religious and Ethnic pulls of Kashmir Militant Movement", *Journal of Peace Studies,* 1(1), November-December 1993, p. 42.

25. Kalim Bahadur, "Regional Implications of the Rise of Islamic Fundamentalism in Pakistan", *Strategic Analysis,* 30 (1), Jan-March 2006, pp. 17-18.

26. *Task Force on Terrorism and Unconventional Warfare, US House Republican Research Committee,* "The New Islamist International", February 1, 1993. Also cited in K. Warikko, no. 22, p. 37.

27. Andreas Behnke, no. 18, p. 300.

28. Elena Pavlova, no. 19, p. 30.

29. Jonathan Stevenson, no. 16, p. 11.

30. See Iraq Study Group (USIP'S) website at http://www.usip.org/isg/iraq study group report/report/1206/iraq study group re port.pdf

31. Rohan Gunaratna, "Al Qaeda's Origins, Threat and its Likely Future", in Rohan Gunaratna (ed.), *Terrorism in the Asia-Pacific: Threat and Response,* Singapore, Eastern Universities Press, 2003, p. 139.

32. *Ibid.*, p. 140.

33. Bruce Hoffman, "Islam and the West : Searching for Common Ground - The ferrorist Threat and the Counter-Terrorism Effort", *Testimony presented to the Senate Foreign Relations Committee on July 18, 2006, RAND Corporation,* pp. 3-6, available at www. rand.org.

34. See Sujit Lahiry, "Human Security: A Conceptual Idea", *Punjab Journal of Politics,* 29(1), 2005, p. 85.

35. UNDP, "An Agenda for the Social Summit" and "New Dimensions of Human Security", *Human Development Report 1994,* New Delhi, Oxford University Press, 1994, p. 3 and p. 22 respectively. Also cited in Ibid., p. 84.

36. Sujit Lahiry, no. 34, p. 95.

37. S. Chesterman quoted in Rosemary Foot, "Human Rights and Counter-terrorism in America's Asia Policy", *Adelphi Paper 363, International Institute for Strategic Studies (IISS),* New York, Oxford University Press, 2004, p. 22. For details, please see S. Chesterman, "Humanitarian Intervention and Afghanistan", in J. Welsh (ed.), *Humanitarian Intervention and International Relations: Theory and Practice,* Oxford, Oxford University Press, 2003, Chapter 9.

38. Rosemary Foot, "Human Rights and Counter-terrorism in America's Asia Policy", *Adelphi Paper 363, International Institute for Strategic Studies (IISS),* New York, Oxford University Press, 2004, pp. 9-11.

39. Jonathan Stevenson, no. 16, p. 19.

40. Rosemary Foot, no. 38, p.6.

41. *Ibid.*, p. 13.

42. US *Department of State, India, Country Reports on Human Rights Practices, 2005,* Released by the Bureau of Democracy, Human Rights and Labour, March 8, 2006, p. 2.

43. *Ibid.*

44. *Ibid.*, p.6

45. Manoranjan Mohanty, "Duality of the State Process in India: A Hypothesis", *Bharatiya Samajik Chintan,* 12 (1-2), March-June 1989.

46. Jonathan Stevenson, no. 16, p.93.

47. *Ibid.*, p.28, emphasis mine.

48. Brian Michael Jenkins, "Safer, But Not Safe", *RAND Commentary,* September 10, 2006 available at http://www.rand.org/commentary/091006SDUT.html. This commentary appeared in *San Diego Union-Tribune* on September 10, 2006.

49. Bruce Hoffman, "Combating Al Qaeda and the Militant Islamic Threat", *RAND Testimony presented to the House Armed Services Committee, Subcommittee on Terrorism, Unconventional Threats and Capabilities* on February 16, 2006.

50. Jonathan Stevenson, no. 16, p. 28.

51. *Ibid.,* pp. 102-103.

52. Lawrence Freedman quoted in Jonathan Stevenson, no. 16, pp.101-

102. For details, refer Lawrence Freedman, *Deterrence,* Cambridge, Polity Press, 2004, pp.127-130.

53. Bruce Hoffman, no. 33, pp. 17-18.

54. Sujit Lahiry, no. 34, p. 95.

55. Sujit Lahiry, "State of Human Rights in India : A Wider Perception", *Social Sciences Research Journal, Panjab University, Chandigarh,* 9 (2), 2001, p. 70.

56. Dipak K. Gupta, no. 8, pp. 27-29.

21

A New Nepal and Her Threat Perception Towards India

Dr. Anshuman Behera

Any collapse of law and order in Nepal has no serious impact on any other country except India. Because India shares a long and open boundary of 1,470 kilometer with Nepal which covers some of the major states of India like West Bengal, Bihar, Uttar Pradesh, Uttarakhand and Himachal Pradesh. The geo-strategic location of Nepal between two Asian giants, China and India, and its open border with both the countries causes definite worries for the security concerns of India. In the past, the British-India recognised Nepal as a buffer zone between the Russian and Indian empires. With changing scenario in the course of time, when china annexed Tibet in 1950, the independent India began considering Nepal as its 'principal barrier' defending the northern frontiers. With Tibet coming under the Chinese control, the security interest of India over Nepal has become more serious. So the geo-political location of Nepal has been transformed to a new buffer zone between India and china. This buffer state assumes more importance because of the emerging political developments in a new Nepal. Nepal no longer remains a kingdom and has been transformed to a republic. The centuries old monarchy has been dethroned by a popular movement against the king by the political parties of Nepal including the Maoists. The success of the movement against the monarchy, to a great extent, gives credit to the Maoists. The Maoists after a long violent struggle of 12 years have joined the mainstream and constitute a major share in the newly elected Constituent Assembly of Nepal. So what worries India, at this particular juncture, is that, whether the Maoists dominated Nepal would come under the influence of the china and what would be Nepal's India policy hereafter, which may pose a potential threat to India's security interests.

The present paper is an attempt to analyse the threat perception that India gets with the changing political scenario in Nepal. While doing so, the paper goes back to the history of Indo-Nepal relations till date. India's response to the Maoist insurgency in Nepal and Maoist version of India's role in Nepal is also covered in this paper. Since China is a major Asian power and located on the other side of Nepal, the paper tries to cover in details the Chinese influence on Nepal and its impact on India's security interest. India itself is faced with rebel groups in various configurations. With the success of the Maoists in Nepal who have strong linkages with similar groups in India constitutes a serious worry for India. With an open border, which provides easy access to many illegal activities, the border is a grave concern for India.

Indo-Nepal Relation: An Overview

Indo- Nepal relations have been characterized by three important factors: long and open boundary, their socio-cultural and historic ties and interdependence between the two countries - India for its security interests and Nepal for its economic compulsions. Looking into the socio-cultural and historical ties, one would find both the countries share strong social and cultural ties. In the past, Nepal was the only Hindu kingdom. It shared similar culture with the Hindu majority India. Starting from the spread of Buddhism to the rule of Indian dynasties like Mauryas, Guptas and Lichchhwis, many historical landmarks representing Indo-Nepalese culture exist in Nepal. These socio-cultural similarities and personal contacts between two countries play an important role in deciding the shape of their political relations. Coming to the position of India in South Asia region, one would find that India connects its border with all other countries while no other country shares a border with each other. India with its size, population strength, and economic status is often felt insecure by all other six countries and Nepal is no exception. In the course of time, the above mentioned socio-cultural and historical bondings have been domineering, providing India bashing grounds for the opponents of India in Nepal. The unstable political development in Nepal, since 1950s, has somehow been linked to the highhanded intrusion of India into the affairs of Nepal. As Prof. S.D. Muni rightly mentioned, "any problem that arises between two close neighbors like India and Nepal or any other smaller South Asian country, is usually explained away in terms of India's bigness and its over bearing and big brotherly behaviour"[1]. Further he says Indo-Nepal relations are unequal relations[2].

The Indo- Nepal bilateral relations have been influenced, in the course of history, by the changing conditions of the South and South-Asia region. The first ever agreement between the two countries (Rana- Nepal with independent India) came to the picture in 1950. The independent India signed a treaty of peace and friendship with the Rana rulers of Nepal that year. Both the countries had similar kind of interest for signing this treaty. If the Indian rulers were under the dire need to go for the same treaty as a response to the presence of the communist China in Tibet, the same was the situation with the than Ranas. As rightly mentioned by Lok Raj Baral, "Any Nepal ruler could have done the same as the Ranas did, through the Ranas were under dire need of cultivating India for the survival of the beleaguered regime as well as to insulate Nepal from the threat of communism"[3].

The 1950 Treaty of Peace and Friendship is considered the bedrock on which Indo- Nepal relations are built. The treaty addresses the security as well as the economic aspects of both the countries. More than any other aspect, the security aspect was given more importance. Important clauses spelt out in this treaty relating to the security state that, both countries would have understanding leading to mutual security, and would inform each other of any misunderstanding between two with any other country which may cause a threat to the friendly relations between the two countries. There are many other important clauses which include: Nepal would import arms or warlike weapons with assistance and agreement of India. Both the countries would not employ a foreigner whose activities would be perceived prejudicial to the security of the other. One more aspect of the treaty addresses in its Article 6 is to give residential status and equal opportunity to the citizens of both the countries in each other's territory. Looking into the provisions of the treaty there are varieties of opinions from both the countries. To Nepal, in most of the cases, this treaty is regarded as a sort of India hegemonic intrusion over the sovereignty of Nepal and the same is responsible for all the mishappenings in Nepal. For India, the treaty is total package which includes aspects like security, economic, social and political. It was only after this treaty was signed, large scale migrations of Nepalese were accommodated in various fields in India. But, unfortunately, for the political elites in Nepal, the treaty remains, as they say, India sided and the only cause for strained relation between the two countries.

India, in its Nepal policy, always favors a 'twin pillar policy'. This includes a constitutional Monarchy and a democratic form of government. This was the reason why New Delhi interfered in the internal affairs of Nepal. When through India's mediation, a century old Rana Regime was overthrown and Monarchy was re-established along with constitutional and democratic form of government through what was known as 'Delhi Settlement' in 1951. All the efforts of India towards Nepal and the spirit of the 1950 Treaty of peace and friendship went in vain when Nepal tried to come closer towards China. In 1954, in a process to go closer to China, Nepal recognised Tibet as an Autonomous Region of China and tried to establish formal diplomatic relation with China. Though it went against the spirit of the treaty, still it was not objected to by India.

The early 1960s witnessed a political change in Nepal and a strained relationship of India with China as well as with Nepal. In Nepal, the new king Mahendra introduced a system of Party-less Panchayat democracy. All the political parties were banned and the king exercised the absolute power. At the same juncture, India developed a dispute with China over border issues and both waged a war in 1962. The war of 1962 made India to pay a heavy price when it lost some of its territory to China.

In this difficult situation what was a matter of greater concern was Nepal's tilt towards China. King Mahendra used his China card more successfully. Nepal signed a treaty of peace and friendship with China in 1960, road construction project from Kathmandu to Kodari in 1961 which coincided with the strained relation between China and India. The Kathmandu-Kodari road construction started in 1963, just after the war, and completed in 1965. This road has immense strategic importance because it is a major breach of Nepal Himalayas from the North from where there is connectivity to India. Making friendship or establishing diplomatic relation with any country is nothing wrong but Nepal did not show any reciprocity in understanding India's security interest. Analyzing king Mahendra's tilt towards China, one would find that, he used his China card to serve a double purpose: he wanted concession from India as well as from China. Secondly, he wanted his regime of panchayat system to be recognized by India as a genuine one. And he proved to be successful in his approach.

India perceived a security threat with the construction of the road from Kodari to Kathmandu. As mentioned earlier, the road connects Nepal with China via Tibetan route. If Nepal was not able to resist China, an attack through this road, the Indian heart land would be easily be opened up to China. And this caused a grave concern for India and forced India to recognize the panchayat regime of king Mahendra in 1965. An agreement was concluded regarding supply of arms to Nepal. This meant, India was forced to restart the links of mutual security concerns of the two countries[4]. This development of mutual security concern did not last long, when Nepal asked India to withdraw its personnel at the Nepal-Tibet check post in 1970. All these reactions of Nepal towards India can be viewed as an indirect approach to under cutting the spirit of the 1950 Treaty of Peace and Friendship.

Change of kingship, succession of king Birendra to the throne experienced no significant change in Nepal's policy towards India. Unlike king Mahendra, he took a different line to pressurize India and to undermine the treaty of 1950. A new idea of recognizing Nepal as a zone of peace was propounded by Mahendra. He wanted to maintain an equidistance from India and China, theoretically if not practically. Because his proposal at non-aligned conference in Algeria in 1973 for declaring Nepal as a zone of peace was nothing but to dilute the spirit of 1950 treaty. India, on the contrary, neither endorsed nor supported the proposal. Relations between two countries experienced some improvement during Janata, Government in India and under B.P. Koirala's Prime Ministership in Nepal. Prime Minister Moraji Desai's visit to Nepal in 1977 added strength to the relationship. During Indira Gandhi's period in 1980 emphasis was given on promoting bilateral trade and transit.

But again the security interest of India came under threat when Nepal bought arms from China in 1988. This move of Nepal not only undermined the spirit of the 1950 treaty but also violated the understanding of 1959 and 1965 which had provisions that disallowed Nepal purchasing arms without India's approval. Adding to this, Nepal, once again, imposed restriction on the movement of Indians into its territory. On the economic side, the Nepali government imposed a heavy tariff of 55 per cent on Indian goods entering into Nepal.

Indo- Nepal relation from 1950 to 1990 was more or less strained. Nepalese elite as well as the intellectuals interpret that some action of India towards other countries created a sense of insecurity in the minds of the Nepalis. To them India's role in dividing Pakistan in 1971, the accession of Sikkim to India and India's silence over Soviet Union's invasion of Afganistan created a fear of Indian domination over Nepal. But the facts remain otherwise. As mentioned by Padmaja Murthy, "Till 1990, a singular contradiction running through Indo-Nepal relation was the desire of the Monarchy to wield power and the belief in India that only a democratic government would give Nepal stability. This contradiction led Nepal to dilute the spirit behind the 1950 treaty and build new linkage. Even though after sometimes India supported the monarchy and the panchayati regime that Nepal introduced, the suspicions continued"[5].

The year 1990 marked re-emergence of democracy through a popular movement against the panchayat regime in Nepal. An interim government under the Prime Ministership of K.P. Bhattarai came into force. Here a sign of improved relationship was seen. All the border points were reopened. Nepal, showing reciprocity, refrained from taking the last consignment of Chinese arms. This was perhaps, for the first time in 40 years, Nepal showed reciprocity to India's security concerns. Following this, for the first time, the Nepalese prime minister on a visit to India, formally made a request to review and amend the 1950 Treaty of Peace and Friendship. Indo- Nepal relation in subsequent years reached new heights. Various projects like Integrated Development of Mahakali River Treaty in 1996, Gujural Doctrine in the same year added to a healthy relationship. At this point of time Indo- Nepal relation was once again put under a question mark. Nepal faced a serious internal problem in form of the Maoist insurgency in the year of 1996.The hijacking of IC 814 after leaving Kathmandu in December, 1999, and discovery of fake Indian currency from a Pakistani embassy employee in Nepal was really a testing time for Indo- Nepal relation.

The Maoists in Nepal and India's Response

The emergence of the Maoists in the rural areas of Nepal and their spread over all parts of Nepal in the subsequent years caused a debacle in Indo-Nepal relation. Since the Maoists, from their very beginning sounded anti-India, India tactically tried to take the monarchy and the democratic forces into its confidence. Initially India was of the opinion that, "Maoist problem is a law and order problem and an internal affair of Nepal". During 1996-2001, India's response was rather causal. Once the talks between the government of Nepal and the Maoists broke down, emergency was declared in Nepal. For the first time India responded seriously to the insurgency. Another factor that fuelled India's response was U.S.A.'s reaction after 11th September incident and its efforts to fight against the 'global terrorism'. India was one of the first countries to support the state of democracy and foreign minister Jaswant Singh was the first to declare the Maoists as the 'terrorists'. Prime Minister, Atal Bihari Vajpayee, called up the Nepalese King and the Prime Minister of Nepal offering whatever assistance is required in their fight against the Maoists. Military hardware and two scouts of helicopters were provided by India. In May 2002, India's Army Chief, General S. Padmanabhan, visited Nepal and some of the Maoist hit districts. He promised royal Nepalese Army more military hardware. He observed : "We can provide training assistance whenever required and anything Royal Nepalese Army requires. India will stand by Nepal in every possible way. If there is a requirement of military assistance we will be glad to share what we have with Nepal"[6].

Besides its assistance to Nepal against the Maoists, Indian created a special joint force in nine states-Andhra Pradesh, Bihar, Chhatishgarh, Jharkhand, Madhys Pradesh, Maharastra and Odisha in order to control the border and go after Nepalese Maoists who may be trying to enter the Indian side. These initiatives taken by India gave importance to its twin pillar policy. The Royal take over in October, 2002, was seriously condemned by India. While India criticized the Royal takeover, it supported the twin-pillar policy, emphasizing upon the importance of both the monarchy and the political parties to Nepal's political stability. Till this point India remained converged with the monarchy. Because India was well aware of the fact that any initiative against the King might strengthen the Maoists which indirectly may have a proportional effect on India's own Naxalite problem. India stressed on the need for a dialogue process between the King, political parties and the Maoists to bring stability in Nepal. India did not stop supplying arms and intelligence sharing till February 2005, when king Gyanendra dismissed the government and took direct control over the Council of Ministers for three years. Once again showing its commitment to democracy, India suspended its arms supply to Nepal, in a reaction to the King's takeover. It agreed to provide non-lethal military supplies to Nepal if the king facilitated the restoration of democracy in Nepal.

In spite of all these efforts, India was not left uncriticised by the Nepali King and the parliamentary forces. The Maoists were also not left behind in criticizing India. From the government side, Nepal kept blaming India that the Maoists were operating from the Indian soil. Links between the Maoists in Nepal and the like minded groups in India created suspicion for Nepal Government. The Times of India, the largest circulated Indian daily, it was revealed for the first time that the People's War group was planning to create a compact Revolutionary zone from Hyderabad to Kathmandu, taking Madhya Pradesh, Bihar and Jharkhand into its areas of influence with the help of other outfits[7]. Coinciding with this report, with in month's time, Co-ordination Committee of Maoists Parties and Organisations of South Asia (CCOMPOSA) was launched on July 1, to unify and co-ordinate the revolutionary process in the region. Supporting the emergency, India's foreign spokesperson, Nirupama Rao promised that India would not allow its territory to be used by those inimical to Nepalese interest[8]. However, the Maoist leaders appeared to be able to function without restriction in Delhi. They issued frequent statements and talked to the world media-from New Delhi[9]. Despite the fact that India arrested some of the top Maoist leaders like, Matrika Yadab, Suresh Ale Magar and C.D. Gajural and banned Maoists' front organization, Akhil Bharatiya Nepali Ekta Samaj under the prevention of Terrorist Act (POTA), still, the Maoists felt fully assured of being able to co-ordinate their activities from the Indian soil. There were many instances of Maoists conducting several secret meetings on the Indian soil. The Maoists continued to get moral and material support both from the like minded groups in India and from Indian black market. While talking to Dinanath Sharma, Chief-Whip Maoist parliament committee and secretariat member Maoist, it was revealed that a large number of arms were purchased by the Maoists from the Indian police officers of Border States[10]. This was in fact a matter of grave concern for India. Not only the failure of Indian administration raised suspicion in minds of the Nepali government but Nepal was, in fact, shocked by the support of Indian intellectuals towards the Maoists. Maoist news portal reported that, a meeting was held 'right under Nepali Embassy's nose', where thousands of Nepalese raised slogan against the monarchy. It also reported that several Indians, also attended the meeting[11]. All these developments not only created suspicion for the Nepali government but also brought debacle in Indo-Nepal relation.

On the other side, the Maoists were next to none in criticizing India's twin pillar policy. King Gyanendra's visit to India was severely criticized by the Maoist leadership. In words of Baburam Bhattarai, a Maoist leader :

The hightened bonhomie between the ruling Hindutva forces in India and so-called incarnation of Vishnu within the Nepalese Royal palace particularly during and after Gyanendra's visit to India. It is there for all to see. The ban imposed on the All India Nepalese Unity Society under the draconian POTA on July 2, arrest and deportation of four journalists.... and capture from New Delhi on September 5 were clearly designed to appease the monarchy[12].

Again he suspected that, "Indian rules are deliberately propping up an unpopular and weakened king so as to further aggravate the ongoing civil war and to military intervene with the king's formal initiation in a grand strategy of 'Bhutanisation' and 'Sikkimisation' of Nepal[13].

Looking into India in this period of 1996 to 2005, one would find that India's position was caught in between the Maoists and the political parties under the influence of the Nepalese Monarchy. From the government side, there were the constant demands to arrest the Maoist activists, operating from Indian soil though India was committed itself to the supplying of arms and intelligence sharing with Nepal, still the suspicion from Nepali Government remained unchanged. Reacting to the King's takeover in 2005, when Indian Government suspended arms supply to Nepal, Nepal immediately played its China card and China made an agreement to supply arms to Nepal. On the other hand, in spite their connection with the Indian Maoists and like minded groups and operating frcm the Indian soil, the Maoists kept on criticizing India for supporting the monarchy and the government under it. In the Maoist literature, Maoist leader like Baburam Bhattarai and Prachanda labeled India an imperial and expansionist country and responsible for all the underdevelopment in Nepal. In contrast, they never criticized China, though China always branded them as anti-government. The Maoists were likely to be more comfortable towards China on the basis of their ideological affiliation. So the period of 1996 to 2005 India found itself in a very critical situation in its Nepal policy.

The Changing Situation in Nepal and Threat Perception Towards India

As mentioned earlier, the Royal takeover in 2005, was condemned by India, India kept on demanding for talks between the Monarch, political parties and Maoists for a peaceful solution that would bring political stability in Nepal. Importantly, India in its Nepal policy had given importance to democracy. This time again, India played an important role for mediation between the Seven Party Alliance and the Maoists. An Indian politician, part of the UPA coalition Government, Sitaram Yechury, was instrumental in the formation of the 12 point agreement and bringing the Maoists and the political parties to protest against the monarchy. His four point formula comprising restoration of parliament; appointment of an interim government; holding elections to a new constituent assembly and formally inviting the Maoists for talks with the government, proposed as a road map for democracy was accepted in Nepal[14]. The joint protest by the Maoists and the Seven Party Alliance brought the monarchy down in April 2006. Nepal went for a Constituent Assembly election where the Maoists were elected in majority to the parliament. Subsequently, Nepal has elected its first President. These new developments in Nepal have satisfied India's long policy orientation and support for democracy. But these developments in Nepal in no way brought down the security concern for India. India today is concerned more for its security for the following reasons.

The China Factor

Nepal's friendly relation with China, a move against its relation with India, has always been a threat towards India. In Nepal, an anti-India sentiment has always been used as a synonym with nationalism. Irrespective of the political linkages and ideological differences, the political elite suspects India and holds India responsible for its underdevelopment. The monarchy since 1960s used the China card either to blackmail India to get some concession or to show its separate identity against it. In a way, as K.V. Rajan, former ambassador to Nepal, states,

> "Nepal's anxiety to satisfy Chinese objectives, its apparent psychological compulsion to be seen as constantly 'standing up' to India, not only gives China the possibility of maintaining a privileged position in Nepal, without too much effort, but also send alarm bells ringing about its intentions vis-à-vis India, almost at will"[15].

On the other hand, China embraced Nepal for the following reasons. First, China is concerned about its security interests in Tibet as the region is dependent on the neighbouring countries for trade. Thousands of Tibetans regularly move into Nepal and India as refugees every year. The Chinese objectives emphasise on nullifying any negative fall out of Tibetan refugees from these countries[16]. Secondly, China is certainly aware of a parallel Asian power at the neighbourhood, India. India's close relations with Nepal, accession of Sikkim, strong cultural tie of Tibetans have forced China to support Nepal. Thirdly, the presence of the United States, in Nepal, in the name of fighting against the global terrorism, has caused worries in China. So China strategically wants to have closer ties with Nepal in order to check the influence of U.S. in Nepal in particular and South Asia in General.

What India perceives as a threat is the closer ties between Nepal and China. Both Nepal and China, these days, are planning for economic linkages and in the areas of constructing road connections between two countries. There is a promise from China to construct a railway line at Nepal-China border, from Lhasa to Khasa. China has agreed to provide financial assistance to Nepal for the construction of Syaphrubesi-Rasuwagdhi Road. At Indo-Nepal border, there has been a rising of China study center (CSC) from 7 in 2005 to 19 till February 2008. These centers were initiated in 2000 to promote cultural interaction between Nepal and China. These days they are being used to disseminate the Chinese perspective on key issues concerning Nepal and India's hegemonic intentions[17]. Soon after the people's movement in 2006, and with the end of monarchy in Nepal, China has shifted its stand on Nepal very tactically. Till 2006, China was very much in favour of the King and supplied arms to fight against the Maoists labeling them as anti-government. But after the success of the Maoists and the Seven Party Alliance (SPA), China stated that, "key to resolution of crisis in Nepal lies in conciliation among the 'Constitutional Forces'. And urged the King to reach to the political parties to restore democracy and peace in the country"[18]. Comparing China's Nepal policy with India's policy with Nepal, one would find that, while India-Nepal relations blew hot and cold, China, by contrast, had established itself as Kathamandu's all weather-friend[19].

Threat from Indo-Nepal Border

Both India and Nepal share a long and open border with each other. This border is free from any natural barrier. The 1950 Treaty of Peace and Friendship alllows citizens of both the countries to travel freely. Though there are fifteen check posts between two countries to check human traffic, only seven of them are functional. In absence of formidable apparatus along the border, the Maoists in countries, ISI activities and illegal smuggling of drugs and war like weapons have caused concern for India. What is really a matter of worry for India, more than, anything else, is the activities of the ISI in Nepal soil and at the Indo-Nepal border area. The ISI activities in Nepal mainly involved in creating anti-India sentiment, anti-India propaganda and promotion of Islamic fundamentalism and mobilization of Muslim communities, concentrated along the border. There has been a rise of madrasas, Islamic schools, along the Indo-Nepal border. In the past there were instances where some of the terrorists were irrlisted through the network of some madrasas[20]. Apart from the ISI, there are exchange of intelligence of Maoists in Nepal and the like minded groups in India. Free flow of fake Indian currency and drugs and weapon through Indo-Nepal border is a grave concern for India.

The Maoists

The Maoists, right from their emergence, have a negative view towards India. In all the Maoists literature the Maoist leadership had labeled India as 'expansionist' 'imperialist', colonial power, and responsible for all underdevelopment in Nepal[21]. They have criticized India for all sorts of help towards the monarch and the Nepali Government against them. The strongest of the criticism was given by Prachanda in September, 2004. He accused India of trying to bring Nepal under its security and economic umbrella. He also appealed to all patriotic and self respecting Nepalese to oppose the surrender by Nepal's rulers to India and India's expansionist intervention. Further he said Indian rulers want conflict, instability and anarchy in Nepal instead of, development and peace"[22].

The suspicious anti-Indian stand of the Maoist has not changed drastically. Answering to a question at Observer's Research Foundation at Delhi, Prachanda, said the anti-Indian sentiment in Nepal is being spread out by un-democratic forces [23]. But at the same time they are likely to be more comfortable with China and not India. The Maoists are in majority now in the constituent Assembly. The earlier mentioned agreements with China relating to construction of railway and roads support their close links with China. Though China, during the 10 years of insurgency, called them as anti-government, yet the Maoists till date never have a negative remark against China. Like any other political elite in Nepal, the Maoists also want to review all the treaties with India and Nepal. To them treaties like Treaty of Peace and Friendship of 1950, Integrated Mahakali River Treaty are made such a way that, it satisfied the interest of India more than Nepal. There are reports that two of the Chinese companies are already there to take up the hydro-electricity project in Nepal. These developments are not at all a good sign for the India's interests in Nepal.

The above mentioned political development in Nepal, China's close relation with Nepal in various fields and demands to review the treaties between India and Nepal are clear indications that India's interests in Nepal are sliding downwards. In the past, India has committed mistakes in its Nepal policy. At a time when Nepal was under triangular forces (King, political parties and the Maoists), India could not bring either of them into its confidence. Though India was very much firm on its twin pillar approach, its inability to check the operation of the Maoists from its soil invited criticism. India failed to foresee the Maoists victory in the Constituent assembly election. With all these mistakes, it can be said that India is a failure and this failure is of its own making in Nepal. Now it is time for India to rectify its mistakes and try to have policies towards Nepal keeping in mind china's involvement in it. While doing so India has to make sure that the success of the Maoists in Nepal and its impact on Indian rebel groups does not influence administration.

Endnotes

1. S.D. Muni, *India and Nepal: A Changing Relationship*, New Delhi, Konark Publishers, 1996, p.1.

2. *Ibid.*
3. Lok Raj Baral, Behind India- Nepal Relations, http: www. kantipuronline.com/kolnews, Accessed on 29. 07. 08.
4. Padmaja Murthy, Nepal's Foreign Policy: King Gyanendra's Quest for Legitimacy, *World Focus*, Vol. 27, No. 5, May 2006, p.4.
5. Padmaja Murthy, India and Nepal: security and economic Dimension, *Strategic Analysis*, Vol.23, No 9, December 1999.
6. "India Hounds Nepal Maoists", Revolutionary Worker, August 2002, http://rwor.org.
7. Times India, April 16, 2001.
8. See Rabindra Mishra, India's Role in Nepal's Maoist Insurgency, *Asian Survey*, Vol. xliv, No.5, Sept/Oct 2004, pp.637-38.
9. Interview conducted by Rabindra Mishra, Ibid. pp.638.
10. Interview conducted by the Author with Dinanath Sharma, on 12.02.08. at Kathamandu.
11. Krishna Sen online, http://www.cpnmaoist.org/index/krishna sen/ newsksna.htm, cited in Rabindra Mishra, No.8, P.641.
12. Baburam Bhattaai, "Triangular Balance of Forces", *Economic and Political Weekly*, Vol. 37, No. 46, November 16-22, 2002, pp. 4609.
13. *Ibid.*
14. Priyanka Singh, India-Nepal Relations: Rickety Roadmap, *World Focus*, Vol. 27, No. 5, 2006, p. 26.
15. K.V. Rajan, Crisis in Nepal and the China Factor, World Focus, Vol. 26, No.1, January 2005, p.18.
16. Kondapalli Srikanth, China's Forays into Nepal, *World Focus*, Vol. 27, No. 5, May 2006, p. 35.
17. Abanti Bhatacharya, China and Maoist Nepal: Challenging for India, http://www.idsa.in/publication/statements/Abanti Bhatacharys, 230508.htm, accessed on 29.07.08.
18. *Ibid.*
19. Abanti Bhatacharya, Chinese Perception of Developments in Nepal, *World Focus*, Vol. 26, No. 7, July 2007, p. 279.
20. For ISI network in Nepal, see Anil Kambej, Nepal: Alarm Bells on Indo-

Nepal Border, *World Focus*, Vol. 27, No.3, May 2006, pp.29-34, and Anil Kumar Singh, indo-Nepalese Relations and India's Securtity, *Indian Defence Review*, Vol.19, 2004, pp. 57-8.

21. See Baburam Bhatarai, *Political-Economic Relation of People's War in Nepal*, Janadisha Publication, Nepal, 2004.
22. *The Hindustan Times*, September 16, 2004.
23. See *ORF Discourse*, Vol.1, no. 3, December 2006, ORF, New Delhi.

Index

I

R

U

V

X

Y

Z